Henry Martyn Hoyt

Protection versus free trade

The scientific validity and economic operation of defensive duties in the United

States

Henry Martyn Hoyt

Protection versus free trade

The scientific validity and economic operation of defensive duties in the United States

ISBN/EAN: 9783337278359

Printed in Europe, USA, Canada, Australia, Japan

Cover: Foto ©Suzi / pixelio.de

More available books at **www.hansebooks.com**

PROTECTION

VERSUS

FREE TRADE

THE SCIENTIFIC VALIDITY AND ECONOMIC
OPERATION OF DEFENSIVE DUTIES
IN THE UNITED STATES

BY

HENRY M. HOYT

THIRD EDITION REVISED

NEW YORK
D. APPLETON AND COMPANY
1, 3, AND 5 BOND STREET
1886

PREFACE.

THE following pages are the result of a friendly challenge to me by an eminent Professor of Political Economy in a New England college to investigate that science, especially its teaching in relation to protective tariffs. The challenge was accompanied by the confident prediction: "If you pursue it to any length, you will certainly come to throw overboard, with scorn, the Pennsylvania notion that the way to grow rich is to stop, by law, profitable production"; together with the Professor's formulated conclusion: "Protection, poisonous in every root and fiber, droops and dies the moment the light of common sense and rational inquiry falls upon it."

Layman though I was, I could not well refuse to take up the gauntlet thus thrown down by the Professor.

In the intervals of business engagements I have undertaken the investigation. It has been done with reasonable thoroughness, and, so far as I know, with impartiality and freedom from desire of controversy. If it betrays a controversial spirit, it is because it is provoked; and even that may add something of interest to a discussion otherwise rather dry and abstract. What "common sense" and faculty of "rational inquiry" I possessed have been fairly given to the work. It could not be denied that I started with a certain prejudgment in favor of the protective scheme. That, however, was no other than the general conviction, expressed by Dr. William Roscher, the distinguished Professor of Political Economy at the University of Leipsic, that "the person who has only a modest opinion of the power of his own reason, and therefore a just one of the reason of other men and other times, will not believe that a system like the industrial protective system, which the greatest theorizers and practitioners favored for centuries, and which governed all highly developed countries in certain periods of their national life, proceeded entirely from error and deception." Nor, again, did I believe that, in a nation with the quick and trained commercial instincts of the Americans, such a system could be founded in mere greed, jobbery, and congressional log-rolling. If the practice had been found expedient, some reasons could be found justifying it.

The inquiries, then, necessarily led to a study of the play and interaction of the economic forces, as ordinarily expounded in the formal treatises on political economy. I found, in detail and specifically, what I had only felt before in a general way, that the whole underground of that science had been wrongly chosen, and that the whole superstructure was now being taken down by the younger school of economists, both in Europe and the United States. I have deemed it proper to submit, at some length, the destructive criticism to which the current official political economy has been subjected.

Of all the forces and their combinations, as usually treated, I find only four pertinent to the discussion proposed:

First. The object of all our efforts is "the satisfaction of our desires." This will be found to be a more manageable motive than "wealth" for the labor and abstinence of men gathered together in society.

Second. "Commodities are paid for with commodities." In international commerce, imports must be paid for with exports—in the long run, imports must balance exports.

Third. While "division of labor" has been the pivot, the fulcrum on which the industrial world has been moved, and while the special aptitude of each individual producer furnishes the materials for domestic exchange, and superiority, at some point, the materials for international trade, the law announced by Adam Smith is the law of the case: "Division of labor is limited by the extent of the market." That is, in other words, the advantages of a "division of labor" may be lost by the want of an adequate market in which the products of the labor at the point of superiority, embodied in commodities, may be sold.

Fourth. In a given area, as of a nation, where the owners of capital and the owners of labor speak the same language, live under the same laws, and act under the same moral, political, social, and economic motives, thus rendering labor and capital therein substantially mobile, the competition of capital with capital and of labor with labor is effective. Over such an area, competition tends to equalize the recompense of all the capitals and the rewards of all labor. A monopoly in such a nation is impossible.

The inquiry, also, involved an analysis of the nature and number of the desires for which a given people seek satisfaction, and the means of satisfying them. It proved not at all impossible to deal with the aggregate desires of a nation as a unit, and to treat the problem as if it was the case of an individual.

Suppose an individual, an average American farmer, with a number of workmen, all of high skill, energy, and industry, in possession of certain fertile fields, with stores of building-material, stones, timber, fuel, and certain machinery, out of which, by his labor, he could supply a large proportion of his and their wants directly by production, and the remaining portion of their wants, indirectly, by exchanging the surplus of their natural products. Let him be surrounded, at a greater or less distance, by neighbors who have fields like his, only less productive, with artisans who could make his sleds, harrows, harness, cotton and woolen goods, dishes, and so on, the product of handicraft industries; not with less labor, but for lower money-price; and besides, stocks of merchandise, consisting of tea, coffee, sugar, tropical fruits, drugs, medicines, and, if you please, wines and cigars. The farmer now works his lands to their capacity, and gathers his crops of wheat, food, cotton, and tobacco. He already thus has, in his garnered fruits and grains, something more than half the subsistence of himself and workmen. For the rest, he proposes to exchange his surplus—to trade the things he does not want for the things he does want. We will suppose (for it will subsequently appear that if anything is legitimate in the science of political economy, it is a *supposition*) the annual value of his crops to be $10,000. To feed his family and pay the cost of raising the things he raises on his fields will cause him an outlay, say, of $6,700. This leaves him $3,300 with which to supply his outstanding want of clothes, carpets, nails, hats, farming-utensils, tea, coffee, sugar, medicines, fruits, wine, and cigars. The inherited traits and historical traditions of this farmer are such as to make all these wants legitimate; they are desires which he is willing to gratify. Upon making the effort to market his surplus he finds he can only sell $700 worth; his neighbors will only buy, because they only want, $700 worth. Of this sum he spends half—$350—for drugs, medicines, fruits, wine, tea, coffee, and sugar, which climate and other reasons forbid him to produce. The other half—$350—he lays out in certain commodities which he and his workmen have not as yet the skill and patience to undertake to produce. There remains yet on his hands $2,600 with which he would, if he could, buy his hats, coats, carpets, shirts, dishes, nails, etc., for himself and his workmen. But there is no market to take them off his hands in excess of $350 worth, in addition to the $350 worth already sold; nor did his neighbors ever have a surplus of manufactured goods equal to his demand. According to the abstract principles of political economy, his neighbors on the poorer soils ought to stop cultivating them to the extent of the additional $2,600 worth of his products, and turn their skill and energy to the production of the hats, coats, etc., that he wants to buy with that surplus. But, in point of fact, the farmer finds that they do not do so; that they do, under natural causes and inherited traits, still till their native soils to within a narrow margin of their fertility. Besides, laborers move freely to the farm from the neighborhood, still further disturbing the commercial equilibrium between the two communities; but this only made the farmer less dependent on his neighbors to make things for him, for now the migration of the workmen themselves takes the place of a trade in the products of their labor.

Therefore, finding upon examination that he can make all these things on the farm, and with as small an expenditure of labor and skill (both of which he has) as his neighbors, he proceeds to make them. Why? Because he found no other way to satisfy all his desires. Although up to $700 worth he could buy them abroad and cheaper, beyond that amount he must make them himself or go without them, for he can not *buy* them at all, for the reason that he does not bring acceptable purchase-money in his hands. Rather than go without them, he proceeds to make them on the best conditions attainable under his natural and acquired resources. The desires are natural to him, and the manufacture is natural to him. The manufacture of the $2,600 worth is *natural*, but it is more, it is necessary, and is an indispensable part of his supply. Its *naturalness* does not depend on the price his neighbors charge, nor their willingness to accept the commodities he offers in exchange, but upon the actual amount of labor it costs him to produce them.

If this had been merely an industrial group, formed on strictly commercial principles, there would have been no more workers in it than were necessary to produce the $700 surplus. But this society happened to be formed of men fleeing from the hardness and oppressions of life elsewhere, and who were not moving on economic motives alone. It was composed of picked men, of the highest type, brooking no masters, having the common bonds of kindred, language, habits, laws, love of religious liberty, and self-government—all of which our benignant farmer permitted them to enjoy in the fullest degree. The group made by these social, moral, and political considerations determined the size of the industrial group. The political entity became the industrial entity. This made them sufficiently numerous to disturb their commercial equilibrium with their neighbors, and consequently the $2,600 surplus lay useless in their hands. When they found that their labor in factories, furnaces, and machine-shops, on looms and potter's wheels, was as productive as that on fertile fields, the surplus food recovered its utility and exchange value, as subsistence for the laborers whom all these inducements had drawn together. The farmer now proceeds to "organize the industries" of that political entity; especially, as he has never experienced any lack of capital in any enterprise which promised adequate returns.

This farmer, in this determination, has simply accepted the limitations imposed on his external exchanges. His mental resolution, thus forced on him, not to try to *buy*, but to *make*, has imposed *a prohibitory tariff* upon all that portion of his necessary supply which he does make. He has now, in the language of the economist, imposed *restrictions* on his exchanges; that is, he does restrict the exchanges with his neighbors, but, to a greater extent, he enlarges the exchanges which take place on his own farm. He has got himself in a place where, in the language of the free-trade writer, he *collects taxes* of himself. It is not *taxation*, it is simply *the cost* of the increased comfort which follows upon the increased consumption he is now enabled to indulge. If it be *taxation* it is voluntary, inasmuch as it is undergone for the sake of the satisfaction of his desires. He can stop the taxation if he will lessen his satisfactions. Abundance and cheapness have been equalized upon the lowest and only terms open to him. He has, however, subserved his true economic purposes, and has realized the true end of all his efforts. The ratio between effort and enjoyment has, in his case, been reduced to a *minimum*. He was reduced to the alternative of wanting fewer things, or making them, on his farm, for himself. Being a civilized man, he chose the latter; being a vertebrate, he could not do business on the basis of being a hermit-crab.

But, inasmuch as the constant pressure of the neighbors to sell the paltry amount of $350 (which he could really better do without, but which some of his people insisted on having) introduces confusion and friction between his own producers and consumers, stops his mills, makes his workmen stand idle, and prevents him and them getting what they want, he imposes an *import duty* on these goods, sufficient to equalize their cost with that of his home product; and the sum thus received goes into his treasury, for the common use of himself and all his laborers. This farmer, now, has imposed on himself "a *tariff for revenue*," "*with incidental protection*," or rather a tariff for *protection*, with *incidental revenue*.

All this time there were certain dogmatic thinkers (very few of them were hand-workers) who said they, personally, could make better bargains away from home, if, having got into their pockets the high wages which they had received for "services" rendered to their co-workmen, they might be allowed to spend it among the neighbors to whom they had rendered no services; and urged their inalienable right to pursue their own interests, so destructive to the interests of the little community. But, the farmer seeing that they, at best, could only get a part of the \$350 worth of imported manufactures, and that the rest of his workmen must go without the \$2,600 worth which they might otherwise make and enjoy, acting for the society, promptly put his foot down on this line of uneconomic as well as selfish conduct.

I think it will not be questioned that, *if* a farmer found himself in these surroundings, he could only supply all his wants, and those of his workmen, in the way supposed; and that, by so doing, he would not only increase the population and "wealth" of the community on the farm, but, thus "regulating commerce," would promote their "general welfare"; and he would do this on the true premises of political economy.

If we find a nation relatively in the like condition and environment, the principles of the science of political economy will be equally applicable to it. This applicability will depend on the closeness of the correspondence in the facts. The analogy will be found unexpectedly complete; especially in the fact that, in any event, about nine tenths of the manufactures in the "protected" industries must be produced at home, under American conditions. What the tariff does—and all it does—is to compel the foreign producer to spend as much in getting into the American market for the other tenth as the American producer does.

Our question is, therefore, I conceive, a national question and not a cosmopolitan one.

The operation of the four principles indicated is seen in the illustration:

First. The satisfaction of the farmer's desires; these, in their number, kind, and intensity, will depend on the kind of man he is, and will determine the kind of effort he makes to satisfy them.

Second. His "imports must be paid for with his exports"; that is, by his external trade he can get nothing *into* his territory except in pay for what he sends *out* of his territory.

Third. "Division of labor is limited by the extent of the market"; that is, if he can not sell the total product of his work, when applied to his most advantageous industry, his labor will not be as profitable as it might otherwise be, and he might as well stand idle for a part of the time. What he makes when he would otherwise be idle *costs* him nothing.

Fourth. When he turns his labor and capital to his own fields and workshops, under effective competition and the perfect mobility of these factors of production, no monopoly can grow up within his little territory.

When the individual or the community discover that they need certain commodities, but can not buy more value than they can sell, by reason of not offering acceptable pay, and, at the same time, can produce them with no greater cost of labor and abstinence in overcoming the obstacles which nature presents than other individuals or other communities, they *naturally* set about making them by the direct act of production. In the case of a nation, the national legislature provides for the domestic production and exchange, by imposing some sort of restriction on the foreign exchange.

Possibly, my friend the Professor is not aware of the full contents of "the Pennsylvania notion." He seems to think pig-iron is the only god of that people. The first corporate determination of that State, at least, shows what one great Commonwealth, finding itself in the predicament of our farmer, did, and exactly the reasons for doing it. In the preamble to her tariff act, passed on the *20th day of September, 1785*, just one hundred years ago, it was thus recited:

"An act to encourage and protect the manufactures of this State, by laying additional duties on the importation of certain manufactures which interfere with them. *Whereas*, divers useful and beneficial arts and manufactures have been gradually introduced into Pennsylvania, and the same have at length risen to a very considerable extent and perfection, insomuch that during the late war between the United States of America and Great Britain, when the importation of European goods was much interrupted, and often very difficult and uncertain, the artisans and mechanics of this State were able to supply, in the hours of need, not only large quantities of weapons and other implements, but also ammunition and clothing, without which the war could not have been carried on, whereby their oppressed country was greatly assisted and relieved: and, whereas, although the fabrics and manufactures of Europe and other foreign parts, imported into this country in times of peace, may be afforded at cheaper rates than they can be made here, yet good policy and a regard to the well-being of divers useful and industrious citizens, who are employed in the making of like goods in this State, demands of us that moderate duties be laid on certain fabrics and manufactures imported, which do most interfere with, and which (if no relief be given) will undermine and destroy the useful manufactures of the like kind in this country; for this purpose:

"SECTION 2. Be it enacted, and it is hereby enacted, by the Representatives of the Freemen of the Commonwealth of Pennsylvania, in General Assembly met, and by the authority of the same, that further and additional duties, hereinafter specified, shall be levied, collected, and paid, on the importation into this State of certain goods, wares, and merchandise, enumerated and particularized in this act"—and the act goes on to enumerate more than seventy articles.

Herein will be found, I think, a fair exposition of the motives NOT "to stop by law profitable production," but rather, by enlarging the domestic exchanges, to substitute a new form of production in order to provide for the "satisfaction of the desires" of all the people. "The freemen of the Commonwealth of Pennsylvania" then knew what they wanted, and the most feasible and cheapest scheme for supplying their wants. They stood at the beginning of things, and saw them clearly enough. The "notion" spread rapidly through all the States of the confederation; so much so, that the purely commercial convention, called by the late colonies in 1786, resulted in the formation of the Constitution of the United States in 1787. The present Constitution was undeniably dictated by commercial necessity. Mr. Webster said, in his speech to the citizens of Buffalo, in June, 1833: "The protection of American labor against the injurious competition of foreign labor, so far, at least, as respects general handicraft production, is known, historically, to have been designed to be obtained by establishing the Constitution." And Mr. Choate, in the Senate, March, 1842, said: "A whole people, a whole generation of our fathers, had in view, as one groundwork and purpose of their new government, the acquisition of the means of restraining by governmental action the importation of foreign manufactures for the encouragement of manufactures and of labor at home; and desired, and meant to do this, by clothing the new government with this specific power of *regulating commerce.*"

There is, then, the jural power, under the Constitution, to enact a prohibitory tariff even, if economic principles justified it. Whether they do or not, it is the purpose of the following pages to determine. Anyway, such a tariff is not unconstitutional.

I have not dealt in statistics, which are liable to no end of combinations and no end of disputation. Comparisons are impossible for want of the second term of the comparison, to wit, another people, like ours in traits and physical resources, developed under free trade.

There have been no assumptions made in the argument. The contribution made by American labor in the commodities produced in the protected industries is a necessary part of the full supply of the whole demand. They are, therefore, natural and necessary.

On the other hand, the advocates of freedom of trade proceed entirely on the assumptions that foreigners have the capital, labor, and skill to make a surplus of manufactured commodities which will supply our demand, and that there is a foreign market adequate to take the surplus of all our products made "under freedom," and that we can exchange one surplus for the other, and thus *buy* the satisfaction of our remaining desires. Neither of these assumptions is true. This is a question of history and fact, and not of *a priori* hypothesis. If the following pages show some repetition—even to tediousness—on this point, it is because it crops out from whatever direction the subject is explored, and it is unavoidable. If the main line of the argument is well chosen, I have no fears but that writers on economy will appear who can use a more rigorous logic and wield more facile pens. They will make the necessary generalizations in the debate, and blaze the desirable "short cut" through the discussion. I have reached very positive convictions of my own, in the progress of my study, upon the scientific validity of defensive duties in their operation on industry in the United States.

I am persuaded that a people such as ours, acting under physical conditions such as ours, were driven by the very nature of the case to the course of development which we took. At the same time I am not unmindful of the danger in economic discussion alluded to by Mr. Mill, "the danger of overlooking something." If I have incurred the danger, sharp criticism will detect and point it out. I am sure that neither the writer nor any of his fellow-citizens can have any interest in this great debate except to get at the right and truth of the matter.

What we are, the census and the national landscape show —what *might have been*, under free foreign trade, has never been made to appear. Until the economist of free trade makes some demonstration in this line, he must rest under the condemnation which Dr. Johnson has thus expressed: "He who will determine against that which he knows, because there may be something which he knows not, he that can set hypothetical possibility against acknowledged certainty, is not to be admitted among reasonable beings."

It is evident enough from numerous extracts, intended to be duly credited, that I have borrowed freely from the writings of many authors; but I should fail to pay a positive and distinct debt, if I omitted acknowledgment of my obligations to the late George Basil Dixwell, of Boston.

H. M. H.

WILKES-BARRE, PA., *December, 1885.*

TABLE OF CONTENTS.

CHAPTER I.

PAGE
PRELIMINARY—SOME DEFINITIONS 1

    The question of protection and free trade still awaits a practical settlement—A question partly of science and partly of art—The unsatisfactory state of the science of political economy—Many questions still unsettled—Colonel Torrens—Prof. Perry's disappointment—Definitions of the science of political economy—Sir James Steuart—Adam Smith—J. B. Say—Mr. McCulloch—M. Sismondi—M. Storch—Prof. Senior—Mr. Mill—Prof. Roscher—M. Bastiat—Henry C. Carey—Prof. Francis A. Walker—Prof. Sidgwick—Prof. Bowen—Prof. Perry—Prof. Cairnes—M. de Laveleye.

CHAPTER II.

SCIENCE OF POLITICAL ECONOMY—THE MECHANISM OF PRODUCTION 13

    The method of the development of the science—The instruments of production, labor, capital, land—Supply and demand, competition—Labor, its definitions—Capital, its definitions—Rent, its definitions—The division of labor, theory of free trade based on it—Its limitations—The distinction between utility and value—Societary association—Credit—Money the instrument of association—Malthus's theory of population—The wages-fund theory.

CHAPTER III.

THE MOTIVE-POWER OF PRODUCTION—THE ECONOMIC MAN . 84

    Mr. Mill's abstraction—Prof. Senior's four propositions—Prof. Sidgwick's view—Satisfaction of desires the real pursuit—Prof. Perry—Henry C. Carey—Prof. Walker—M. Bastiat—Which the cheapest and which the dearest market—Prof. Perry's inadequate premises—He omits consumption, a vital consideration—Prof. Jevons—The real man—Walter Bagehot—Prof. Leslie—Mr. Ruskin.

CHAPTER IV.

WHO IS BOUND BY THE SCIENCE—ITS JURISDICTION OVER THE LEGISLATOR 60

Mr. McCulloch—Prof. Senior—Mr. Mill—Prof. Jevons—Walter Bagehot—Prof. Leslie—Frederic Harrison—Dr. John K. Ingram—Stephen Colwell—Prof. Rickards—Prof. Sumner—Destructive criticism on the science in its present state—Deductive science powerless without observation and experience—No laws of political economy of universal application—The opinion of Napoleon—M. Thiers—Thomas Carlyle—Table of contents of Adam Smith's "Wealth of Nations."

CHAPTER V.

LAISSEZ FAIRE—NOT A SCIENTIFIC DOGMA. 88

Adam Smith's doctrine of natural liberty—The basis of his theory of free trade—He reduces political economy to a theory of egoism—Prof. Cairnes's criticism on him—Origin of *laissez faire*—M. Colbert's achievements—M. Wolowski on the *rôle* of authority—Prof. Perry's concession—M. Bastiat, mere liberty powerless—*Laissez faire* a fiction of ancient philosophy—Prof. Cairnes says it is a pretentious sophistry—Rejected by Prof. Jevons and Prof. Walker—Individual and national interests are not identical, demonstration by John Rae—Mr. Mill's concession to protection—Protest by Prof. Bonamy Price and Prof. Thorold-Rogers—Mr. Mill reaffirms—Judge Phillips—*Laissez faire* discredited as a scientific dogma.

CHAPTER VI.

THE REAL QUESTION—NOT ONE OF TAXATION—INVOLVES THE ECONOMIC EFFECTS OF RESTRICTION 112

Misstatement of the issue by Profs. Perry and Sumner—Distinction between taxation and the regulation of commerce—The four legitimate issues as raised by Prof. Sumner—What his abstract system overlooks—Prof. Perry's exclusions—Analysis of foreign trade—Prof. Perry's six questions and their answers—Prof. Perry's impregnable position—Its weakness.

CHAPTER VII.

THE ALTERNATIVES OFFERED—WHAT WE BUY AND WHAT WE SELL 131

Two sets of alternatives offered by the free-trader—The first set necessarily rejected—The second set the nation undertook to accept—The assumptions on which they were based turned out to be wrong—First, that there is a market abroad for the surplus of productions in the most advantageous industries—Disproved by Benjamin Franklin, Alexander Hamilton, James Madison, John C. Calhoun, Andrew Jackson, Daniel Webster—Failure of Prof. Perry's equation of international demand—Unprofitable industries—What we sell and what we buy—The balances of trade on the exports to and imports from the other nations.

CHAPTER VIII.

ADAM SMITH—SOME FACTS IN OUR HISTORY 165

The second assumption of the free-trader—That the exchangeable value of our exports would not be reduced, and that the exchangeable value of our imports would not be increased—The problem submitted to Adam Smith—Discussion of it on the principles of the "Wealth of Nations"—The satisfaction of the desires of all the people by exchanges in a foreign market impossible, for two reasons: the foreign market does not contain the surplus we wish to buy, nor will it take the surplus we wish to sell—We are thrown back on the domestic manufacture—The facts in our early history—Growth of domestic industries during the Napoleonic wars—The English blockade, the Berlin Decree, Orders in Council, the Milan Decree, all operated as restrictions—Jefferson Davis on the compensating effects of restriction in the Confederacy—Effect of restrictions from 1807 to 1816 on the cotton, woolen, and iron industries—Prof. Taussig's concession to the economic effect of restrictions.

CHAPTER IX.

THE ECONOMIC QUESTION—THE SCIENTIFIC QUESTION . . 189

The two ideals of the end we desire to reach—The problem as proposed by Prof. Jevons realizes all the satisfactions which our labor and capital can accomplish—Reached by restrictions—The problem as proposed by Prof. Sumner, the maximum of material good for a given effort—Will realize the satisfaction of the desires of only some of us—The exertions of all of us can not realize in the foreign market the satisfaction of the desires of all of us—Supplying the demand of the foreign market will not call into activity all our resources and all our energies—Some exchanges in the foreign market advantageous—All exchanges not advantageous—Competing industries—The fatal results of overproduction of food and raw materials — The impossibility of purchasing twenty-six hundred million dollars' worth of imports with seven hundred million dollars' worth of exports—We fail in the satisfaction of our desires—The railroad trip between New York, Philadelphia, and Trenton.

CHAPTER X.

THE POLITICAL QUESTION—THE POPULAR QUESTION . . 213

The supposition that we were the only nation on the planet—In what respect the introduction of the elements of other nations should affect us—The distinction between an organism as a whole and the units composing it—What is called the liberty of the unit is necessarily absorbed to a greater or less extent by that of the whole—Protection in the United States arose out of the facts of our early history—Some of these facts set forth in detail—The relations between agriculture, manufactures, and commerce—The aggregate of the desires of the people of the United States—Their satisfactions can not be purchased in a foreign market—Satisfactions must be made at home—The price of them is the cost of living, and not taxation.

CHAPTER XI.

SCHEDULE "A"—PRODUCTION UNDER FREEDOM . . . 240

Mr. Springer's schedule of incidental taxation—Intended to show the taxation which protection imposes on consumers—Hon. Frank Hurd's assumption—The industrial organization out of which the farmer, the laborer, and the professor get their compensation—It must come from the exchange of services between them—Exports must pay for the imports—Free-traders victims of the fallacy of division—Why the atomistic view of society fails—The individual peddler—The Minnesota farmer—Prof. Sumner's iron problem—We must fall back on the domestic production—That must be put beyond the reach of contingency—Why destroyed industries can not spring up again—Capital and labor not reservoirs of pure force, to be turned on and off at pleasure—America as a manufacturing competitor—The law of indifference—The conditions on which free trade is possible—Prof. Cairnes and Mr. Mill's accounts of its operations on us—Mr. Carey's account of the necessary sequence of adopting it.

CHAPTER XII.

COST OF PRODUCTION—A PARADOX 277

Attempt of free-traders to solve the question on consideration of cost of production—Our high wages a detriment to competition—David A. Wells—Sir Thomas Brassey—Prof. Cairnes—Prof. Cairnes's paradox, that a high rate of wages means a low cost of production—What it proves—Lands us back into the group of agricultural industries—Prof. Perry's inventory of our resources—Why we have failed to enter into their possession under free trade—The "something else" we can do if we abandon the protected industries—English free-traders invite us to go into the general business of civilization for the benefit of the whole family of mankind—Our present mission rather to make commodities cheap and abundant for ourselves.

CHAPTER XIII.

A CASE IN POINT—THE AUSTRALIAN EPISODE 302

Gold in Australia and California—The cases of these countries illustrate how advantageous industries and cost of production operate in international commerce—The advantage of the industry depends on the command which its product has over the markets of the world—Food and gold—The relative efficiency of food and gold in making foreign exchanges—The decline in the productiveness of her mines resulted in the social, political, and pecuniary progress of Australia—Industrial growth not measured by extent of external trade—In the United States, what are called the advantageous industries, food and raw materials, never procured in foreign markets the other commodities we needed—A *dernier ressort* to domestic manufacture under protection.

CHAPTER XIV.

COMPETITION IN A FOREIGN MARKET COMPELS US TO EXPORT OUR GRATUITIES 311

Our so-called advantages lie in our natural resources—International commerce sets competition in operation—It gives us pay only for our onerous contribution to value—We export the gratuities for nothing—Rigid demonstration of this proposition by M. Bastiat—Cheap foreign labor not a gratuity to us—Bankruptcy and fire-damaged goods not a reliable source of supply—Our warfare is against nature and not against humanity elsewhere—The high-priced human instrument of production—Free trade enables Prof. Bonamy Price and Prof. Thorold-Rogers to call our Western prairie lands English farms—Mr. Carey's maxim, whoever is compelled to seek a market must pay the cost of getting to it.

CHAPTER XV.

GENERAL THEORY OF WAGES—HIGH RATE OF WAGES IN THE UNITED STATES 324

There is no general formula which can settle the exchange relations of capital, labor, and commodities—Supply and demand no solution—Commodities and laborers not produced upon the same motive—High wages here not based on exchange value of agricultural products—The theories of Profs. Perry, Sumner, and Walker examined—Competition of the farm with the shop—Independent proof that the protective tariff does not permit one citizen to collect taxes of another—High rate of wages in the United States based on the energetic character of people using highly productive instruments in field, forest, seas, and mines—Engaged principally in making commodities to be consumed by the laborer himself—The case as put by George Basil Dixwell and Prof. Sumner.

CHAPTER XVI.

WHY INDUSTRIAL ENTITIES SHOULD CORRESPOND WITH POLITICAL ENTITIES 361

The question only applicable to a group of freely trading nations—No such group on the earth as yet—To form such a group would lead to a redistribution of the capital and labor of the nations forming it—The group as a whole might gain, any member of it may lose—The cases in Germany and France—Free trading in France, Holland, Belgium, and Austria under Napoleon—The case of the thirty-eight States of the Union—The industrial entity not determined by economic motives—The reasons for maintaining the political entity are social and political—The economic results flow from them and are subsidiary—The conditions on which universal free trade can be realized.

CHAPTER XVII.

A Fallacy which Free-Traders put in the Mouths of Protectionists—Creating Industry 378

The professors ask, Can taxes make capital out of nothing?—Restrictions do not create productive energy—They permit a different distribution of existing energy—They awaken slumbering energies—The English Navigation Act—Adam Smith calls it "that great prohibitive and protective law, the wisest of all English commercial regulations"—What it did for English supremacy in trade—The fallacy of the syllogism of Mr. Mill—A question of fact, answered by Mr. Dixwell.

CHAPTER XVIII.

Industrial Results Achieved—Some Practical Maxims of Tariff Reform 391

The true grounds of our argument—How our landscape would have looked under free trade—The assault by American capital and labor on nature—Its grand results in increasing utilities and diminishing values—Leisure not possible to men of our race—Cheapened American products—Our contribution to the world's civilization—Has raised the *morale* of labor everywhere—The free-trader's proposals to export food, raw materials, and manufactured goods—An impossible proposal: it leaves nothing for other nations to do for us—Exports and imports no criterion of real growth—We are about to assert our supremacy on the ocean—Mr. Gladstone's Godspeed to us—Tariff reform, removing protective duties according to science—Horizontal reductions—The distinction between duties for revenue and protection—What consumers have a right to—The incidence of customs duties deduced from experience—The practical maxim for the future.

PROTECTION *VS.* FREE TRADE.

CHAPTER I.

PRELIMINARY—SOME DEFINITIONS.

It is a hundred years since Adam Smith published the "Wealth of Nations." After a century of theoretical discussion, the question of "free trade" and "protection" still awaits a practical settlement. Scholars have written essays, professors have written books, and statesmen have filled volumes of debates, without producing any settled reasons for their convictions on the subject in the minds of the majority of the people in any country. To-day it is an absorbing topic in America, and administrations and policies will be determined by the decision of the voters of the United States upon economic consequences involved in it. One great school of political economy conceive that they have established a series of propositions compelling belief in the doctrine of free trade, to which every intelligent mind must assent—asserting with more vigor than courtesy that, if a man has not yet made up his mind on this subject, it is because "he has no mind to make up." By virtue of much iteration they have persuaded themselves, and seem to have induced a wide-spread conviction in the public mind, that somewhere and somehow in *the science* of Political Economy are imbedded principles which establish this theory; that there are definite data in that science from which their conclusions inevitably flow; that there are certain scientific postulates from which can be unalterably deduced the economic policy of free trade. They assert that this science "belongs to no nation and is of no country." If such be the case—if the *theory* is a universal one and true; if science terminates in the theory—that should be the end of discussion. If the theory be true, the practice of it in accordance will be right. If it be demonstrable that free trade leads to the greatest economic gains for the people of the United States, then the statesman of the United States must practice in the art of political economy that which the philosopher teaches in the science of political economy. If there be any irrepealable laws of human nature, operating in the domain of this science, of universal application—appropriate to all people, at all times and under all circumstances—then we ought to know what they are and submit to this constitution of things. If there be no such general laws, we ought to know that. In that event we are remanded to the study of *the facts* in our situation *as a nation*, and shall be at liberty to adopt that policy which a fair rational judgment upon our own case shall dictate. The mere political economist is in the habit of laying down the conclusions of his science—its theoretical deductions—and then, when brought face to face with a practical question upon which action must be taken, he abdicates in favor of the "statesman." The modern economist has found it necessary to work out his problem as if *wealth* were an end in itself, leaving statesmen to take up his results and place them in their due relation to the wider purposes and aims of society. He deliberately forgets or suppresses the fact that society has other purposes and aims. He is uncertain whether his abstractions will find any corresponding reality in men and things. As an expert, he carries on all his processes on the assumption that he is operating in a vacuum, but as a layman he finds that the medium—human society—with which he is dealing is not a vacuum, but, on the contrary, is filled with resistance and obstructions, and his science avails nothing for conduct.

The pretensions of this school of economists whose logical outcome is free trade are entitled to examination. Most writers in England since the days of Adam Smith, and many in the United States, have insisted that the result of sound discussion in political economy leads to the doctrine of freedom of trade between all nations; and that irrespective of the fact that all nations do not adopt it. Inasmuch as all sentiment, all considerations of patriotism, of charity, of religion, of domestic ties, of honor, are by the very definition of political economy excluded from the field of the science by this school of economists, they must mean that by a system of free trade *the wealth* of any particular nation will be in the largest way promoted; that the necessaries, conveniences, and luxuries of its inhabitants will be supplied with less cost of labor *indirectly*, by means of foreign trade, than *directly* by the process of production. Neither the economist nor the statesman can be engaged in any more vital inquiry than whether this is indeed true. This inquiry is to be pursued, we are told, in the formal treatises on political economy. In that science, it is insisted, is a body of reasoned truth upon which we may take our stand; in it is a coherent system of doctrine which leads us to actual verities accessible to all men of average comprehension, equally available to the professor and the merchant, the farmer and the manufacturer, the student and the statesman. Surely, if there be such a system, the millions of quick, acute, and trained minds engaged in the wonderful industrial and commercial enterprises of our own times must come to some agreement touching first principles, and the inevitable consequences flowing from them; the student in his closet, and the business-man at his desk, ought to agree as to the truth, if there is ascertainable truth in the case. Probably it must be admitted that the majority of men in the various pursuits, even the most intelligent, have had neither the time nor opportunity to become familiar with the formulated propositions of the professional writers on political economy. That the science has never had very much practical effect in the conduct of men need not be adverted to; nor, indeed, that most men have been suspicious of the science. Nor has the dislike of the science, as a safe guide in affairs, ever been more intense than to-day. One has only to read the able and earnest essays of the best writers in England, the Continent, and the United States, to be persuaded of the doubt, the unrest, and the distrust pervading the most thoughtful minds as to the present condition and future standing of the science. As now taught, the dissatisfaction with its premises and its conclusions is wide-spread and intense. This dissatisfaction is confined to no school, and is equally felt by and expressed by all—free-trader as well as protectionist.

We propose to make an analysis of the teachings of the science of political economy, as touching the debate between "free trade" and "protection." If there be any "inmost nature" in the subject, we propose, under the guidance of the economists, to explore it. We propose briefly to inquire what this science is about, where its teachings begin, and where they end. A careful and an intelligent student ought to have no real difficulty in testing the validity of the definitions and the methods employed; and a sincere and a candid student should not hesitate to yield his intellectual assent to what is truth. That we may do *the science* and its professors no injustice, we must begin with them at the beginning, we must state all their premises, examine all their processes, and accept legitimate conclusions. That we may not be the victims of mere sophistry and rhetoric, we must watch them closely. If we see them floundering in the quagmire of the assumptions and deductions into which they have plunged, it is not necessary that we should leave solid ground. To garner the really few grains of truth which they have thrashed out, it will not be necessary to encumber ourselves with their bushels of chaff. The results, when reached, should be impersonal, and should be the triumph of the right, of clear and absolute knowledge. Prof. Cliffe Leslie says, in one of his essays: " The scientific spirit is not a triumphant and boastful one, fired with a sort of intellectual *chauvinism*, seeking polemical distinction and a path to promotion in the field of party war. A cavalry-officer of the period of the Crimean War, when that branch of the army was distinguished by the glory of a mustache, used to say that no man could conceive the pitch to which human conceit could soar, unless he had served in a light-dragoon regiment. He was, however, mistaken. There was a being yet more elate with a sense of superiority over his fellow-creatures in the economist who had Bastiat at his finger-ends, and who looked on political economy as a weapon by which he could discomfit political adversaries, and on free trade as a personal triumph, though he had as much claim to renown for it as a passenger in a Cunard steamer to the fame of Columbus." Prof. Bonamy Price, in his " Chapters on Practical Economy," does condescend to reargue the question, but he commiserates the dullness which resists his demonstration, " conspicuous and complete," and adds, " one is tempted to feel something of that mortification which a mathematician would experience if he was compelled to demonstrate anew the principles of the multiplication-table." Prof. Cairnes, so lately as 1874, in " Some Leading Principles of Political Economy newly Expounded," laments the necessity of restating axioms: "Nevertheless I am unwilling to leave the subject of these chapters without some fuller consideration than has yet been given to it of the great controversy not yet, unfortunately, extinct, of free trade *vs.* protection. I have said, 'not yet extinct'; perhaps I should rather have said even now active and glowing with something of its pristine fervor; for we have only to turn our eyes to France or to the United States, not to speak of our own colonies, to see with what vigor, and, I regret to say, with what success, the venerable sophism still maintains itself, alike in the public press and in national legislation."

Nor can we withhold a measure of sympathy with our own Prof. Perry. In the edition of his " Political Economy," 1873, with true prophetic fervor he had said: " This doctrine, clearly an outgrowth of the mercantile system, is now something more than two hundred years old, and is everywhere in its decrepitude. An incurable wound was inflicted on it by the publication of Adam Smith's ' Wealth of Nations,' in 1776; the centennial of that event and of American independence will probably witness very little practical vitality in it anywhere in the world; it has died out utterly in Great Britain, where it once had a vigorous life; it colors scarcely at all the revenue systems of the German and Austrian Empires; it still lingers feebly in Russia; it has had a recent temporary revivification in France; and, though steadily and rapidly declining in the United States, it has been strong enough here to control the national legislation of the past decade."

In 1883, with somewhat baffled expectation, the language is: "The taint, however, of its birth and breeding rests on it like a curse; even if let alone, it would now have been in its decrepitude owing to the poisons in its blood; but an incurable wound was inflicted on it in 1776 by one Adam Smith, hastening it toward its burial; the centennial of that event and of American independence found it a lingering energy of evil, especially in the United States" (the professor might have added, under the malign and crude empiricism of such statesmen as Bismarck and Thiers, also in Germany and France; and, as if in the very irony of science, in Canada and Victoria); "and political economy, denouncing it as the enemy of mankind, hopes soon to throw upon its loathsome carcass the last shovelsful of cleansing earth."

Unfortunately for the political economists, protection is no "carcass." It is still a live subject for vivisection, and the "cleansing earth" seems rather to withhold its offices for those who are now wielding the scalpel and the dissecting-knife over it. It will be evident, indeed, that there are still many "unsettled questions in political economy," as there were when John Stuart Mill wrote his elaborate essay under that title. In his "Essay on the Production of Wealth," Colonel Torrens, more than sixty years ago, said: "With respect to political economy, the period of controversy is passing away; and that of unanimity is rapidly approaching. Twenty years hence there will scarcely exist a doubt respecting any of its fundamental principles." At the end of the twenty years Prof. Senior pointed out the want of definiteness and certainty of meaning in the terms "value," "wealth," "labor," "capital," "rent," "wages," and "profits." These are the principal terms in the science of political economy. "When," he says, "we read the most eminent of the recent writers on the subject, we find them chiefly engaged in controversy. Instead of being able to use the works of his fellow-laborers, every economist begins by demolition and erects a new edifice, resting perhaps in a great measure on the same foundation, but differing from all that have preceded it in form and arrangement."

Mr. Mill has said of Adam Smith's "Wealth of Nations" that "it is in many parts obsolete and in all imperfect"; and Stephen Colwell, a competent witness, testifies that the successors and disciples of Adam Smith "have not hesitated to cut and carve, and apply the caustic until there is scarcely an important passage in the whole work ('Wealth of Nations') which some one of his friends has not detached from his system as wrong or branded as absurd." The fate of some of these words has been "settled" by the late economists. Prof. Perry, of Williams College, abolishes the word "wealth" outright, and Prof. Jevons does the same by "value." Of Colonel Torrens's "unlucky prophecy," so eminent a writer as Prof. Cairnes, as lately as the year 1874, says, "So far from the period of controversy having passed, it seems hardly yet to have begun—controversy, I mean, not merely respecting propositions of secondary importance, or the practical application of scientific doctrines, but controversy respecting *fundamental propositions*, which lie at the root of its reasoning, and which were regarded as settled when Colonel Torrens wrote."

As all this testimony comes from well-known teachers of the "orthodox" English economy, it will serve to put us on our guard as we go with them hastily through the science, its definitions and development. We have not the space to pause and indicate the want of unanimity in definitions and ambiguity and confusion in their application, except so far as they bear on the controversy in hand.

Adam Smith (1776) gives no definition of his science. His work is entitled "An Inquiry into the Nature and Causes of the Wealth of Nations." "Political economy," he says, "proposes two distinct objects: first, to provide a plentiful revenue or subsistence for the people, or, more properly, to enable them to provide such a revenue or subsistence for themselves; and, secondly, to supply the state or commonwealth with a revenue sufficient for the public service. It proposes to enrich both the people and the sovereign."

Sir James Steuart (1767): "The principal object of the science is to secure a certain fund of subsistence for all the inhabitants, to obviate any circumstance which may render it precarious to provide anything necessary for supplying the wants of the society, and to employ the inhabitants (supposing them to be freemen) in such manner as naturally to create *reciprocal relations and dependencies between them*, so as to make their *several interests lead them to supply one another with their reciprocal wants*. . . . *Political economy in each country must necessarily be different.*" This proposition has been attacked as heterodox, but it will be seen that the very latest writers of the orthodox school have been compelled to accept it.

M. Say: "Political economy is the economy of society; a science combining the results of our observations on the nature and functions of the different parts of the social body."

Mr. McCulloch: "The science of the laws which regulate the production, accumulation, distribution, and consumption of those articles or products that are necessarily useful or agreeable to man and possess exchangeable value"; and that "its object is to point out the means by which the industry of man may be rendered most productive of wealth, to ascertain the circumstances most favorable to its accumulation, the proportions in which it is divided, and the mode in which it may be most advantageously consumed."

M. Sismondi: "The physical welfare of man, so far as it can be the work of government, is the object of political economy."

M. Storch: "Political economy is the science of the natural laws which determine the prosperity of nations, that is to say, their wealth and their civilization."

Prof. Senior: "That science which treats of the nature, the production, and the distribution of wealth."

Mr. Mill: "Writers on political economy profess to teach or to investigate the nature of wealth, and the laws of its production and distribution, including, directly or remotely, the operation of all the causes by which the condition of mankind or of any society of human beings in respect to this universal object of desire is made prosperous or the reverse."

Prof. Roscher: "By the science of national or political economy we understand the science which has to do with the laws of the development of the economy of a nation. . . . It inquires how the various wants of the people of a country, especially those of food, clothing, fuel, shelter, etc., may be satisfied; how the satisfaction of these wants influences the aggregate *national* life, and how in time they are influenced by the *national* life."

M. Bastiat: "Every effort, capable of satisfying, on condition of a return, the wants of a person other than the man who makes the effort, and consequently the wants and satisfactions relative to this species of effort, constitute the domain of political economy. . . . Political economy is the theory of exchange."

Henry C. Carey: "The science of the laws which govern man in his efforts to secure for himself the highest *individuality* and the greatest power of his *association* with his fellow-men."

Prof. Francis A. Walker: "Political economy or economics is the name of that body of knowledge which relates to wealth. Political economy has to do with no other subject whatever than wealth. Especially should the student of economics take care not to allow any purely political, ethical, or social considerations to influence him in his investigations. All that he has as an economist to do, is to find out how wealth is produced, exchanged, distributed, and consumed.

"It will remain for the social philosopher, the moralist, or the statesman to decide how far the pursuit of wealth, according to the laws discovered by the economist, should be subordinated to other, let us say higher, considerations. . . . It can not be too strongly insisted on that the economist as such has nothing to do with the questions—what men had better do—how nations should be governed—or what regulations should be made for their mutual intercourse. His business is simply to trace economic effects to their causes, leaving it to the philosopher of every-day life, to the moralist, or the statesman, to teach how men and nations should act in view of the economical principles so established. The political economist, for example, has no more call to preach free trade, as the policy of nations, than a physiologist to advocate monogamy as a legal institution."

Prof. Sidgwick: "Political economy, in England. at least, is now almost universally understood to be a study or inquiry concerned with the production, distribution, and exchange of wealth."

Prof. Bowen: "On what principles do men readily exchange these articles" (the aggregate of things which we call wealth) "for each other; and what motives, what general laws, regulate their production, distribution, and consumption? Political economy undertakes to answer this question, and is therefore properly considered one of the moral sciences."

Prof. Perry classes economics as a moral science with metaphysics and ethics. "Is there a single class of facts, easily conceived of and defined as such, . . . with which alone political economy has to do? We answer: Yes. *Sales* are a very definite thing. They are never confounded with gifts, and they are never confounded with thefts. . . . Political economy is the science of sales or exchanges. Anything whatsoever that is *salable*, or can be made so, comes within its view, and, scientifically, *it cares nothing whatever for anything else.*"

Prof. Cairnes: "The science which traces the phenomena of the production and distribution of wealth up to their causes in *the principles of human nature* and the laws and events, *physical, political*, and *social*, of the external world."

With this diversity in premises, it is manifest that there is a wide margin for diversity in the conclusions reached by the professors of the science.

The most manageable definition, and the one from which advance may most easily be made into the region of actual experience, is that of M. de Laveleye. It is the one upon which the discussion which follows is based:

"Political economy may therefore be defined as the science which determines what laws men ought to adopt in order that they may, *with the least possible exertion, procure the greatest abundance* of things useful for the *satisfaction* of their *wants*, may distribute them justly and consume them rationally."

CHAPTER II.

THE SCIENCE OF POLITICAL ECONOMY—THE MECHANISM OF PRODUCTION.

HAVING thus made his definitions and set the limits to the "field of the science," let us see briefly how the political economist proceeds to develop his subject. The method will be familiar to every student and high-school pupil. He attempts an analysis of the social structure. By close and accurate observations he undertakes to ascertain what is going on in the organism about him. He takes account of the activities in operation and endeavors to trace the details of these operations. The motive power he finds in human nature. It is the "satisfaction of human wants," "with the least possible effort." It is not alone the cravings of hunger and thirst, the effects of heat and cold, of drought and damp. The satisfaction of every lower want in the scale creates a desire of a higher character. No limit is thus set to the labors of humanity. As the satisfaction of our desires can not be had except on the condition of being consumers, purchasers, each one is, in the main, under the necessity of producing that which he exchanges. "Every man who puts forth an effort to satisfy the desire of another, with the expectation of a return, is a producer." To the extent to which he directly satisfies his own wants by his own labor, he is not in the contemplation of the political economists. The man or the nation which can satisfy its own wants by its own labor, neither needs foreign exchanges nor the aid of any science of foreign exchanges. "When a man shaves his own face, our science has nothing to say—when the barber shaves him for a fee, it has a good deal to say."

The instruments of production are labor, capital, and land, or natural agents. "The produce of the earth—all that is derived from its surface by the united application of labor, machinery, and capital—is divided among three classes of the community: the proprietor of the land, the owner of the stock, or capital necessary for its cultivation, and the laborer, by whose industry it is cultivated. To determine the laws which regulate this distribution is the principal problem in political economy." This is Mr. Ricardo's formula. These laws operate independently of human interference, and, by consequence, he did not consider wealth in connection with human welfare.

The share of the proprietor of the land, or other natural agent, is called rent; the share of the owner of the stock, or capital, is called profit; the share of the laborer is called wages. Whatever may be the nature of the finished product, whether of an agricultural or a manufacturing process, the problem of the science is to ascertain the share which goes to each of the agents concerned in its production. Really preliminary to the actual process which issues in the product is an inquiry involving data lying still deeper in human nature, to wit, the impulse under which men engage at all in societary co-operation. This leads to the science of society or sociology. Passing that for the present, we endeavor to ascertain the laws which determine the distributive share of each in the joint result.

It may as well be confessed, at the outset, that no laws can be laid down which give us the slightest assurance that true sequence of facts and their relation has been ascertained. Competition has been supposed to be the optimistic (or pessimistic) Jack-of-all-trades which brings about the equilibrium of the contesting claimants. Competition between the owners of capital lowers interest and profits; between landlords it lowers rent; between laborers it lowers wages.[1] In all these cases, the value of the services offered are said to depend on "supply and demand," or the price of commodities is said to depend on cost of production, or the cost of reproduction. The cost of production is said to consist of "wages and profits," or the expectation of profits. Sometimes it is said the price varies with the demand, and again, that the demand varies with the price. Or, again, the supply is said to determine the price, and still again, the price is said to create or determine the supply. In all this ceaseless round of human activities, it seems to be agreed that no law has been discovered which awards the results of labor on the maxim, either "to each according to his wants"—"to each according to his work"—or "to each according to his sacrifice." It can not be doubted that, if the science of political economy could discover any laws which would lead to a just scheme of distribution, they would be recognized and enforced.

"It is only exertion which demands for itself something in exchange that is, technically, labor. . . . So far as exertion, physical or mental, is put forth for amusement, physical or mental, it has nothing to do with political economy."

"Labor," says Adam Smith, "was the first price, the original purchase-money paid for all things, and it constitutes *the ultimate* and *real standard* by which their *value*

---

[1] Herein is seen the underlying fallacy of much of the agitation and discussion which assumes that "capital" and "labor" are in competition. They are not. The competition is that of capital with capital, and labor with labor.

can be estimated and compared." The *natural* price of labor, according to Ricardo, is "that price which is necessary to enable the laborers, one with another, to subsist and perpetuate their race without increase or diminution."

The text-writers usually divide it into common, skilled, and professional labor. Following Adam Smith, they lay it down that the rate of wages will be determined, in their action on the supply of labor, by the agreeableness or disagreeableness of the employment; the easiness and cheapness, or the difficulty and expense, of learning the different employments; the constancy or inconstancy of employment; the amount of trust involved; the probability of success; custom, prejudice, and fashion; legal restrictions and voluntary associations (under this head is discussed the operation of guilds and trades-unions); and the mobility of laborers, or the lack of it. The last consideration has an important economic bearing on the question of international trade, and we shall have occasion to recur to it.

Many recent economists have recognized a distinct class of "laborers," whom, for the want of a proper English word, they call *entrepreneurs* (undertakers). These are the organizers of our great industries, and their compensation is referred to the head of " profits." They receive what is called the " wages of management." The modern industrial organization is, indeed, based upon the high executive skill of this class of men.

" Capital" has had almost as many definitions as there have been writers on the subject, and does not appear as yet to have any generally received meaning. The distinction between " capital " and " money " is all-important, and must be borne constantly in mind.

Mr. Carey defines it as "the instrument by means of which man obtains mastery over Nature," and includes the mental powers of man himself as well as his physical powers. Macleod calls capital "any economic quantity used for the purpose of profit." Prof. Senior defines it as "an article of wealth, the result of human exertion, employed in the production and distribution of wealth."

Adam Smith: "That part of a man's stock which he expects to afford him revenue is called his capital."

Ricardo: "Capital is that part of the wealth of a country which is employed in production, and consists of food, clothing, tools, raw materials, machinery, etc., necessary to give effect to labor."

J. S. Mill: "The distinction between capital and not-capital does not lie in the kind of commodities, but in the mind of the capitalist—in his will to employ them for one purpose rather than another; and all property, however ill adapted itself for the use of labor, is a part of capital so soon as it, or the value to be received from it, is set apart for productive reinvestment. The sum of all the values so destined by their respective possessors composes the capital of the country."

Prof. Sidgwick does not define capital, but he adverts to the fact that a different signification is given to the term capital by the man of business and the economist. The former understands by it "wealth employed so as to yield a profit," whether this profit be gained by increasing the whole stock of wealth in the country, or by getting possession of the wealth of others, in exchange for services. The latter understands it as "wealth employed in production." This distinction will be useful.

Prof. Perry: "Anything valuable *outside of man himself* which becomes a means in further production." This definition excludes physical and mental powers, skill, honesty, etc. The reward for these is wages. But, while not capital, these are agencies in production, quite as indispensable as conditions. "Capital is some product, always a commodity or a claim, reserved for the sake of an increase to present values through its employment productively, which increase is called profits."

Prof. Jevons: "Capital, as I regard it, consists merely in the aggregate of those commodities which are required for sustaining laborers of any kind or class engaged in work." A stock of food is the main element of capital. The current means of sustenance constitute capital in its free or unassisted form. "The function of capital is to enable the laborer to await the results of his labor."

"A claim" is "a right to demand in the future." Prof. Perry says this is capital—a position much controverted. "Credit" represents the outcome of those claims, and we all know how enormously they have been extended in modern times. "Credit not only convenes exchanges but also *creates* them; it brings something new into the world of traffic, a new class of things bought and sold, values that would not otherwise have existed at all. It enlarges the field of political economy, and makes a new grand division of time pay tribute to the world of sales. The past is represented in commodities, the present in personal services, and the future in credits. . . . The chief gain for individuals and for the whole community in the use of proper credits . . . is found in the fact that *a new capital* is thereby created, a new purchasing power, something in the world of values *additional* to what existed before."

Are intellectual and moral powers capital? Prof. Senior has said, "It is not on the accidents of soil or climate, or on the existing accumulation of the material instruments of production, but on the quantity and the diffusion of this immaterial capital" (knowledge, skill, education), "that the wealth of a country depends." If, as we shall have occasion to see, political economy undertakes to exclude these considerations from its economic view, so much the worse for the science.

Economists, then, divide capital into "fixed" capital and "circulating" capital—into "consumers'" capital and "producers'" capital. "Circulating capital is all new materials—all wages paid out in view of ultimate profit—completed products on hand for sale—all products bought and held for the sake of resale. Fixed capital will be found under one or other of the following heads: all tools and machinery—all buildings used for production purposes—all permanent improvements on land—all investments in aid of locomotion, such as railroads, canals, ships, and everything subsidiary to them—all products loaned or rented or retained for that purpose—and the national money as a whole." (Prof. Perry.)

Capital is the result of saving. It results from the act of a person who either abstains from the unproductive use of what he can command, or prefers the production of remote to that of immediate results.

Prof. Senior very philosophically substituted the word "abstinence" for "profit." It expresses the act or conduct of which profit is the reward, and which bears the same relation to profit that labor does to wages. "By the word abstinence we wish to express that agent, distinct from labor and the agency of nature, the concurrence of which is necessary to the existence of capital, and which stands in the same relation to profit as labor does to wages."

Capital may be indefinitely increased by using the results of saving, or the products of labor and the other instruments of production, for the purpose of further production.

"Productive consumption is that use of a commodity which occasions an ulterior product. Unproductive consumption is, of course, that use which occasions no ulterior product. The characteristic of unproductive consumption is, that it adds to the enjoyment of no one but the consumer himself. Its only effect upon the rest of the community is to diminish *pro tanto* the mass of commodities applicable to their use."

The remuneration to the proprietor of land is called rent. Land, in this connection, includes mines, rivers, and ports—indeed, any appropriated natural agents, limited in extent or number. The definitions of rent given below will show the different theories upon which it is supposed rent accrues.

Ricardo: "Rent is that portion of the produce of the earth which is paid to the landlord for the use of the original and indestructible powers of the soil." This view of rent has been adopted by Prof. Senior, John Stuart Mill, and the great body of English economists.

Prof. Perry defines rent (edition of 1883) as follows: "The rent of leased lands is the measure of the service which the owner of the land thereby renders to the actual cultivator of it," (having added in the edition of 1873) 'and does not differ essentially in its return from the rents of buildings in cities or from the interest of money." The philosophy of Henry C. Carey and Frédéric Bastiat, whom Perry follows, led them to this conception of the nature of rent, because they held that in all schemes of production *the utilities of nature were gratuitous.* Prof. Perry says, after Carey and Bastiat, that there are no "original and indestructible powers of the soil, and, if there were, they are God's gifts, and no one is authorized to take pay for their use. Land derives its value from the onerous contributions of man." We shall have a necessity further on to look into this matter. A correct understanding of the nature of rent is a fundamental one in social science. Of Ricardo's "Theory of Rent," including "the law of diminishing production from land," Mr. Mill has said: "This general law of agricultural industry is the most important proposition in political economy. Were the law different, nearly all the phenomena of the production and distribution of wealth would be other than they are."[1]

Under the head of land, the economist usually treats of the tenure under which lands are held, the laws of descent, etc.

Where the proprietor and the cultivator are the same person, he is the recipient of both rent and profit in virtue of the double relation he bears to a natural agent of production.

Writers on economics generally hold that the proceeds of a given product are distributed in the following order: First, rent; second, interest; third, profits; fourth, wages.

The conditions of successful production are: Association, the coming together of men of various desires, various capacities, and various employments; division of labor, in which connection international commerce has been designated as making "territorial division of labor" possible; and invention, by which, to a greater and greater extent, we are enabled to employ the gratuitous forces of nature by means of mechanical and chemical discoveries.

We may as well pause here long enough to indicate that the entire theory of free trade is based on the notion of "division of labor." In short, it is this: "The only reason why men ever exchange services at all is on the ground of relative superiority at different points. The tailor makes the blacksmith's coat and the blacksmith shoes

---

[1] "Rent is the surplus of the crop above the cost of cultivation on the least productive lands contributing to supply the market. Admitting the private ownership of land, that surplus, necessarily, so far as economic forces are concerned, is left in the hands of the landlord. There, so far as economic forces are concerned, it must remain."—PROF. FRANCIS A. WALKER.

the tailor's horses for no other reason in the world except that each has a relative advantage of the other in his own work, and therefore there is a mutual gain in their exchanging works." It is manifestly assumed in this *régime* that the tailor has a market for all his products *as a tailor*, and that he can expend *all his time and skill* in the production of commodities in which he has this relative advantage, and that *he has a market* for these commodities.

And so of the blacksmith. If there is not a market for all the commodities which he can produce *as a blacksmith*—the occupation in which he has the greatest relative advantages—he must embody his surplus time and skill in the production of some other commodity or stand idle. Thus much of individuals.

The same of nations. The diversity of relative advantages at different points exhibited by different nations is the basis of international exchanges.

"The various countries of the earth have received from the hands of God a diversity of original gifts, in soil, natural productions, position, and opportunity. This diversity exists for a good design" (note the subtle introduction of theological predilection in this phrase), "and can never be substantially reduced by man, even if there were, as there is not, any good reason for desiring to reduce it. Besides original diversity in these respects, there has been developed in the history of the inhabitants of these countries a diversity of tastes, aptitudes, habits, strength, intelligence, and skill to avail themselves of the forces of nature around them. These differences are somewhat less inherent and more flexible than the others, but they exist and always have existed, and in a greater or less degree always will exist, and it is in these diversities, original, traditional, and acquired, that international commerce depends. . . . There is no mutual gain in any series of exchanges, unless each party has a superior power in producing that which is rendered, compared with his power in producing that which is received." (Prof. Perry.)

This is a correct exposition of the motive and conditions of foreign trade. The free-trader assigns to the United States the production of the things in which we have the superiority over other nations; and on these products we accept our assignment in "the international division of labor." But we accept this rôle on the further unalterable alternative presented by Adam Smith in the "Wealth of Nations":

"*The division of labor is limited by the extent of the market.* Before any man, or any set of men, can, in common prudence, devote themselves to any particular employment, they must be assured that they can dispose of the commodity which their exertions in the prosecution of that employment will produce. In situations where there is not a sufficient number of customers near at hand to consume the manufactured article" (in our case, for "manufactured article," substitute "food and raw material"), "or where it can not with advantage be transported to those at a distance, the making of that article can never become the exclusive employment of any man or set of men. *Where, therefore, there is not a sufficiently extensive market, labor can not be so much subdivided as it otherwise would,* and *its productive powers are cramped for want of room in which to exert themselves.*"

We venture to anticipate the discussion so much as to predict that Prof. Perry's premises, Adam Smith's dictum, the productive forces of the United States, and the world's market, will, when put in conjunction, constitute a quadrilateral within which free foreign trade in America must perish of inanity.

The causes which determine the productiveness of labor

are, first, the personal character of the laborer, his corporeal, intellectual, and moral qualities; secondly, the degree in which he is assisted by natural agents; thirdly, the degree in which he is assisted by capital; fourthly, the degree of freedom with which he is allowed to direct his industry. (Prof. Senior.)

Inasmuch as almost all commodities are produced, or most efforts are put forth, for the purpose of being exchanged, we come to the conditions under which exchanges are made: "Men have desires, are capable of making efforts to meet those desires, and experience a satisfaction when the desires are met. . . . Desires, efforts, satisfactions, constitute the one circle of political economy, and value arises in every case from a comparison of two corresponding efforts. Efforts are naturally irksome. Everybody wishes to realize as large a satisfaction as possible from a given effort. If, by making that effort for another, a larger satisfaction will be realized than by expending it directly for one's self, there is an immediate and pressing motive to make the effort for another, and to reach the satisfaction not directly, but indirectly, that is, by exchange." (Perry.) The adoption of a system of exchanges makes the possession of value of any kind equivalent to the possession of the objects of personal desire. *Value*, then, is the mediator between exchanges. Perhaps the common sense of mankind has had no practical difficulty with this word, but the mode in which the conception is generated has been wrestled with by professional writers. Henry C. Carey was the first one who worked it out by means of any wide view of the nature of the social structure, and the action and interaction of the powers of man and nature. In a general way, it had been treated as growing out of labor—as affected by the scarcity of the commodity in which it was incorporated—by supply and demand, by utility, capability of accumulation, conservability, and so on. Mr. Carey says: "*Utility* is the measure of man's power over nature, *value* is the measure of nature's power over man. The former grows, the latter declines, with the power of combination among men." These definitions are exceedingly abstract, but they logically contain the philosophy which Mr. Carey promulgated. They are the first disclosure of a scheme which gives *valuable things, wealth,* their true function in a human progressive society. They are the basis of the optimistic view which he, and after him Frédéric Bastiat, takes of the final outcome of human society. The latter's correlative propositions are: " In the state of isolation, our wants exceed our powers; in the social state, our powers exceed our wants." The result of this exposition of the whole of social science is thus expressed: " *The constant approximation of all men toward a level, which is always rising;* in other terms, *improvement and equalization;* in a single word, HARMONY."

The general notion is thus developed by Bastiat: " Let us accustom ourselves to distinguish *utility* from *value;* without this there can be no economic science. I give utterance to no paradox when I affirm that *utility* and *value*, so far from being identical, are ideas opposed to one another. Want, efforts, satisfaction: here we have man regarded in an economic point of view. The relation of utility is with want and satisfaction. The relation of value is with effort. Utility is the good, which puts an end to the want by the satisfaction. Value is the evil, for it springs from the obstacle which is interposed between the want and the satisfaction. But for these obstacles there would have been no effort either to make or to exchange. Utility would be infinite, gratuitous, and common, without condition, and the notion of value would never have entered the world. In consequence of these obstacles, utility is gratuitous only on condition of efforts exchanged, which, when compared with each other, give rise to value. The more these obstacles give way before the liberality of nature and the progress of science, the more does utility approximate to the state of being absolutely common and gratuitous; for the onerous conditions, and consequently the value, diminish as the obstacles diminish. I shall esteem myself fortunate if, by these dissertations, which may be subtile, I succeed in establishing this encouraging truth, *the legitimate property* of value, and this other truth, equally consoling, *the progressive community* of utility." These considerations certainly open a hopeful view of the future supremacy of the human family over the forces of nature. If the logic and rhetoric of Bastiat had stood him in as good stead in the whole of his discussion, he need not have separated from Mr. Carey on the question of "protection."

"The utility involved in every valuable service is derived from two sources—the free contribution of nature and the onerous contribution of man. If the service be unique, if only one person or a few be in a position to render it, no useful principle can be laid down which shall discriminate the two component parts of the utility; but in respect to the vast mass of services, of which a market rate can be predicated, it is very clear that the competition with each other of those who are ready to render them will fix the current value at a point which shall just about compensate for the onerous element involved. That portion of the utility which is the free gift of nature will be very nearly a common factor in that whole set of services. *The action of competition will eliminate this common factor, and tend constantly to determine value on the basis merely of what man has done to impart utility to those services,*" (Prof. Perry.)

Value is not in the material thing, it is no quality of the commodity. But, inasmuch as services are mainly incorporated in material things, it seems likely that the human family will continue to exchange their products and services without much regard to the metaphysics of the case.

Value, then, is "the relation of mutual exchange established between two services by their exchange."

As men can not, as a general thing, exchange their products directly with each other—as barter is impossible in any extended commercial organization—the invention of some medium of exchange was natural and necessary. Money is that medium. It is the great economic agent to bring the producer and consumer together. It is the great instrument of association between men. Coin, token-coin, convertible and inconvertible notes, legal tender and not-legal tender, bankers' credits, checks, mercantile bills, exchequer bills, and many other forms of credit, may be called *money*. While it is a purely human device and was adopted for man's convenience, it has often seemed to master society and thwart its purposes. In its essence and functions it ought to be neither complicated nor mysterious. The basis of gold and silver has been settled upon by the common consent of the nations, but there are yet outstanding many unsettled questions: the possibility and advisability of a bimetallic standard, the amount which the exchanges of a nation require, the relation of paper money to coin, and the real nature of the credit which paper currency stands for, are sufficiently undetermined to render their discussion, even, at times dangerous to the stability of trade and finance. All of us are familiar with the unaccountable phenomena of commercial crises. Money may be abundant, enterprises may invite to effort, labor may be standing waiting in its market, but a pall hangs over society activities. Credit has departed from men. Want of confidence paralyzes all industrial movement. It is a time of panic, and no science can predict the future. Indeed, science can not account for the past. In such crises we hear much of over-production, under-consumption, and under-production. It is an idle jangle of words, and neither describes nor explains anything.

It would seem as if some phases of the money question ought to be settled by this time, but controversies go on. Inasmuch as "money is the current and legal measure of values," the material of which money itself is made must be a commodity having value. The only real dollar known to the commerce of the world is the coin dollar. This proposition, however, is still in dispute.

But there is another kind of money, the paper dollar—the promise-dollar. Inasmuch as it is the sign and not the thing signified; is "the representative of something and not that something itself," the promise-dollar ought always to be convertible into the real dollar. As a measure of value or of exchange the paper dollar must be redeemable; redeemable in a real commodity—also a proposition still disputed.

Money performs functions as a medium of exchange, a measure of value, a standard of value, and a store of value.

"The whole question," says Henry C. Carey, "and all the philosophy of money is, however, settled by the simple proposition, of universal truth, that in the natural course of human affairs the prices of raw and finished commodities tend to approximate, the former rising as the latter fall, and the rapidity of the change increasing with every increase in the supply of *those metals* which *constitute the standard with which prices need be compared*. . . . Approximation in the prices of the raw material and the finished commodity is the one essential characteristic of civilization. . . . *Money* is *the instrument of association*—the cause of motion and power in a society."

As accounting for much of the want and misery in the world the orthodox economist, in some form or other, makes use of Dr. Malthus's "Theory of Population." In this way he undertakes to give the reasons why, in the case of so many millions of the human race, "effort" is not rewarded by "satisfaction." The Malthusian theory is this: "According to the principle of population, the human race has a tendency to increase faster than food. It has, therefore, a constant tendency to people a country fully up to the limits of subsistence; meaning by those limits the lowest quantity of food which will maintain a stationary population."

Mr. McCulloch thinks that "the power of increase in the human species must always in the long run prove an overmatch for the increase in the means of subsistence." Mr. Mill's statement is that "the tendency of population to increase in most places faster than capital is proved incontestably by the condition of the population in most parts of the globe." This tendency to increase in population can be only held in check by moral self-restraint or by the scourges of famine, pestilence, and war. The doctrine has been made to play a decisive part in some of the speculations of famous writers. Prof. Perry dismisses it thus: "Malthusianism, as it has been called, is really a topic of physiology and not of political economy at all. Political economy presupposes the existence of persons able and willing to make exchanges before it begins its inquiries and generalizations. How they come into existence, the rate of their natural increase, and the relation of this increase to food, however interesting as physiological questions, have clearly nothing to do with our science." But in the matter of "exchanges," we shall find that the wages question, as related to the demand and supply of labor, and the distinction between *labor* and *the laborer*, have something to do with our science.

What is called the wages-fund theory has been made an important part in the process of production and distribution. Adam Smith had laid down, as quite fundamental, this proposition: "The general industry of the society never can exceed what the capital of the society can employ. As the number of workmen that can be kept in employment by any particular person must bear a certain proportion to his capital, so the number of those that can be continually employed by all the members of a great society must bear a certain proportion to the whole capital of that society, and can never exceed that portion." In Smith's discussion, this is one of the pillars of his free-trade system. We shall see later on the essential vice of this statement as a statement of fact. It is not true that industry is limited by capital, and, as a matter of fact, there has never been any limitation on the employment of labor by reason of lack of capital. It is one mode of formulating the wages-fund theory.

Mr. Mill states that theory in these words: "There is supposed to be at any instant a sum of wealth which is unconditionally devoted to the payment of wages. This sum is not regarded as unalterable, for it is augmented by saving and increasing with the progress of wealth; but it is reasoned upon as at any given moment a predetermined amount. More than that amount it is assumed that the wages-receiving class can not possibly divide among them; that amount, and no less, they can not but obtain. So that, the sum to be divided being fixed, the wages of each depend solely on the divisor, the number of participants." In other words, the quotient, wages, would be increased in the ratio in which the divisor, laborers, were decreased.

Now, it is still a disputed question whether wages are paid out of capital at all; whether the laborer does not advance his labor to the capitalist. Under the attack of Mr. Thornton, Mill himself abandoned the wages-fund theory. Prof. Walker and Mr. Longe both repudiate it. Prof. Cairnes, even after Mill's defection, returns to its defense. Prof. Perry holds to a form of it, somewhat modified. Some of them seem to think that in some way or other the doctrine of free trade could be best maintained on the assumption of the truth of the theory.

Prof. Jevons thus disposes of this question: "There is another inversion of the problem of economics which is generally made in works upon the subject. Although labor is the starting-point in production, and the interests of the laborer the very subject of the science, yet economists do not progress far before they suddenly turn around and treat labor as a commodity which is bought up by capitalists. Labor becomes itself the object of the laws of supply and demand, instead of those laws acting in the distribution of the products of labor. Economists have invented, too, a very simple theory to determine the rate at which capital can buy up labor. The average rate of wages, they say, is found by dividing the whole amount of capital appropriated to the payment of wages by the number of the laborers paid; and they wish us to believe that this settles the question. But a little consideration shows that this proposition is simply a truism. The average rate of wages must be equal to what is appropriated to the purpose, divided by the number who share it. The whole question will consist in determining how much is appropriated for the purpose; for it certainly need not be the whole existing amount of circulating capital. Mill distinctly says that because industry is limited by capital we are not to infer that it always reaches that limit; and, as a matter of fact, we often observe that there is abundance of capital to be had at low rates of interest, while there are also large numbers of artisans starving for want of employment. The wages-fund theory is, therefore, illusory as a real solution of the problem."

"Another part of the current doctrines of economics determines the rate of profit of capitalists in a very simple manner. The whole produce of industry must be divided into the portions paid to rent, taxes, profits, and wages. . . . Eliminating rent and taxes as exceptional, we thus arrive at the simple equation—

Produce = profit + wages.

A plain result also is drawn from the formula; for we are told that if wages rise, profits must fall, and *vice versa*. But such a doctrine is radically fallacious: it involves the attempt to determine two unknown quantities from one equation. I grant that, if the produce be a fixed amount, then, if wages rise profits must fall, and *vice versa*. Something might perhaps be made of this doctrine if Ricardo's theory of a natural rate of wages—that which is just sufficient to support the laborer—held true. But I altogether question the existence of any such rate."

"The view which I accept concerning the rate of wages is not more difficult to comprehend than the current one. It is that the wages of a working-man are ultimately coincident with what he produces, after the deduction of rent, taxes, and the interest of capital. I think that, in the equation—

Produce = profit + wages,

the quantity of produce is essentially variable." Prof. Walker agrees to this, and thinks from the total produce is first deducted rent, then interest, then profits, and that "labor is the residual claimant to the product of industry."

We have now the clew as to the amount of capital

which will be appropriated to the payment of wages in any trade: "The amount of capital will depend upon the amount of *anticipated* profits, and the competition to obtain proper workmen will strongly tend to secure to the latter all their legitimate share in the ultimate produce."

"The fact is that labor once spent has no influence on the future value of any article; it is gone and lost forever. In commerce, by-gones are forever by-gones, and we are always starting clear at each moment, judging the values of things with a view to future utility. Industry is essentially prospective, not retrospective, and seldom does the result of any undertaking exactly coincide with the first intention of its promoters." Mr. Carey's theorem was that "value depends on the cost of reproduction."

We now have a sketch of the mechanism of the industrial organism. We see how the economic man tends to behave. Unfortunately for the scientific value of the conclusions to be drawn, we have little more than *tendencies*, and all along there are occasions for "allowances," "corrections," "friction," and "disturbing elements."

CHAPTER III.

THE MOTIVE TO PRODUCTION—THE ECONOMIC MAN.

WE, following the economist, turn then to the motive power of this mechanism. We are to explore the mental characteristics of the man who is to put it all in motion. We turn from the external world to mental phenomena— the behavior of a being having desires, intellectual and moral capabilities, and will. From this point forward the data of investigation are psychical. They are in the field of moral science, and not in the region of things—external objects. The method is a metaphysical one. The validity of our results depends on deductions—conclusions reached by an *a priori* process. The consequences will be as might be expected. We shall find no realities in the world to correspond with the abstraction from which we start out. The underlying motive has been described by different writers from different points of view. Adam Smith, it may readily be conceded, attempted the first systematical explanation of the phenomena of an industrial and commercial society. Most writers in England since his day have endeavored to unfold more accurately his ideas. Of these writers, one of his most learned and distinguished disciples has approvingly said: "They have not hesitated to cut and carve, and apply the caustic until there is scarcely an important passage in the whole work which some one of his friends has not detached from his system as wrong, or branded as absurd." In his theory of wealth, man is considered as actuated solely by Selfishness; in his theory of morals, he is considered as actuated by Sympathy. Among the premises of his work are these: "Men are prompted to expend by the desire of present enjoyment—a passion only momentary and occasional. They are prompted to save by the desire of bettering their condition—a passion which comes with them from the womb, and never leaves them till they go to the grave. . . . The principle exciting to frugality, the uniform, constant, and uninterrupted effort of every man to better his condition, produces both public and national as well as private opulence, and is frequently more than sufficiently powerful to counteract the extravagance of government and the greatest errors of administration. . . . Alone and without any assistance it is capable, not only of carrying on the society to wealth and prosperity, but of surmounting a hundred impertinent obstructions with which the folly of human laws too often encumber its operations." In these passages we come upon the doctrine of *laissez faire*, which it has been attempted to erect into a scientific principle, on the assumption that the individual knows his own interests in the sense in which they are identical with the interests of society. This principle and this assumption will engage our attention further on. We return to our motive powers. M. Rossi groups them in this wise: "Our power over things by means of labor; our inclination to saving if a sufficient interest stimulates us; our inclinations to unite our exertions for a common purpose; our instincts of property, and of exchange or trade. These are the facts of every time and of every place; these are the general facts of political economy." This is a much more satisfactory generalization. It puts more flesh and blood upon the skeleton, which most economists start with as their "economic man."

Mr. Mill, in his essay on "Unsettled Questions in Political Economy," has once for all determined, for the English school, the method of the science, and defined the economic man with which it deals. The revolt against his abstract science and its *a priori* method is now well-nigh universal. He says:

"What is now commonly understood by the term 'political economy' is not the science of speculative politics, but a branch of that science. It does not treat of the whole of man's nature as modified by the social state, nor the whole conduct of man in society. It is concerned with him solely as a being who desires to possess wealth, and who is capable of judging of the comparative efficacy of means for obtaining that end. It predicts only such of the phenomena of the social state as take place in consequence of the pursuit of wealth. It makes entire abstraction of every other human passion or motive, except those which may be regarded as perpetually antagonizing principles to the desire of wealth, namely, aversion to labor and desire of the present enjoyment of costly indulgences. These it takes, to a certain extent, into its calculations, because these do not merely, like others and occasionally, conflict with the pursuit of wealth, but accompany it always as a drag or impediment, and are therefore inseparably mixed up in the consideration of it. Political economy considers mankind as occupied solely in acquiring and consuming wealth. Under the influence of this desire, it shows mankind accumulating wealth, and employing that wealth in the production of other wealth. Sanctioning, by mutual agreement, the institution of property; establishing laws to prevent individuals from encroaching upon the property of others by force or fraud; adopting various contrivances for increasing the productiveness of this labor; setting the division of produce by agreement, under the influence of competition (competition itself being governed by certain laws, which laws are therefore the regulators of the division of produce); and employing certain expedients (as money, credit, etc.) to facilitate the distribution. . . . The science then proceeds to investigate the laws which govern these several operations, under the supposition that man is a being who is determined, by the necessity of his nature, to prefer a greater portion of wealth to a smaller in all cases, without any other exception than that constituted by the two counter-motives already specified. *Not that any political economist was ever so absurd as to suppose that mankind are really thus constituted*, but because this is the mode in which science *must necessarily proceed*. . . . The manner in which it necessarily proceeds is that of treating the main and acknowledged end *as if* it was the sole end, which, of all hypotheses equally simple, is nearest the truth. . . . In this way a nearer approximation is obtained than would otherwise be practicable to the real order of human affairs in those departments. This approximation is, then, to be corrected by making proper allowance for the effects of any impulses of a different description. . . . The conclusions of political economy, consequently, are only true, as the common phrase is, *in the abstract*. . . . All that is requisite is that the political economist be on his guard not to ascribe to conclusions which are grounded upon an hypothesis *a different kind of certainty* from that which really belongs to them. . . . That which is true in the abstract is always true in the concrete, *with proper allowances.* When a certain cause really exists, and, if left to itself, would infallibly produce a certain effect, that same effect, modified by all the other concurrent causes, will correctly correspond to the result really produced."

This is the "orthodox" statement of the case. We shall find that when the "allowances" and "modifications" are properly made, we have passed into entirely different premises. Even though the premises were true and the reasoning correct, the conclusion is inadequate and utterly useless. "A bone fairly enough represents the sort of wealth coveted by a dog, who has a comparatively simple cerebral system, and few other objects. Yet you can not predict the conduct even of a dog from his love of bones, or not one would be left in the butchers' shops. The dog has a regard for his master and a fear of the police, and he has other pursuits."

According to Prof. Senior, the general facts on which the science of political economy rests are comprised in these four general propositions:

"1. That every man desires to obtain additional wealth with as little sacrifice as possible."

This is a matter of consciousness. It is the motor which instigates human activity. It takes effect subject to the conditions imposed by these facts:

"2. That the population of the world, or, in other words, the number of persons inhabiting it, is limited only by moral or physical evil, or by fear of a deficiency of those articles of wealth which the habits of the individuals of each class of its inhabitants lead them to require.

"3. That the powers of labor and of other instruments which produce wealth may be indefinitely increased by using their products as the means of further production.

"4. That, agricultural skill remaining the same, additional labor employed on the land, within a given district, produces in general a less proportionate return; or, in other words, that though, with every increase of the labor bestowed, the aggregate return is increased, the increase of the return is not in proportion to the increase of the labor."

These facts are matters of observation.

The second is "the Malthusian law of population."

The third is made available by the "effective desire of accumulation"—present saving with the purpose of future enjoyment.

The fourth is "the law of diminishing returns."

Prof. Senior goes on, and says of the *desire for distinction*, that it is "a feeling which, if we consider its universality and its constancy, that it affects all men and at all times, that it comes with us from the cradle and never leaves us until we go into the grave, may be pronounced to be the most powerful of human passions." He thus subordinates wealth to the desire for distinction. He adds, as if conscious of an undue limitation of the motive force behind human beings, under all conditions and in all states of progress: "the nature and urgency of each individual's wants are as various as the differences in individual character. Some may wish for power, others for distinction, and others for leisure; some require bodily and others mental amusement; some are anxious to produce important advantage to the public; and there are few, perhaps there are none, who, if it could be done by a wish, would not benefit their acquaintances and friends. Money seems to be the only object for which the desire is universal, and it is so because money is *abstract wealth*. Its possessor may satisfy at will his ambition, or vanity, or indolence, his public spirit or his private benevolence."

He might have added, further, that "the desire of wealth" itself is only a generalized form of an indefinite number of more particular impulses. He continues:

"The proposition in question" (the desire to obtain additional wealth with as little sacrifice as possible), "though we are not aware that any one has thought that it required to be formally stated, is assumed in almost every process of economical reasoning. It is the corner-stone of the doctrine of wages and profits, and, generally speaking, of exchange. In short, it is in political economy what gravitation is in physics, or the *dictum de omni et nullo* in logic: the ultimate fact, beyond which reasoning can not go, and of which almost every other proposition is merely an illustration."

Bastiat surrounds the subject with his usual rhetorical success: "Political economy regards man only in one aspect, and our first care must be to study man in that point of view. This is the reason why we can not avoid going back to the primary phenomena of human sensibibility and activity. . . . The general idea of sensibility springs from other ideas which are more precise: pain, want, desire, taste, appetite, on one side, and, on the other, pleasure, enjoyment, competence. Between these, his extremes, a middle term is interposed, and from the general idea of activity spring the more precise ideas of pain, effort, fatigue, labor, production. In analyzing sensibility and activity we encounter a word common to both—the word pain. . . . This advises us that here below we have only a choice of evils. In the aggregate of all these phenomena, all is personal, as well the sensation which precedes the effort as the satisfaction which follows it.

"We can not doubt, then, that *personal interest* is the great main-spring of human nature."

Mr. Henry Sidgwick, speaking of the fundamental assumption which economists make, says: "The first and most fundamental is that all persons engaged in industry will, in selling or lending goods, or contracting to render services, endeavor, *cæteris paribus*, to get as much wealth as they can in return for the commodity they offer. This is often more briefly expressed by saying that political economy assumes the universality and unlimitedness of the desire for wealth. Against this assumption it has been urged that men do not, for the most part, desire wealth in general, but this or that particular kind of wealth; in fact, that 'the desire of wealth is an abstraction compounding a great variety of different and heterogeneous motives which have been mistaken for a single homogeneous force.'. . . At the same time, it is equally true that there are other things obtainable by labor besides wealth, which mankind generally if not universally desire, such as power and reputation; and it is further undeniable that men are largely induced to render services of various kinds by family affection, friendship, compassion, national and local patriotism, and other kinds of *esprit de corps* and other motives. The amount of unpaid work that is done from such motives, in modern civilized society, forms a substantial part of the whole, and political economists are perhaps fairly chargeable with an omission in making no express reference to such work—with the exception of the mutual services rendered by husbands and wives and by parents and children."

Prof. Perry does make "express reference" to these motives and the exchanges growing out of them. He sweeps them completely out of the field of the science of political economy. Having found the word "wealth" a veritable "slough of despond," he dropped it as both a useless and a confusing term. After the manner of Bastiat, he deals with our "desires" and their "satisfactions." "The desires of men are not only various in kind and indefinite in degree, but also tend to increase in variety and extent by the progress of knowledge and freedom. To the gratification of almost all these desires, however, there are obstacles interposed, some of which are physical and some moral; and these obstacles are so great, in all directions, that the powers of the individual man are utterly incompetent to surmount them. They mock at his weakness and throw him back upon his destitution. Without association with his fellow-men there is no creature so helpless, so unable to reach his true end, as is man; and therefore it is that the impulse to association is one of the strongest impulses of our nature. *Men come together, as it were, by instinct, into society.* And *associating together in a society,* it is very soon discovered, not only that there are various desires in the different members of the community which are now readily met by co-operation and mutual exchange, but also that there are very different powers in the different individuals in relation to those obstacles which are to be surmounted." As a circumlocution for getting, not "wealth" but "satisfaction of desires," at the least possible sacrifice, he quotes approvingly, as the unyielding iron law of our nature, under which we are impelled, the words of President John Bascom: "Between one dollar and two dollars a man has no choice, he must take the greater; between one day and two days of labor, he must take the less; between the present and the future, he must take the present. This is not a sphere of caprice, nor scarcely even of liberty; the actions themselves present no alternative."

Henry C. Carey seized upon the "impulse to association" (which Prof. Perry denominates as *one* of the strongest impulses of our nature) as *the* strongest impulse of our nature. The whole scheme of human "exchanges" grew out of this "association," and not the "association" out of the "exchanges." Mr. Carey undertook to show that the United States, one of the "societies," one of the "communities" to which Prof. Perry alludes—the nation—was sufficiently large in the extent of its territory, the variety of its soil and its climate, in the mountains to be pierced, in its rivers to be bridged, in its forests to be leveled, in its fields to be made fertile, in its mines to be opened, in its useful products to come into existence, in the scope of the moral and intellectual talents of its population, in its capacity for the minutest division of employments and its skill in mechanism, and in the vast variety of the desires, satisfactions, and aspirations which its people could and must provide for and gratify, to afford the very highest illustration of *the power of association*, and in its highest degree, which had been yet seen on the earth.[1] They separated on a question of fact, and not on a dogma of science. At the point where they separated, neither of them was within the limits of the field of political economy, as defined by the English school and Prof. Perry.

Prof. Francis A. Walker, after quoting John Stuart Mill's description of his "abstract" man, goes on and adds:

"We have here all the elements of the economic man. He is taken as a being perfectly capable of judging of the comparative efficacy of means to the end of wealth. That is, he will never fail, wherever he may be, or wherever he may live, whether capitalist or laborer, rich or poor, taught or untaught, to know exactly what course will secure his highest economic interest, that is, bring him the largest amount of wealth."

Of course, we know that this is not true, at all, to the facts, in the conduct of the actual man.

"Moreover, that end of wealth he never fails to desire with a steady, uniform, constant passion. Of every other human passion or motive, political economy makes entire abstraction; love of country, love of honor, love of friends, love of learning, love of art, pity, honor, shame, religion, charity, will never, so far as political economy cares to take account, withstand in the slightest degree, or for the shortest time, the effort of the economic man to amass wealth. . . . There are, however, two human passions and motives, of which political economy takes account as perpetually antagonizing principles to the desire of wealth, namely, aversion to labor and desire of the present enjoyment of costly indulgence; that is, indolence and gluttony."

---

[1] The census of 1880 has given the most complete proof of causes and their effects.

Frédéric Bastiat starts out with the proposition, "The subject of political economy is man." He at once proceeds to divest his science of human interest by eviscerating it after this fashion: "But it does not embrace the whole range of human affairs. The science of morals has appropriated all that comes within the attractive regions of sympathy—the religious sentiments, paternal and maternal kindness, filial piety, love, friendship, patriotism, charity, politeness. To political economy is only left the cold domain of personal interest. Dispute its right to exist as a science, but don't force it to counterfeit what it is not and can not be."

Of this economic man Mr. Carey had said: "Modern political economy has made for itself a being which it denominated man, from whose composition it excluded all those parts of the ordinary man that are common to him and the angels, retaining carefully all those common to him and the beast of the forest. It has been forced to exclude from its definition of wealth all that pertains to the feelings, the affections, and the intellect. It sees nothing but material things."

His own definition of "wealth" is "the power to command the ever-gratuitous force of nature."

This definition is the logical basis of the system of Carey, Bastiat, and Perry—though the latter sometimes calls wealth property. It contains the germs of a really philosophical system of social science, but out of this system Prof. Perry has cut a thin slice—so much only as is included in the operation of "a sale" or "an exchange." In the last edition of his "Political Economy," issued in 1883, he seems to have reached what he deems solid ground. He seems to have found satisfactory answers to the questions which he says he has been for thirty years, "and increasingly as the years went by," asking himself: "What is political economy about? Within what precise field do its inquiries lie? Is it possible clearly and simply to circumscribe that field?"

In the process of answering these questions he has developed his view of political economy, as he defines it, with great clearness and simplicity. Adopting the language he applies to one of his predecessors, he shows himself to be "original, over-confident, sometimes careless, controversial, exasperating, almost belligerent, and always indefatigable." While we can not help admiring his dialectic push, there are many wide and impassable gaps between his premises and his conclusions. We shall therefore look carefully and somewhat in detail into them. We have already given his definition. Political economy is the science of sales or exchanges. "Anything whatsoever that is salable or can be made so comes within its view, and scientifically it cares nothing whatever for anything else. . . . Before anything is sold, or is being ready to sell, it cares not what other science employs itself on that thing; after the thing is sold, economy loses its interest in it, and other sciences may take it up, if they choose. *Salableness* is the one quality that constitutes the class of things with which the science is conversant, and it claims complete jurisdiction over all things just as far forth as they have this quality, and no further."

The exclusions thus made at the threshold he thinks entitle him to make this criticism: "They show that the leaders of the second school" (including, as he classifies them, Adam Smith, Ricardo, Senior, and Mill) "are inconsistent with themselves in their general conceptions of the subject-matter of the science. They begin nowhere. They have no steady class of facts to deal with. They have, indeed, demonstrated many important truths, and they have done excellent practical service for mankind, but in the entirety of their scientific work we can take but little satisfaction. It is on account of this comparative failure in their scientific outset that the second school have declined in influence and are now likely to be superseded." With his own "outset" he thinks a true and lasting science may be obtained, "provided only the next right steps be taken" also. Where do the school of Prof. Perry begin? What is their "scientific outset"? What is their "next step"? They simply throw overboard, at once, the word "wealth" as incapable of any definition for scientific use. The motive power of the elder economists—the desire of every man to obtain additional wealth with as little sacrifice as possible—is moved further back, is sunk in the wider generalization, "satisfaction of desires." We shall see what success attends this legitimate change of base. It renders the science more human, but introduces many elements besides economic gains.

Again: "There is one word that marks and circumscribes the field of ethics, and that is *ought*. There is one word that marks and circumscribes the field of economics, and that word is *value*. . . . It favors honesty and morality, indeed, because they facilitate exchanges. It puts the seal of the market upon all of the virtues. It condemns slavery, not so much because it is ethically wrong, as because it is economically ruinous. . . . But let us here add once for all the grand truth that *political economy does not cover the entire relations between employer and employed, and between buyers and sellers* generally; it covers perfectly their economical relations, the relations between buyers and sellers *as such;* but morality and religion have *additional*, but not incompatible, words to utter when this science *becomes silent;* mutual forbearance and concession, mutual affection and helpfulness, are duties enforced by higher considerations than those of gain." True, indeed, the whole scheme of societary co-operation is based on these *additional sanctions.*

The professor is here at least good enough to give us a human reality and not a mere economist's "abstraction" to deal with; and yet he falls into the old rut of dealing with only a part of the real man. We had good reason to hope that this many-sided man, with desires and passions and moral nature and a will, would, under their operation, put himself, as a whole, into an "exchange" as he would into any other act, that he would not operate in sections, so to speak, but would and must act as an integer. But we are first to find a part of him in the old, hopeless, impracticable pursuit of "wealth": " In thus circumscribing the field of political economy and yielding ground that has been sometimes claimed as falling within it, we all the more assert complete jurisdiction over the territory as thus defined. No other possible science can have anything to do with the gaining of property by means of exchanging. Theft is out of the question here; so are gifts. It makes no difference what a man's *motives* may be in buying and selling; it makes no difference what his *ultimate purposes* may be as to the results of his buying and selling, *the buying and selling* must proceed in accordance with the principles of this science."

Inasmuch as "buying and selling" had been going on for some centuries before this science had been worked out, one might have thought that, logically and chronologically, it might more properly have been asserted that the "principles of the science" must proceed in accordance with the "buying and selling."

Again: "Saint and sinner must plow with the same heifer. The laws of value are absolutely universal. One man may get rich for the sake of making a display, and another man may get rich for the sake of doing good; but the *getting rich* is one and the same process forever. As John

Bascom well says: 'Whichever one of a thousand motives engages man in the pursuit of wealth, once in that pursuit, these all conform to one method and acknowledge one law.' ... Whatever others have done, therefore, or may hereafter undertake to do, we propose solely to investigate the motives and the conditions that govern men in their exchanges." But it had just been said by our author that "it makes no difference what a man's motives may be in buying and selling."

We are remanded, then, to "the conditions" that govern men in their exchanges. We prefer to restore the discarded terms. The motive is to procure the "satisfaction" of some "desire." The condition under which we prefer to make it is, at the least "expenditure of effort," or, to take the terminology of the second school, "to get additional 'wealth' at the least possible sacrifice." Translated into the language of commercial life it means, "Buy in the cheapest and sell in the dearest market"; and in case he repeats the operation often enough a man will be getting rich. But what determines *the vital fact, which is the cheapest and which the dearest market?* Is there any market in the world, except the home market, in which fifty million Americans can supply their wants *by exchange?* Can the "satisfaction" of all their "desires" be had on any condition except that of *direct production?* For answers to these questions we shall ransack treatises and essays in vain. The answers lie, obviously, *in facts* which are open before us on the pages of American experience.

Now, as political economy is a moral science and has its base in our mental characteristics, we would seem to have exhausted it in ascertaining the attitude of the mind as influenced by various passions, desires, hopes, fears, and the like. The "satisfaction" of "desires," "the desire for additional wealth," is the mental affection. Of that we are conscious; that we know by the act of introspection. The "least effort," the least possible sacrifice, is an external fact. The measure of resistance to us can only be reached by experience. Which is the "cheapest market" and which is the "dearest market" is an external fact to be ascertained by experiment, as is the fact whether we can supply our wants by a resort to that market. The data for the settlement of these questions are not to be found in the science; they depend on external material conditions which change every day and every hour. We can follow the changes which take place in our own desires and the things which satisfy those desires, but the means of satisfaction lie outside of ourselves, and which is the "cheapest" and which is the "dearest" means of reaching them can only be found out upon actual trial. Political economy tells us how we shall act when we come to it, but does not know how we shall come to it. It is silent before the great class of satisfactions which we seek, when strength of desire is overruling all considerations of *cost* in exchange value; and when even the world's market does not need and will not take enough of the commodities we offer in exchange to enable us *to buy* what we need. It happens that, in the divine ordering of the nations, the people of America can *make* what they need.

But we return to the platform which Prof. Perry has laid down for himself to stand on : " When a man shaves his own face, our science has nothing to say; when the barber shaves him for a fee, it has a good deal to say. . . . Efforts of all kinds that find their purpose and end in an exchange are production; efforts put forth for amusement, for self-improvement, for benevolence, for personal or family gratification, are not production. Political economy has to do with processes only as those are related to sales, and it makes no difference what kind of processes they are if they have that design and issue."

The system, then, takes cognizance only of individuals and of no motive except personal gain. It excludes all altruistic motives, and at a blow cuts out parental, patriotic, charitable, and religious considerations. It can have nothing to do with art, or beauty, or ethics. It dissects out of the corpus of human life a body of experience which, out of relation to its antecedents and consequents, is without significance. It takes out of the conduct of sentient beings, having thoughts, affections, and will, exactly the portion in which, by and in itself, resides neither intellectual nor moral value. We have found a definite field of the science, but is it worth exploring? We have found the limits of political economy, but we can not stir hand or foot without passing them. In this little kingdom, we no sooner leave "John o'Groat's" than we are at "Land's End." We chafe against the bounds set to our inquiries, but in vain. There is no germinal idea in the premises we have imposed on ourselves. While they are true in point of fact, they are bald, barren truisms. The premises are true, the reasoning correct, but the conclusions are useless. They are unrelated propositions, have no fructifying contents, and are incapable by themselves of leading to one additional inference. In the words of Prof. Leslie, a protesting disciple of the English school: "Yet without the family, and the altruistic as well as the self-regarding motives that maintain it" (and the same may be said of the sentiment of nationality), "the work of the world would come to almost a stand-still; saving for the remote future, would cease; there would be no durable wealth; men would not seek to leave anything behind them; the houses of the wealthiest, if there were any houses at all, would be built to last only for their own time."

In this scheme, the climax of life only comes at the point where something is being made ready to sell—the crisis of affairs lies in the "swap." The laboring-man who has, with some success, fought his way through the dreadful competition of life, sits down with his wife to brood over the destiny of the son who has been born to them. In a large way, he has learned to appreciate the value of some equipment besides a pair of hands with which the lad may be made ready for his battle. Out of the depths of their parental affections they conclude upon a liberal education for the son, and prepare for the strain upon their narrow resources. Among institutions of equal facilities to give educational "services" for this laboring-man's money, it is quite certain he will choose the one requiring "the least sacrifice" on his part; he "will buy in the cheapest market." But what is essentially the human element in this determination of parental instincts? The overmastering love of that father and mother? or the mere higgling for the price of tuition?

A distinguished commander of the Army of the Potomac dies in the city of his birth. Prompted by an effective union of many honorable motives—love of country, pride, comradeship, homage to patriotic worth—the survivors of the marches and battles and victories in which they participated under the dead general feel impelled to erect a commemorative statue, and as an appeal to coming generations. It may or may not be that in the selection of artists and contractors to execute their purpose they will consult "market values." Does the center of forces impelling them lie in the earnest and honorable impulses of humanity which suggested the enterprise, or in the contract stipulating for the "purchase-money"?

The officials of a great and populous town resolve upon appropriate public buildings. Instead of stopping at mere "utility," they resolve upon a structure which shall be a worthy symbol of the enterprise and civilization of their day. They summon architects who may be able to embody their purposes in symmetrical and artistic lines. Their applauding fellow-citizens co-operate, and at last emerge the "plans and specifications" of the structure which for them and their children promises to be an educational force—"a thing of beauty and a joy forever." In the final analysis, would the social value of the transaction reside in the refined and trained impulses of the community, or would its whole virtue be concentrated in the advertisement for "sealed proposals," and the whole enterprise culminate in the "awarding of the contract" to "the lowest bidder"?

Within the memory of most of us, three millions of men in the United States, with no reference to exchange values, took their lives in their hands to wage a war with their own countrymen and kinsmen. They went to render "services" in sufferings, pain, and death under a "strip of painted canvas"—the flag of their country, and the symbol of its majesty. These services they conceived involved whatever of chivalry, patriotism, and morality was appropriate to them as citizens of a definite nation. The exchangeable value of their services was thirteen dollars per month. To obtain these thirteen dollars they left comfortable homes, lucrative employments, and enterprises of great worth and moment. Will it be said that this was not an economic act, and that political economy takes it out of its purview? But a science which deals with these men must deal with them as wholes. If economic considerations disappear so readily out of their conduct, it is hardly worth while to attempt any scientific theory of the mere phalanges which political economy amputates from such a body—to deal with the body without the soul. The economic harmonies can only be evolved when we ennoble self-interest as the spring of industry with the tones of domestic affection, public spirit, the sense of duty, inherent energy, intellectual tastes, and moral judgments.

A science which sees nothing of economic forces in this series of human, every-day transactions, can possess little human interest. To abstract out of these only the idea of "exchangeable value" is to have a residuum unworthy of further analysis. So much for the motives to production which the science leaves out of the pale of economics.

"But," say the professors, "after the thing is sold, economy loses its interest in it." As, in its language, "consumption is purchase," the science takes no account of consumption—takes no account of what becomes of things —what disposition is made of "wealth" after it is purchased.

"We know not of any laws of the consumption of wealth, as the subject of a distinct science; they can be no other than the laws of human enjoyment." But does not the science obviously rest on the laws of human enjoyment?

Mr. Mill had said that there was no "science of consumption"; Prof. Perry considers consumption as not being in view of political economy. Prof. Jevons, on the contrary, says, "The whole theory of economy depends upon a correct theory of consumption." In this proposition Mr. Sidgwick mainly concurs. Writers who hold to the stricter definition of political economy as the science of exchanges have a very good reason for excluding the topic of consumption. Consumption, when dealt with as a social fact, leads out of economy to sociology; and if any word can enrage a modern free-trade economist it is the word "social science," or "sociology," unless we except the word "national" in this connection. Political economists have a right to define their science, but then they are bound by their own definitions, and other people have a right to insist on their staying within the limits they themselves have prescribed. Prof. Walker has presented some urgent reasons why economy does not stop at production and the "exchange."

"It is in the use made of the existing body of wealth that the wealth of the next generation is determined. It matters far less for the future greatness of a nation what is the sum of its wealth to-day, whether large or small, than what are the habits of its people in the daily consumption of that wealth; to what use those means are devoted, whether to ends which inspire social ambition, which restrict population within limits consistent with a high *per capita* production, which increase the efficiency of the laborer and supply instrumentalities for rendering his labor still more productive, or to ends which allow the increase of population in the degree that of itself involves poverty, squalor, and disease, which debauch the laborer morally and physically, striking at both his power and disposition to work hard and continuously, and which waste, in idle or vicious indulgences, the wealth which should go to increase capital.

"To trace to their effects upon production the forces which are set in motion by the uses made of wealth, to show how certain forms of consumption clear the mind, strengthen the hand, and elevate the aims of the individual economic agent while promoting that social order and mutual confidence which are favorable conditions for the complete development and harmonious action of the industrial system; how other forms of consumption debase and debauch man as an economic agent and introduce disorder and waste—here is the opportunity for some great moral philosopher to write the most important chapter[1] in political economy, now, alas! almost a blank."

---

[1] This chapter has been written; it is "The Economics of Consumption," by Robert Scott Moffat.

Mr. Walter Bagehot has something to say on this head: "Just as this science takes an abstract and one-sided view of man, who is one of its subjects, so it also takes an abstract and one-sided view of wealth, which is its other subject. Wealth is infinitely various; as the wants of human nature are almost innumerable, so the kinds of wealth are various. Why man wants so many things is a great subject, fit for inquiry; which of them it would be wise for men to want more of, and which of them it would be wise to want less of—are also great subjects equally fit. But with these subjects political economy does not deal at all. It leaves the first to the metaphysician, who has to explain, if he can, the origin and order of human wants, and the second to the moralist, who is to decide, to the best of his ability, which of these tastes are to be encouraged and when, which to be discouraged and when. The only peculiarity of wealth with which the economist is concerned is its *differentia specifica*—that which makes it wealth. . . . He regards a pot of beer and a picture, a book of religion and a pack of cards, as all equally wealth, and therefore, for his purpose, equally worthy of regard."

Prof. Leslie restores the relation of the parts of the science in correspondence with the relation between actual human attributes: "The love of gin is the love of one kind of wealth which too often competes in the mind of a poor man with the love of a decent dwelling. . . . One of the most important economic inquiries relates to the changes which take place in the direction of the chief wants of mankind and the species of wealth which they call into existence. The main object of industry and accumulation on the part of the French nation is landed property; the chief impulse determining the national economy is the desire of it; in England the desire is absent among the nation at large, and the one which totally takes its place with no small number of Englishmen is the love of beer. Happily in England there is a still more general object of desire in the house, and the house owes its structure, perhaps its very existence, to the institution of the family. . . . The formula of demand and supply is still supposed by some economists to explain everything fully, but both demand and supply have in every case a long history. . . . It is a misrepresentation of the Mercantile System [to say] that its adherents considered nothing but money as wealth; still they did attach undue importance to it, and the consequence of the excessive estimation in which they held it demonstrates the absurdity of basing either the economic prosperity of nations or economic science on the abstraction, which is the corner-stone of both, in the deductive system."

And then Mr. Bagehot comes in again and brings us around to the point where we started: "Of course this reasoning implies that the boundaries of this sort of political economy are arbitrary, and might be fixed here or there. But this is already done when it is said that political economy is an abstract science. All abstractions are arbitrary; they are more or less convenient fictions made by the mind for its own purposes. An abstract idea means a concrete fact or set of facts *minus* something thrown away. The fact or set of facts were made by nature, but how much you will throw aside of these and how much you will keep for consideration you settle for yourself. There may be any number of political economies, according as the subject is divided off in one way or another."

Imagine this mode of dealing with such sciences as geometry, chemistry, botany, dynamics, physiology, statics, etc.! Under this conception of a science its professors and teachers have about the advantages which the inventors of chess-problems have in chess. The chances are that they will, in the main, be able to solve their own problems.

But in actual life we do not invent our own problems. They are made ready to hand for us, and Nature makes no "allowances" for our mistakes in their solution. Take up any systematic treatise on economy, and the "suppositions" are made upon which the author is to proceed. The "answer" will correspond to no actual state of facts, and will be reached after divers "but according to the original hypothesis," "allowances for disturbing causes," "other things being equal," and the like dove-tailed devices. It is true that "the desire of wealth" and "the aversion to labor" are facts of man's nature. While they are antagonistic principles, they are not ultimate principles, and they are mingled, in operation, with a multitude of other principles. Any inference drawn from the operation of these two alone must, as Prof. Cairnes says, "land us in conclusions which have no resemblance to existing realities." Or, recurring to Mr. Ruskin's case of the professor of gymnastics who began his instructions by the assumption that the "human body was constituted of muscles and flesh, without any bones." Having, "under this supposition," ascertained what exercises his "abstract" man could perform, he introduced the skeleton as a "disturbing element." His theory was open to the single objection, at least, that it was "deficient in application." This is not one whit more grotesque and unphilosophical than the economists' treatment of man in dealing with his moral structure. They have endeavored to give to their "rude generalizations" the authority of "laws."

What are the conditions which direct the energies and determine the actual occupations and pursuits of mankind in different ages and countries? This is the main problem. In its application to the United States, it is the problem for the American statesman and the American voter to determine. How far, then, does the science of political economy enable us to separate the elements of the case? What binding force can its scientists assert over the conduct of the governing power?

No perfection of mechanism in a steam-engine would be of any avail unless connected with a nest of boilers. Provision must be made for "letting on" steam, as well as a pipe prepared for the "exhaust." The machine can not run by force of steam confined in a closed circuit. So with the energies of a people. The greater their productive force, the more "efforts" they make, the greater will be their creation of commodities—the "satisfactions" they will experience. "Satisfactions" are the motive to "effort." "Desires" of one kind and another are the motive force, and grow out of the inherited traits and historical traditions of the particular people. They may have the inherent power and the physical conditions to satisfy them by a direct effort of production, at a less cost of labor and sacrifice than by the indirect process of exchange. *Some* of their desires they can manifestly procure at less cost of labor and sacrifice by exchanges abroad. So many as we can thus procure it is our manifest advantage to procure; if we can procure *all* of them in this way, very good. It may very well be that *some* exchanges abroad are advantageous, and so it is; it may very well be that *all* exchanges made abroad would not be advantageous, but, on the contrary, would be *impossible—and so it is*. It depends upon the particular facts of our situation as a nation: how much we want; how many and of what kind are our desires; what we have got to pay for them with, and how much foreigners want of what we have to offer in exchange. It is manifest that it is a special problem, depending on a special collocation of facts. So far as our surplus will be salable in foreign markets, we are interested in the foreign trade; so far as our wants are too numerous to be supplied by the things we can buy and *pay for* abroad, we must supply them at home. Provision must then be made for supplying them by home industry. The only condition by which the last alternative can be realized is by saving more or less of the domestic market by *restrictions* on the import of foreign commodities. One form of this is a protective tariff.

It is our interest to buy all we can with our cotton, tobacco, wheat, and beef. The limit of our purchases will depend, not on our desires, or our capacity to produce at home, but on the demand for these products in the foreign markets. No treatise on political economy will ever tell us how much and what to desire; how much agricultural produce we can raise, or how much the foreign markets will take, or its price. In the main, we must depend on our own direct efforts, as the facts of our history have demonstrated.

CHAPTER IV.

WHO IS BOUND BY THE SCIENCE—SOME DESTRUCTIVE CRITICISM.

AFTER this disagreement upon fundamental propositions, we shall not, perhaps, be amazed at the general disclaimer on the part of its most eminent teachers of the jurisdiction of the science over the legislator.

This disclaimer on the part of some of its professors grows out of their consciousness of its unreal and artificial nature; on the part of others of its professors, it does not grow out of modesty.

Mr. McCulloch says that "the economist who confines himself to mere enunciation of general principles or abstract truths may as well address himself to the pump at Oldgate as to the British public. If he wish to be anything better than a declaimer, or to confer any real advantage upon any class of his countrymen, he must leave general reasoning and show the extent of the injury entailed upon the community by the neglect of his principles."

Nassau William Senior, the eminent Professor of Political Economy in the University of Oxford, who wrote since the date of the free-trade agitation in England, with great emphasis indicates the agencies of government to which the conclusions of so hypothetical a science do not extend. He says:

"These inquiries involve, as their general premises, the consideration of the whole theory of morals, of government, and of civil and criminal legislation; and, for their particular premises, a knowledge of all the facts which affect the social condition of every community whose conduct the economist proposes to influence. . . . The questions to what extent and under what circumstances the possession of wealth is on the whole beneficial or injurious to its possessor, or to the society of which he is a member? What distribution of wealth is most desirable in each different state of society? And what are the means by which any given country can facilitate such a distribution? All these are questions of great interest and difficulty, but no more form part of the science of political economy, in the sense in which we use that term, than navigation forms part of the science of astronomy. The principles supplied by political economy are indeed necessary elements in their solution, but they are not the only or even the most important elements. The writer who pursues such investigation is in fact engaged on the great science of legislation; a science which requires a knowledge of the general principles supplied by political economy, but differs from it essentially in its subject, its premises, and its conclusions. The subject of legislation is not wealth, but human welfare. Its premises are drawn from an infinite variety of phenomena, supported by evidence of every degree of strength, and authorizing conclusions deserving every degree of assent, from perfect confidence to bare suspicion. And its expounder is enabled, and even required, not merely to state general facts, but to urge the adoption or rejection of actual measures or trains of action. . . . His (the economist's) premises consist of a very few general propositions, the result of observation or consciousness, and scarcely requiring proof, or even formal statements which almost every man, as soon as he hears them, admits as familiar to his thoughts, or at least as included in his previous knowledge; and his inferences are nearly as general and, if he has reasoned correctly, as certain as his premises. . . . The confounding the science of political economy with the sciences and arts to which it is subservient, has reduced economists sometimes to undertake inquiries too vague to lead to any practical results, and sometimes to pursue the legitimate objects of the science by means unfit for their attainment. To their extended view of the objects of political economy is to be attributed the undue importance which many economists have ascribed to the collection of facts, and their neglect of the far more important process of reasoning accurately from the facts before them; . . . but the facts in which the general principles of the science rest, may be stated in a very few sentences, and, indeed, in a very few words. But that the reasoning from these facts, the drawing from them correct conclusions, is a matter of great difficulty, may be inferred from the imperfect state in which the science is now found after it has been so long and so intently studied."

Many millions of men in America have been waiting years for a demonstration "in a very few sentences, and, indeed, in a very few words," or, indeed, in many words and many sentences, of the economic propriety of the application of principles of free trade to these United States.

We proceed to state at considerable length the attitude of John Stuart Mill toward the practical value of the conclusions of the science:

"In the definition which we have attempted to frame of the science of political economy, we have characterized it as essentially *an abstract science*, and its method as the method *a priori*. Such undoubtedly is its character as it has been understood and taught by its most distinguished teachers. It reasons, and, as we contend, must necessarily reason, from assumptions, not from facts. It is built upon hypotheses strictly analogous to those which, under the name of definitions, are the foundation of the other abstract sciences. Geometry presupposes an arbitrary definition of a line—'that which has length but not breadth.' Just in the same manner does political economy presuppose an arbitrary definition of man, as a being who invariably does that by which he may obtain the greatest amount of the necessaries, conveniences, and luxuries of life with the smallest quantity of labor and physical self-denial with which they can be obtained in the existing state of knowledge." Lamenting the want of opportunity to make, in the science, an *experimentum crucis,* he proceeds:

"How, for example, can we obtain a crucial experiment on the effect of a restrictive commercial policy upon national wealth? We must find two nations alike in every other respect, or, at least, possessed in a degree exactly equal of everything which conduces to national opulence, and adopting exactly the same policy in all their other affairs, but differing in this only, that one of them adopts a system of commercial restriction and the other adopts free trade. Doubtless this would be the most conclusive evidence of all if we could get it. But let any one consider how infinitely numerous and various are the circumstances which either directly or indirectly do or may influence the amount of the national wealth, and then ask himself what are the probabilities that in the longest revolution of ages two nations will be found which agree and can be shown to agree in all those circumstances, except one."

Noting, then, that the actual facts do not happen as the theory provided that they should, he goes on:

"The discrepancy between our anticipations and the actual fact is often the only circumstance which would have drawn our attention to some important disturbing cause which we had overlooked."

It is to be noted that this confessional passage contains the germ of all the reasons for the discrepancies in the science.

"Nay, it often discloses to us errors in thought, still more serious than the omission of what can with any propriety be termed a disturbing cause. It often reveals to us that the basis itself of the whole argument is insufficient; that the data from which we had reasoned comprise only a part, and not always the most important part, of the circumstances by which the result is determined. Such oversights are committed by very good reasoners, and even by a still rarer class, that of good observers."

How, then, are we to still this "jumping Jack"? Why, go back to the *a posteriori* road, which we should have taken in the first place, and sift and scrutinize *the facts*:

"Without this, he" (the Professor of Political Economy) "may be an excellent professor of abstract science; for a person may be of great use who points out correctly what effects will follow from certain combinations of possible circumstances in whatever tract of the extensive region of hypothetical cases those combinations may be found. He stands in the same relation to the legislator as the mere geographer to the practical navigator; *telling him the latitude and longitude of all sorts of places, but not how to find whereabout he himself is sailing*. If, however, he does no more than this, he must rest contented to take no share in practical politics, *to have no opinion*, or *to hold it with extreme modesty*, on the application which should be made of his doctrines to *existing circumstances*.

"No one who attempts to lay down propositions for the guidance of mankind, however perfect his scientific acquirements, can dispense with a practical knowledge of the actual modes in which the affairs of the world are carried on, and an extensive personal experience of the actual ideas, feelings, and intellectual and moral tendencies of his own country and of his own age. The true practical statesman is he who combines this experience with a profound knowledge of abstract political philosophy. Either acquirement without the other, leaves him *lame* and *impotent,* if he is *sensible of the deficiency;* renders him *obstinate* and *presumptuous,* if, *as is more probable, he is unconscious of it.*"

Contrasting the student in his closet and the man of business in the outward world:

" The one despises all comprehensive views, the other neglects details. The one draws his notion of the universe from the few objects with which his course of life has happened to render him familiar; the other, having got demonstration on his side, and forgetting that it is only a demonstration *nisi*—a proof at all times liable to be set aside by *the addition of a single new fact to the hypothesis*—denies, instead of examining and sifting, the allegations which are opposed to him."

The reconciliation will be found in him " who can make the anticipations of the philosopher guide the observation of the practical man, and the specific experience of the practical man warn the philosopher when something is to be added to his theory."

In the preface to his treatise, " Theory of Political Economy," Prof. Jevons takes occasion to say : " The conclusion to which I am ever more clearly coming is, that the only hope of attaining a true system of economics is to fling aside, once and forever, the mazy and preposterous assumption of the Ricardian school. Our English economists have been living in a fool's paradise. . . . When at length a true system of economics comes to be established, it will be seen that that able but wrong-headed man, David Ricardo, shunted the car of economic science on to a wrong line, a line, however, on which it was further urged to confusion by his equally able and wrong-headed admirer, John Stuart Mill. . . . It will be a work of labor to pick up the fragments of a shattered science and to start anew; but it is a work from which they must not shrink who wish to see any advance of economic science." And his last word is a protest against " the noxious influence of authority."

" There is ever a tendency of the most hurtful kind to allow opinions to crystallize into creed. Especially does this tendency manifest itself when some eminent author, enjoying power of clear and comprehensive exposition, becomes recognized as an authority. His works may, perhaps, be the best which are extant upon the subject in question; they may contain more truth with less error than we can meet elsewhere. But to err is human, and the best works should ever be open to criticism. If, instead of welcoming inquiry and criticism, the admirers of a great author accept his writings as authoritative, both in their excellences and in their defects, the most serious injury is done to truth. In matters of philosophy and science, authority has ever been the great opponent of truth. A despotic calm is usually the triumph of error. In the republic of the sciences, sedition and even anarchy are beneficial in the long run to the greatest happiness of the greatest number. . . . Show us the undoubted, infallible criterion of absolute truth, and we will hold it as a sacred, inviolable thing; but, in the absence of that infallible criterion, we have all an equal right to grope about in our search of it, and nobody and no school nor clique must be allowed to set up a standard of orthodoxy which shall bar the freedom of scientific inquiry.

" I have added these words because I think there is some fear of the too great influence of authoritative writers in political economy. I protest against deference for any man, whether John Stuart Mill or Adam Smith or Aristotle, being allowed to check inquiry. Our science has become too much a stagnant one, in which opinions rather than experience and reason are appealed to."

This is the testimony of Englishmen who have actually built up what is called and taught as the official science of political economy. Many more names, expounders of the same system, might be added, with the same general reservation which they make to the practical untrustworthiness of the science. They have had misgiving as to its value in affairs, but, in a half-hearted, reluctant sort of way, have seemed to think that, while it was an artifice, it might still pass as a scientific one.

The name of Mr. Walter Bagehot will be recognized as that of a man eminent among recent students in various departments of economy and politics, as well as a man of great business aptitude. He is also well known as an orthodox believer in the Manchester school of political economy—at least as applied to England at this date. He quarrels with its "postulates" and its "preliminaries," but on the whole he holds its conclusions applicable, *but applicable only to the existing commercial facts in England.* After commenting on the circumstances, often noted, that those who are conversant with its abstractions are usually without true contact with its facts, and that those who are in contact with its facts have usually little sympathy with and little cognizance of its abstractions, he gives the reasons why he thinks the science is held in so low an estimate:

"Dealing with matters of business, it assumes that man is actuated only by motives of business. It assumes that every man who makes anything makes it for money, that he always makes that which brings him in most at least cost, and that he will make it in the way that will produce most and spend least. It assumes that any man who buys, buys with his whole heart, and that he who sells, sells with his whole heart, each wanting to gain all possible advantage. Of course, we know that this is not so, that men are not like this, but we assume it for simplicity's sake as an hypothesis." He further comments:

"First. It has often been put forward, not as a theory of the principal causes affecting wealth in certain societies, but as a theory of the principal, sometimes even of all, the causes affecting wealth in every society. And this has occasioned many and strong doubts about it. . . . No doubt almost every one—every one of importance—has admitted that there is a friction in society which counteracts the effect of the causes treated of. . . . Now, *I hold these causes are only the main ones in a single kind of society— a society of grown-up, competitive commerce, such as we have in England;* that it is only in such societies that the other and counteracting forces can be set together under the minor head of 'friction,' but that in other societies there are other causes, in some cases one, and in some another are the most effective ones, and that the greatest confusion arises if you try to fit on uneconomical societies the theories only true of, and only proved as to, economical ones. We need not that the authority of political economy should be impugned, but that it should be minimized.

"Secondly. I think, in consequence of this defect of conception, economists have been far more abstract, and in consequence much more dry, than they need have been. If they had distinctly set before themselves that they were dealing only in causes of wealth in *a single set of societies*, they might have effectively pointed their doctrines with facts from their societies. But so long as the *vision of universal theory* vaguely floated before them, they shrank from particular illustrations.

"Thirdly. It is also in consequence, as I imagine, of this defective conception of the science, that English economists have not been as fertile as they should have been in verifying it. They have been too content to remain in the 'abstract' and to shrink from concrete notions, because they could not but feel that many of the most obvious phenomena of many nations did *not look much like their abstractions*. ... If you try to give *a universal reason* why nations are poor and why nations are rich, you will not be able to arrive at any useful answer. Some will be poor because they are cooped up on poor soil; some because they have a religion which disinclines them to make money; some because they have ancient rules, which helped them to make a beginning but now retard them; some because they have never been able to make a beginning, and many other causes might be given. *The problem taken up in that form is indeterminate; why nations are rich or poor depends on the whole intrinsic nature and all the outward circumstances of such nations.* There is no simpler formula to be discovered, and a science which attempted to find one would of necessity have to deal with the whole of physical science; it would be an account of all men and all the earth."

This is something in quite a different vein from the high-sounding proclamation of Mr. Lowe (Lord Sherbrooke) so often quoted as ending all controversy: "Political economy belongs to no nation; it is of no country. It is the science of the rules for the production, the accumulation, the distribution, and the consumption of wealth. It will assert itself whether you wish it or not. It is founded on the attributes of the human mind, and no power can change it."

It would be unjust and absurd to pretend that in all these years the economists have not accumulated a large body of related facts, gathered from observations on the conduct of man in the social state. The physical order in which we produce exchangeable commodities, and the mental habits which so order, have been thrown into a certain kind of correlation. Certain tendencies have been detected, telling the average of human conduct. It is these *tendencies* which have been mistaken for "laws." The generalizations about the different forces which stimulate us to action have in certain aspects more or less truth in them. But the fundamental and fatal error in the English school has been to identify a single one of these forces as the resultant of them all. However useful and meritorious they may have been as first attempts to untangle the causes and sequence of economic phenomena, they have been barren of results, and still remain useless terms in "the solemn humbug of economic orthodoxy."

As might have been expected after a curious inquiry through many decades into the reasons for the totally inconsequential character of the science, the reasons themselves, at last, have passed into the alembic of final analysis. It is not too much to say that, at last, the science has been subjected to a destructive criticism. This it has received at the hands of Prof. Cliffe Leslie, Mr. Frederic Harrison, and Dr. John K. Ingram—not that these learned and skillful essayists have been the only ones to put the dissecting-knife into the body of this science, but it is to them we shall principally refer in reviewing this autopsy.

M. Comte, in the course of the long and friendly correspondence which took place between John Stuart Mill and himself, first pointed out the utterly inadequate nature of the groundwork of the science of political economy as such, and as Mr. Mill had expounded it. The latter was compelled to summon all the resources of his dialectic skill in reply.

In M. Comte's conception of the whole line of inquiries involved in the investigation of the social organism, society should be contemplated in the totality of its elements. No investigation should or could be undertaken into any portion of these elements, except in constant connection with parallel investigations, carried on contemporaneously into all coexisting portions of the complex whole. The facts of wealth are, in the form in which they are presented to us, so inextricably woven with facts of a different order—with facts of the intellectual, moral, and political order—that the determination of them is possible only when considered in connection with associated facts. All isolated study is doomed to failure, and consequently a science of political economy is impossible. The method of dealing with the organic world and the inorganic world must be different—the former must be dealt with as an *ensemble.*

On this Frederic Harrison makes this comment: "*Every organism* is an *ensemble.* The organic means something which has *a complex function over and above any of its elements.* The study of the organism is the study of this function. Chemists may and must study the gastric juices, but generations of chemists could not explain the physiological process of digestion. Just so, a pure economist, studying the facts of wealth apart, gives only a sort of chemical explanation of the social nutrition. The really organic theory of this function of the social system he is precluded from touching by the very terms of his science. . . . *There is no such thing in nature as a purely industrial human being*, nor, indeed, *any purely industrial act.* The laws of the industrial nature are incapable of being stated, except with or in terms of *the character as a whole.*"

Stephen Colwell, the writer of the preliminary essay in the American edition of Frederick List's "System of National Economy," makes his criticism to the like effect:

"The absurdity of divorcing wealth from its indispensable union with human interests, and from its dependence upon considerations and motives higher than wealth, is in no respect more striking than in the attempt to separate it from national polity and politics. Whether this serious mistake arose from the exigencies of logic or from neglecting the distinction between science and art, it was equally fatal to clear perceptions. The assumption that the whole range of interests and subjects usually embraced in political economy, that is, all that relates to industry, to trade, and social amelioration, should be withdrawn from the domain of politics and from the discretion of legislators and statesmen, and be committed to political economists, was so bold, if not so presumptuous, that it could not have been made except by men laboring under some great delusion; and when we reflect upon the unsettled state of the science, by the light of which political economists in their closets were to decide upon the well-being of millions upon millions of people, and upon the fate of nations, we can not but wonder that such an idea was ever entertained for a moment by men of intelligence. . . . There is a certain order of minds which, abhorring details and feeling unable to grapple with them, gladly take refuge in rules and generalities, and to this must belong those who imagine that the science of political economy is entitled to take precedence of political wisdom and experience."

In a somewhat similar strain, Prof. Rickards, who succeeded Prof. Senior at the University of Oxford, discloses the opinion of a man who knew something of human affairs: "It is well known that Napoleon Bonaparte, who possessed one of the most powerful understandings of modern times, entertained a rooted antipathy to political economy. It was a saying of his that 'if an empire were made of adamant, the economists could grind it to powder.'

He looked upon the lucubrations of economical writers as he looked upon one of the ready-made political constitutions of Abbé Sieyès—as an artificial creation of speculative brains. He regarded them as a collection of technical rules and dogmas, devised by ingenious theorists and men of the closet, setting up to instruct the rulers of mankind how to conduct the commercial and financial affairs of their governments."

In 1876 appeared Prof. Cliffe Leslie's interesting article "On the Philosophical Method of Political Economy." It came from a source which compelled respect and attention. We can, at most, indicate the points at which he aimed his criticism. His aim was to show that the *a priori* and deductive method failed to throw any light on the nature of wealth, its differences in kinds and constituents, and that the causes which affected *the economic condition of different nations* at different times *must be sought in the entire state of society;* that the amount of wealth depended on the conditions determining the direction and means of supply; that the distribution of wealth was not the result of exchange alone, but also of moral, religious, and family ideas and sentiments, and the whole history of a nation:

"The bane of political economy has been the haste of its students to possess themselves of a complete and symmetrical system solving all problems before it with mathematical certainty and exactness. The very attempt shows an entire misconception of the nature of those problems, and of the means available for their solution. . . . The truth is, that the whole economy of every nation, as regards the occupation and pursuits of both sexes, the nature, amount, distribution, and consumption of wealth, is the result of a long evolution, in which there is both continuity and change, and of which the economic side is only a particular aspect or phase. And the laws of which it is the result must be sought in history, and the general laws of society and social evolution.

"The succession of the hunting, pastoral, agricultural, and commercial states is commonly referred to as an economic development, but it is, in fact, *a social evolution, the economical side* of which is indissolubly connected with its *moral, intellectual,* and *political sides*.[1] To each of these successive states there is a corresponding moral and intellectual condition, with a corresponding polity. With the changes from savage hunting-life to that of the nomad tribe, thence to fixed habitations and the cultivation of the soil, and thence to the rise of trade and towns, there are changes in feelings, desires, morals, thought, and knowledge, in domestic and civil relations, and in institutions

---

[1] Prof. Sumner, while disclaiming the old abstract premises, in terms, still travels in the old abandoned *a priori* rut: "We have to understand that an *economic* investigation may be carried on just as independently as a chemical or physical or biological investigation. The economist does not need to be on the lookout all the time to correct his results by reference to some outside considerations, or to the dogmas of jejune and rickety systems of metaphysical speculation. On the contrary, he should regard the introduction of extraneous elements, no matter under what high-sounding names of *moral, political,* and *social,* as sure signs of impending confusion and fallacy." ("Princeton Review," March, 1882.)

We leave the Professor to settle that with Leslie, Ingram, and Bagehot. His form of economic investigation might be adequate to effect the immediate exchange of commodities existing on a given day. It would not account for the existing stock, nor could it furnish a clew to the nature or amount of to-morrow's supply, or where to-morrow's supply was to come from. A given kind of moral, political, and social man must, at last, be a definite kind of economic man, in correspondence with himself. His wants are peculiar to his traits, and the preparation to meet them must grow out of his environment. You can not expect a human being, with one sort of aptitudes, to go off and live in a part of the world and in pursuits which do not engage those aptitudes. He will make the arena of his struggle such that it will engage his best efforts, physical, mental, and moral. Then the economic results will take care of themselves.

and customs, which show themselves in the economic structure of the community, and the nature, amount, and distribution of wealth. . . . *A priori* political economy has sought to deduce the laws which govern the directions of human energies, the division of employment, the modes of production, and the nature, amount, and distribution of wealth, from an assumption respecting the cause of conduct prompted by individual interest; but the conclusion which the study of society makes every day more irresistible is that the germ from which the existing economy of every nation has been evolved *is not the individual*, still less the mere personification of an abstraction, but *the primitive community—a community one in blood, property, thought, moral responsibility, and manner of life,* and that *individual interest* itself, and *the desires, aims, and pursuits of every man and woman* in the nation, have been molded by and received their direction and form from *the history of that community.*

"Both the desires of which wealth of different kinds is the object, and those which compete with them, are in every nation the results of its historical career and state of civilization. What are called *economic forces* are not only connected, but *identical with* forces which are also *moral* and *intellectual*. . . . Recent apologists for the *a priori* and abstract method of economic reasoning feel themselves constrained to confine its application to the most advanced stage of commercial society; they seem even prepared to concede its *inapplicability to every country save England, and to confine it to the latest development of English economy.* . . . They thus abandon at once the claim formerly made on behalf of political economy to the character of a universal science founded on invariable laws of nature. . . . It is, in fact, as inapplicable to the most advanced stage of commerce as to that primitive state of nature from which

Ricardo deduced it, by a process which deserves a high place in the history of fallacies; and which was not present to Mill's mind when arguing that 'no political economists pretend that the laws of wages, profits, values, prices, and the like, set down in their treatises, would be strictly true, or many of them true at all, in the savage state.' . . . Every successive stage—the hunting, the pastoral, the agricultural, the commercial stages, for example—has an economy which is indissolubly connected with the physical, intellectual, moral, and civil development; and the economical development of English society at this day is the outcome of the entire movement which has evolved the political constitution, the structure of the family, the forms of religion, the learned professions, the arts and sciences, the state of agriculture, manufactures, and commerce. The philosophical method of political economy must be one which expounds this evolution." Such an exposition would be the *science of sociology.*

Then came the address of John K. Ingram, LL. D., on "The Present Position and Prospects of Political Economy," read in 1878 before the British Association for the Advancement of Science. It assailed with great skill and vigor the current political economy on four grounds:

First. The attempt to isolate the study of the facts of wealth from that of other social phenomena.

Secondly. The metaphysical or viciously abstract character of many of the conceptions of the economists.

Thirdly. The abusive preponderance of deduction in their processes of research; and

Fourthly. The too abstract way in which their conclusions are conceived and enunciated.

It will be impossible to indicate the acute and searching analysis to which he subjected orthodox economy by any detached extracts. His general conclusions were that the results arrived at by the dominant school need not be thrown away as valueless; that they shed important partial lights on human affairs, and afforded salutary partial guidance to public action. The task incumbent on sociologists in general was to incorporate the truths already elicited into a more satisfactory body of doctrine, in which they will be brought into relation with the general theory of social existence, and to utilize such materials as their predecessors had accumulated. The current economy was provisional and preparatory, and was not entitled to acceptance if regarded as a final systematization of the industrial laws of society: " In human affairs it is in general impossible to solve special questions correctly without just conceptions of *ensemble*—all particular problems of government, of education, of social action, whatever kind connect themselves with the largest ideas concerning the fundamental constitution of society, its spontaneous tendencies, and its moral ideals."

This address was received with sullen respect. Mr. Lowe came to the rescue. He was more especially concerned to defend Adam Smith, who, he conceived, had been attacked in the strictures on the deductionists. But, in truth, Adam Smith had never pretended to deduce the science from the assumption of the "desire of wealth and aversion to labor." This had been the attempt of his successors. Because the "Wealth of Nations" was mainly the result of observation and classification and not of deductive reasoning, it had been indicated by Dr. Ingram as a proper basis for a real science of sociology.

"A science is not created by adducing arguments to show that it is possible," says Mr. Lowe. "The 'Wealth of Nations' does not owe its success to a peculiar method of treatment, but to the peculiar nature of the subject of which it treats. . . . All that political economy pretends to is that when and in proportion as these things" (labor, wages, rent, commerce, taxes) "come into existence, the principles which apply to them come into existence also, and that, though as society becomes more complicated these things become complicated too, they do not change their nature, but retain the qualities with which they were originally imbued. There is a point where the doctrine of *laissez faire* ceases to be applicable, as in the case of children. . . . As to the future of political economy, I do not profess to be very sanguine that many new or striking discoveries are in reserve for it. If I have stated correctly the cause of its success, any attempt to widen its field will only deprive it of that basis of certainty which it derives from the practical uniformity of the feelings and wishes of mankind in regard to wealth. The future is all for the sociologists, and I am inclined to think it will remain so."

After speaking of its brilliant and lasting successes as compared with other moral sciences, he adds: "To the labors of these men, whose methods are so erroneous, we owe, among other things, the repeal of hundreds of galling taxes on almost all the comforts of life and on the food of the people—the repeal of the corn and navigation laws, etc. Those are some of the achievements of the past, and I may be excused if I prefer them to the shadowy and unrealized anticipations of the future." To which Prof. Leslie replies that these achievements which Mr. Lowe arrogates were not triumphs "for his own economic method. Those he refers to were achieved by *the opposite method of reasoning from observation and experience.*"[1]

---

[1] "But it is obvious that, while free trade was being introduced into England, many other causes of prosperity were also coming into action—the progress of invention, the construction of railways, the profuse consumption of coal, the extension of the colonies, etc., etc. Although, then, the beneficent

So, then, the free-trade legislation of England has not grown out of the body of doctrine which constitutes the modern English political economy. Prof. Leslie says distinctly that the most arduous problem respecting the separation of occupations, namely, "What are the causes governing its actual course, determining the direction of the national energies, the employments of different classes and of both sexes in different ages and countries?" has never even occurred to the deductive school.

The economic structure of any given community, the direction taken by national energies, the occupation of the different classes and of both sexes, the constituents and the partition of movable and immovable property, the progressive, stationary, or retrogressive condition in respect to productive power, and the quantity and quality of the necessaries, comforts, and luxuries of life, are insoluble by the science of political economy. Why? Because these are "the results not of special economic forces, but of all the social forces, political, moral, and intellectual as well as industrial." The inquiry, then, is a *national* one. We have escaped the weak, purposeless conclusions suggested by cosmopolitanism. Every distinct community, society, state, nation, every *political entity*, is to be discussed as *an industrial entity*. It is impossible to conceive of the terms of an industrial economic problem except under the condition of nationality. The only *universal* principles of political economy assumed or established are as applicable to men in a savage state as in the civilized state. "Exchange" goes on in one exactly as the other—the eternal laws of value are as true in Patagonia as in France.

---

results of free trade are great and unquestionable, they could hardly be found to exist *a posteriori*."—JEVONS, "Theory of Political Economy," p. 20. Prof. Jevons omits the great factor—the discovery of gold in Australia and California.

The difference between civilization and barbarism lies in the desires to be satisfied, the things to be exchanged, and their mode of production. These depend on moral, intellectual, and political considerations as well as economic. If, then, they are to be ascertained, we must part completely with the old friends with whom we started out, from Prof. Senior to Prof. Perry. "The science of exchanges" is of no help to us in the business of nation-making.

Mr. Mill has pointed out the fallacy of treating political economy as the "science of exchanges." That definition "omits the most important condition determining the production of wealth, and overlooks the truth that human institutions, laws of property and succession, are necessarily chief agencies in determining its distribution." If the science of English political economy has not served to guide English statesmen in the affairs of England, it will not serve to guide American statesmen in the conduct of the affairs of America. If English statesmen at last fall back on "observation and experience" of English facts in the conduct of English industry and commerce, American statesmen will be compelled to fall back on "observation and experience" in the conduct of American industry and commerce. As between free trade and protection, we have not seen as yet in this hasty review what course "observation and experience" will commend to us. There is an end, however, to the conceit and dogmatism which asserts that there are any irrepealable "laws" of political economy of universal application, a science which "belongs to no nation, is of no country," which must dominate our policy. We certainly have reached no standing room in any science which reverses the judgment which Prof. Senior puts in the mouth of Napoleon, viz.: "That he believed free trade between independent states to be like gambling between individuals, and therefore mischievous to the one or the other; mischievous, in fact, to the one which, in the ultimate settling of accounts, had to pay a balance in money."

We have found nothing which justly enables Prof. Perry to say of Daniel Webster and his speech on the tariff in 1828, "He then and afterward brought forward in defense of protection arguments which political economy pronounces unsound":

Nothing which convicts M. Thiers of false economics when, in answer to the question, "Why do you give these bounties to the French sugar-refineries?" he replied, "I wish the tall chimneys to smoke":

Nothing to disarm the criticism which Mr. Bagehot says foreigners make to English free-traders: "Your English traders are strong and rich; of course, you wish to undersell our traders, who are weak and poor. You have invented this political economy to enrich yourselves and ruin us; *we will see that you do not do so.*"

We have seen that not a few of the "respectable professors of the dismal science" have been reached by the words of Mr. Carlyle:

"For many sins I have read much in those inimitable volumes of yours; really, I should think, some barrowsful in my time—and, in these last forty years of theory and practice, have pretty well seized what of Divine message you were sent with to me. Perhaps as small a message, give me leave to say, as ever there was such a noise made about before. Professors of the dismal science, I perceive that the length of your tether is now pretty well run, and that I must request you to talk a little lower in future."

The topics and the order of their exposition adopted by Adam Smith have been followed by almost all subsequent writers. This will appear from the table of contents of the "Wealth of Nations,"[1] which is given below. It will be noted that the larger portion of his work is merely descriptive of what happens in the course of the business of men, and the order in which external things follow each

---

[1] "The Wealth of Nations"—its table of contents:

BOOK I.

Of the causes of improvement in the productive power of labor, and of the order according to which its produce is naturally distributed among the different ranks of the people.

Chapter 1. Of the division of labor.

(As domestic exchanges grow out of the divisions of callings, trades, and pursuits in which men render services to each other, so foreign commerce has its origin in a kind of "international division of labor" in which the different nations enter upon the production of the commodities in which respectively they have some absolute or relative advantage over each other.)

Chap. 2. Of the principles which give occasion to the division of labor.
Chap. 3. Division of labor is limited by the extent of the market.
Chap. 4. Of the origin and use of money.
Chap. 5. Of the real and nominal price of commodities, or of their price in labor and their price in money.
Chap. 6. Of the component parts of the price of commodities.
Chap. 7. Of the natural price and market price of commodities.
Chap. 8. Of the wages of labor.
Chap. 9. Of the profits of stock. (Capital.)
Chap. 10. Of wages and profits in the different employments of labor and stock.
Chap. 11. Of rent of land.

BOOK II.

Chap. 1. Of the divisions of stock.
Chap. 2. Of money as a particular branch of the general stock of the society.
Chap. 3. Of the accumulation of capital—or of productive and unproductive labor.
Chap. 4. Of stock lent at interest.
Chap. 5. Of the different employments of capital.

BOOK III.

Chap. 1. Natural progress of opulence.

(This chapter is mainly historical. It goes into the discouragement of agriculture in Europe after the fall of the Roman Empire, the rise and prog-

other. It is the work of a close observer, simply. When he comes to his deductions from human nature—from the universality and intensity of the desire of each man to promote his pecuniary interest—he assumes as a fact what even his most loyal disciples have advanced as an assumption only. As has been observed, "Adam Smith thought there was a Scotchman inside every man."

Adam Smith attacked with great vigor the colonial system of England. While England, for commercial and dynastic reasons, was girdling the earth with her colonial

---

ress of cities and towns, and how the commerce of the towns contributed to the improvement of the country.)

BOOK IV.

Chap. 1. Of the principles of the commercial or mercantile system.

(The doctrine erroneously imputed to the mercantile school was that money was the only wealth, and that the gains in foreign trade would be largest when the exports most greatly exceeded the imports, and when the balance was paid in money, gold or silver. Adam Smith's doctrine was that wealth consisted chiefly in consumable commodities—in what he calls "the necessaries, conveniences, and luxuries of life," and not solely in money. Trade-balances may turn against a nation—to pay them, the nation may be drained of specie; whether it leads to panic, commercial crises, destruction of industries, depends on a variety of co-operating causes. This is not the place to go into this. In the long run the imports and exports of a nation must balance. "Products in market are a market for products"; "if a nation *will* not buy of foreigners, it *can not* sell to them"; "if foreigners *will* not buy of a nation, it *can not buy* of them," are different sides of the same truth. The mercantile system is no part of the protectionist's political economy.)

Chap. 2. Of restraints upon the importation from foreign countries of such goods as can be produced at home.

Chap. 3. Of the extraordinary restraints upon the importation of goods of almost all kinds from those countries with which the balance is supposed to be disadvantageous.

Chap. 4. Of drawbacks.

Chap. 5. Of bounties.

Chap. 6. Of treaties of commerce.

Chap. 7. Of colonies.

acquisitions, Adam Smith contemplated them from the commercial stand-point alone. He saw that the effort was to provide in the colonies a market for English manufactures, and to make them sources of supply for food and raw materials. This was the purpose of the restrictions which England everywhere imposed upon the colonies, by positive enactments and trade regulations. These American colonies were brought under the dominion of British rule not less by parliamentary bonds growing out of political sovereignty than by economic fetters growing out of mercantile theories. The Navigation Act, passed in the middle of the seventeenth century, made everything on the land and on the seas tributary to the mother-country. At last the American Revolution came—evolved from a long series of events possessing political and economic significance.

"American independence, like the great rivers of the country, had many sources, but the head-spring, which colored all the stream, was the Navigation Act," says Mr. Bancroft. It is doubtful if Adam Smith had any conception of the marvelous development of industries which this century has seen, and that England would become the workshop of the world, and must be compelled to buy the food which supported her workmen. Indeed, he says: "to expect that the freedom of trade should ever be entirely restored in Great Britain is as absurd as to expect that an Oceania or Utopia should now be established in it," and that "her master manufacturers would set themselves against every law which is likely to increase the number of rivals in the home market." But the day came when, under the facts of English history, it seemed sound political economy for those same English "master manufacturers" to invoke the help of free-trade policies. It turned out, apparently, that the theory of free trade, put into practice, would work for British manufacturers and American food-raisers, in the nineteenth century, the precise economical results which commercial restrictions and parliamentary statutes had worked between the mother-country and her colonies in the eighteenth century. The political rebellion and the economic rebellion had their origin at the same source. The remedy for the double mischief lies, still, in political and industrial freedom—unrestricted freedom of production between the fifty millions of the citizens of the new republic. Free trade with England *restricts our industries* and *our domestic exchanges* in the same sense, and with the same economic results, which the false application of the Mercantile Theory did. The unrestricted workings of free trade with England operated upon us in the same manner, and to the full measure of subjugation which accompanied the omnipotence of the parliamentary decree.

In the foregoing view of the "Wealth of Nations," we are fairly in possession of the field of the science of political economy. It is aside from any useful purpose to go on and indicate any one of the "ninety-odd blunders and fallacies" which have been attributed to that work. They do not touch our controversy; they only go to the validity of the claims which the science may set up to be a science.

On two points of some relevancy I venture to adopt the criticism of Mr. Bagehot:

"But, when we pass from the refutation of ancient errors (especially the error that wealth consists solely in money, or, in gold and silver) to the establishment of coherent truth, we shall not be equally satisfied. Students are, indeed, still sometimes told that they will find such a truth in Adam Smith; but those who had nothing else to read, and who wanted to read accurately, did not find it so. What, in fact, a student will find in Adam Smith, is a rough outline of sensible thoughts, not always consistent with themselves, and rarely stated with much precision, often very near the truth, though seldom precisely hitting it; a great mental effort in its day, though often deficient in the consecutiveness required by careful learners, and, except for the purpose of exciting an interest in the subject, altogether superseded and surpassed now."

Adam Smith made a serious attempt to demonstrate that "the capital employed in agriculture not only puts into motion a greater quantity of productive labor than any equal capital employed in manufactures, but in proportion, too, to the quantity of productive labor which it employs, it adds a much greater value to the annual produce of the land and labor of the country, to the real wealth and revenue of its inhabitants."

Mr. Bagehot's comment is: "In fact, probably few passages in so eminent a writer on the subject for which he is eminent, contain so much curious falsehood. If nature does nothing in manufactures, in what is it that it does anything? Manufactures are but applications of natural forces, just as agriculture is another application, and the reasoning assumes that the natural causes which produce dear things are more beneficial to mankind than those which produce cheap things, though, had Adam Smith seen that he was making such an assumption, he would have been the first to reject it."

A successful attempt to refute Adam Smith's doctrine was made by Alexander Hamilton in his celebrated "Report on the Treasury in 1791."

Of Adam Smith's exposition of the causes which give exchangeable value to commodities—the central inquiry in the whole science—Mr. Bagehot says: "Although, therefore, Adam Smith had the merit of teaching the world that the exchangeable value of commodities is proportioned to the cost of their production, his analysis of that cost was so very defective as to throw that part of political economy into great confusion for many years, and as quite to prevent his teaching being used as an authority upon it now."

These extracts are made at some length, for the reason that the general public is probably not aware of the force and destructiveness with which the science has been analyzed and criticised. The political economy of the future will possess an entire change of spirit. As Prof. Ely, of Johns Hopkins University, says ("The Past and the Present of Political Economy"): "It (the younger political economy) does not acknowledge *laissez-faire* as an excuse for doing nothing while the people starve, nor allow the all-sufficiency of competition as a plea for grinding the poor. It denotes a return to the grand principle of common sense and Christian precept. Love, generosity, nobility of character, self-sacrifice, and all that is best and truest in our nature, have their place in economic life."

CHAPTER V.

LAISSEZ FAIRE—NOT A SCIENTIFIC DOGMA.

We have, in this synoptical view of society in its efforts to satisfy its various desires, seen how it goes about the various processes of production, viewed its instruments of production, the considerations of utility, of value, which put them in operation, and the functions of money, credit, and so on, to facilitate their exchange.

Some of these exchanges terminate in the procuring of commodities to be used in further production, and the accumulation of these constitutes capital, the result of parsimony, saving, the effectual desire of accumulation—a contemplation of the future rather than the present; other exchanges terminate in the gratification of the passions in profligacy, in luxury, in charity, in objects of fashion and distinction, but which do not result in economic gains, that is, "wealth." We have seen the process by which individuals may acquire wealth. This they may obviously be able to do either by the creation of new objects having exchangeable value, or by the acquisition, from other people, by exchange—by a sufficient number of opportunities to "buy cheap and sell dear," or by the socially unprofitable industry of speculation. A nation, a people as such, never has and never can get rich by the latter method alone. Traders may get rich while the nation as a whole is growing poorer.

A nation must acquire wealth by the increase of its

"stock," by making new things, or by bringing into its boundaries new things, possessing exchangeable value.

Adam Smith has said, "The annual revenue of every society is always precisely equal to the exchangeable value of the whole annual product of the country, or rather, is precisely the same thing as that exchangeable value."

We have as yet been put in possession of no tests by which we may ascertain when "the annual revenue of the society" is at its greatest. The real problem is, then, to ascertain how the industry of a nation may be made to yield the greatest annual product. The economic man we have been contemplating so far was an individual with a salable thing in his hands, running about the planet to find a purchaser, a unit doing the best he can to promote his own interests, as he understands them.

We now find him a member of a society in which his liberty to do as he pleases is restrained by considerations of what is called the general welfare of that society. He can not escape the limitations which his citizenship in a definite nation puts upon him, if he would, and there can be no intelligent apprehension of his industrial relations to the world, except as a member of that society. We come then, at last, upon ground which contains the problem in hand. From this time forward we shall be in debatable territory. Some of the contentions before us will grow out of *doctrine* and some out of *facts*. We may as well, then, begin at the beginning. The entire premises of free trade were laid by Adam Smith. They will be found in these extracts from Book IV, "Wealth of Nations":

"But the principle which prompts us to save is the desire of bettering our condition; a desire which, though generally calm and dispassionate, comes with us from the womb, and never leaves us until we go into the grave. In the whole interval which separates these two moments, there is scarce perhaps a single instant in which any man is so perfectly and completely satisfied with his situation as to be without any wish of alteration or improvement of any kind. . . .

"The natural effort of every individual to better his own condition, when suffered to exert itself with freedom and security, is so powerful a principle, that it is, alone and without any assistance, not only capable of carrying on the society to wealth and prosperity, but of surmounting a hundred impertinent obstructions with which the folly of human laws too often encumbers its operations; though the effect of these obstructions is always, more or less, either to encroach upon its freedom or to diminish its security. . . .

"Every system which endeavors, either by extraordinary encouragements to draw toward a particular species of industry a greater share of the capital of the society than what would naturally go to it, or by extraordinary restraints to force from a particular species of industry some share of the capital which would otherwise be employed in it, is in reality subversive of the great purpose which it means to promote. It retards instead of accelerating the progress of society toward wealth and greatness, and diminishes instead of increasing the real value of the annual produce of its land and labor. . . .

"All systems, either of preference or restraint, being completely taken away, the obvious and simple system of natural liberty establishes itself of its own accord. Every man, as long as he does not violate the laws of justice, is left perfectly free to pursue his own interest in his own way, and to bring both his industry and capital into competition with those of any other man or order of men. The sovereign is completely discharged from a duty in attempting to perform which he must always be exposed to innumerable delusions, and for the proper performance of which no human wisdom or knowledge could ever be sufficient: the duty of superintending the industry of private people, and of directing it toward the employments most suitable to the interests of society."

It is not certain that in this last paragraph Adam Smith meant more than that, within the limits of a given nation, industry and trade should be free. In paragraph after paragraph in the book he insists on the supreme importance of the domestic commerce, the home market, and to an extent which has met with dissent from many of his more intensely free-trade followers. When he wrote, England was filled with monopolies holding special and valuable privileges, and the home trade was under many systems of preference and restraint imposed by royal license. In a country in which absolute free domestic trade prevailed, in which the industry and capital of each is in perfectly free competition with that of all, as in the United States, his criticisms would be disarmed of their force.

But, taking the widest application his words are capable of, we proceed to an analysis of his propositions. They are two:

The first is, that men are purely egoistic, are capable of perfectly perceiving their separate interests, and are not hindered by feelings of any other kind from their pursuit.

The second is, that every man, in pursuing his own advantage, at the same time furthers the good of all.

Together they constitute the doctrine, which is the "last word" the science of political economy has to utter, *laissez faire*, "letting things alone," out of which the practice of free trade, it is insisted, flows with scientific rigor.

His economic force is "the natural effort of every individual to better his condition." As the individual achieves wealth, the society will be carried to opulence and prosperity. The effort to "better his condition" is at last generalized under the name of "wealth," as much so as that of the Epicurean under the name of pleasure. Philosophically, this is materialism, and reduces political economy to a theory of egoism.

To get at it, we are invited to a short excursion into metaphysics, which we must accept. We are told the solution lies in a psychological pool, and we must plunge in. In essence, we are still dealing with an abstraction. It greatly simplifies the problem if we conceive of man as purely selfish. But we delude ourselves if we proceed on this assumption as the principle of human intercourse. This is to confound the "rules of the market" with "the rules of life"—with the elementary laws of human nature. The simplification is carried too far.

It is safe to say that society could not exist a single day with this one-sided force alone in operation.

The same Adam Smith who wrote the "Wealth of Nations" also wrote a "Theory of Morals." In this treatise Sympathy was assumed as the basis of moral sentiments. Neither selfishness nor sympathy form a scientific basis for conduct. "In the race for wealth, and honors, and preferments, he may run as hard as he can and strain every nerve and every muscle in order to outstrip all his competitors, but if he should jostle or throw down any of them, the indulgence of the spectators is entirely at an end," says Adam Smith.

Justice, then, is a constituent in conduct, and conscience, even if it be only the sense of "tribal approval or disapproval." It takes effect as an ingredient in the "condition" which we desire "to better." The family is a relation in which egoism is largely substituted by altruism. In a less degree, the nation is an instance, for we suppose there is such a sentiment as patriotism. The sense of community is an effective and ever-present force, economic force, which we can not rid ourselves of. Whatever may be the antithesis between governmental interests, dynastic interests, and free private interests, here at least there is a measurable merging of the egoistic principle into the principle of community, which is the government. The sense of the predominance of common aims weakens the force of motives terminating in self. When men are relieved from the burden of procuring the necessaries of life, the various ambitions which play so large a part in life, the consciousness of efficient co-operation with one's fellowmen is a dominant pleasure and a powerful motive. It will, on reflection, appear evident enough that neither political economy, nor any other science having to do with social facts, ever can exist if self-interest were the only spring of human action. From self through the family, the nation, to humanity in general, there is an extension of altruistic feelings, weakened in degree only, not different in kind. This is our human nature.

Mr. Mill, in a passage in his "Autobiography," gives us this as his ideal of the social life which we are likely to attain: "While we repudiate, with the greatest energy, that tyranny of society over the individual which most socialistic systems are supposed to involve, we yet look forward to a time when society will no longer be divided into the idle and the industrious; when the rule that they who do not work shall not eat will be applied, not to paupers only, but impartially to all; when the division of the produce of labor, instead of depending, as in so great a degree it now does, on the accident of birth, will be made by concert on an acknowledged principle of justice; and when it will no longer either be, or be thought to be, impossible for human beings to exert themselves strenuously in procuring benefits which are not to be exclusively their own, but *to be shared with the society they belong to.*"

The precise and abstract rules of political economy meagerly embrace the ruling laws of nature, everlastingly and invariably guiding the machinery of human toils and struggles. We have not only sympathy and the sense of community, as illustrated in the family and in the State, mitigating the selfish pursuit. We have further, the antagonistic forces of indolence and habit, the struggle between the desire of immediate enjoyment and the desire of accumulation. All these motives this egoistic political economy adds to and subtracts from, as if they were in a state of mechanical mixture, and were capable of separation in action. Human motives can not thus be added and subtracted. By their co-operation in the individual they become different from what they are in themselves. They constitute one new composite entirety. No dynamometer can measure out the force contributed by each to the general resultant. There is not one side of a man which is employed in selfish barter and another in unselfish benevolence. Men are not built in compartments, in one of which egoism is supreme, and in another sympathy, in another justice. The whole composite nature of the man acts. Oxygen and hydrogen constitute water, but water is a new and different compound. Its behavior, as water, in no way conforms to the behavior of the oxygen and hydrogen, as such. So far as conduct is concerned, it in no way aids us to know that water is composed of the two gases, and no amount of knowledge or speculation as to the conduct of oxygen and the conduct of hydrogen, separately, furnish the slightest clew to the conduct of water.

Prof. Perry says that political economy does not "cover the *entire* relations of buyers and sellers, but only the relations of buyers and sellers *as such;* morality and religion have *additional* but not incompatible words to utter when this science *becomes silent.*" There are no "buyers and sellers *as such*." The words which morality and religion utter to them are not *additional*, they are synchronous. The resultants of our social life are the product of all the capabilities of the composite man, buyer, seller, father, citizen, lazy, industrious, hopeful, honest, poor, unjust, prudent, or reckless. It is an orchestra whose balanced melodies are not the consecutive notes of instruments alternately played upon, but the joint contemporaneous and instantaneous concord of the whole. The sensuous effect of the orchestral harmony is irresolvable into the contribution of each performer. It is a chorus in which there are no solos. If the buyer and seller "*as such*" are operating under the axioms of pure selfishness, there can be no guarantee that the transaction will not result in a theft and not a sale. The sole pursuit of the economic gain which egoism provokes, may provoke justice to reward it with the penitentiary. If the motives inspiring us, which we ordinarily call moral motives, were dropped out of the lives of any of us, the daily record of conduct would be a blank. Any such purely atomistic conception of society is worthless for this or any other science. Moral motives not only do not drop out, but they can not be made to drop out. If they could drop out, the race would cease to be human. The economists first empty their economic man of all the aptitudes and attributes which they conceive, for the sake of simplicity, are not involved in the "buyer and seller as such," and, having ascertained how they think such a suppositious creation would comport itself, they conclude that the actual human being will bring his acts into conformity with their theoretic laws.

Prof. Cairnes, in criticising Bastiat's economic philosophy, it seems to me, removed the foundation of the whole science as developed by Adam Smith and his successors : " It is much as if a chemist were to propound, as a solution of the problem of the composition of bodies, that matter is compounded of elementary atoms, omitting to classify the various forms of matter according to their elementary constitution, or to say in what proportion in each class the elements combine. Such a generalization is no generalization in the scientific sense of the term: it is a compounding of a crowd of unanalyzed phenomena under an ambiguous word." Still less of scientific value would the solution have, if the forms of matter were incapable of classification, or if it was impossible to discover, or say, in what proportion the elements in hand did combine.

The synthesis of moral and mental forces in the actual human being is insoluble, and all fancied analyses must be remanded to the limbo of speculation in which the human family have indulged, with little profit and no conclusions, since the days of Plato. At the same time, while they have been baffled by the speculation, they have gone on and made great communities and systems in which politics, commerce, war, religion, morals, and love have been mingled with the desire of wealth in ever-varying proportions and energy. We have evidently not identified the central agent in the "desire of wealth."[1]

---

[1] "Another consideration occurs in this connection. It is impossible to separate the individual from his surroundings in state and society. In the strictest sense of the term and from a purely scientific standpoint, we do not live for ourselves alone but for one another as well as for ourselves. We are inextricably and organically bound up in state and society. What we call self-interest is *as a rule* not interest for one individual. It is a desire for the welfare perhaps of two, three, or four united in a family, perhaps of a circle of friends or relatives, perhaps of a town, city, or state. How many men toil for the *ego* alone? Assuredly very few. What we call egoism is usually only relative. We mean the circle is too narrow. Of course all this does not deny the existence of such a thing as downright egoism or selfishness, any more than it denies the fact of the existence of robbery, falsehood, and murder.

"All this proves that it is not individual self-interest, certainly not indi-

In the second place, we then come to the real premise of the doctrine of *laissez faire*, that "every man in pursuing his own advantage at the same time furthers the good of all."

Now, this is not laid down as a practical rule which in the greater number of instances it will be safer to follow. It is set up as a scientific principle to be universally applied to every social or industrial organization. The binding implication is that, taking human beings as they are, in the actual state of moral and intellectual development they have reached; taking account further of the physical conditions with which they are surrounded in the world; lastly, accepting the institution of private property as understood and maintained in most modern states, the promptings of self-interest will lead individuals, in all that range of their conduct which has to do with their well-being, spontaneously to follow that course which is most for their own good and for the good of all. That is, "first, that the interests of human beings are fundamentally the same; that what is most for my interest is also most for the interest of other people; and, secondly, that individuals know their interests in the sense in which they are coincident with the interests of others, and that, in the absence of coercion, they will, *in this sense,* follow them."

When Colbert, the great finance minister of Louis XIV, asked the merchant Legendre as to the best means of protecting French commerce, the answer was, "*Laissez faire, laissez passer.*" Colbert reorganized French industry by *protective* measures, by making manufacturers and com-

---

vidual selfishness, but *social considerations, which are the first and foremost factor in economic life in modern times.* It is a social consideration which induces the English capitalist to prefer 'eight or ten per cent profit with English society to the quadruple returns of California or Australia.' "—PROF. ELY.

merce free, for the first time, *within the limits of the French Empire*. He broke down the cordon of customhouses and regulations and restrictions which hampered French industry within the lines of French territory. He first gave their industry *national* form and *national* extent. His achievements have justly attracted the praise and approval of historians and economists. Quesnay, the head of the French economists, the Physiocrates, exalted the words of Legendre into an absolute scientific axiom. M. Wolowski, who wrote the Preliminary Essay to Roscher's "Political Economy," says of it:

"There is need of *institutions* to complete the exercise of the independence acquired by labor, and of laws to regulate that exercise. The *laissez faire* and *laissez passer* of economists is in no way like the absolute formula, which some have denounced and others sought to utilize, as relieving authority of all care and all intervention.

"To understand this maxim aright we must go back to the oppressive *régime* of ancient society. Quesnay's formula was, first of all, a protest against the restraints which hampered the free development of labor. But it did not tend to abrogate the office of legislator, nor to deprive society or the individual of the support of *the public power* which watches over *the fulfillment of our destiny*.

"It may have seemed convenient to find in the gravity of a politico-economical principle an excuse for the sweets of legislative and administrative *far niente*, but it is generally conceded that *the rôle of authority has grown* rather than diminished under the *régime* of the liberty of labor. The task is in our day a hard one, both for individuals and nations, for liberty dispenses its favors only to the masculine virtues of a laborious and an enlightened people.

"The mission of authority is not to constrain but to

counsel; not *to command*, but *to help accomplish;* not *to absorb* individual activity, but *to develop* it."

Prof. Perry says: "Each man's right of freedom is limited, of course, by every other man's right of freedom, which he is not at liberty to infringe; and also, in certain respects, by what is called *the general good*, of which the judge must be the government under which he lives."

How far, then, is the *laissez-faire* axiom of itself likely to result in the good of the whole, or to affect the effort of the individual for his own good?

Individuals may be relied upon to pursue their own interests according to their knowledge, experience, and capacity; how far, necessarily and as a fact in practice, will their interests be coincident with that of others and of the whole?

"Human interests are harmonious," exclaims Bastiat; "let them alone, and, under the supreme law of competition, we shall have the equalization of individuals on a higher plane of conciliation." He no more than we could shut his eyes to the ugly facts of industrial ills about him; we no more than he can suggest the remedy. But it is not to be found in *laissez faire*. Speaking of those who live by wages, he can not help saying: "The situation of men of this class is essentially precarious. As they receive their wages from day to day, they live from hand to mouth. In the discussion which, under a free *régime*, precedes every bargain, they can not wait: they must find work for to-morrow on any terms under pain of death. The result is that wages tend to fall to the lowest rate which is compatible with bare subsistence, and in this state of things the occurrence of the least excess of competition among the laborers is a veritable calamity. To deny the sufferings and wretchedness of that class of men, who bear so material a part in the business of production, would be to shut our eyes to the light of day. It is, in fact, this deplorable condition of a great number of our brethren which forms the subject of what has been justly called the *social problem;* for, although other classes of society are visited also with disquietudes, suffering, sudden changes of fortune, commercial crises, and economic convulsions, it may nevertheless be said with truth that *liberty* would be accepted as a solution of the problem, did mere *liberty* not *appear powerless* to cure that rankling sore which we denominate pauperism."

Here, then, our rule breaks down, even though in the presence of our ignorance and powerlessness we know no other solution. "Letting alone" does not work harmonious or just results, and political economy does not and can not accept it as one of its scientific "laws."[1]

Where the "law" could be reversed with reasonable success, it has been. All laws for common schools, all poor-laws, all factory legislation fixing the hours of labor and the ages of children who may be employed as laborers, all legislation directed to the "truck system," are instances of governmental interference with the freedom of contract. The "Irish Land Bill" is a very signal instance of legislative invasion of what, in all Anglo-Saxon history, have been considered "vested rights." We shall see, later on,

---

[1] "If all that Bastiat and his confrères write only held in real life, the solution of the Social Problem would indeed be an easy task. Business men know, however, that the share of the produce of labor and capital received by labor diminishes by so much the profits of capital, and that, *cæteris paribus*, the larger the proportion of profits received by capital, the smaller the proportion received by labor. That there is an entire harmony of interests between the different classes of society, is at complete variance with the teachings of modern science, and 'is at best a dream of human happiness as it presents itself to a millionaire.' It is possible to reconcile the different classes of society only by a higher moral development. The element of self-sacrifice must yet play a more important rôle in business transactions, or peace and good-will can never reign on earth."—Prof. Ely, *ut supra.*

how considerations of the *general welfare* have justified this course of administrative action. More especially in England, parliamentary interference has been denounced as contrary to the sound conclusions of political economy.

Adam Smith did not attempt to philosophize over the process by which the unrestrained pursuit of his own good by the individual led, unconsciously to that individual, to the general welfare. He generalized from a few very inadequate particular instances. He boldly went into the domains of theology in order to help out his political economy. "Each member of the community is led in this, as in many other instances, by an *invisible hand* to promote an end that was no part of his intention."

In contrast with this view of Adam Smith, let us see what our American Prof. Francis A. Walker says: "Political economy owes nothing to natural theology. The economist is under no obligation to any assumptions derived from that source. He has, indeed, no more right to start with the theory of an order of nature which is purely beneficent, than he would have to start with the opposite theory of an order of nature wholly maleficent. As an economist, he has no mission to 'vindicate the ways of God to man.' He is to investigate the laws of wealth; that duty he will best discharge by reasoning, as justly as his mental powers enable him to do, from economic premises which have been established by adequate induction, and from such only."

But the fact seems to be that there is no such coincidence between the interest of the individual and the society.

Prof. Cairnes has not hesitated to say that he holds it, as usually understood, to be a pretentious sophistry, destitute of foundation in nature and fact, and rapidly becoming an obstruction and nuisance in public affairs:

"Now I beg you to mark the strange assumptions that

underlie this reasoning. Human interests are naturally harmonious, *therefore* we have only to leave people free, and social harmony must result: as if it was an obvious thing that people knew their interests in the sense in which they coincide with the interests of others, and that, knowing them, they must follow them; as if there were no such things in the world as passion, prejudice, custom, *esprit de corps*, class interests, to draw people aside from the pursuit of their interests in the largest and highest sense. Here is a fatal flaw on the very threshold of Bastiat's argument, and it is a flaw which no follower of Bastiat has repaired, which, for my part, I believe to be irreparable. Nothing is easier to show than that people follow their interests. But, between this and following their interest, in the sense in which it is coincident with that of other people, a chasm yawns. This chasm, in the argument of the *laissez-faire* school, has never been bridged. The advocates of the doctrine shut their eyes and leap over it."

Prof. Jevons rejects the doctrine: "It is fatal to attempt to uphold, in regard to social legislation, any theory of eternal fixed principles or abstract rights. The whole matter becomes a complex calculus of good and evil. All is a question of probability and degree. I venture to maintain that we shall do better in the end if we throw off the incubus of metaphysical ideas and expressions. We must resolve all those supposed principles and rights into the facts and probabilities which they are found to involve when we inquire into their real meaning.

"The right of a man to dispose freely of his labor, means the recognition by the legislature that, in the majority of cases, a man is the best judge of his own interests in disposing of his labor. In a number of cases specified in the statute-book, the legislature recognizes an opposite state of things.

"The principle of the freedom of trade stands on the same footing; it is a probability of advantage which, however, must be set aside in case of a greater probability of evil."

Prof. Francis A. Walker thinks that the free-trade economists have taken "an unjustifiably lofty attitude on this subject; practically refusing to argue the question at all, as one of national expediency, contenting themselves with occupying the high ground of *laissez faire*.

"Now, the doctrine of *laissez faire*, although established by the English economists to their own satisfaction, as containing a principle of universal application, and thus deemed by them a conclusive answer to all arguments specially directed to justify restrictions upon international trade, has never been accepted in the fullness of significance given to it by them throughout any wide constituency, not even by any large proportion of the educated classes—not even generally by publicists, or statesmen, or men of affairs."[1]

---

[1] "The truth is, the stern necessities of political life compelled statesmen to violate it in England itself, even when proclaiming it with their lips. This was first done apologetically, and each interference was regarded by the 'school' as an exception to the rule; but it finally began to look as if it were all exception and no rule. Interference was found necessary in every time of distress, as during our late civil war, when Government borrowed money for public works to give employment to the Lancashire operatives, at the time of the cotton famine. Every reform in the social and economic institutions of Great Britain has been accomplished only by the direct, active interference of Government in economic affairs. When Gladstone began his work of conciliating Ireland in 1869, he found it expedient to grant loans of public money to occupiers who wished to improve their holdings, and to proprietors to reclaim waste lands or to make roads and erect buildings, enabling them thereby to employ labor. In 1880 the Government of Ireland again decided to alleviate the sufferings of the Irish by making an advance of £250,000 out of the surplus of the Church funds, for public works of various kinds, in order to provide employment for those needing it. The recent Irish acts interfering between tenant and landlord in the matter of rent, and offering

The whole series of parliamentary acts regulating factory administration, first passed more than half a century since, have been based on principles of restriction. By means of governmental interference hours of labor have been limited, night-work in certain cases forbidden, the employment of children has been prohibited, holidays have been prescribed, and sanitary inspection by officials has been provided for. In his "Reign of Law," the Duke of Argyll remarks that "during the present century two great discoveries have been made in the science of government: the one is the immense advantage of abolishing restrictions upon" (English) "trade; the other is, the absolute necessity of imposing restrictions upon labor."[1] Yet this whole system of legislation was resisted by the economists as opposed to their eternal fixed principles, or abstract rights.

"They asserted," says Prof. Walker, "the entire competence of the laboring classes to protect their own interests; they repeated their maxims, *laissez faire, laissez aller*, just as confidently as they do when 'protective' duties

---

the assistance of the state to tenants in arrears, violate all the principles of *laissez-faire* economists, and are nevertheless applauded by the wisest and best men of all lands. *Laissez faire* was tried in the early part of this century in English factories, with results ruinous to the morality of women and destructive of the health of children. Robert Owen, himself a large and successful manufacturer, declared that he had seen American slavery, and, though he considered it bad and unwise, he regarded the white slavery in the manufactories of England as far worse."—Prof. Ely, *ut supra*.

[1] Prof. Van Buren Denslow adds: "The Duke of Argyll forgets that the discoveries in government are four, not two. The other two were the discoveries made by mothers—first, that their daughters ought all to be able to swim; secondly, that they should on no account go near the water. The latter is exactly on a par with the notion that it can be an economic doctrine that the worker, in trading in his work, or in that which his work produces, shall not be free; but that the trader, in trading in the product of another's work, shall be free."

are proposed; they put themselves on record in the most formal manner against all measures of restriction upon factory and workshop labor; they cast their lot with the opposition to this class of legislation, and staked the reputation and influence of political economy upon their being right in this matter. But it did not turn out so. Although in the first instance, that of the act of 1842, Sir Robert Peel, the elder, had been so solicitous not to violate the principle of the self-sufficiency of labor that he made the bill apply only to apprentices, the wards of the state, the political rightfulness and the economical expediency of regulating the contract for labor so grew upon the public mind of England that act after act extended the supervision of the state over factory and workshop, until the policy of restriction had vindicated itself to the complete satisfaction of the working classes, even in the main of the master class themselves, and of the statesmen of the kingdom and publicists almost without exception." [1]

Then social, political, and economic reasons united in justifying interference with the freedom of contract; and we have the dread alternative of Prof. Perry, that "there can be no science of exchanges if economical reasons can be given for *restricting* exchanges."

---

[1] "In our own country it is curious to note how the advocates of *laissez faire* abandon position after position. First, tenements are exempted from what is considered the general law, because experience has shown that 'nothing short of compulsion will purify our tenement districts.' Then it is discovered that the ordinary laws of supply and demand are not preserving our forests; consequently, that individual and general interests do not harmonize. The inadequate action of competition in regulating and controlling great corporations gives another excuse for governmental interference. 'Corners' in necessaries of life call for a further abandonment of the *laissez-faire* dogma, as does also the success attendant on the establishment of government fisheries. The list might be extended almost *ad libitum*, and every day adds to it. Thus has *laissez faire*, one of the strongholds of past political economy, been definitely abandoned."—PROF. ELY, *et supra*.

It is agreed that the "obvious and simple system of natural liberty" is an offshoot of the ancient fiction of a code of nature, and "a natural order of things" is a form given to that fiction in modern times, by theology on one hand, and a revolt against the tyranny of the folly and inequality of such human codes as the world had known on the other.

A criticism directed against the oppressions, political and industrial, of mediæval times, could have no application to the United States, in any stage of its career, since it was an organized government. Adam Smith's "Wealth of Nations" must be read in connection with his "Theory of Moral Sentiments." "Abstraction would never have played so great a part in Adam Smith's philosophy, would never have resulted in such sweeping generalization respecting the beneficent and equitable economy resulting from the play of the natural inclinations and individual interests of men, had not the classical conceptions of nature's harmonious code become blended with the theological conception of that great benevolent and all-wise Being, who directs all movements of nature, and who is determined to maintain in it at all times the greatest possible quantity of happiness. It is incontrovertible that historical investigation convicts the nature hypothesis of reproducing a mere fiction of ancient philosophy." (Prof. Leslie.)

The "principle of liberty" as a practical guide, and *laissez faire* as a philosophical maxim, fall to the ground.

In his "Statement of some New Principles on the Subject of Political Economy," published in Boston in 1834, John Rae undertook to demonstrate that, in the nature of things and as a fact, "individual and national interests are not identical." The demonstration is complete. Indeed, the whole book is a capital example of calm, dispassionate exposition, and of clear, logical argument. Mr. Mill, whose own writings show, through and through, familiarity with John Rae, says, "In no other book known to me is so much light thrown, both from principles and history, on the causes which determine the accumulation of capital."

The difference in the causes which give rise to individual and to national wealth are clearly pointed out. His argument is conducted upon underlying principles. I quote one of his illustrations:

"Let any one, in any country, in Great Britain for instance, trace backward for fifteen or twenty years the mutations that have occurred in the fortunes of the persons with whom he is acquainted, and he will find that there are few whose circumstances are not very much changed from what they were. Good conduct, good fortune, and frugality have made many rich who were then poor; imprudence, misfortune, prodigality have made many poor who were then rich. But, while that man has been adding house to house, and farm to farm, and this has been giving up one portion of property after another, till he finds all he once possessed in the hands of another, the whole mass of houses, lands, and wealth has undergone but little alteration: the national capital itself remains, comparatively, but little changed. It is not by the acquiring wealth previously in the possession of others, that nations enrich themselves. But a very small part of the capital of any community can, I suspect, be accounted for by tracing its passage from any other community. Instead of one nation growing rich and another poor, we rather see many neighboring nations advancing at the same pace toward prosperity and affluence, or declining equally to misery and want. As individuals seem generally to grow rich by grasping a larger and larger portion of the wealth already in existence, nations do so by the *production of wealth that did not previously exist.* The two processes differ in this, that one is an *acquisition,* the other a *creation.*"

He was no believer in "administrative nihilism." "The community adds to its wealth by creating wealth, and if we understand, by *the legislator, the power acting for the community,* it seems not absurd or unreasonable that he should direct part of the energies of the community toward the furtherance of this power of invention." ("Invention is the only power on earth that can be said to 'create,'" he says.) "In the following cases it would seem, at least, not improbable that the power of the legislator so directed might be beneficial:

"I. In promoting the progress of science.

"II. In promoting the progress of art—1. By encouraging the discovery of new arts. 2. By encouraging the discovery of improvements in the arts already practiced in the country. 3. By encouraging the discovery of methods of adapting arts already practiced in other countries to the particular circumstances of the territory and community for which he legislates.

"But a case of the circumstance of a country being so peculiarly favorable to the practice of a foreign art that, in the very first essays it makes in it, it can successfully compete with another, where that art has been long established, is assuredly rare; and, if any such case occur, we may be satisfied that the manufacture might, *with much advantage, have been previously introduced.* The only difference between us" (Adam Smith and himself) "is, that the doctrines he advocates teach us to wait till the miscalculations of some unfortunate projector confer on us a public benefit. I hold that it would be more just and judicious that the necessary first cost of the scheme should be borne by the whole community; more just, as thus the burden necessary to be borne to procure a common benefit will be divided among all, instead of being sustained by one; more judicious, as the society will not have to wait for the attainment of a desirable object, on so doubtful a chance as the folly of projectors."

These extracts naturally lead up to, and probably suggested, the concessions made by Mr. Mill himself in favor of *protection*, a concession which Prof. Thorold Rogers, Prof. Price, Prof. Cairnes, Prof. Sumner, all agree "is perpetually quoted and is perpetually mischievous, . . . ought never to have been made," but which logically involves all that has ever been urged by protectionists in the United States. Mr. Mill had admitted the reasonableness of granting patent-rights and copyrights, and then guardedly proceeds:

"The only case in which, on mere principles of political economy, protective duties can be defensible, is when they are imposed temporarily (especially in a young and rising nation), in hopes of naturalizing a *foreign industry*, in itself perfectly suitable to the circumstances of the country. *The superiority of one country over another in a branch of production often arises only from having begun it sooner. There may be no inherent advantage on one part, or disadvantage on the other, but only a present superiority of acquired skill and experience.* A country which has this skill and experience yet to acquire may, in other respects, be better adapted to the production than those which were earlier in the field; and, besides, it is a just remark that nothing has a greater tendency to promote improvements in any branch of production than its trial under a new set of conditions. But it can not be expected that individuals should, at their own risk, or rather to their certain loss, introduce a new manufacture, and bear the burden of carrying it on until the producers have been educated up to the level of those with whom the processes are traditional. *A protective duty, continued for a reasonable time, will sometimes be the least inconvenient mode in which a nation can tax itself for the support of such an experiment."* [1]

All that the protectionists in the United States ask of the doctrine of *laissez faire* is " let alone," as between the fifty millions of us who have our hands on all the levers of

---

[1] This passage in Mr. Mill, which seems on its face to embody so much plain common sense, has been roughly attacked. Prof. Bonamy Price places an alarming estimate on the mischief it has wrought. He says (" Practical Political Economy," p. 315): " No name of high celebrity is put forward so incessantly as the shield of their doctrine, by the advocates of protection, as that of Mr. Mill, and so great is the support which it gives to a policy so profoundly injurious to *the happiness of mankind* " (isn't this a rather euphemistic exaggeration for the only thing the professor can mean, the prosperity of the present generation of English manufacturers?), " that it may almost be questioned whether Mr. Mill has not done more harm to the welfare of the human race by the countenance he has given, though limited, to protection, than he has done good by all his other writings on political economy."

Prof. Thorold Rogers re-enforces Prof. Price:

" Few statements made by any writer have, I am persuaded, been more extensively though unintentionally mischievous than this admission of Mr. Mill. The passage has been quoted over and over again in the United States and in the British colonies as a justification of the financial system which these communities have adopted. The circumstances in which they are situated exactly square with the hypothesis of Mr. Mill. The countries are young and rising—industries, as yet nascent, are thoroughly *suitable to the natural capacity of the region and of the people,* the latter being of the same stock with the mother-country, whose manufactures they prohibit and discourage. There is *no reason,* apparently, except that of priority in the market, *why the industry of the old country should not be transplanted to the new.* Hence, I repeat, Mr. Mill's concession is perpetually quoted, and is perpetually mischievous."

" Mr. George W. Smalley (of the ' New York Tribune ') asked Mr. Mill, during his later years, ' whether he still adhered to this statement ? ' ' Certainly,' was his answer. ' I have never affirmed anything to the contrary. I do not presume to say that the United States may not find protection expedient in their present state of development. I do not even say that, if I was in America, I should not be a protectionist.' "—PROF. THOMPSON, " Political Economy," p. 250.

industry possible to any people—" hands off," as to the rest of the industrial world. Government can arrange these conditions for us, and conserve in the completest manner " the obvious and simple system of natural liberty "—our own natural liberty—to have access to our own resources.

Judge Phillips says, wisely: " Legislators can not stand neutral, as mere lookers-on at a drama, in the catastrophe in which they have no hand. They are the appointed responsible actors and agents, and the result, whether success or ruin, is of their achievement.

" The false pretense of free trade not to act, is, in fact, positively and directly, in the most efficient manner possible, taking sides with the foreign competitor. The pretense that the Government is to be neutral in this contest is as preposterous as to pretend that it is to be neutral in the case of hostilities with any foreign country."

James Madison easily formulated out of the facts of our history this conclusion: " To allow trade to regulate itself is not, however, to be admitted as a maxim universally sound; *our own experience* has taught us that it is, in certain cases, the same thing as allowing one nation to regulate it for another."

As a rule of individual or national conduct we may, then, dismiss *laissez faire*, not only as a pretentious sophistry, but as a very pretentious humbug.

CHAPTER VI.

AN ANALYSIS OF FOREIGN TRADE—THE REAL QUESTION AT ISSUE.

WE have now come into sight of the problem of political economy. It is, namely, to investigate the nature, the causes, the amount, and the distribution of wealth in human society, and the laws of coexistence and sequence discoverable in this class of social phenomena. The solution offered by current orthodox deductive economists, and the one to which we have been giving attention somewhat in detail, may be briefly but accurately summed up as follows:

"The nature of wealth is explained by defining it as comprising all things which are objects of human desires limited in supply and valuable in exchange. Of the causes governing its amount and distribution the chief exposition is that the desire of wealth naturally leads, where security and liberty exists, to labor—accumulation of capital, appropriation of land and its resulting rent, division of labor, or separation of employments—commerce, and the use of money. Whence a continual increase in the total stock of wealth and its distribution in wages, profit, and rent, followed by the prices of products in proportion to the labor, sacrifice, amount of capital, and quantity and quality of land contributed by each individual to production. Inasmuch as human fecundity tends to augment population in a geometrical ratio, while the productiveness of the soil is limited, the proportion of rent to wages and profit tends to increase in the progress of society." This is the entire framework upon which different authors put the flesh and muscles to suit themselves.

The question we are about to investigate is not one of *taxation*. We may as well get this clearly fixed in our minds. "Taxation is no part of the science, and there can be no true science of taxation. Nature has given no whisper that we can hear about any taxes," says Prof. Perry; and Prof. Sumner holds that "there are no scientific laws of taxation, because there are no natural laws of taxation. Nature has not provided for taxation as she has for production, exchange, distribution, and consumption. Taxation is part of the co-operation of society for its own defense against the evil and destructive forces within itself."[1]

The question involves, first and last, the economic effects of *restriction*. Restriction is an effort of a nation to provide against destructive forces from without. It assumes the existence within that nation of productive forces which are natural and proper to its people, and it undertakes to use them. In our own case, it undertakes to make it an inducement to the people of other lands to come here and enter into the joint possession of them, and to set no domestic limit to the forms of industry within reach. Our activities are to be measured by our capacities and numbers, and are not to be restricted to the supply of the demand of other nations, based on exchange values.

It may be that this proposal will run foul of some economic doctrines which would provide a comparatively

---

[1] Even though it were a question of raising surplus money for public purposes—taxation—it might be good economy. Prof. Senior gives a clew to the secret of meeting enormous indebtedness and consequent taxation: "A country which has been forced into raising a large public revenue, suffers far more from the indirect than from the direct effect of taxation—suffers more by being *prevented from producing*, than from being *obliged to pay*." The progress in the payment of our own war-debt is in point.

sparse population on a rich soil with the means of a comfortable, lazy existence through exchanges made in products which cost us little labor, little effort and sacrifice. A restricted number of human beings might live here with entire scientific precision, and in close and strict subordination to the technical rules of an abstract system, but they must forego their mission, not alone of creating new values —"wealth"—but also of nation-making and of historical standing. The orthodox scorn and despise the sentiment of nationality in these discussions; but if the satisfaction of desires be the true end of human effort, the insatiable aspirations of the men of America for a true citizenship and a national individuality will be found no less potent and irrepressible impulses than the desire for wealth. Wealth is only one of the objects the successful pursuit of which has created the fullness and perfectness of life here. It has not been an object of distinct pursuit, it came along as one of the many ends in which our efforts culminated—working out, as a whole, the general welfare.

And, then, Profs. Perry and Sumner[1] distort the whole discussion of the *protective* system, effectuated by *restrictions* upon foreign exchanges, as though it were a question of *taxation*. This is done deliberately to cover the confusion and fallacy which that mode of treatment enables them to import into the debate. One mode of reaching protective results is by imposing import duties upon foreign manufactures. In this case, it is not the revenue, the proceeds of that particular form of taxation which we are after, but the restriction of the market *pro tanto* to a

---

[1] I name these two very distinguished professors because they are able, alert, and have made the only scientific contribution to American free trade. They are controversialists, and have not always, under their fervor of conviction and impatience with dissent, preserved the amenities of debate. If they are met in the same spirit, it is not intended as disrespect to them.

home-producer. The economical effects could be reached as effectively by prohibitory legislation as by tariffs for revenue which result incidentally in protection. The whole contention between the protectionist and the free-trader may be carried on without the slightest recurrence to the word "taxation," either in fact or idea. Having made the protectionist say that *taxation* has some *creative* power, Prof. Sumner rudely challenges him to the proof thus: "The rest is all phrases intended to occupy attention while the thimble-rigging is going on. If this is not so, let some protectionist analyze the operation of his system and show by reference to undisputed economic principles where and how it exerts any effect on production to increase it." If the protective tax, as the professor insists on calling it, should prove the means of *removing the obstacle* to the best distribution of the population and natural employment of their efficiency, the epithet "thimble-rigger" might be unpleasantly applicable elsewhere.

If the distinction between *taxation* and the *regulation of commerce* has never been known to these gentlemen, it is time they took a glance at the ante-Revolutionary debates both in the British Parliament and Colonial Assemblies. The speeches of Lord Chatham and Edmund Burke in defense of the colonies contain long arguments based on the distinction. Indeed, the Revolution did not have its origin in any denial of the parliamentary right to impose limitations for "the regulation of commerce," but it arose distinctly out of the effort to tax the colonies directly for the purpose of raising *revenue*. The legal power of Parliament "to regulate commerce" was not disputed by the colonists, but they protested against its economic effects on them. The power to *levy taxes* was instantly resented, unless accompanied with the right of representation. The legal power in Congress "to regulate commerce" includes the power to lay *protective duties*, and, if economic reasons justify it, *prohibitory duties*. Any device is authorized which promotes "the general welfare." The Constitutional grant is, "to regulate commerce."

Prof. Perry breaks out into very intemperate words in this connection. He confuses means with ends: "We have seen abundantly already what protection in the false sense is, as complicated and comprehensive *taxes*, and it is a piece of pure and plausible deceit to apply a word so diffused with wholesome association to a thing so penetrated with loathsome selfishness. *Government*, which is *nothing but a committee of citizens to attend impartially to certain great needs of the whole*, is thereby prostituted to the end of the possible enrichment of the few at the cost of the certain impoverishment of the most." We may as well carry along with us the professor's definition of *government*.

It is one of the unaccountable things that a layman is expected to draw calm and lucid conclusions from the furious and lurid rhetoric with which the professors of political economy always go about it to lay down their premises in this department of their science. In his address before the Tariff Commission, Prof. Sumner starts off in this wise:

"Who is the beneficent genie now, who works all the magic of the protectionist's system? It is *a tax*. If *taxes* are only rightly adjusted, says the protectionist, they make wages high and low, and prices high and low, all at the same time. When one hears this kind of nonsense, one is forced to believe that the sum of superstition in the world is a constant quantity. Superstition is a defective sense of causation. . . . The protectionist legislator lays *a tax*, and goes home secure in the faith that wages will be high, prices low, and prosperity stable, as if there were a fixed, direct, and inevitable law of nature connecting taxes with social welfare, and nothing else. . . . This superstition is more wild than fetichism or astrology."

It is a perfectly legitimate demand, which the parties to this discussion have a right to make on each other, that there should be some common understanding of the terms involved, some adequate analysis of the facts with which they deal, and some adequate conception of the principles of political economy, or the practical maxims of business, and of the proper application of the one to the other.

Mr. David A. Wells, more temperate, but still inaccurate, defines the protective system as one which maintains "that a state or nation can most surely and rapidly attain a high degree of superior prosperity by protecting or shielding its domestic industries from the competitive sale or exchange with the products of all similar foreign industries; the same to be effected either by direct legislative prohibition of foreign commerce, or by the imposition of such discriminating taxes (duties) on imports as shall, through a subsequent enhancement of prices, interfere to a greater or less extent with their introduction, free exchange, and consumption. An explanation of either of the terms 'free trade' or 'protection' involves, therefore, a presentation of the arguments based on *theory* or *experience* which may be adduced in support of the respective economic systems of which they are the expression."

But our aggressive friend Prof. Perry will not admit the possibility of either theory or experience in the case of protection : " This explains a peculiar and long-noticed fact, namely, the protectionist talkers and writers rarely or never use radical analysis. They rarely or never begin at the beginning, take simple cases and follow them on, try to show why and how *high taxes* on certain things promote the public prosperity, and thus connect cause with effect and premise with conclusion. On the contrary, they talk endlessly *about* protection, ascribe to it marvelous efficacy, often refer to it as if it were a leading factor in the development of industry, without ever once *taking it to pieces* before our eyes and showing us that it is adapted in its very nature to bring about the results ascribed to it. The truth is, *an honest analysis is fatal to it*, and so recourse is had to smooth words and deceptive phrases and ornamental epithets, non-suggestive even of the real nature of the thing."

We shall try to take it to pieces and venture on the analysis suggested.

In a very incisive paper, "The Argument against Protective Taxes" ("Princeton Review," March, 1881), Prof. Sumner concedes two possible positions which the protectionist may assume. Whenever Prof. Sumner undertakes to state his adversary's premises, it must be noticed that his attitude is not a judicial one. Very grave allowances must be made both for over-statements and under-statements of his opponent's position, and very thorough filtration must be made of the prejudgments and unfair and untrue perversion which he thrusts to the fore as his adversary's premises and conclusions. Making allowances for rhetorical sophistries, we may come to a kind of an understanding of the doctrines which a protectionist may be thought capable of entertaining from these paragraphs, taken from the paper referred to. The italics indicate points at which some adjustment of words to things is to be made. "Mischievous thing," "isolation," "antagonism of nations," are the professor's glosses on alleged doctrines which nobody holds :

"1. He may boldly declare that there is a science of wealth based on restrictions ; that he can discover the principles of it and reduce them to a theory ; that trade between countries is *a mischievous thing*, at least if it runs on parallels of latitude; that *isolation* and *antagonism of nations* is the *law of nature* upon which wealth and civilization depend; that there is therefore *no universal science of wealth*, but only *a national science of wealth*, and that this science is, in its final analysis, only a generalization from certain empirical maxims of economic policy.

"2. The other ground which the protectionist may take is that protection does not increase wealth, but is, for some reason or other, expedient."

Prof. Perry says, frankly and once for all, that "there can be no science of exchanges" (i. e., no such science as political economy) "if any *economical* reasons can be given for *restricting exchanges*."

Now, the protectionist and the free-trader are dealing with the same economic forces. What these are we undertook to summarize at the opening of this chapter. If they start from the same premises, there must be some fallacy in reasoning or mistake in fact somewhere, for their conclusions are radically at opposites. The free-trader thinks protection is a fatal economic and political blunder. Whatever estimate we may make of our progress in accumulating wealth in the United States, we are, he thinks, infinitely worse off than we should have been under free trade. It is quite difficult to imagine what the idea of a free-trader is as to the goal we *might have* reached. And it may be a question of the *ideals* from which we start and of the ends to be attained. The end he contemplates, perhaps, is not to be viewed from the national stand-point, but from a cosmopolitan. But surely, if the protectionist and free-trader start together, and do not arrive together, the cross-roads where they separated ought to be discoverable. Let us start, then, with the two distinguished American professors whom we have had occasion to quote so often. Prof.

Sumner, in his "Princeton Review" essay, affects to state the issue, "free from all sentimental and pedantic rubbish." As is his custom, he asks his pupil to look at his landscape through glasses which he has colored in advance, and he always faces him in his own direction before he starts him. At least, he is a master of the art of so putting a problem that his solution is disclosed in the very form of its statement. Here are his four questions, and we shall try to answer them, although each question is already *enceinte* with the answer he has carefully prearranged. They impliedly contain the whole argument against Defensive Duties. The italics are not his:

"The *economic* question about the tariff is, Does it enable the population of the country to command *greater material good* for a *given effort?*

"The *political* question about protection is, Does the statute enacted by the legislature *alter the distribution of property* so that one man enjoys *another man's earnings?* Has the state a law in operation which enables one citizen to *collect taxes* of another?

"The *scientific* question about protection is, Does it lessen *the ratio of effort* and *sacrifice* to *comfort* and *enjoyment?*

"The *popular* question about protection is, Does it prevent me from *supporting myself and my family* by *my labor* as well as I could do it if there were no *protective taxes?*"

These questions raise legitimate issues, which will be discussed, *infra*, Chapters IX and X.

These inquiries are made by a scholar thoroughly trained in a science, and one who, year after year, has guided bright and inquisitive minds over the whole field, and who, it may be assumed, see and understand all the contents of that field. Such a one must be assumed to be able to apply the abstract and general propositions which belong in his science to the concrete facts of a specific problem. The conclusion he reaches ought to be true in some sense; if not to the actual facts of the case in hand, it possibly *might have* been true in some supposititious case—it might be made to correspond with certain ideal presuppositions. Of course, there would have been some sort of definite industrial organization here under free trade. It becomes the professor to let us know, in detail, what it would have been. It is certain that the commercial and industrial ruins which the United States now present to a sympathizing world are not nearly so wide-spread as the theory of Prof. Sumner says they ought to be. The dilapidation is not total, and he is compelled to admit that we have "accumulated capital faster in the United States than in any country in the world." The economic history of the country under the highly protective tariff of 1861 has been a standing wonder to the free-traders of England and America. It yields readily to adequate analysis. Its phenomena are explicable under very obvious principles. Protection worked the results intended, and *the why* lies not very deep.

Mr. Mill says: "If a political economist, for instance, finds himself puzzled by any recent or commercial phenomenon; if there is any mystery to him in the late or present state of the productive industry of the country which his knowledge of principles does not enable him to unriddle, he may be sure that *something is wanting* to render his system a safe guide in existing circumstances. Either some of the facts which influence the situation of the country and the course of events are not known to him, or, knowing them, he knows not what ought to be their effects. In the latter case, *his system is imperfect, even as an abstract system*. It does not enable him to trace correctly all the consequences even of assumed premises. . . . Against false premises and unsound reasoning, a good mental discipline may secure us, but against the danger of *overlooking something*, neither strength of understanding nor intellectual cultivation can be more than a very imperfect protection."

In the nature of the case Prof. Sumner must see very definitely the course of economic development which would have taken place under free trade. Any of us—all of us—can figure it out with reasonable completeness. It contemplates the arrival on the shores of America of a limited number of men acting solely under economic impulses. Tied by economic considerations to European commercial centers, extending by concentric lines of growth exactly in accordance with the stimulus furnished at those centers, it contemplates the arrival on these shores of no more men and women than may supply the demand for the raw materials which their old home market would take up. That is what the English statesmanship which founded these colonies avowedly proclaimed and intended. Indeed, these emigrants would, it must be supposed, always consider that old center of trade as their ultimate political center, nor would they deem themselves, in thus surrendering to merely commercial considerations, as the nucleus of a new center of activity—of a nation. The theory overlooks the arrival on these shores of the multitude fleeing from the workshops of Europe and the religious and political oppressions which had compelled them to expatriate themselves, and the vast occupation of the new opportunities here afforded, and which would produce, when referred to old industrial centers, an unsymmetrical industrial growth. With the full play of both sets of agencies, political and industrial, in operation, we are in the presence of an entirely new problem. The evolution of industries and of population, if made here in strict correlation to European development, would have presented a case for the application of, or rather would have illustrated, some of the well-known principles of the science of political economy. It assumes that we are built upon the precise kind of prevision with which the founders of great industries endeavor to adjust supply to demand. The community growing up under these limitations would have been demonstrably inferior in acquisition, in energy, in civilization, and in wealth.

Things have not, however, turned out in the United States as English statesmen and the free-traders predicted. We are indubitably prosperous—which they, of course, deny. They have failed in correct predictions of economic events, because the realization of the result has been contingent on the action of contemporaneous agencies not included in their economic premises. Their prevision is an attempt to forecast, not events, but *tendencies*, and these tendencies have been counteracted by others, of which the free-trader is determined to take no account. When reproached that they can not even explain the present, they reply, "Oh, now, you are outside your science!"

Our early history negatived their presuppositions. Prof. Sumner has said, with great emphasis and with entire accuracy, that "what we are is the result of our *inherited traits and traditions* and of *our physical surroundings.*" Herein he fairly jumps the inclosure within which the definitions of the *science* confine him, and yet he betrays his contempt at the effort to mix up economic and "sociological" considerations. Unfortunately for him, the Creator of the human family so mixed the ingredients in human nature.

The economic phenomena of America are incapable of being interpreted upon any principle of exchange. It was a case in which the productive forces of men and material conditions—" inherited traits and traditions *and* physical surroundings "—being such as they were, must, when brought into mutual action and reaction, eventuate as they did, and in which economic, moral, and political motives conspired to force us to the line of development which we took. In our human nature there were other *desires* just as natural as " trading." It can be shown that sound economic considerations alone not only justified but compelled our policy, and vindicate our career. Before proceeding to answer the four questions asked by Prof. Sumner, let us see what we mean by " trade," " commerce," " exchanges," foreign or domestic, free or restricted.

We shall find no more "exasperating, almost belligerent" controversialist than Prof. Perry. Taking up his " Political Economy" at the chapter on " Foreign Trade," let us go through a simple supposed case with him—the trade between England and France in cotton and silks.

" *The first question* is, When will it be mutually profitable for England to send cottons to France to buy silks with, and France to send silks to England to buy cottons with? The answer is easy: The trade will be mutually profitable when efforts bestowed in France upon silks will procure, through exchange with England, more of cottons than the same amount of efforts bestowed in France upon cottons will produce of cottons directly; and then, when efforts bestowed upon cottons in England will procure more of silks, through exchange with France, than the same amount of efforts bestowed in England upon silks will produce of silks directly. So long as there is a difference of *relative efficiency* in the production of the two commodities in the two countries, so long, setting cost of carriage aside, may there be a profitable exchange of the two. To make such an exchange profitable to both parties, it is not at all needful that the cottons exchanged for the silks shall have cost the English as many days' labor as the silks have cost the French; or that the silks shall cost the French as much as the cottons cost the English. It is not a question of the absolute cost of either commodity to the parties producing it" (it does not appear whether the Professor means *cost*—measured by "labor and abstinence," or by "wages and profits," a distinction of great importance, because, in one case, cost may be equalized by competition, in the other, not); "but a question of the relative cost of that produced in either country, compared with what would be the cost of the other commodity were it to be produced in that country. *A demand in each country for the product of the other is, of course, presupposed in the illustration.*"

This proposition, stuck in parenthetically, is vital, and must be borne in mind. The whole trade in each country is founded on a demand in the other for the surplus of the product in which it has the greater relative efficiency. With no foreign market, it is compelled to sell a surplus product in the home market at a reduced average efficiency. It will then, by home production, get all its supplies at the cheapest rate possible to a country so situated. If it had, what it has not, an adequate foreign market, it would preserve its highest efficiency by exchanging in that market. An overpopulation in a country, resulting in overproduction, would be an economic blunder: and overpopulation in the United States is really the point at which the free foreign trader ought to direct his economic criticisms. Having such an overpopulation, it is the business of an American economist to furnish the "services" which they may render each other, or witness their exodus.

Prof. Perry goes on:

"In effect, the Frenchmen ask, Can we get more and better cottons by working in silks and then trading them off for English cottons, than we can get by the same efforts in working on cottons at home? The Englishmen ask. Can we get more and better silks by working in cottons and then trading with France for silks, than we can get by trying to make silks at home?"

Yes, if all the silks wanted in one country just pay for all the cottons wanted in the other, and they acted solely on present economic motives: if England quits making silks and France quits making cottons.

"*The second question* is, How does the diversity of relative advantage practically work in foreign trade?

"In the majority of cases, doubtless, foreign trade takes place in articles, in the production of one of which each of the respective countries has an *absolute advantage* over the other, but an every way advantageous trade may be carried on in articles in the production of both of which one nation shall have an absolute superiority over the other, provided only that this superiority be *relatively diverse* in the two articles."

This is a rare case in international trade. The case of Barbadoes and the United States is in point. The inhabitants of Barbadoes, favored by their tropical climate and fertile soil, can raise provisions cheaper than we can in the United States. And yet Barbadoes buys nearly all of her provisions from this country. Why? Because, though Barbadoes has the advantage over us in the ability to raise provisions cheaply, she has a still greater advantage over us in her power to produce sugar and molasses. These she exchanges with us for flour. If there were no foreign market for her sugar and molasses, Barbadoes would be compelled to raise her own flour, or go without it. It may be as well to bear this in mind: that she could buy no more flour than her sugar and molasses would pay for.

"*The third question* is, What are the extreme limits of the value of cottons and silks in the case supposed, and when will a third nation be able to undersell either in the ports of the other?"

The answer to this raises no question germain to our discussion.

"*The fourth question* is, How does the varying play of the international demand affect the value of articles in foreign trade?

"The answer is, If the demand for French silks in England *just answers* to *the demand for English cottons* in France, so that the *silks* offered by France *just pay for the cottons* offered by England, then, cost of carriage aside, the gains of the trade will be equally divided between the two nations. . . . This case of equalization, though possible, is rarely likely to occur in practice. In any terms of exchange first offered, there is likely to be a stronger demand in one country for the product of that. This will lead to *a change of value* and *a new division of profits*. The product for which *the demand is less* will find *its market sluggish*, and, in order to tempt further and brisker exchanges, will be compelled to *offer more favorable conditions*. He who enters a market *in quest of what is more in demand*, with a service in return *which is less in demand*, will *have to lower his terms* or *not trade*." Prof. Bowen states the same principle in these words: "Whichever nation is under the strongest temptation or necessity to buy from others—*whichever needs to buy more value than it can sell*—that nation labors under a disadvantage in the traffic, and *must offer its own commodities at the lowest possible price*."

"It follows from these principles," continues Prof. Perry, "that what a nation purchases by its exports, it purchases by its most efficient labor, and consequently at the cheapest possible rate to itself. Only those things, for the procuring of which a nation possesses decided advantages relatively to other nations and relatively to its own advantages in producing directly what is received in return, are ever exported, and hence the return cargoes, no matter what they have cost their original producers, are purchased by this nation as cheaply as if they had been produced by its own most advantageous labor. *This is a wholly impregnable position, and the advocates of restricting foreign trade are challenged to try their hand a little at its defenses.*"

This impregnable position lacks the only basis of fact in America upon which it can possibly stand. The consumption of goods in the United States—the product of the competing or protected industries—is larger than we have ever been enabled to buy in the world's market with any or all of our exportations which the world's market would buy of us: nor has the world's market ever contained a surplus of the products of such industries sufficient for our wants, even if we had the proper purchase-money. Our wants have been such that to have supplied them all abroad, we should have been compelled to buy more value than we can sell.

"*The sixth question* is, Which party in foreign trade pays the costs of carriage, or does each pay them in equal proportion?"

This question is confessedly insoluble by any economist. Our Professor's answer is: "That will depend on the equation of international demand. Nothing in the nature of things hinders that each party shall, in effect, pay the freights of the other, or *one even pay the freights of both.*"

"These, then," concludes the Professor, "are the essential principles of foreign trade, . . . and in the light of their principles it is very clear that foreign trade is just as legitimate as domestic trade; that it rests on the same ultimate principles in the constitution of man and in the providential arrangements of nature; . . . that to prohibit it or restrict it, otherwise than in the interest of morals, health, or revenue" (why not add, the general welfare?), "must find a justification, if at all, outside the pale of political economy. That to say to any body of men who wish to render merely commercial services to foreigners, to receive back similar services in return, that such services shall neither be rendered nor received, is not only to destroy *a certain gain*, but also to interfere with a *natural* and *inalienable right.*"

This last proposition, if true, would end the discussion. It is not, however, a proposition in political economy. It is a theorem which must be established in the science of law or morals or sociology. It never has been proved, and we may pass it with the assumption that it never can be. Prof. Walker cheerfully concedes that "the claim to freedom of trade as a 'natural right' is not one of which the economist can properly take account."

Of such attempts to treat an art like a science, "to found theories of politics on what is called abstract rights," Prof. Cairnes says: "They are a species of hybrid philosophy. . . . The argument is involved at the outset in a *petitio principii*. The question, What is? and the question, What ought to be? are distinct questions. It may be that the answers to them coincide: that *that which is* is also *that which ought to be;* but then this is a thing to be proved, not to be taken for granted."

To this analysis of foreign free trade ought to be added an argument for free trade which the Professor emphasizes throughout his treatise : "If a nation *will* not buy of foreigners, it *can* not sell to them. This is the universal and fundamental objection to "protection," so called, that, if legal barriers *keep out* a dollar's worth of foreign goods which *want to come in*, they thereby and necessarily *keep in* a dollar's worth of domestic goods which *want to go out.*"

There are plenty of goods which we want, but foreigners do not have for sale all we want—they have some only. There are plenty of domestic goods which want to go out, and foreigners do not want them. Protective tariffs do not stop the trade. Our purchasing power is not of the right kind to take effect in the foreign market. Our surplus is in the wrong kind of merchandise; their surplus is not large enough for our needs. We want the foreign goods, but under the facts of our case we must go without them, or, if we want them "bad enough," we must go to the labor and cost of making them under American conditions—which is not feasible or possible "under freedom." If foreigners would stop competing with us in raising food and cotton, and give us the market, we could do better, so far as mere trade is concerned—but they don't stop and they won't stop. If foreigners *will* not buy of us, we *can not* buy of them. We can not buy of them for two reasons: their market can not offer as much as we would buy; it will not take as much as we would sell. This state of things drives us to competition.

CHAPTER VII.

THE ALTERNATIVES OFFERED US—WHAT WE BUY AND WHAT WE SELL.

The decks are now fairly cleared for action. The first step is to determine the industries in which we have an absolute superiority over other nations.

There is a general agreement among free-traders that "they are all 'land' industries."[1] The whole stress of the free-trade argument is that we ought to pursue these industries and supply our wants of other commodities by exchanges of them effected through free foreign trade. For all the purposes of the argument, the products of these industries are, up to this date in our history, cotton, tobacco, food (in the various exportable forms of wheat, corn, meats, cheese, butter, hops, etc.), and the precious metals—to which, latterly, may be added, petroleum.

One of two sets of unalterable assumptions must be made in putting this scheme of "international division of labor" into practical operation in the nation which we call the United States.

I. One set is this:

1. That we shall in the United States raise so much food

---

[1] The ground idea of them all is well expressed by Prof. Cliffe Leslie: "The best economy, of course, would have been for American capital to confine itself to the fields in which it had superior productiveness, awaiting a rise of wages and in the cost of coal-mining in England for competition in others." ("Fortnightly Review," October, 1881.)

and raw materials as the foreign markets will take, and no more.
2. That our population shall increase no faster than the number of laborers involved in that production shall require.
3. That increase of capital shall keep pace with that order of development.
4. That the total annual produce of the industry and capital of this country shall be kept down to these dimensions.

The "industrial entity," the nation, so formed, is the one upon which the science of free-trade economy has fixed its ideal expectations. The rate of growth and ultimate size reached under the conditions thus prescribed are those which the science says *ought* to have been. It contemplates us as coming all the way across the Atlantic to start a food and raw-material factory, limited and adjusted to foreign conditions. We were simply to be a *truck-farm* for Europe. Now, whatever *ought to have been*, and whatever *might have been*, the wrong kind of men came to make that a possible result. The early settlers here did not found a penal colony. It was *morally* impossible that they could have accepted this set of conditions. Under them the case was settled adversely by the course of our actual history, and the whys and wherefores are too numerous to discuss.

II. The other set is this:
1. That there is a market abroad for the whole surplus of these productions in our most advantageous industries.
2. That all our capital and labor could be employed in their production.
3. That under these circumstances the exchangeable value of our exports would not be reduced.

4. That the exchangeable value of our imports would not be increased.

5. That our wants are such that we are not compelled to buy more value than we can sell.

Of the alternatives offered, we undertook to accept the second. We did not attempt to take our place in the world's industry according to the exact rules of political economy, because, in the first place, we did not come in pursuance of mere commercial instincts; in the second place, we were not that kind of men; and, in the third place, too many of us came. We therefore rejected the first alternative.

We did undertake to accept the second, because, while we came to found homes and institutions, it seemed as though, proceeding in accordance with these conditions, we *might* reach the expansion which our inherited traits would work out of our physical surroundings. We then saw no reason why our industrial entity should correspond with our political entity. Upon making the experiment, we soon found that they must correspond. Why this was so, the free-trader will find out if he will read the history of his country, or will consult any practical American farmer now. And if he wishes to fortify his judgment by authority, let him buy a copy of Adam Smith's "Wealth of Nations" at the nearest second-hand bookstore.

I have said we undertook to organize our national industries on these assumptions:

1. That there is a market abroad for the whole surplus of the productions in our most advantageous industries.

2. That all our capital and labor could be employed in their production.

3. That, under these circumstances, the exchangeable value of our exports would not be reduced.

4. That the exchangeable value of our imports would not be increased.

5. That our wants are such that we are not compelled to buy more value than we can sell.

We failed in this attempt, because *every one of these assumptions turned out to be wrong*, as we now proceed to show.

This is a proper place to lay down two or three general principles in the science which no one is interested to dispute.

Prices are in the main determined by supply and demand. But the market for the special products of our food-industries is limited by the number and capacity of the stomachs depending on us for food. It is a well-understood fact that, in civilized nations, more value is consumed in manufactured goods than in food. In the United States the tea, coffee, sugar, and the like tropical fruits which we consume must be brought from abroad, and they have hitherto been paid for by exports of raw material.

It is agreed that a nation pays for its imports with its exports, and that in the long run the whole imports will be equal to the whole exports; unless it is when a nation is borrowing, as the United States did on a great scale during the war, and in the growth of its railroad enterprises; or unless a nation is in the receipt of income for foreign loans and investments, as is the case with England at present. Her imports exceed her exports by a hundred million pounds annually—an apparent unfavorable balance, but it is really the income she receives from foreign investments and freight earnings in the carrying trade.

But the imports and exports between any two nations may or may not balance. What is meant by the "equation of international demand" is that the imports and exports of each nation with all foreign countries must in the long run balance. The tea we buy of China is paid for in cotton we sell to England, or the coffee we buy from Brazil may be paid for in tobacco sold to France. The balance in the long account current with all foreign countries is paid in money. The free-trader is fond of saying that protection is "the loathsome offspring" (!) of the old mercantile theory of political economy, according to which a nation thought it made the greatest gains when it had the largest "balance of trade," payable in money, in its favor. When all other arguments fail, he hurls this old boomerang. A protectionist has no more call to believe in the mercantile theory than the free-trader. In fact, bullion plays a very small part in foreign commerce. When large exportation of that is required, trade stops.

Less than one half of all the merchandise imported into the United States is in manufactured goods; and of these very much the larger parts consist of silks and velvets, and fine woolen goods and kid gloves, French wines and china, which are articles of luxury.

However much we might be disposed in the United States to look to other countries for our supplies of manufactured goods, we can only obtain them to the extent to which other countries need our products. Our consumption of such goods will, therefore, be not in proportion to the power of domestic production and the wants of the people here, but to the desire of other countries to have our commodities.

So that we may invert Prof. Perry's key-stone, "If a nation *will* not buy of foreigners, it *can* not sell to them," and say, "If foreigners *will* not buy of us, we *can* not *buy* of them," and then his arch is liable to fall. But then it will not fall far, and, besides, it was not much of an arch anyway.

If we confine ourselves to the production of our fertile fields, to what extent will the markets of the world take them? This is the everlasting issue in the case, as raised by the scientific free-trader, who insists on *science*. From 1789 to 1885 it has been unceasingly asked by statesmen, by farmers, by laborers. I notice that the theoretical professors never attempt an answer. Why do not the pupils who sit under their teachings insist on a definite, specific answer to it, and insist that there shall be no flinching? For myself, I make no question that, with free trade, agriculture would, by this time, have been so unprofitable that "mills and factories" would have come in naturally. We would have been so poor that we could have competed, under the *régime* of low wages, with Europe; rather, we should neither have had anything to sell nor wanted to buy anything. We should have backslidden out of the contest.

It is before this question that the American people and the American farmers have balked, and have refused to trust in free trade. That instinct was correct, and can not be overridden by anything but stern facts—theoretical disquisition about what might have been or what ought to have been, fail to convict their judgment.

I wish the professors would try their hand at this, as a question of fact.

Alexander Hamilton, in his Treasury Report of 1791, laid the basis for the protective system, and it was in the presence of this unanswered question that the protective policy was adopted. Washington, Franklin, Jefferson, Madison, Monroe, and Jackson are all distinctly on record as solicitous to find a vent for our surplus food-products. Failing to see any adequate foreign market, they turned to the much-derided *home* market. Distinguished professors affect to believe that they have undone its economic effects when they dismiss it, as one professor did in his address before the recent tariff commission, with the contemptuous, "Oh, that is the famous truck-farm argument." Hamilton's report will be referred to in other connections.[1]

It must be borne in mind that Hamilton, Franklin, and their associates were gazing into the inmost nature of the problem when its elements were simple and capable of disentanglement, when there was no danger of falling into an ambuscade of intricate figures or bad logic. They knew what they wanted, and adopted the only plan open to them to supply their wants.

Franklin, writing from London in 1771, says:

"If our Country People would well consider that all they save in refusing to purchase foreign Gewgaws and in making their own Apparel being apply'd to the Improvement of their Plantations, would render those more profitable, and yielding a greater Produce, I should hope they would persue resolutely in their present commendable Industry and Frugality. And there is still a further Consideration. The Colonies that produce Provision grow very fast. But of the Countries that take off those Provisions, some do not increase at all, as the European Nations; and others, as the West India Colonies, not in the same proportion. So that, tho' the Demand at present may be sufficient, it cannot long continue so. Every Manufacture encouraged in our Country, makes part of a Market for Provisions within ourselves, and saves so much Money to

---

[1] Hamilton's Treasury Report is the great magazine of the scientific weapons of the protectionist. No improvement has been made in the formulation of his propositions; but they have been made luminous by the facts of our history. No free-trader has ever leaped the ditches or scaled the parapet of his impregnable fortress. His bastions command the entire front. The professors hurled their little hand-grenade, "mercantile theory," at him. But when he himself denounced it as "the vain project of selling everything and buying nothing," that dynamite failed to explode.

the Country as must otherwise be exported to pay for the manufactures he supplies. Here in England it is well known and understood that wherever a Manufacture is established which employs a Number of Hands, it raises the Value of Lands in the neighboring country all around it, partly by the greater Demand near at hand for the Produce of the Land; and partly from the Plenty of Money drawn by the manufactures of that Part of the Country. It seems, therefore, that the Interest of all our Farmers and Owners of Lands, to encourage our young Manufactures in preference to foreign ones imported among us from distant Countries."

Upon the market for surplus agricultural products Hamilton says:

"But it is also a consequence of the policy which has been noted that the foreign demand for the products of agricultural countries is, in a great degree, rather casual and occasional than certain or constant. To what extent injurious interruptions of the demand for some of the staple commodities of the United States may have been experienced from that cause, must be referred to the judgment of those who are engaged in carrying on the commerce of the country; but it may be safely affirmed that such interruptions are at times very inconveniently felt, and that cases not unfrequently occur in which markets are so confined and restricted as to render *the demand* very unequal to the supply.

"Independently, likewise, of the artificial impediments which are created by the policy in question, there are natural causes tending to render the external demand for the surplus of agricultural nations a *precarious reliance*. The differences of seasons, in the countries which are consumers, make immense differences in the produce of their own soils in different years, and consequently in the degrees of their necessity for foreign supply. Plentiful harvests with them—especially if similar ones occur at the same time in the countries which are furnishers—occasion, of course, *a glut in the markets of the latter.*[1]

---

[1] "As to the creating, in some instances, a new, and securing in all a more certain and steady demand for the surplus produce of the soil:

"This is among the most important of the circumstances which have been indicated. It is a principal means by which the establishment of manufactures contributes to an augmentation of the produce or revenue of a country, and has an immediate and direct relation to the prosperity of agriculture.

"It is evident that the exertions of the husbandman will be steady or fluctuating, vigorous or feeble, in proportion to the steadiness or fluctuation, adequateness or inadequateness of the markets on which he must depend for the vent of the surplus which may be produced by his labor; and that such surplus, in the ordinary course of things, will be greater or less in the same proportion.

"For the purpose of this vent a domestic market is greatly to be preferred to a foreign one, because it is, in the nature of things, far more to be relied upon.

"It is a primary object of the policy of nations to be able to supply themselves with subsistence from their own soils; and manufacturing nations, as far as circumstances permit, endeavor to procure from the same source the raw materials necessary for their own fabrics. This disposition, urged by the spirit of monopoly, is sometimes even carried to an injudicious extreme. It seems not always to be recollected that nations who have neither mines nor manufactures can only obtain the manufactured articles of which they stand in need by an exchange of the products of their soils, and that, if those who can best furnish them with such articles are not willing to give a due course to this exchange, they must of necessity make every possible effort to manufacture for themselves; the effect of which is that the manufacturing nations abridge the natural advantages of their situation through an unwillingness to permit the agricultural countries to enjoy the advantages of theirs, and sacrifice the interests of a mutually beneficial intercourse to the vain project of selling everything and buying nothing." (We shall have occasion, hereafter, to note the impossible feat which certain known reformers in our day propose, to wit, to export both food, raw materials, *and* manufactured goods to the rest of the world. This starts the natural query, What, then, is the rest of the world to do for us?) . . .

"Considering how fast and how much the progress of new settlements in the United States must increase the surplus produce of the soil, and

James Madison (message, February, 1815):

"But there is no subject that can enter with greater force and merit into the deliberations of Congress than weighing seriously the tendency of the system which prevails among most of the commercial nations of Europe, whatever dependence may be placed on the force of natural circumstances to counteract the effect of an artificial policy, there appear strong reasons to regard the foreign demand for that surplus as too uncertain a reliance, and to desire a substitute for it in an extensive domestic market.

"To secure such a market, there is no other expedient than to promote manufacturing establishments. Manufacturers, who constitute the most numerous class, after the cultivators of land, are for that reason the principal consumers of the surplus of their labor.

"This idea of an extensive domestic market for the surplus produce of the soil is of the first consequence. It is of all things that which most effectually conduces to a flourishing state of agriculture. If the effect of manufactories should be to detach a portion of the hands, which would be otherwise engaged in tillage, it might possibly cause a smaller quantity of lands to be under cultivation; but, by their tendency to produce a more certain demand for the surplus produce of the soil, they would, at the same time, cause the lands which were in cultivation to be better improved and more productive. And while, by their influence, the condition of each individual farmer would be ameliorated, the total mass of agricultural production would probably be increased, for this must evidently depend as much, if not more, upon the degree of improvement as upon the number of acres under culture.

"It merits particular observation, that the multiplication of manufactories not only furnishes a market for these articles which have been accustomed to be produced in abundance in a country, but it likewise creates a demand for such as were either unknown or produced in inconsiderable quantities; the bowels as well as the surface of the earth are ransacked for articles which were before neglected, animals, plants, and minerals acquire a utility and value, which were before unexplored.

"The foregoing considerations seem sufficient to establish as general propositions that it is the interest of nations to diversify the industrious pursuits of the individuals who compose them. That the establishment of manufactures is calculated not only to increase the general stock of useful and productive labor, but even to improve the state of agriculture in particular, certainly to advance the interests of those who are engaged in it. There are other views that will be hereafter taken of the subject, which, it is conceived, will serve to confirm these inferences."

a consideration of the means to preserve and promote the manufactures which have sprung into existence, and attained an unparalleled maturity throughout the United States during the period of the European wars. This source of national independence and wealth I anxiously recommend, therefore, to the prompt and constant guardianship of Congress."

John C. Calhoun (speech, Tariff Act, 1816):

"When our manufactures are grown to a certain proportion, as they will under the fostering care of the Government, the farmer will find a ready market for his surplus produce, and, what is of equal consequence, a certain and cheap supply for all his wants. His prosperity will diffuse itself to every class in the community, and, instead of the languor of industry and individual distress now incident to a state of war and suspended commerce, the wealth and vigor of the community will not be impaired."

Andrew Jackson (Coleman letter, 1824):

"This tariff—I mean a judicious one—possesses more fanciful than real danger. I will ask what is the real situation of the agriculturist? Where has the American farmer a market for his surplus product? Except for cotton, he has *neither a foreign nor home market*. Does not this prove, where there is no market, either at home or abroad, that there is *too much labor employed in agriculture*, and that the channels for labor should be multiplied? *Common sense points out the remedy.*" [1]

---

[1] In 1824 Andrew Jackson wrote to Dr. Coleman *inter alia* these words: "This tariff—I mean a judicious one—possesses more fanciful than real danger. I will ask, what is the real situation of the agriculturist? Where has the American farmer a market for his surplus product? Except for cotton, he has neither a foreign nor home market. Does not this clearly prove, where there is no market either at home or abroad, that there is too much labor employed in agriculture, and that the channels for labor should be multiplied? *Common sense* points out the remedy. Draw from agriculture

Mr. Webster[1] (speech on the Tariff Act, 1824):

"Sir, that is the truest American policy which shall most usefully employ American capital and American labor, and best sustain the whole population. With me it

---

the superabundant labor; employ it in mechanism and manufactures, thereby creating a home market for your breadstuffs, and distributing labor to the most profitable account and benefits to the country. Take from agriculture in the United States six hundred thousand men, women, and children, and you will at once give a home market for more breadstuffs than all Europe now furnish us a market for. In short, we have been too long subject to the policy of British merchants. It is time that we shall become a little more Americanized, and instead of feeding the paupers and laborers of England, feed our own; or else, in a short time, by continuing our present policy, we shall be rendered paupers ourselves."

[1] Mr. Webster saw the beneficent operation of the tariff of 1828—the "tariff of abominations" for which he voted—the disappearance of societary activity under the horizontal *ad valorem* tariff of 1832, and the refluent wave of prosperity under the tariff of 1842. It was observation and analysis of those phenomena which transferred Henry C. Carey from the atomistic views of the free-traders, with whom he stood when he wrote his unpublished "The Harmony of Nature," in 1836, to an advocate of protection in 1844. They had both outgrown the atomistic view of society as a mass of independent units, each taking care of himself in the markets of the world. What men in society need is the wages of labor—returns for employment. If Mr. Webster did not understand political economy in 1824, as is charged, he seems to have come in sight of some of its doctrines in 1846. In his speech in the Senate in that year he said: "To diversify employment is to increase employment, and to enhance wages, and, sir, take this great truth, place it on the title-page of every book of political economy intended for the use of the United States, put it in every 'Farmer's Almanac,' let it be the heading of the column in every 'Mechanic's Magazine,' proclaim it everywhere and make it a proverb that, *when there is work for the hands of men, there will be work for their teeth.* When there is employment there will be bread. It is a great blessing to the poor to have cheap food; but greater than that, prior to that, and of still higher value, is the blessing of being able to buy food by honest and respectable employment. Employment feeds and clothes and instructs. Employment gives health, sobriety, and morals. Constant employment and well-paid labor produce, in a country like ours, general prosperity, content, and cheerfulness. Our destiny is labor. What is the first great cause of prosperity with such a people? Simply employment. Cheap food

is a fundamental axiom, it is interwoven with all my opinions, that the great interests of the country are united and inseparable, that agriculture, commerce, and manufactures will prosper together or languish together." . . . While he was opposed to total prohibition, to the attempt " to raise up at home manufactures not suited to the climate, the nature of the country, or the state of the population, there were substantial distinctions to be made," and it was possible " to awaken a home competition in the production of some articles. . . . I think freedom of trade to be the general principle, and restriction the exception, and it is for every state, taking into view its own conditions, to judge of the propriety in any case of making an exception. . . .

" In the next place, there never was any reason to expect that the *increase of our exports of agricultural products* would keep pace with *the increase of our population.* That would be against all experience."

It is sad to think how many economical blunders these statesmen have worked into these short paragraphs. In order to confer some *exchange value* on the farmer's products, and to have them consumed at home, in the interest of the greatest annual product of American industry, and to the end of securing the greatest annual income of the American people—the highest aggregate of their gross annual rent, wages, and profits—out of which each worker gets his share, Washington, Hamilton, Jefferson, Madison, Calhoun, Jackson, and Webster proposed, in the language of the modern *a priori* college professors, " to take away one man's earnings to give them to another," " to enable one citizen to collect taxes of another," " to confer a favor on one group of its population by an equivalent oppression

---

and cheap clothing are very desirable; but they are not the first requisites. The first requisite is that which enables men *to buy food and clothing, cheap or dear.*"

exerted on another," " to produce forced monopolies and distorted industrial relations," " to introduce that industrial abomination, an industry that does not pay," " to create parasite industries to live on the exuberant productions of the natural industries"; " pauper, of course, is one of those silly and invidious terms which have been introduced into this discussion, in the interest of falsehood and folly"; and, finally, they are " Anglophobists"! And all this evolved out of " common sense"! All this trouble, in order " to build up *competing* manufactures"! exclaim the professors.

The demand of the outer world for the food and raw materials of this country never has increased, and never will increase, as fast as our population; besides, we can export no part of our perishable products. At the moment in 1885 when these lines are being written, there is no demand in any European market for American flour, and its exchange value in the home market is greater than that in the foreign market, and this in the face of the fact that nearly one quarter of our population has been diverted from agricultural to mechanical pursuits! If all American labor and American capital had been devoted to our "most advantageous industry," is there any rational doubt of the destructive terms on which we should have supplied our wants of foreign commodities by exchange?[1] What does the farmer think?

Between 1784 and 1884, without attempting any historical details, there have been years when, under a succession of bad harvests abroad, coinciding with good crops at

---

[1] We are now, as indeed we always have been, in the dilemma above quoted from Prof. Perry: " The product for which the demand is less will find its market sluggish, and, in order to tempt further and brisker exchanges, will be compelled to offer more favorable conditions. He who enters a market *in quest of what is more in demand*, with a service in return which is *less in demand*, will have *to lower his terms, or not trade*."

home, we have reaped enormous gains; and there have been years in which corn has been burned on the Western prairies for fuel. A nation of fifty millions of people will scarcely risk their economic welfare on chances so doubtful as these.

It follows from his principles, says Prof. Perry, "that those men, who deem it needful that each nation should be able to *compete* with other nations, are shallow thinkers. Why are they not consistent enough to apply their favorite doctrine of 'competing' to domestic exchanges also, and demand that the clergyman shall have facilities for 'competing' with the lawyer, the tailor with the blacksmith, the farmer with the manufacturer, the publisher with the author? Will people never learn that all exchanges, domestic as well as foreign, depend on relative superiority at different points, and that a nation which should try to make its success in production equal at all points, would be as foolish as an artisan trying to learn and practice all trades at once? Suppose the nation to succeed, what then? It would supply its wants at a certain average efficiency of effort; whereas, by a thorough development of all its own peculiar resources, it could command by exchange the products of the world at a cost not exceeding that of its own most productive and efficient exertions."

If the Professor had included all his qualifying doctrines and all the facts of our commerce, and had not interjected irrelevant matter into these few lines, there would be left no subject of dispute. The insurmountable fact, which the Professor omits, is that the world's market has never offered the chance to us to buy the manufactured goods we consume, and that we are compelled to make a portion of them, and for that portion we are necessarily in "competition" with foreign labor and capital.[1] He is dis-

---

[1] In his water-level illustration used above, the Professor says that the conditions of a trade equally profitable to both parties require "that the de-

cussing the *rôle* which the United States ought to play in the "international division of labor." An artisan's efficiency may well lie in a single direction, but a nation is many-sided — the United States is well-nigh all-sided: it has proved its capacity "to learn and practice all trades at once."

He is endeavoring to ascertain what we ought to produce so that we may not commit the absurdity of "competing" with other nations. If there was not anything that we could do to more advantage than any other nation, that would be an indication, on his economic argument, either that we ought not to have come here at all, or that some of us ought to emigrate forthwith. But suppose we have the same advantages as other nations? If there was no work for the clergyman, the lawyer, the tailor, or the blacksmith, as such, then none of them ought to exist, as such, exclusively, and probably they would not exist long. But each man primarily pursues one of these callings for the sake of making a living, and he expects to do this by the exchange of services with others. So far forth as there is no demand for his services in his special calling, so far forth he must "try to learn and practice" some other calling in connection with it — he must average his efforts. With a full opportunity to sell all the products of his own calling, he will have to "compete" with nobody except

---

mand for French silks in England *just answers* to the demand for English cottons in France, so that the silks offered by France *just pay* for the cottons offered by England." Translated into the language of our American problem that would be, "that the demand for American food and raw materials in Europe and Great Britain *just answers* to the demand for foreign manufactured goods in the United States, so that the food and raw materials offered by the United States *just pay* for the manufactured goods offered by Europe and Great Britain." The argument doesn't fit, and the illustration lacks applicability. Europe and Great Britain have never yet taken enough of our food and raw materials to pay for one tenth of our demand for manufactured goods. (See Chapter X, *infra*.)

those in the same industry. He will have no "competition" with his customers. If he can not live on his salary as a clergyman, he may be compelled to eke out his livelihood by "competing" at times with the schoolmaster. If he is not "all-sided," he must come under the very first limitation imposed by Adam Smith in his chapter on the "Division of Labor," the most important chapter in his "Wealth of Nations," "The division of labor is limited by the extent of the market." Smith cites the manufacture of pins in illustration: In his day ten men, by division of labor, could make 48,000 pins a day; whereas, without it, they could only make 200. Suppose, now, the artisans who supervise the process can make 48,000 pins, and that there is only a demand for 24,000 pins a day. In that case, the artisans must be idle half the time. Production at that establishment would be most profitable only when the market took an output of pins to the number of 48,000. *An overproduction of pins would lead to loss and waste unless they could be utilized as a first step in the production of something else, for they would possess no exchange value as pins.* Now, Prof. Perry wants the international division of labor so made among the different nations of the earth that the United States shall enter upon that industry upon which it can expend "its own most productive and efficient industry." This is agriculture. As in the case of the individual artisan, the people of the United States are here, primarily, to earn their subsistence and supply their various wants and not to produce exchange values. As between themselves, the division of labor has received its perfect development; as between the United States and the other nations, we will exchange the surplus of production in the most advantageous industry so far as there is any market for it.

The most perfect machinery, and the most absolute

superiority over other producers, would avail nothing to the manufacturer if the market would not take his pins. But if pins were a preliminary stage of some other salable product for which there was a market, he would still hold his advantage. He might then manufacture pins to any extent. Convert them into the next form of commodity, and *the original superiority he possessed would accompany the new industry.* It *might* or *might not be less profitable* than *pin-making, which exactly supplied the market and occupied his whole capital and labor*, but it would be more profitable for him than to remain idle, and would add more to the gross annual product of the country in which he lived than if he took the establishment to some other land. The surplus food of America fulfills its best purpose when it furnishes subsistence to the domestic artisans who are producing the other commodities we use —the surplus is only preparation for the next stage of our industrial labors. Here we come again upon the triple fallacy which the free-trader must employ—that all capital and labor can be put upon the most advantageous industry —that all men work all the time as hard as they can, and that there is a foreign market for all the products of that industry.

If the extent of the foreign market is not sufficient to take up the surplus, we must consume it in process of further manufacture "on the premises," as in the case of the pin-manufacturer. But when we come to see in what form it shall be consumed, we find at once that we are in "competition" with other nations. Unless we waste our surplus, and waste our time and keep standing idle the labor which produced the surplus, we must "compete," and we can only successfully "compete" by *restriction*. We do not seek "competition"; it is forced upon us. If our wants are to be supplied, it may be compulsory upon us to satisfy them ourselves at "a certain average efficiency of effort." Our division of labor has been pushed too far; we have accepted a line of industry—agricultural—which keeps us on half-time to avoid overproduction. The alternative is to adopt other industries in connection with them, which may indeed reduce us to some "average efficiency" only; or, to dismiss our laborers, remit our capital, and redistribute them to other national departments of the international division of labor. The world's commerce did not need us all to supply its deficiencies at the point of our relative superiority. We in this political body-politic miscalculated our functions in the cosmopolitan industrial body-politic; our structure was on too large a scale, and our functions cease. The result is we have miscarried; we are prematurely on hand. "Will people never learn" that if the inhabitants of the United States are here to supply certain exchange values to international trade, there are too many of us, and our "own peculiar resources" are too prolific for current commercial needs? "Will people never learn" that if the inhabitants of the United States are here to earn the means of subsistence by honest, honorable, cheerful work, *all* "our most productive and efficient exertions" can not be put forth in the presence of a foreign "competition" which drives us out of the field? So many of the products of the world as we can not command from our own most productive forces, we must be willing to procure by domestic exchanges made at only "a certain average efficiency of effort."

But there is a still further limitation to the division of labor—the nature of the employment. Of all the departments of industry, agriculture allows of the least division of labor, and, at best, the labor is rude. Machinery has been used with some efficiency, but no machinery can overcome the loss of time, the delay of the seasons, which must attend the processes of planting, growing, and reaping. The natural industries of this country are the ones in which increased productions are made under increasingly higher cost; labor, expended on the soil, will reap rewards constantly growing less. Exchange values may not decrease from this cause, but the increased cost of production will diminish the farmer's profit. Agriculture is subject to "the law of diminishing returns."[1]

There were moral and economic reasons why Washington, and Hamilton, and Jefferson, and Madison, who stood at the beginning of things, deemed it a betrayal of the interests of their posterity to limit the productive energies of the people to raw materials, and then to such quantities only as the exigencies of foreign markets might take off our hands. When the authors of our Constitution invited immigration of laborers from all the world—opened their ports to free trade in labor itself—they, by a happy consistency, shut their ports to the products of foreign labor. Why does not the free-trader inveigh against the first as well as the last? The one was the cause of the other, and this illimitable supply of labor the primary cause of the failure of his theories.

But the increase of population and of the power to produce raw materials in excess of any foreign demand has in an inconceivable degree outrun the ideas of these early statesmen. There is, indeed, an immeasurable power in America for these products, and there is an immeasurable superiority at these points. But the absolute superiority in these advantages disappears at the instant when excess of

---

[1] Improved machinery, inventions, new modes of fertilization, may retard the effect of the law. If the farmer cheapens food by raising more of it at less cost of production, he is not the loser. But if food is cheapened by reason of an unsalable surplus, he is a loser. Cheap food is as desirable to a society as cheap anything else, but the cheapness ought to be the result of more efficient processes, not of overproduction.

production terminates in loss of exchange value. Then the product must be converted into some manufactured commodity. Alongside of these absolutely superior advantages are others which, in comparison with these, may be relatively less profitable. Compared with wheat, here and now, under existing conditions, iron, cotton, woolen, glass, and pottery may (or may not, for nobody can tell) be less profitable, in view of exchanges abroad; but in these enumerated manufactures, in what consists our inferiority relatively to like products abroad? First and last, it is in the higher rate of wages paid laborers in them. Higher wages mean greater comfort for the men and women who earn them. After all the discords in our system are run through the scale, they are located in wages. It is like the tuner of the piano. Absolutely exact intervals and harmonious chords are impossible over the whole key-board, so the piano-tuner pushes the discords all together—accumulates them all in what he calls "the wolf"—and locates them on a single string. This gives us the key to the situation. If the higher cost of production, reckoned in wages, is traced to the laboring-man, and goes into the wages which purchases his comforts and composes his welfare, we have taken all discord out of the diapason—want of skill, or capital, or efficiency, is no longer the source of the trouble. We shall now see that the pursuits of other industries, while *less* profitable (than food-raising under conditions which may be conceived, but were never actual), are *not unprofitable;* we shall see why, if they pay less, they may still pay, and we shall see that, to the extent to which they pay, they are clear gain; and that if they were not carried on here, the men and money employed on them could not be employed at all in this country, and their presence here would be an economic blunder.

To provide for diversification in the pursuits of a people is not an abuse of power on the part of the Government. Rather, we adopt the judgment of M. Chevalier, an authority the free-trader will not care to challenge: "On the contrary, it is the accomplishment of a positive duty so to act at each epoch in the progress of a nation as to favor the taking possession of all the branches of industry whose acquisition is *authorized by the nature of things.*" Protection does not propose to enter upon unnatural industries nor to repel the gratuities of nature; but an industry in America in which the only inferiority is in a higher rate of wages is not for that reason either unnatural or unprofitable: nor are the products of cheap foreign labor a *gratuity* morally or economically. The true struggle of humanity is against nature, and not against itself; it is not the struggle of humanity in one part of the world against humanity in another part. Nature is the obstacle to be overcome, and not other men. "And here," in the language of Prof. Cairnes, "I must in the first place insist that *cost* means sacrifice, and can not, without risk of hopelessly confusing ideas, be identified with anything that is not sacrifice. It represents what man parts with in the struggle between him and nature, which must be kept eternally distinct from *the return* made by nature on that payment. This is the essential nature of cost, and the problem of cost of production as bearing on the theory of value is to ascertain how far and in what way the payment thus made by man to nature in productive industry determines or otherwise influences the exchange value of the products which result. Given the productions of a man's industry, this alone will not determine the amount of his remuneration. In order to do this we must know, further, the proportion in which what he produces will exchange for what he wants—that is to say, for the articles of his consumption."

When we have once supplied the demands of the market with the products of our most efficient industry, the acceptance of the fruits of a day's labor expended abroad, under natural conditions similar to ours, whether cheap or dear, is the exclusion of the products of a day's labor expended here, cheap or dear. It is only a question whether the laborer shall live in America or Europe. If he is to live here, the industry which employs him must have protection if it is to survive. The free-trader is compelled to conclude that he ought not to live here.

It is a fundamental *assumption* of the free-trader here that the exchange value of raw produce would be kept at present absolute rates if the whole productive energies of the United States were employed on them. If there are any facts to make good this assumption, it would justify his doctrine, economically. But if his assumption is indefensible, then the whole question of superior advantages disappears and the advantages with it. Raising raw materials is only the most profitable industry because there are high returns of raw products for little labor; but the rewards of the labor when exchanged depend on the market price of the products. What fair, decent claim is there, then, for the clamorous assertions that this state of prices would continue under free trade? On the sole condition that the relative price of agricultural products remains as it is, has the free-trader any warrant to call them the most advantageous industries. What scientific warrant is there, then, to declare the protected industries unprofitable? Confessedly they are only less profitable relatively to an agriculture whose products could be sold in a market adjusted, with ideal accuracy, to a prearranged demand. Conceivably, such a market might be arranged in *the abstract;* it has never existed as a concrete fact.

There may be great returns in wheat and corn per acre

in Iowa and Dakota, but whether the industry is relatively profitable depends on the market value of these products. The free-trader always takes it for granted that there is a normal, absolute, unvarying rate of agricultural profits under freedom. This is the most profitable industry, and all others are "unprofitable." Up to a certain point the production of a certain amount of agricultural produce is profitable. After that point is reached who can say what is the most advantageous industry? Is the ability to export it the test? Then we are to keep on exporting grain so long as we compete successfully with them in the world's market. Suppose the world-market is supplied without us; what then? Why, then, having wasted our patrimony, the freemen of America are forced to take up other employments and acquire the skill which will enable us to organize and undergo the competition which the violated laws of common sense and nature now at last thrust upon us. Under defensive duties we are enabled to undergo it now and set in motion our industrial machinery, *once for all*.

The economists are unceasingly saying that there is a gain in every exchange, or else the parties to it would not trade. There is neither historical nor logical truth in this. Life, unfortunately, is filled with the mistakes of men in production and exchange, and the miseries which have flowed from men not understanding their own true interests. If the gain which a man reaps by exchanging his estate for the means of vicious indulgences is summed up in "the gratification of his desires," very good. The science has jurisdiction over him. All satisfactions come from the proceeds of industry. All the creations of industry are distributed in the forms of wages, rent, and profits. There will be most to divide when the most is produced. If all production can not go forward in the most advantageous work, we take up the next most productive. We not only proceed thus, but we are compelled to proceed after this fashion. Such tirades as this are an inexact description of the facts: Says Prof. Perry: " The original trade interfered with by protective taxes is always profitable; otherwise it would not be carried on, and only asks to be *let alone* to maintain itself as profitable." The original trade of hauling merchandise from Philadelphia to Pittsburg in Conestoga wagons was natural and profitable. It was the best we could do in the way of transportation. Railroads came along, and it ceased to maintain itself as profitable. Western grain was laboriously carted from Buffalo to New York. It was profitable, otherwise the business would not have been carried on. The Erie Canal cuts off, in whole or in part, this *natural* industry, and, by *restricting* carriage by horses and wagons, compels the traffic to be carried on in canal-boats. The original and natural industry of weaving by hand was profitable; it has been sadly interfered with by the power-loom. Does Prof. Perry expect society to be petrified in its present tracks?[1]

---

[1] Prof. R. Ellis Thompson pertinently asks: " Is it 'natural' that any nation should keep its farms on one continent and its workshops on another? Is it 'natural' that cotton, on its way from the grower to the weaver, should go half-way round the globe and back? Is it 'natural' that a large part of the race should be employed in carrying bulky articles—raw materials and coarse goods—from some countries to others in the same climate and of the same general capacity? Is it 'natural' that a country with millions of tons of iron on the surface of her soil, and square miles of coal not far below it, should send thousands of miles for railroad-iron?" ("Social Science.")

Frédéric Bastiat recognizes the "unnatural" and artificial conditions under which European exchanges have grown up. The United States have no occasion to extend their exchanges into such a system. The effort it will exact from us will exceed the effort which it saves. He says: " It is thus we see important branches of industry established where they ought not to

"There is a *natural market* for the things a nation has to sell in the *foreign things* offered against them," exclaims the Professor. Why do these people everlastingly look to the foreign market? The domestic market can be made to offer the same commodities against our exportables.

"Now, when this profitable interchange is going forward, protection steps in and cuts off in part or in whole this *natural market,* and compels the home things to be sold in a *restricted* and *less profitable* market, by putting heavy taxes on the introduction of the things seeking these home products in exchanges; . . . the advocates of protection do not claim that branches of business which would otherwise be profitable and self-supporting should be protected, but only the weak and *less profitable* kinds; let it be noted that the 'protected' branches of manufacture are, by supposition" (?) "and confession" (!), "*unprofitable,* otherwise it would be idle to try to persuade the people to be taxed to keep them along; and so, to bolster up these, protective taxes *virtually destroy* other branches of industry, which only ask that their *natural market* shall be let alone, in order to maintain an independent and profitable existence." [1]

---

be. France makes sugar." (He did not anticipate, when he wrote in 1850, the triumph of protection which the sugar interests in France would illustrate in 1884.) "England spins cotton brought from the plains of India. Centuries of war, torrents of blood, the dissipation of vast treasures, have brought about these results, and the effort has been to substitute in Europe sickly and precarious for sound and healthy enterprises, and to open the door to commercial crises, to stoppages, to instability, and finally to pauperism."

This is the "clash of chaotic cupidities" amid which free trade invites America to cast her fortunes. The central trouble with the world is that it seems to have grown up on the political and not on the economic movements of the race.

[1] Prof. Sumner states a similar series of propositions with his usual crisp-

One can scarcely deal patiently with such a bundle of assumptions and fallacies. This *natural market* is confessedly limited, and is not natural to us. Profitable interchange can only go forward so long as our production is kept within its limits—if we ingeniously hit the mark, very well—but the overproduction sets us back to other industries; and it has been the part of wisdom to provide these other industries while we are rich enough to average our efficiency. A farmer may begin operations by cultivating his most fertile and profitable fields, but if his family increased indefinitely, he would extend his cultivation over more remote and possibly less productive domains. His average results might be proportionately less for a given expenditure of effort, but it is the best he can do, and his absolute results are increased.[1] If no children came to

---

ness and dogmatism. Like his brother professor, he assumes the existence of an illimitable foreign market for the products of the group of most advantageous industries: "If an industry does not pay, it is an industrial abomination. It is wasting and destroying. The larger it is, the more mischief it does. The protected manufacturer is forced to allege, when he asks for protection, that his business would *not pay* without it." (It would not "pay" *him*, the manufacturer, without protection, that is certain. The real practical, common-sense question is, Will it pay the society of which he is a member, in the long run, if, once for all, it organizes the new industry at a present extra cost?) "He proposes to waste capital. If he should waste his own wealth, he would not go on long. He, therefore, asks the legislature to give him power to *lay taxes* on his fellow-citizens, to collect from them the capital which he intends *to waste*, and good wages for himself while he is carrying on that business besides. This is what is called 'developing our industries,' and the operation of the law is such that the waste and destruction can go on indefinitely. Either an industry can pay under freedom, in which case it does not need protection, or else it would not pay under freedom, in which case it is wasting the wealth of the nation as long as it goes on."

[1] The Pennsylvania Railroad, with its main line and branches, is a complicated organism. Its main line has a great earning capacity. Many of its branches are run, possibly, at a loss as branches. The main line, operated alone, shows the highest efficiency—is the most profitable industry. It can only be worked, including its branches, at a certain average efficiency, or, if

him, he could keep possession of his original field, and maintain his original advantage. The people of the United States have simply acted on his maxims. Immigrants and natural increase of population have driven them to occupy industries, possibly less profitable, but far from unprofitable. They can only escape the unprofitable consequences of overproduction, for a limited foreign market, by forbidding immigration or driving labor to other countries.

The industries which pay "under freedom" have a relative superiority so long as their products maintain their present exchangeable value in the foreign market. Rigidly maintained within the limits of that market, they pay. Finding the labor and capital of the country in excess of the requirements of such industries, the legislature, acting for the whole people, provides that the people may engage in the next most profitable industry. Unless employed, the capital and labor must and ought to leave the country. The " protected manufacturer " asks nothing of the people. All-of-us, the State, simply determine to enter upon all these industries indispensable to our supply of needed commodities. When organized they *pay*—possibly pay less than agriculture under the ideal presuppositions which have never been realized since the Government was organized. There is no waste and destruction, but the whole outcome is pure gain. The product would not exist else,

---

you please, reduced *rate* of average earnings. And yet it is manifest that the joint effect of the main line and branches is not a losing one, and is more profitable—the earnings are absolutely larger—than if the main line alone were operated and the branches were idle. Yet, in a certain sense, the main line is *taxed* by the branches. Treated as a whole, there is no *tax* in the case—no " waste."

What the economists call the unprofitable industries in this country are "the branches" which Nature herself has built for us, and which the human nature with which God has endowed us, qualifies and urges us to operate.

for the men and the money could not be employed in America on the most advantageous industry itself without causing that industry to cease to "pay under freedom." We come back again to the eternal fact of the incapacity of the foreign market to absorb the commodities which the international division of labor has assigned to our productive energies. The nation has simply extended its operations over fields which yield less average profits, but the operation still pays.

We have so often come upon this dilemma of the free-trader in finding a market abroad for all the products of our most advantageous industries, that we may as well examine the case somewhat in detail.

For the fiscal year ending June 30, 1883, the total exports from the United States were, in round numbers, $804,000,000.[1]

---

[1] Agriculture, 77 per cent of the whole............. $619,269,449
Manufactures, 13·91 per cent of the whole.......... 111,890,001
Mining industry and oils, 6·40 per cent of the whole.. 51,444,857
Forestry, 1·24 per cent of the whole............... 9,976,143
Fisheries, ·78 per cent of the whole............... 6,276,375
All others, ·67 per cent of the whole............. 5,366,807

Agricultural exports amounted to 77 per cent of our whole exports, or to $619,269,449, made up as to its principal items as follows:

Cotton.. $247,328,721
Bread and breadstuffs......................... 208,040,850
Provisions.................................... 107,388,287
Tobacco....................................... 22,095,229
Animals living................................ 10,789,268
    Total..................................... $595,642,355

or 96 per cent in these five items.

The exports of manufactured products were $111,890,001.

In detail they were made up of:

Manufactures of wood.......................... $26,793,708
  Iron and steel.............................. 19,165,321
  Cotton...................................... 12,951,145
  Leather..................................... 7,923,662

The imports were $723,180,914.[1]

The tables subjoined show the course of trade, and the trade balances, between the United States and each of the

Turpentine	$4,366,229
Agricultural implements	3,883,919
Drugs, chemicals	3,306,195
Sugar and molasses	3,266,581
Sewing-machines	3,061,639

These nine items constitute about 75 per cent of our exports of manufactures. The remaining items embrace a little of almost everything.

[1] The main items were:

Sugar and molasses	$99,326,395
Wool, raw and manufactured	55,224,283
Silk, raw and manufactured	50,807,616
Chemicals, etc	43,126,285
Coffee	42,050,513
Iron and steel	40,796,007
Cotton	37,654,221
Hides and skins	27,640,030
Tin	23,917,837
Flax	19,737,542
Fruits	19,313,041
Tea	17,302,849
India-rubber	15,844,302
Jute, etc	12,646,513
Breadstuffs	15,830,605
Wood	14,857,578
Leather	13,104,415
Tobacco	11,771,596
Provisions	10,653,273
Earthen, stone, and china	8,620,527
Fancy goods, perfumery, etc	8,358,471
Furs	7,959,759
Glassware	7,762,543
Precious stones	7,692,385
Paper materials	5,329,876
Hemp	5,118,508

The remainder of the list includes a great variety of things—books, pictures, musical instruments, and the like—no one item of which amounts to one half of one per cent of the total imports.

other countries, taken from the Bureau of Statistics for the year ending June 30, 1883. Any other recent year would show about the same state of trade:

VALUE *of the* IMPORTS *of* MERCHANDISE *from, and of the* EXPORTS *of* MERCHANDISE *to, those countries in our commerce with which the value of* EXPORTS EXCEEDED *the value of* IMPORTS *during the year ended June 30, 1883.*

Order.	COUNTRIES.	Imports of merchandise into the United States.	Exports of domestic and foreign merchandise from the United States.	Exports in excess of imports.
1	Great Britain and Ireland...	$188,622,619	$425,424,174	$236,801,555
2	Russia..................	2,599,995	19,141,751	16,541,756
3	Spain..................	7,794,345	16,931,287	9,136,942
4	Germany................	57,577,728	66,169,929	8,792,201
5	Mexico.................	8,177,123	16,587,620	8,410,497
6	Netherlands.............	12,253,733	18,919,583	6,665,850
7	British possessions in Australasia................	4,021,395	9,795,656	5,774,261
8	Belgium.................	23,161,200	27,778,975	4,617,775
9	Portugal................	1,093,476	5,485,037	4,391,561
10	Denmark................	302,886	4,508,876	4,205,990
11	Chili...................	435,584	2,860,496	2,424,912
12	Hong-Kong..............	1,918,894	3,777,759	1,858,865
13	British North American possessions...............	44,740,876	46,580,253	1,839,377
14	United States of Colombia...	5,171,455	6,868,971	1,697,516
15	Sweden and Norway.......	1,831,171	2,824,548	993,377
16	Gibraltar................	4,573	627,816	623,243
17	British possessions in Africa and adjacent islands.....	1,840,020	2,438,069	598,049
18	Azores, Madeira, and Cape Verd Islands............	70,689	631,089	560,400
19	Miquelon, Langley, and St. Pierre Islands...........	17,370	451,887	434,511
20	Danish West Indies........	384,003	702,126	318,123
21	Hayti..................	2,971,515	3,223,101	251,586
22	Liberia.................	71,888	182,010	110,122
23	French Guiana...........	18,437	102,084	83,647
24	Portuguese possessions in Africa and adjacent islands..	2,665	5,012	2,347
	Other countries, the exports to which exceeded the imports..................	290,200	439,690	149,490
	Total.............	$365,173,846	$682,457,799	$317,283,953

VALUE *of the* IMPORTS *of* MERCHANDISE *from, and of the* EXPORTS *of* MERCHANDISE *to, those countries in our commerce with which the value of* IMPORTS EXCEEDED *the value of* EXPORTS *during the year ended June 30, 1883.*

Order.	COUNTRIES.	Imports of merchandise into the United States.	Exports of domestic and foreign merchandise from the United States.	Imports in excess of exports.
1	Cuba	$65,544,534	$15,103,703	$50,440,831
2	France	97,989,164	58,682,223	39,306,941
3	Brazil	44,488,459	9,252,094	35,236,365
4	British East Indies	19,467,800	2,185,804	17,281,996
5	China	20,141,331	4,080,322	16,061,009
6	Japan	15,098,890	3,376,434	11,722,456
7	Spanish possessions, other than Cuba and Porto Rico.	10,617,563	324,474	10,293,089
8	Hawaiian Islands	8,238,461	3,776,065	4,462,396
9	British Guiana	5,946,429	2,035,156	3,911,273
10	Venezuela	5,901,724	2,403,705	3,498,019
11	Porto Rico	5,477,493	2,164,708	3,312,785
12	Central American states	5,121,315	2,003,467	3,117,848
13	Argentine Republic	6,192,111	3,543,196	2,648,915
14	Uruguay	3,980,110	1,452,818	2,527,292
15	Peru	2,526,918	493,894	2,033,024
16	Italy	11,909,658	10,313,558	1,596,100
17	Austria	2,984,923	1,779,904	1,205,019
18	Greece	1,231,580	91,017	1,140,563
19	French West Indies	2,895,857	1,813,555	1,082,302
20	Turkey	2,168,967	1,369,703	799,264
21	Dutch West Indies	882,058	589,612	292,446
22	Dutch East Indies	2,645,917	2,407,131	238,786
23	British West Indies	8,736,112	8,502,153	233,959
24	San Domingo	1,417,519	1,201,874	215,645
25	French possessions in Africa and adjacent islands	388,483	257,898	130,585
26	Greenland, Iceland, and the Faroe Islands	97,400		97,400
27	British Honduras	531,839	504,417	27,422
28	Dutch Guiana	473,043	451,349	21,694
	All other countries, the imports from which exceeded the exports	4,911,410	1,221,369	3,690,041
	Total	$358,007,068	$141,381,603	$216,625,465

It thus appears that of our exports, agriculture furnished 77 per cent, manufactures 13·91 per cent, and mining and mineral oils 6·40 per cent.

Of food-products, we sent abroad values to the amount of $325,000,000, less than 10 per cent of our products. This was consumed in Great Britain and the people living along the western water-front of Europe. England is compelled to buy about one half of the food of her population abroad, but America is by no means the only country in the world which raises a surplus accessible to her. France can feed herself, and Germany. The extension of railroads through Europe into the food-raising areas of Poland, Hungary, and Russia, has brought down all prices in Mark Lane. Asia has now fairly brought her agricultural products into competition with ours.

On inspection of the tables given above, we find that the balance of trade against us in Cuba, France, Brazil, China, Japan, Spanish possessions, and Venezuela, is nearly two hundred millions. We sell no food to them. For our sugar, French wines and articles of luxury and elegance, tea, tropical fruits, raw hides, and a large list of commodities which we can not mention, we pay in cash or its representative, and not in exports direct. The balance of trade is in our favor in the cases of Great Britain, Russia, Spain, Germany, Netherlands, Belgium, Portugal, and Denmark. From them we get the bankers' bills of exchanges which settle the adverse balance elsewhere. What is left we can take out in manufactured goods from England, Germany, and France. With England alone there is a balance of trade in our favor of $236,000,000. But that does not mean that we can take pay in British goods. We sent there $425,000,000 worth of exports, and took from there $188,000,000 in merchandise. The difference was sent in bills of exchange for our account to pay our debts to France, Cuba, Brazil, China, and Japan. We paid England, Germany, and France, for manufactured goods made of wool, silk, iron and steel, and cotton alone, $185,000,000.

These goods could have been made at home, and it is all that our surplus food, which the foreign market would take, enabled us to buy. We should then have been compelled by free trade to have gone without all these commodities which the protection tariff enabled the home industries to produce here. Besides the $600,000,000 which the American farmer sold abroad, he sold more than $1,500,000,000 at home. We bought abroad, in round numbers, $723,000,000, for about half of which we paid in food and provisions. Let us now see how exchange values on exports and imports will be affected according to some principles we find laid down in Adam Smith's "Wealth of Nations." We come to the third and fourth propositions in the second alternative set we are considering.

CHAPTER VIII.

ADAM SMITH—SOME FACTS IN OUR HISTORY.

Accordingly, let us invite the free-trader, supposing him to be honest and fair-minded, to propose to Adam Smith the foregoing data to determine the relative exchange values in a foreign market of raw produce in a state of overproduction, and certain manufactured commodities in a state of underproduction. America, by underselling all other countries, has, succeeded in getting rid of $700,000,000 worth of her products, of which about half were food and provisions. For this she got in exchange some $350,000,000 in articles of the uses, decencies, elegancies, and luxuries of life becoming a highly civilized society—tropical fruits and products unfitted to her climate and the capacities of her labor; besides, she took in exchange some $350,000,000 of manufactured goods which under existing conditions she does not undertake to produce. Her domestic manufactures produce some $8,000,000,000 of value from their industries annually, of which probably $2,500,000,000 come from competing industries which commenced to exist mainly by virtue of protective laws, and industries related to and dependent on them. They employ one quarter of the population of the land.

"It is proposed, Mr. Smith, that, inasmuch as at present we get fair returns from labor in fertile fields, the surplus produce of which has a home market for $1,500,000,000 worth annually, and a present foreign market for an additional $700,000,000, we all take to this most advantageous industry and abandon the protected industries. We are all going into the industry which 'pays under freedom.' We shall then want to buy in foreign markets the $700,000,000 as now, and besides the $2,500,000,000 worth of the products which our 'distorted industries' now furnish us; besides, our surplus productions in agriculture will then be swelled by the whole amount which one fourth of our population, released from protected industries, can add to them. On the whole, we shall need to find a market abroad for our surplus products to the amount of quite two thousand five hundred million dollars.

"'Why are we compelled to carry our bulky produce nearly three thousand miles?' Because the workshops of the world are there, and men work cheaper and their wages are low.

"No; there are no disadvantages against our labor except the necessity of paying our workmen higher wages. They are freemen, accustomed to comfort, educate their children, and have a general purpose to get on in the world. They are great producers, and are also great consumers. There is a very energetic state of things, indeed, among them. And these great wages come from the commodities they make.

"No; there is no country in which the soil, climate, and natural productions are more varied. No country has any peculiar advantages over us—no country, at least, inhabited by civilized man. No country exceeds us in the amount of capital it possesses, nor in the skill and willingness to work. Indeed, capital is so plentiful, and labor so abundant, that a few years ago in a sudden emergency more than three million men went into the industry of a civil war. They invested more than six thousand millions of dollars in the business. Both the men and the money were promptly forthcoming. Of course, when you wrote the 'Wealth of Nations' you seemed to think 'industry was limited by capital.' In America what is wanted is not capital, but a field of employment. The world has gained in the last hundred years, and you have no idea how things have gone on.

"Yes, I recall what you wrote: 'The natural advantages which one country has over another in producing particular commodities are sometimes so great that it is acknowledged by all the world to be in vain to struggle with them. By means of glasses, hot-beds, and hot walls, very good grapes can be raised in Scotland, and very good wine, too, can be made of them at about thirty times the expense for which at least equally good can be brought from foreign countries. Would it be a reasonable law to prohibit the importation of all foreign wines merely to encourage the making of claret and burgundy in Scotland?'

"But I could not honestly say that the protected industries in America answer at all to that description. They are not 'such employments.' The climate of Scotland is a permanent obstacle to grape-raising. I could not say that the production of a ton of iron or a yard of cloth requires any more capital and labor than it does in England. It costs no more to overcome the obstacles which nature presents in America than it does in Great Britain. Its increased cost is principally in the wages of the laborer. The protectionist seems to hope that that disadvantage will be permanent. I recall that you have said that 'labor is the first price—the original purchase-money paid for all things.'

. . . .

"And so you now think that it is no economic disadvantage to the nation, *as a whole*, that its labor is better paid? That, if the industry is natural to a country, the *increase in wages costs the nation nothing?* That, because the laborer can afford increased consumption, and does afford it, the consumer of his products gets it all back again, and that in the final division all labor gets distributed into rent, wages, and profits, and universal activity is the result? That industrial competition equalizes remuneration to sacrifice, and that the country is the richer by the new thing produced?

"Ah! then I see how, the natural facilities being the same and the skill the same, it modifies what you wrote in these words: 'Whether the advantages which one country has over another be natural or acquired is in this respect of no consequence. As long as the one country has those advantages and the other wants them, it will be always more advantageous for the latter rather to buy of the former than to make. It is an acquired advantage only which one artificer has over his neighbor who exercises another trade, and yet they both find it more advantageous to buy of one another than to make what does not belong to their particular trades.' You mean, if the Americans are all-sided and have brought the division of labor to perfection, that the acquired advantage stands on equally high and strong grounds with natural advantage, and that it was worth while to acquire the new advantage. I do now recollect that John Rae showed the respects in which an individual and a nation became opulent by means of entirely different orders of procedure. I see clearly why your illustration lacks application to a state of things you had never conceived. There had been no parallel case in your experience.

"No; there is no scarcity of labor. There must be nearly seven hundred thousand laboring-men added each year to the population of the United States by natural increase and immigration. Such a fact, which in its magnitude could not have been in your cognizance, completes the equipment of America in its land, its capital, and its labor, the great trinity from which alone can come national opulence. And yet, in your inductive reasoning, you had betrayed your true insight into the divine efficacy of their unity. 'Nations,' you said, 'can only advance in greatness and prosperity as the numbers of their inhabitants increase. Whatever the natural fertility of the soil, however genial the climate, and however well fitted the whole country may be for the practice of every species of industry, yet if it be deficient in population, these natural riches can never be elaborated, and it must hold a poor and inconsiderable rank in the scale of nations.' (Adam Smith here was very near the outside limits of his science, and gave sure sign of 'impending fallacy and confusion' as he approached the confines of social science, and hinted at moral considerations.) 'A confined and comparatively barren territory, filled with a numerous industrious population, exceeds the most fertile and extensive country, scantily peopled. *It is the people that make the state*—its real riches lie in its inhabitants.'" (Is it possible that Adam Smith is going to solve an *economic* problem by introducing *moral* and *political* elements?)

Adam Smith, *loquitur:* "No, my free-trade friend, you misconceive the philosophy of the 'Wealth of Nations.' I have treated a nation as a society in possession of certain instruments of production. They are engaged in procuring for themselves the necessaries, conveniences, and amusements of life. It is true that, when I wrote, this flame of industrial conquest had not lighted up the world and made life a scene of industrial warfare. Men had not wrested fire and steam and electricity to human uses.

"They were still tugging away with human muscles. I had pointed many paragraphs of my book against the vileness and injustice of the English colonial policy, and its evident purpose to enslave the industrial impulses of her colonists. I said: 'To prohibit a great people, however, from making all they can of every part of their produce, or from employing their stock and industry in a way that they judge most advantageous to themselves, is a manifest violation of the most sacred rights of mankind.' I did this because its effect was to suppress the industrial freedom of the colonies and to hold them in commercial slavery to the ambitious designs of English statesmen and English manufacturers; yet it seems that free foreign trade now works precisely the same results. I taught that all systems, either of preference or restraint, being taken completely away, 'the obvious and simple system of natural liberty establishes itself of its own accord.' And I discharged the sovereign from 'the duty of superintending the industry of private people, and of directing it toward the employments most suitable to the interests of society.' When I wrote, the steam-engine was not perfected, and the spinning-jenny and power-loom had not been invented. Iron was brought to England from America. The two or three millions of people who occupied America were strung along the coast, and had scarcely got west of the Hudson, and had not reached the Ohio and the lakes. Population was sparse, and their few and simple wants were supplied by household industries and a little commerce with England and the West Indies. As things were then, they were simply productive agents thrown to the periphery of the industrial wheel by force of the central agencies at work in England and Europe. They were subordinate members of the industrial structure, and performed subordinate functions. They had even then no market for their surplus. Their agriculture of itself, at that time, produced them poverty, not wealth; rudeness, not comfort; scarcity, not plenty, as you now seem to understand these things. The

Revolution, which they began the same year my 'Wealth of Nations' was published, made them a new political center. It was the genesis of a new nation. The aspirations of mankind were kindled afresh. There was a movement of all people and all tongues to the shores of the Western empire. Freedom was the word, and civil liberty and religious emancipation were the watchwords. Men sought Columbia for homes, the chances for plenty and freedom. They went under domestic, social, political, ethical, national motives, as well as a regard for economical results. Once settled under their own roof-trees, they turned to the practical affairs of life. More laborers went to America under the impulses of the great uprising of humanity which urged them than, under 'the obvious and simple system of natural liberty,' could retain normal and profitable relations to European commerce. They took to the most advantageous industries, but after the war there were ruin, bankruptcy, and distress. From 1783 to 1789 they had the policy of absolute free foreign trade. There was no sale for the products of their industry in the foreign market. The instinct of liberty had distributed these men in America in a proportion out of any ratio which mere considerations of economic prudence would have inspired. Too many had come. Some must remain idle, return, or pursue other industries. I had never said, in the 'Wealth of Nations,' that if a country had some natural and highly advantageous industry, God had intended that no more people should live and work in that country than could work at that industry. I had never said that a man should learn a trade, unless he could sell the products of his labor in that trade. I had never said that, if men flocked to a new country under the stimulus of the highest motives possible to human beings, there were any economic doctrines which compelled them to be idle and starve. I have said they could always produce for the home market, and in some score of places in my book I have insisted on the superiority of that market. For instance, 'Whatever, then, tends to diminish in any country the number of artificers and manufacturers, tends to diminish the home market—the most important of all markets for the rude produce of the land.' More specifically I have said these words: 'Capital employed in purchasing in one part of a country in order to sell in another part the produce of the industries of *that country*, generally *replaces*, by such operation, *two distinct capitals* that had both been employed in its agriculture or manufactures, and thus enables them to continue that employment. The capital used in buying foreign goods for domestic consumption, when the purchase is made by the produce of domestic industry, replaces also two distinct capitals, but *one of them only supports domestic industry, the other supports foreign industry*, and, *therefore, foreign trade* will give but *one half the encouragement* to the industry or *productive labor* of a country that *domestic* or internal trade does.'

"My chapter, 'Of the Natural and Market Price of Commodities,' teaches what the natural price would be when the component parts of the cost are taken into account. There is no market price in a market where there is no demand. M. Say has tried to prove that there can be no *general glut;* but a glut in overproduction of particular commodities is within the familiar experience of every observer. Agricultural products are steadily renewed from year to year, and the amount of food each person consumes is very definitely determined. The wants of a hungry man are well known, and may be quantitatively provided for. But there is no limit to many forms of human wants, such as clothing, shelter, luxuries, indulgences, artistic longings—engendered by riches, fashion, caprice. The food a given market takes may be determinately ascertained; not so with manufactured commodities. If the people in America overproduce food for the limited markets which depend on them, they pay the same penalty, in loss of market values, as if they overproduced gunpowder or iron—with the certainty that they have strong competitors in all parts of the world. If my doctrine of natural freedom has full play within the limits of the thirty-eight States of the Western Republic, they have satisfied all the conditions I have prescribed.

"If your industries are natural, and not overweighted by the necessity of more labor—sacrifice, effort—for a given product than in other nations; if your pursuits are only those authorized by the nature of things, they are legitimate pursuits for an industrious, skillful people. When there is no difference in natural and acquired advantages, the price of labor—the wages of a day's work—is no decisive test of the productiveness of labor. The abundance of commodities is the test of that; money-prices only confuse the matter in your mind. You have as large a product under a high rate of wages as under a low rate. If all your people can not be employed in the industries which give the highest returns, and unless you find a market which will continue to take them on correspondingly high exchange values, you must take to other industries and consent to certain average returns. It is, at last, the products which you want, not their price. If you can not expend your highest efficiency and receive the highest returns, you must consent to exert a certain average efficiency, and be content with certain average returns.

"If Scotland could acquire the sunny skies and genial climate of France, her hills would be covered with vines instead of heather, and to acquire that advantage it would be worth paying for, even if it took a great expenditure.

'A new channel might be opened from the exhaustless river of human power, springing from the mingled sources of nature and art, so that a plenteous stream would flow in the community, from which individuals drawing might largely add to the general opulence. But some means must be employed to open it up. There is an obstruction in the way that must previously be overcome; a rock blocking it up that must be removed. No individual will open up the channel, because, were he to do so, he could derive no more benefit from the labor than others who had not labored. The whole society, or rather the legislator, the power acting for the whole society, might do so, and in similar cases has done so; and, to judge of the measure by the events consequent on it, with the happiest success.' The Navigation Act was a famous instance.

"National and individual capital do not necessarily increase in the same manner. At least my words in the 'Wealth of Nations' must be taken with the qualifications which suggest themselves if you read carefully and closely —if read literally, they contain an ambiguity, I might say a fallacy, which was not in my mind, but which the facts in America, and the course of modern commerce, render quite apparent.

"In a passage habitually quoted I said: 'It is the maxim of every prudent master of a family never to attempt to make at home what it will cost him more to make than to buy. The tailor does not attempt to make his own shoes, but buys them of the shoemaker. The shoemaker does not attempt to make his own clothes, but employs a tailor. The farmer attempts to make neither the one nor the other, but employs those different artificers. *All* of them find it for their interest to employ *their whole industry* in a way in which they have some advantage over their neighbor, and to purchase with a part of its produce, or, what is the same thing, with the price of a part of it, whatever else they have occasion for. What is prudence in the conduct of every private family can scarcely be folly in that of a great kingdom.'

"Now a tricky logician can make an unfair use of that passage. You will observe that I had said that the different artificers find it for their advantage *to employ their whole industry* in the way in which they have some advantage. It is obvious to any reasonable thinker that he could only retain his advantage on the condition that he could *sell the whole of his surplus produce* and get 'the price of it.' If he remained idle one day or two days a week he would lose his advantage, or, if he kept at work and made more shoes, or clothes, or food than the others wanted, he would be compelled to make such concessions in price as would be fatal to his advantages. In the latter case, the surplus for which there was no demand would bring no price, and he would lose his labor and trouble. If he were idle two days in a week *as a shoemaker*, he could do something else, and what he produced when he would otherwise have been idle *costs* him nothing. So far as it has exchangeable value it would be clear gain to him and to the society in which he lived.

"I must remind you again in this connection of what I said in my chapter of the 'Division of Labor': 'The division of labor is limited by the extent of the market. Before any man or any set of men' (the people of the United States, for instance) 'can in common prudence devote themselves to any particular employment' (the raising of raw produce, for instance), 'they must be assured that they can dispose of the commodity which their exertions in the prosecution of that employment will produce.' This proposition is just as applicable to the international division of labor and the world's commerce as it is to the division of labor in the villages. A nation takes the same risks in undertaking to hold its superiority in prices in the markets of the world, even in an advantageous industry, as the tailor or the blacksmith who produces more than he can sell. The folly of 'a great kingdom' which drives ahead without any true perspective of the wants of the world's commerce is just as egregious and inexcusable as that of the private family which makes unsalable things for the town market. The nation and the family may make the commodity at a small cost of labor, but it can not have the price of it on the basis of superior efficiency. If they can consume it at home and make it the means of further products for which there is a market, they will recover their superiority. What happens in the case you put is this: international commerce will operate as a substitute for competition, and free trade reduces your efficiency and compels you to divide your advantages with foreign nations. Protection enables your people *as a whole*—the nation—to retain them all.

"I thereupon answer your question, and say to you that, if you undertake to sell $2,500,000,000 of products in a market which requires only $700,000,000, you undertake an impossibility. If the trade were possible, you would lose all your relative superiority, and would pay the cost of transportation both ways—the whole expense of the carriage of your exports and of your imports will be paid by the people of the United States. The whole cost of getting to a market to which you are forced to go will be borne by your people. But, more than all, you will starve in the midst of your fertile fields. You can not dispose of the commodities which your exertions have produced.

"The formula, not fully worked out by myself, which Mr. Mill called 'The Equation of International Demand,' is the law of your case. He announced it in these words: 'The produce of a country exchanges for the produce of other countries at such values as are required, in order that the whole of her exports may exactly pay for the whole of her imports.' But, under the conditions of the case you put to me, a large portion of your exports go for necessities which you can not raise, the products of non-competing industries. The portion with which you might purchase manufactured commodities such as you produce in your *competing* industries, 'protected' industries will furnish only a small part of your aggregate demand. The foreign market neither takes nor gives according to your requirements. You must, therefore, make them at home.

"Do it at once, and stop your illogical grumbling about *taxes* and your senseless refinements of carrying on one industry at *the cost* of another. These are the only conditions of 'freedom' left open to you."

The entire consistency of what we have supposed Adam Smith to have said can be maintained from the discussion in his "Wealth of Nations." It is equally certain that, in more than one passage, John Stuart Mill has taken the same ground. It is very true that when the latter contemplates the world of trade from Manchester and looks upon the necessity England is under to procure by exchanges the very food which maintains her labor and the raw materials upon which they work, he wants unrestricted commerce with countries which raise food and raw materials. If the world were a single nation, and population was distributed throughout solely on economic impulses, things would happen as theory presupposes. In point of fact, English commercial agents are in every port in the world for economic purposes. They are members of an industrial and not a political entity. But they are there in the pursuit of fortune, and with no purpose of residence, citizenship, and the founding of a home for themselves and their children. A world built up on scientific economic considerations would be very different from the existing one. It is divided into nations, and economic considerations have had little, we might say no share in bringing it about. If every extension of the habitable globe had reference to the world's commerce, and every new enterprise to market values in that commerce, political lines would be different. It shows what a blunder has been made in the Providential ordering of things, that the structure was not put up according to the plans and specifications of David Ricardo and New England college professors. If men could be born where they pleased, or if men could and would go freely from one country to another when the demand for the products of their industry in their native land failed, or when the pursuit of an occupation in which they had special aptitude is incapable of being carried on—if men did not care where they lived and where they died—we might assent to speculations as to what would be. If, on the other hand, all the motives of life, except economic ones, keep him in his political home, the capacity and opportunity of a man to work at all may depend on governmental restraints on the products of foreign labor, and the industrial entity must be *conterminous* with the political entity. It is not a question of protecting the weak against the strong, or the high-priced laborer against the low-priced laborer. It is giving to the laborer of a given country the market for the products of his labor. It is to prevent the laborer himself from being removed from the country, and substituting therefor a trade in the product of his labor. The argument does go equally well either end first. Germany successfully keeps its lower-priced labor in German industries on German soil by protecting her home market, and so does France. Otherwise it might conceivably happen that there would be no occasion for a German to live in Germany. If a man, in determining in what country he shall have a home, is without sentiment, he may submit to the streams of economic influences and be thrown ashore at the first shoal he strikes. Oppression or disaster may force a man to accept the alternative of expatriation, as many millions have done, but it would be an absurd inversion of the order of events to say that they had done so in deference to the influences of a scientific economy whose central seat was Manchester, say. "Once convince a French peasant," says William Dillon, "that he can get higher wages for his labor and higher interest on his capital in the Western States of America than in France, and, according to the theory of the economist, he may be relied on to go to America. As a matter of fact, we all know that, in ninety-nine cases out of a hundred, he may be relied on to stay at home."

But the present national divisions of the world were not brought about by economic impulses. Free trade, alike in theory and in fact, determines in advance that we shall in America pursue a limited group of industries. The historical and existing fact is that we are not here for industrial considerations solely. Being here, and classifying ourselves, we find we are too numerous to supply all our wants from abroad, and at the same time fulfill the conditions of the equation of international demand. Our wants, as Prof. Sumner says, originate in our inherited traits. We must equate our efforts one with another. We have fertile fields adequate to the supply of all our wants with self-help—the moment we go abroad with our surplus we are as helpless as if that surplus was in nutmegs or bananas, which nobody wanted to buy. The world does not want so many of either, as a population (redundant in this respect) which did not come here for the sole purpose of raising nutmegs and bananas, can supply. It is as if there were too many tailors or too many shoemakers in a village: they must do something else or go elsewhere.

We have now tried our hand at Prof. Perry's "wholly impregnable position," that "what a nation purchases by its exports it purchases by its most efficient labor, and consequently at the cheapest rate to itself." We have seen how its theory is implicated with facts. We have seen how the "division of labor is limited by the market," and that overproduction for a given market breaks down exchange values in which alone resided superior efficiency in production, and that when the point of efficiency was overworked we must either stand idle or fall back to a certain average efficiency in production. What, so much as, it can buy abroad, it purchases by its most efficient labor: but what it can buy in this way is not sufficient to supply its wants.

It remains to glance very briefly at our own history, and to deal, not with statistics, which satisfy nobody, but with great underlying, pervading, distressing facts which marred the happiness and prosperity of the people, and impelled the fathers of the Union to some system of restraints on the importation of foreign goods, and the imposition, as a consequence, of protective duties. They were driven to it by the discovery that the five assumptions they made, and which we have before referred to, were wrong in fact. It was the inauguration of a settled reasoned national policy and economy.

Alexander Hamilton (in 1791) enumerates seventeen branches of manufactures which had been successfully carried on in the colonies—to wit, leather, iron, wood, flax and hemp, bricks, liquors, paper, hats, refined sugars, oils, copper and brass wares, tin-wares, carriages, tobacco, starch and hair-powder, lampblack, and gunpowder.

It would be a mistake to confound the processes then

in vogue with the present organization of industry. Manufactures then were literally HAND-MADE. The people were mostly engaged in agriculture and commerce. Only such blacksmiths, carpenters, masons, shoemakers, and other artisans existed side by side with the farmers as were indispensable. But many tools were then made by the blacksmiths, and many wares by the carpenter, which are now made by machinery on a large scale. All weaving was done on hand-looms. So much of these goods as could be imported, were imported and paid for by agricultural products. But these went mainly to the West Indies, and from this trade was derived the means of payment of the imports from other countries. Then, as now, only the finer textile fabrics were imported. Cloths, linens, and textile fabrics were mostly homespun. Ship-building, of wood, and the carrying-trade, had been natural and profitable industries. The making of pig-iron was substantially an agricultural industry, and could only be carried on where wood was plenty, charcoal being the only fuel used.[1] It was converted into bars under the trip-hammer and slitting-mill. The moderately protective duties provided for in the first tariff act passed, under the present Constitution, on July 4, 1789, had steadied up the domestic manufactures somewhat, and the country was passing the unhappy free-trade crisis of 1783–'89.

The Napoleonic wars produced exceptional and adventitious markets until 1808, when we became involved in European complications. In all these years we had almost a monopoly of the supply to the belligerents of wheat, corn, and meat, the prices of which were high, and the profits on the freight of which were large. In the mean time England had adopted successfully the inventions of

---

[1] See a very faithful and intelligent account of the iron industry in the United States—"Iron in all Ages," James M. Swank, Philadelphia, 1895.

Arkwright and Hargreaves in cotton manufacture, the use of coke in the manufacture of iron, and Cort's invention of puddling and rolling iron. So long as the foreign market held out, we advantageously supplied our need of these products, cheapened by machinery, by our exports. The political and economic effects of the wars of the French Revolution kept the question of protection in the background, but its expediency was never questioned by Hamilton, Jefferson, Madison, Monroe, and, indeed, Calhoun. How purely accidental and contingent our commercial advantages were during the wars, and how dependent upon wars, appears from a single fact. The Peace of Amiens lasted two years, 1802-'3. Our imports fell off from $111,300,000 in 1801, to $76,300,000 in 1802, and $64,700,000 in 1803; our exports, from $94,000,000 in 1801, to $72,000,000 in 1802, and $55,800,000 in 1803. Flour was $10.45 per barrel in 1801, and fell to $6.75 in 1802-'3. This was the effect of peace in Europe. Our prosperity had been artificial.

No nation can count on continual prosperity based on disasters to other nations. In 1806 England had established a blockade of the Continent from Brest to the Elbe. Napoleon followed with the Berlin Decree. Then came the English Orders in Council, and again Napoleon's Milan Decree. In due time came our embargo in 1807—non-intercourse in 1809, and war with England in 1812. What happened? According to Prof. Sumner: "Embargo, non-intercourse, and war, lasting from 1807 to 1815, *created an artificial state of things here*, or, perhaps I should say, the United States was drawn into the *distortion and perversion of industry and commerce which the great wars were producing in Europe*. Manufactories of various kinds sprang up here *to supply the wants of the people*, when cut off from the usual sources of supply by foreign exchange.

They produced articles of inferior quality or design, generally speaking, but *the people had to be satisfied with them*. They were sustained by the artificial difficulties in foreign exchange, and by the *diminished profits* of other industries which *would have been more profitable here*."[1]

The real truth is, our prosperity, between 1792 and 1807, had been artificial and factitious, created by foreign wars, during which our commerce prospered so long as we could maintain our attitude as neutrals. Peace abroad brought us back to our normal condition, as seen in 1802–'3.

According to Prof. Taussig:[2] "This series of *restrictive* measures blocked the accustomed channels of exchange and production, and gave an enormous stimulus to those branches of industry whose products had before been imported. Establishments for the manufacture of cotton goods, woolen cloths, iron, glass, pottery, and other articles, *sprang up with a mushroom growth*."

One is tempted to inquire how our fathers were, else, to find the satisfaction of their desires? Were they to sit

---

[1] Speaking of the "distortion and perversion of industry" forced upon a people by *restrictions*, here is what a very distinguished free-trader has officially said as the grounds for "returning thanks to God." The economic effects of restriction, whether by war or tariffs, is the same, and the "compensation" the same under either cause. In his annual message to the Confederate Congress, in 1863, Jefferson Davis discourses thus:

"The injuries resulting from the interruption of foreign commerce have received compensation by the development of our own resources. . . . Cotton and woolen fabrics, shoes and harness, wagons and gun-carriages, are produced in daily-increasing quantities by the factories springing into existence. Our fields, no longer whitened by cotton that can not be exported, are devoted to the production of cereals and the growth of stock, formerly purchased with the proceeds of cotton. In the homes of our noble and devoted women—without whose sublime sacrifices our success would have been impossible—the noise of the loom and the spinning-wheel may be heard throughout the land. With hearts swelling with gratitude, let us then join in returning thanks to God."

[2] Assistant Professor of Political Economy at Harvard College.

idly until a ukase from the professors at Harvard, Yale, and Williams prescribed the time and conditions under which they might proceed to supply the necessaries and conveniences of life?

"It is sufficient here to note that the restrictive legislation of 1808-'15 was for the time being equivalent to extreme protection. The consequent rise of a considerable class of manufacturers, whose success depended largely on the continuance of protection, formed the basis of a strong movement for more decided limitation of foreign competition."

Some concessions to this feeling came in the tariff act of 1816. Cotton and woolen goods were to pay 25 per cent until 1819.[1] The act was defended with great force by Mr. Calhoun. But there was no general movement made in the direction of protection as such. If there was any expectation that agriculture and commerce would be again as profitable as they were previous to 1808, the people were doomed to disappointment. They were to be led up, by an experience not unlike that of 1783-'89, to a strong public conviction in favor of protecting their industries, and the enactment of legislation to that end. Prof. Taussig shall describe the order of events after the close of the War of 1815: "The harvests in Europe for

---

[1] The *minimum* duties, which so excite the ire of free-traders, first appear in this act. The duty was 25 per cent on cotton cloths. The minimum clause provided that it should not be less than six and a quarter cents per yard; that is, that the goods should be considered to have cost twenty-five cents per yard. Cotton cloths were then worth twenty-five to thirty cents per yard, and the *minimum* did not increase the duty. The price of cotton fell in 1819 to nineteen cents, in 1826 to thirteen cents, and in 1829 to eight and a half cents per yard. The *cheaper* goods became, of course, the larger *per cent* the tariff bears to *the cost*. The nearer we come to supplying the domestic demand by the domestic production, the more it *costs* the consumer! This is a very cheap and superficial fallacy, as is seen in the case of cotton cloth.

several seasons were bad, and caused a stronger demand and higher price for the staple food-products. The demand for cotton was large, and the price high. . . . The prices of breadstuffs and provisions, the staples of the North, and of cotton and tobacco, the staples of the South, were not only absolutely but relatively high, and encouraged continued large production of these articles. The prices of most manufactured goods were comparatively low. After the war, the imports of these from England were very heavy. The long pent-up stream of English merchandise may be said to have flooded the world at the close of the Napoleonic wars. In this, as in other countries, imports were carried beyond the capacity for consumption, and prices fell much below the normal rates. The strain of this oversupply and fall of prices bore hard on the domestic manufacturers, especially on those who had begun and carried on operations during the restrictive period; and many of them were compelled to abandon their works."[1]

Why did not the people of the United States thrive under this inundation of cheap English goods? Prof. Taussig tells us: "Prices began to fall rapidly and heavily, and continued to fall through 1819. *The prices of the agricultural staples of the North and South underwent the greatest change, for the harvests in Europe were again good in 1818, the English corn laws of 1816 went into operation, and the demand for cotton fell off.* . . . The prices of manufactured goods had already declined, in con-

---

[1] "In 1816 the English exported immense quantities of manufactured goods to the Continent and to the United States. The results of these transactions were disastrous. Our paper money here also exercised its influence to encourage overtrading and over-importation. In 1817 the manufacturers were in distress, cries were heard against the inundations of foreign goods, against the drain of specie, and against the balance of trade."—SUMNER, "Protection in the United States."

sequence of the heavy importations in the years immediately following the war; when, therefore, the heavy fall took place in 1819 in the prices of food and of raw materials, in the profits of agriculture, in wages and in rents, the general result was advantageous for the manufacturers. . . . It is easy to see that the whole process was nothing more than the evolution of the new state of things which was to take the place of that of the period before 1808. *Before that year manufactured goods,* so far as they could be obtained by importation, *were imported cheaply* and *easily by means of large exports and freight earnings. These resources were now largely cut off. Exports declined, and the imports in the end had to follow them.*"

Thus, the facts of our external commerce inverted the economic arch upon which *the theory* of Prof. Perry and his school is built.

For all ordinary cotton and woolen fabrics, the industries may be considered as fairly established in 1824–'28. Tariff rates upon them have not increased the cost to the consumer. Iron, pig and bar, has encountered some special difficulties in production.[1]

---

[1] So long as charcoal was the only fuel used in making iron, its manufacture would be confined to countries where wood was abundant, as Norway, Sweden, Russia, and the American colonies. During much of the eighteenth century England imported her crude iron. The use of coke in the blast-furnace came in 1750, and Cort's processes of puddling and rolling in 1783. This worked a revolution in the production of iron. Bar-iron, but no crude iron, was imported into the United States before 1808, although manufactures of iron, nails, spikes, anchors, etc., were imported. In 1816 Congress was asked for the first time to extend protection to pig-iron, hammered bars, and rolled bars. Pig-iron continued to be made of charcoal. The bituminous coal-fields were too distant from the centers of population to render them available for the supply of coke. The process of puddling was not introduced here until 1830. The use of so refractory a fuel as anthracite coal, under a hot blast, was not introduced until 1838. This marked the turning-point in iron-production in the United States. Improved and cheap pro-

These industries had all come into existence between 1808 and 1816, when embargoes and war had operated to *restrict* foreign commerce as effectually as prohibitory duties. What was true of the cotton industry was true of the woolen and iron industries, and all the others.

Prof. Taussig's conclusions, and concessions to the *protective* principle in the case of cotton manufactures, are true of all the others. "Before 1808 the difficulties in the way of the introduction of this branch of industry were such that it made little progress. These difficulties were largely artificial; and though the obstacles arising from ignorance of the new processes and from the absence of experienced workmen were partly removed by the appearance of Slater,[1] they were sufficient, when combined with the stimulus which the condition of foreign trade gave to agriculture and the carrying-trade, to prevent any appreciable development. Had this period come to an end without any accompanying political change—had there been no embargo, no non-intercourse act, and no war with England—the growth of the cotton manufacture, however certain to have taken place in the end, *might have been subject to much friction and loss.* Conjecture as to what might have been is dangerous, especially in economic history; but it seems reasonable to suppose that, if the period

---

cesses in England, and the tariff of 1846, kept the industry in a backward state until 1861. Since then the American production has reached five million tons a year, and has a capacity to supply the domestic demand; and furnaces now make from one hundred to one hundred and fifty tons a day, when the old charcoal-furnaces could scarcely make fifty tons a week. In all essential respects, the industry was only fairly established in 1861. It was then an infant; it is now in robust maturity. It has cost us something, but it was indispensable, and was worth the cost. It has now been incurred " once for all."

[1] An English artisan who came to America in 1789. There were only four cotton-factories here in 1803.

before 1808 had come to an end quietly and without a jar, *the eager competition of well-established English manufacturers, the lack of familiarity with the processes,* and *the long-continued habit, especially in New England, of almost exclusive attention to agriculture, commerce, and the carrying-trade, might have rendered slow and difficult the change,* however inevitable it may have been, to greater attention to manufactures. Under such circumstances there might have been room for the legitimate application of protection to the cotton manufacture as a young industry. But this period, in fact, came to an end with a violent shock, which threw industry out of its accustomed grooves, and caused that striking growth of the cotton manufacture from 1808 to 1815 which has been described. *The transition caused much suffering; but it took place sharply and quickly. The interruption of trade was equivalent to a rude but vigorous application of protection, which did its work thoroughly.* . . . On the whole, although the great impulse to the industry was given during the war, the duties on cottons in the tariff of 1816 may be considered a judicious application of the principle of protection to young industries." (Prof. F. W. Taussig, "Protection to Young Industries, as applied in the United States," p. 36.)

It thus appears that the foundations of our industries were not laid in any ambitious purpose " to compete " with anybody, but a sincere, honest, and compulsory attempt to realize the Satisfactions of life out of the conditions which surrounded our fathers—to secure the only " wealth " accessible to them.

CHAPTER IX.

A FURTHER ANALYSIS—"THE ECONOMIC QUESTION"—"THE SCIENTIFIC QUESTION."

THERE are two points of view from which this whole discussion can take place; there are two ends or consummations which the observer may contemplate. The principles of the science will be equally applicable in the process of passing from the point of view to the end contemplated. The practical maxims of business, as I should prefer to call them, will be the same in each case. The man who enters upon a manufacturing enterprise proceeds, if he is successful, upon these "principles of the science" or "practical maxims of business," and there is no real dispute as to what they are. The man who enters upon a mercantile enterprise proceeds in like manner upon the "principles" and "practical maxims" applicable to his case, and there is no actual contention as to what they are. There is no mystery connected with the conduct of either pursuit. In point of fact, logically and chronologically, men had manufactured and exchanged with varying fortunes, centuries before Adam Smith wrote and before the science of political economy had been thought of. The analysis of the different steps of production, exchange, and consumption, could only be useful and take on a scientific value so far as it conformed to the outward facts. The science, if it is to exist, must proceed in accordance with "the buying and selling," and "the buying and selling" would not be conformed to the mold of the science. The operation of these laws does not depend on their recognition by students—or others.

The economist now comes upon a problem in his science presented by the conditions of the States of the Union on this continent a hundred years ago. He looks upon their natural resources, fertile lands, navigable rivers, harbors, forests, coal, ores, clays, and sands. He takes account of the mental and moral powers of the population considered as instruments for the production of wealth. He takes account of the necessaries, conveniences, and luxuries of life, in which they are wont, by virtue of the civilization they have reached, to indulge—the aggregate of the "desires" for which they are willing to seek "satisfaction" in the consumption of the wealth they have made the exertions to create.

He contemplates that in a hundred years there may be fifty millions of people, soon thereafter to be a hundred millions, and that they will then have overrun, taken possession of, and appropriated all the soil, or all the accessible and valuable portions.

He widens his view and draws within his range the conditions of the people of all the world, their industrial organization, their population, their standard of living, their capacities, and their instruments of production. He finds a vast, complicated, and effective *régime* of industry there. He contemplates the respects in which they possess superiority over the inhabitants of the United States. He inquires into the forces of nature which have been brought into the service of man. He estimates the advantages which steam and machinery have conferred upon different races in their efforts to conquer nature to human uses. He considers whether the people of the United States have the skill, the energy, the impulses, and the ability to extort the highest utility from these natural agents. He reckons the relative cost in labor and sacrifice —the will-power and the muscle-power involved in the production of any commodity, in this land and in foreign lands. He finds there is no product of labor as such, which can be produced by the inhabitants of any land in the same latitude, at a less expenditure of human toil than in the United States. He finds that in the United States we can raise certain food and raw materials from the soil at a much less expenditure of human labor than any other people, and that for these products there is a limited market in Europe. It further appears that the labor—the real sacrifice which a workman in Europe puts into a ton of iron or a yard of cloth—is no less than is required for the like ton or yard here; but the laborer there is content to take less wages and the capitalist less profits. He is willing to put forth an effort for production for which he is satisfied to take less remuneration in money or fewer commodities in the way of food, clothing, and shelter for his wife and children. He finds that the workman in the United States is unwilling to accept industrial employment on these terms. Rather than do that, he will prefer the comfort and the feeling of safety for his wife and children which he can find on the fertile lands which the Government of the United States will give him for nothing—or, at least, on terms which only repay the cost of surveying them for the settler. As the owner of a farm, his wages are now the whole product of his labor, swelled by the whole amount of the gratuitous contribution of the original powers of the soil (or the space which his natural instrument of production occupies)—the gift of this Government. It is not as an *agricultural laborer* that he gets these returns, for the hired labor on a farm is the lowest-priced labor in the country. It is as a *land-owner*—as *the proprietor* of the *natural instrument* of production which the State, for reasons touching the public welfare, had freely presented to him as a gift; for I believe it is conceded that the private title to soil is given to the owner as being simply the most *expedient* device, as yet, for reaching the best cultivation—producing to the society the greatest results. There is no natural inherent right in the case. That the owner pays value for it does not affect the question.[1]

The economist now sees that all the inhabitants, whose efforts are thus supplemented by natural agencies of all kinds, and who are in a situation economic to reap all the fruits of their work, have been enabled to adopt a higher standard of living, compared with a laborer abroad, and, by consequence, all the other people here demand like returns if they enter upon any of the other pursuits which are natural to a people possessed of civilization and the means of illustrating it, and which are necessary, if their various desires are to be satisfied. It is evident that there is a vast amount of comfort, content, and happiness possible to an industrious and intelligent people, thus in possession of the soil of half a continent. The different classes of society which the agriculturists are compelled to have in their midst—their parsons, their school-teachers, their cobblers, their clothes-menders, their cellar-diggers, and their fence-

---

[1] "Private ownership of land is only division of labor. If it is true, in any sense, that we all own the soil in common, the best use we can make of our undivided interests is to vest them all gratuitously (just as we now do) in any who will assume the function of directly treating the soil, while the rest of us take other shares in the social organization. The reason is, because in this way we all get more than we would if each owned some land and used it directly. Supply and demand now determine the distribution of population between the direct use of land and other pursuits. . . . In modern society the organization of labor is high. Some are land-owners and agriculturists; some are transporters, bankers, merchants, teachers; some advance the product of manufacture. It is a system of division of functions."—SUMNER, "Social Classes."

makers—can only be had on the condition that "they are admitted to a participation in the abundance enjoyed" not alone "by the agricultural population," but by the owners of the soil, timber, water-power, sands, ores, etc., in the soil. For the manufacture of their shoes, their clothes, their carpets, their hats, their plows and chains, their cutlery, their glass, their sewing-thread, their salt, their borax, and their quinine, etc., it seems there are people in England and Germany willing to undertake them for less wages, and consequently will furnish them for a less price. The farmer finds that by sending his cotton, his wheat, and tobacco to England and Germany, he can apparently, and for the time being, really get more iron, *or* steel, *or* calico, *or* woolen goods, *or* silks, *or* wines, *or* gloves, for any given amount of his surplus, than his neighbors will consent to supply the same commodities for. But he can only get from abroad these commodities to the extent to which he can pay for them by the surplus of his abundant crops. If he does not already know it, he will speedily find out that, in the long run, he can only get the commodities he needs, the imports, by means of the food and cotton he has to sell, the exports. If he can not sell abroad he can not buy abroad. He will find he can not get his iron, *and* steel, *and* calico, *and* woolen goods, *and* silks, *and* wines, *and* gloves, with the proceeds of what he can sell. His consumption of manufactured goods is so great that he can not purchase them all abroad with the surplus of any salable commodity which he produces.

Our economist here has most of the elements of the problem which the American question presents. The people here who created their government, freed from political alliances with all the other governments, had an option to begin an industrial system undisturbed by any entangling alliances with existing industrial organizations. Contemplating all political, all social, all ethical, all historical, all sentimental, all national, and all ethnological considerations, or looking at economic considerations alone, which of two possible solutions of their problem should they adopt? For the present we shall assume the jural power to adopt either. Divesting themselves of all impulses, except to create the greatest amount of wealth, how should they apply their industry to the materials in hand? Or, taking the more generalized form of the proposition, how should they expend their efforts to realize the greatest amount of satisfactions?

These two problems of economics may be stated thus:

1. In the words of Prof. Jevons: "*Given a certain population, with various needs and powers of production, in possession of certain lands and other sources of materials: required the mode of employing their labor which will maximize the utility of their produce.*" ("Theory of Political Economy," p. 289.)

2. As given by Prof. Sumner: "*Throwing aside all technicalities, the case is to find how, for a given exertion and sacrifice, to get the maximum of material good.*" ("Princeton Review," March, 1881.)

Two distinct forms of possible achievement are open to us, as we work under the first or the second formula—as we *direct* the forces at our disposal—or "let things alone."

Under the first formula we shall pay little or no attention to industrial conditions abroad. We apply *all* the powers, capabilities, and energies of *all* "the population" to *all* "the lands and other sources of our materials." To this end we might invite the people of all the world to come and help us. In fact, we did invite them all (except China), and, in fact, about ten millions did come. This mode of opening up the opportunities for the full action and interaction of our mental endowments and physical conditions would set no limit to the productive creations of our industry, except the limitations of labor (number of laborers) and capital. If we were free from foreign interference—if, for example, we had been the only country on the planet—*cæteris paribus*, no absolute bounds could be set to the increase of improved farms, houses, railroads, engines, looms, tools, carriages, pianos, and the thousands of objects which swell the inventory of national " needs "; no bounds except the desires of the people and the working-power of their brains and muscles. Their production would go on under the laws of perfect competition between labor and capital, and under remuneration in exact correspondence to labor and sacrifice. Our national inventory in 1885, in these items of wealth, reaches the enormous sum of $53,000,000,000.[1]

But we were not the only people on the planet. This *régime* was impossible unless some plan of *restriction* was devised—some exclusion from our market of some of the commodities made abroad, either by the mental resolution of the people, or their statute to that effect. These consequences might be made to flow from the enactment of a positively prohibitory statute as to foreign goods. They might ensue from the indirect effects of foreign political complications, as the " Berlin Decree," " Orders in Council," and the " Milan Decree," during the period of the Napoleonic wars; or they might result from a state of war in which we were parties, as in 1812–'16; or again, they can be made to flow from a " protective tariff."

The distinct end thus proposed could be reached by *restrictions* imposed on the importation of foreign manufactures. The domestic manufacture could thus be *protected*. Under protection, the domestic manufacture *could* be established, for, as we see, it has been established—nay,

---

[1] Mr. David A. Wells puts it at $64,000,000,000.

more, in consequence of, and not in spite of, defensive duties. Nor need the question be complicated with considerations of "revenue." Protection is to be defended or attacked on the merits or demerits of the industrial philosophy underlying it, dissociated from revenue. In its essence it is not a question of *taxation* at all. All attempts to deal with it from that point of view only obscure the issue, and insistence on treating it as a question of *taxation* is intended for dishonesty or sophistry. I do not allege that protection and revenue are exclusive of each other, for I hold it demonstrable that they are not; indeed, Prof. Sidgwick, in his work, the last formal treatise issued from orthodox English economy, has sufficiently proved that taxes laid for revenue may be made to operate protectively and conversely. But, as Prof. Sumner says, "the line between them is sharp and precise, and we can discuss the wisdom of protection, entirely aside from the wisdom of raising revenue from customs duties." I am willing to accede to Prof. Perry's challenge: "If protection be good, it is good in and of itself; if it is bad, it has no business to be begging to lean on something so respectable as revenue. The burden of proof, at any rate, lies upon the man who brings in a theory interrupting the play of natural laws. Let him bring forward and prove his theory of restriction. Let us hear the arguments and see the grounds that justify the prohibition of an advantageous trade." The real question is whether we can induce or stimulate the home industries, by the means of defensive duties, to a production of commodities which will supply all the wants of our people in the greatest ultimate abundance and cheapness.

Nobody has made any proposal to prohibit "an advantageous trade." We are trying to see if we can not do better. We have been exploring the data of our own peculiar case in its peculiar facts to see if it would not be more advantageous to supply our wants without any foreign trade. "Trade" is no very potent word to conjure with. "The trader is a necessity, not a power." If we can dispense with him, we have got rid of a serious source of "taxation." The end proposed by protection is the supply of all our wants, so far as possible, by the use of our own productive agencies.

Under Prof. Sumner's formula, we shall go about our national economy from an entirely different direction. We now take cognizance of what foreign nations have to sell, and the terms on which we can buy. We notice the nature of their wants and the extent to which we can supply them on terms advantageous to ourselves. We shall soon see that their requirements from us will be the gauge of our commerce with them. They have not newly come into the industrial world as we have. The adaptations of their internal trades and exchanges have been already made with substantial fixity. The adjustments of their foreign commerce have come to something like stability—their industrial and commercial systems have been established. This, at once, places us under the necessity of adjustments and adaptations to already existing systems. They may be natural to the original members of the system, because the system is a development, a growth. To us, they are artificial, and we must fit ourselves in and piece them out here and there. Long before we appeared, their industrial procession was formed. And now, on our arrival, we must "fall in" when and where we can squeeze out a place for ourselves. With the procession as a whole we can not keep up, except by staying at the rear.

Their competition is not effective against us in skill, energy, brain-power, and muscle-power. They can not work faster, or more persistently, or more effectively, but they are willing to take less remuneration for their expenditure of labor-power. It is a warfare in which their weakness becomes strength, and we are driven off the field.

But there are fields in which we are their superiors. There is one point at which competition can not drive us out. There are fields in which we have the aid of the forces of nature. Agriculture, the raising of raw products, enables us to summon the original and indestructible powers of the soil to our assistance. The superabundant rewards of fertile acres added to the rewards of our own labor, constitute an aggregate which enables us to re-enter at one point of the international struggle.

In the struggle " a given exertion and sacrifice " at that point will yield a product with an exchangeable value, if not unduly overworked, which equalizes our condition. That product then is the one to which the science of modern English political economy requires us to confine our industrial energies. What of skill and intelligent direction that pursuit requires we are to devote to it. All our industrial efforts are to be adjusted to the production of the commodities in which alone we have the superiority over the foreign producers.

So far as the foreign markets will take the product of the most advantageous industry, so far we shall reap the highest economic gain; just filling the demands of that market we shall be in economic equilibrium. In case we cause an overproduction we shall lose our exchange power. In case there is no market abroad, we shall lose the whole value, and besides be compelled to do without the foreign commodity, for which the only reliance we had was the export of the product of this most advantageous industry.

For "a given exertion and sacrifice" made in our special field we produce, say, twenty bushels of wheat. For a like exertion and sacrifice made in the production

of iron we produce, say, one ton of iron. If the exchange
is made here at home, the ton of iron will require the
whole twenty bushels. If the exchange is made abroad,
we shall get the ton of iron for fifteen bushels of the wheat.
The latter transaction manifestly gives us "the maximum
of material good" for that particular "exertion and sacrifice." But there is a limit to the quantity of wheat which
the foreign market will take on any terms, and there is a
very distinct limit to what it will take from the United
States. That limit is the amount which it takes to feed
the people in other countries, diminished by the total food-product of these other countries. It is fixed by the necessities for food and the supplies of food in these same
foreign countries, and does not in any sense depend on the
amount of their products which we need. There is no
definite limit to the iron and other things which we need.
The case of the ton of iron and the fifteen bushels of wheat
is by itself very plain sailing. But suppose that in the purchase of tea, coffee, and sugar, drugs, dye-stuffs, and chemicals, which are now articles of necessity, and of French
wines and foreign fruits, which are articles of luxury, and
of silks and satins, and fine clothes, which are articles of
fashion, we had supplied the foreign demand for the products of our most advantageous industry: then how is the
ton of iron to be obtained? Or if the iron is obtained, how
are the other things to be procured? One at a time we
can supply our wants. But when the infinitude of our
desires is aggregated, what relation will our exportables, the
purchase-money, bear to the aggregate of importables, the
satisfaction which we must purchase abroad? We have
seen that they break hopelessly down. Can the given "exertions and sacrifices" of us *all* be made in like manner
to result in the maximum of material good to us all?

But there is an outstanding reason to which we have not

yet adverted, which prevents the supply of the wants of all of us by the foreign exchange. This is the fact that there is no market in the world which contains the full supplies which our maximum of good involves. The world has not as yet accumulated the capital, labor, and skill which are adequate to produce the requisite *surplus* of manufactured goods—goods made in the *competing*, "protected" industries—which are natural and necessary to us. No nation or group of nations is rich enough to do this for us. We must make the remainder, then, at home. The argument in hand is only in reply to the logic which undertakes to say what ought to be.

The "given exertion and sacrifice" will yield the product here, but what creates the answering demand there? What principle of the science of political economy correlates the capacity to produce here, with the capacity to consume there? Supply and demand? Then the supply is to be kept down to the demand. We gauge our industry to the foreign capacity to consume, which is confessedly limited. Having filled that capacity, we either do nothing, or, having reduced our most advantageous industry to *nil*, we now take to other industries. That is, having overproduced ourselves out of the foreign market, we are now poor enough to undertake the hitherto "unprofitable" industries; we are compelled to abandon an "advantageous trade."

Bursting suddenly into the industrial world, and producing, without reference to foreign markets, there could in the nature of things be no assurance, not even a chance, that our production would fit the existing conditions of a world's market. There could be no rational prevision of the state of the world's market, and no rational adjustment to its needs. Discarding exchangeable values, we should have gone on producing illimitable supplies; what might have saved us, and what has saved us, was *the nature* of *our production*, and the fact that it *furnished subsistence*, especially to men in our own country. If we had a trade with some other planet—if Mars, for instance, had been an available foreign market—we might have reached the maximum of material good by exchanges. As it was, we had no recourse, except either to consume it at home, in the prosecution of allied industries, or stop making the "exertion and sacrifice" required in its production.

The second formula will do this for us: it will give us the maximum of material good on two conditions, namely: that we make the *precise* "exertion and sacrifice," and no more, necessary to produce *a surplus*, which the *foreign market will take;* and then that we continue only *to need* and *desire* the *number* and *amount* of *things* which *that surplus will pay for.*

Conformity to these conditions could only be realized by legislative omniscience, which the protectionist never ventured to invoke; or the "guidance of an Invisible hand," which even the theology of Adam Smith never recognized as operative. The true problem is, then, *not* "for a given exertion and sacrifice" to get the maximum of "material good." It is rather to so occupy our "field of employment" that we can expend upon it *all* the *exertions* and *all the sacrifices* which we *as a people* are *willing* and *able to make;* to get the maximum for all which is possible, when *all our abilities* and *all our energies* are called into play.

Unless one occupies the point of view from which he can contemplate all the efforts which the whole fifty millions of us are capable of making, and all the good which the whole fifty millions of us are capable of enjoying, he has no business either as the writer of text-books on economy, of essays in reviews, or as a statesman in Congress, to assume to be in intelligent possession of knowledge, or to suggest intelligent legislation on this subject. Such empiricists might as well undertake to make provision for the civic wants of the population of a great city, provide institutions affecting its sanitary, police, and fiscal systems, after having simply explored one of its blind back alleys. Because some of the inhabitants got their water-supply from the town-pump, they assume that all could; or, because one sewer relieved part of the waste, they conclude that it could take it all out of the corporate limits.

Because we have *some* most advantageous industries, which employ *some* of our energies and *some* of our skill, it is decreed that we are not to occupy, with the energies and skill unemployed, any less advantageous ones. Because we can make some exchanges advantageously abroad, it is assumed we can make all our exchanges advantageously abroad. Our national growth and the fullness of our national life are to be adjusted by and adapted to the conditions of the outer industrial world. We are asked to regulate our conduct by the exigencies of exchangeable values, and not by the exercise of all our productive forces. These are to be employed, not with reference to their inherent and natural capacities, but are to be fitted to a Procrustean bed, not made to our measure. Our vast powers of production are to be idle, or to be subordinated to the mere accidents of foreign exchange values—our stream of creative agencies to be kept within the bounds of the foreign estuary into which it flows—our illimitable freedom of scope and variety to be dwarfed into the measure of the comfortless slavery, and consequent want of purchasing and consuming power, of the toiler in other lands. We are to be cast in a mold the size and form of which are not in correspondence with our internal forces, but which conform to the repressive power of an external rigid obstacle.

The advocate, then, of unrestricted trade must contemplate the limitations which thus in the nature of his problem surround the growth of the nation: a certain number of laborers only, and a certain amount of capital only, can profitably enter into the special industries of the country. We take up a limited field in the international division of labor. That "division of labor is limited by the market." There are no canons of the science of political economy by which we can forecast, under this *régime*, the rate of our progress and growth. What may be positively affirmed by any man of average intelligence would be the sharp antithesis between the outcome with "free trade" and "protection." One economist may, in entire good faith, prefer the form of national life which would naturally flow from agricultural pursuits—the comfort, contentment, and intelligence of a people devoted to food-raising. They make their few foreign exchanges without excitement. They are out of the roar and waste of industrial machinery. They are exempt from the suffering and disaster of commercial crises. But they have bought their ease and independence at the cost of "wealth" and higher social life. The decision must turn on the radically different views of human society which the observer takes. The free-trader says: "A new country can not have the higher social development until the population begins to grow dense. It is so with us yet. We have not the literature or the science or the fine arts of the old countries, but we have not their poverty and misery. We must take our advantages and disadvantages together." (Sumner, "Protection in the United States," p. 26.) We are to accept, then, our assignment to the *rôle* of food-raising for other nations. In the long decades of the future we may have a population dense enough to give us a higher social development. It is true there is no case in all history in which such a state of things ever arose in a purely agricultural state, or out of an agricultural state without "a lift." But in time the leveling process will reduce our profits to a point at which manufacturing will come in naturally. We can not force them. We go on rudely competing with all the food-raisers of the world—competing in a market which is limited and variable. We shall have a uniform overproduction, and the market will be a place where we can give away our goods rather than a mart in which we can sell them. The laws of trade and the principles of nature as expounded by Bastiat and Perry compel us to share the "gratuities" of our soil with the foreign nations with whom we trade, and to raze the exchangeable value of our products to the point where the American farmer only gets compensation for his own labor—or his "onerous contribution" to their value. All over the world the food-raisers are making all the crops which are possible—a farm is an instrument of production which the owner is not likely to abandon. In point of fact there are only two or three nations on the whole earth which do not raise their own food. In most countries there is a surplus—an overproduction. Of course, exchange values disappear. At the same time the special characteristics of the commodity in which the overproduction takes place disguise and hide the enormous economic fallacy which urges such an overproduction. The food-raiser can subsist on his food—he can consume his own product—he will not die of starvation. He can, at least, "live and be comfortable." So far in the United States the free-traders have been able to hide away competitors in overcrowded industries on the soil. This device has been open to them. Thus the surplus labor has been kept in abeyance, and has offered no hindrance to the free application of abstract theories. An ugly factor in the problem was thus put out of sight, but not got rid of. The unemployed laborer will soon reappear to us, and provision must be made for him. So special an overproduction in any other industry would be seen to be attended with fatal commercial consequences. Such an overproduction, and so continuous, in calico, or iron, or steel rails, or shoes, would destroy their manufacturers. These must be sold—these must be exchanged. The farmer can eat his overproduction some time or other. The glut is only inconvenient, it is not fatal, industrially. But the manufacturer can not eat his calico, nor the iron-man his steel rails. If they could, we should see overproduction on a large scale.

Inasmuch as things are as they are, the mill-owner, the furnace-man, and the anthracite-coal miner must now " shut down." But the farmer never shuts down. There is neither strike nor " lock-out " in his industry. The enormous commercial gains which the farmer fails to reap—or, rather, the enormous losses which accrue to him by reason of his overproduction—are forever concealed by virtue of the consumable nature of his product.[1] If they were salable, as well as consumable, the wretched waste which we know annually takes place in American tillage would be manifest, and could be avoided. Not only in remote and inaccessible sections, but in regions which may be seen by the traveler from the window of the railroad-car in which he is riding, may be observed wretched evidence of the lethargy and inertia which follow productive fields, careless methods, and unsalable crops. Corn half gathered or in unopened cribs—stacks of unused hay and stalks—ill-fed cattle trampling their fodder under feet—betray the nerve-

---

[1] In 1880 the crop of wheat, corn, oats, barley, rye, buckwheat, and potatoes aggregated 2,885,853,071 bushels, and sold for $1,442,559,918. In 1881, what was called a short crop of the same products—to wit, 2,175,175,-164—sold for $1,570,248,541. In other words, 710,677,007 less bushels sold for $127,488,623 more.

less, motiveless result of using a natural instrument of high productive power, with capacity to keep a man from dying of mere starvation, but which besides possesses little wealth-creating value. The waste of labor, energy, and capital misdirected into these most advantageous industries, with its reaction on the character of the people, has vastly exceeded all the losses incurred by protection in the effort to divert them into "unprofitable" furnaces, factories, and mills.

We are seeking a solution of the question in its economic aspects, and not in its political, moral, and educational aspects. I am not aware that it has ever been contended that the gross annual product of the industry of the United States is not greater under the doctrine of our productive forces than under the notion of exchangeable values—that we can not make more values at home than we can buy abroad; nor am I aware that any free-trader has ever indicated what direction skill and labor were to take if we abandoned the protected industries. They make vague statements that people will find something to do. "As for the scope for varied talents," says Prof. Sumner, answering Alexander Hamilton's celebrated report of 1791, " persons *go to the places* which offer an arena for their talents. They do not sit still and say, 'Let us make an arena here.' . . . As for the varied field for enterprise, *the world* opens that, and our enterprises seek the place of advantage."

Precisely: such "persons" and such "enterprises" can leave the country and seek employment and habitations elsewhere. Thus easily the free-trader whistles one fourth of our population and one half of the value of the nation's property down the wind. In this way he makes the facts conform to his theory, and establishes the ideal of his republic. The protectionist *would* sit still and say: "Let us make an arena *here*. By *restrictions*, industries here will diversify themselves under the operation of natural forces. The development of society will be as regular and natural as that of a plant. There will be no forcing, and the bud will burst into a blossom at the proper moment. Keep the foreign competition off our backs, and we shall at once enter upon the domestic arena in all its dimensions without loss of time, waste of capital, or dissipation or misdirection of energy. It may stimulate us to greater exertions, and we may work harder; but we are capable of the exertions, and are willing to work harder. We reap the reward of our untiring exertions." We see that there is neither a waste of one nor a miscarriage of the other. They will be embodied in articles of material "wealth," and we shall make and have exactly as many as we choose to have. Of this we can have no assurance under the conditions of dependence on foreign commerce and the exchangeable value of our own commodities always determined in a market always oversupplied.

Prof. Perry exclaims, "There can be no science of exchanges if an economic reason can be given for restricting them." Not stopping to expose the ambiguity lurking in his use of the word *restriction*, it is manifest that we have, from our two points of view, a choice between the foreign exchange and the domestic exchange. We can at our pleasure have either, but can not have both at our option at the same time—we can not have the one and then the other by turns—we can not vibrate thus between stagnation and activity—the forces of production can not thus be turned on and off at pleasure. In manufactures, such as can only exist under some form of excluding the foreign product, it is, as we shall see, all or none. So far as we shut out the product of foreign labor we are thrown back to the employment of domestic labor. This you may call "restricting exchanges," if you please—it is restricting *some* exchanges. But we have infinitely enlarged our domestic exchanges. We have exercised our option, and now the number of domestic exchanges has increased many fold. If there is "a gain in every exchange," which is the pet benignity of the science, the exchanges are multiplied, and the gains are shared by our own people. We have provoked a double production and a double consumption. Where is the waste? Where the loss? Where the friction? The only extra *cost to the nation* for all and all kinds of the products of its protected industries is the added comfort, the increased food, better clothes, superior shelter which its laborers have consumed and enjoyed—a result made possible by their higher wages. The American laborer is a higher-priced "tool." But the only true function of a government is to make such tools possible. We scarcely dare use the words *man* and *his welfare* as terms involved in discussing political economy, for fear of being suspected of sociological speculations. If now we take into the account the number of people in the United States and the inventory of their wealth, it is obviously absolutely and proportionally greater than free foreign trade would have given us. If we substitute "satisfaction of desires" for "wealth" as the true end of all our labor and abstinence, we shall the more readily agree to this.[1] The free-trader is confronted with the palpable, undeniable, inex-

---

[1] "*Hence, either prosperity in a free-trade country or distress in a protectionist country is fatal to protectionism, while distress in a free-trade country or prosperity in a protectionist country proves nothing against free trade.*"

This flexible test of results I find in a little book, "Protectionism," issued by Prof. Sumner since the text was in type. Of course, on that test, no argument from experience and observation possesses any validity. Prof. Sumner risks the whole debate on the proposition, "*Free trade is only a mode of liberty.*" Protection is "a social abuse, an economic blunder, and a political evil." In dealing with it in "Protectionism," he says he has not troubled himself "to keep or throw off scientific or professional dignity." His last

pugnable fact that the domestic production and exchange have resulted in an inestimable increase of the products, things, commodities, the property, the fixed and floating capital of the nation, as well as the population of the nation. In the nature of things, if all the men engaged in rendering mutual "services" to each other live here, there must be more products on this area than if half of them lived three thousand miles away. The free-trader keeps up his monotone that protection "does not increase wealth. It is mathematically demonstrable that it lessens wealth." He only means that some-of-us might have more comfort with less work if the others had not entered into this arena of the world's industry alongside of that some-of-us. He probably assumes, and justly, that free trade would have kept them away.

Under the second formula, then, *a given exertion and sacrifice*, by some-of-us, may yield *the maximum of material good* to some-of-us—the others not being in America. But all the exertions of all-of-us expended in view of foreign exchange may only yield the minimum of material good. Our imports are limited by, and must be paid for, by our exports. The moment we have supplied the foreign demand, that moment we must quit wanting more foreign things, quit having more population, and quit making more agricultural products. The maximum of material good will be derived only by that some-of-us who own the soil, and the others-of-us have no call to live in the United

---

work shows no new ground occupied by him. I do not say that Prof. Sumner is not right in this business; I only say I am unable to see that he is right.

Believing he can safely stand on his abstract maxim, he deals with protectionism as "deserving only contempt and scorn, satire and ridicule."

If he is right, he can afford the air of the burn-your-bridges-behind-you young man which, intentionally, is made to pervade "Protectionism." If he is not right, his book is about the worst piece of professional insolence yet put into print.

States, and no calling if we live there. If, after that, all of us go on producing food, we can only procure the "satisfaction" of our "desires" for manufactured goods by producing them at home, and under the conditions of *protection*. A farmer is just as capable of forming a correct judgment on the purchasing power of his products under these limitations as any college professor.

More than that, we shall fail to get the commodities we need, and which constitute our "material good." Of such commodities—the product of the competing protected industries—the people of the United States consume annually about $3,000,000,000. We import about $400,000,000 of like commodities, and about $300,000,000 worth of merchandise, which we can neither raise in this climate nor manufacture. If we went without the latter, we should still (unless our nature was changed by rude labor) desire $2,600,000,000 of goods made in protected industries. We can export only $700,000,000 in agricultural products. How are we to get this $2,600,000,000 of "satisfaction" of "desires"? for this is what constitutes the maximum of material good—our welfare. This is, at last, the use of "wealth."

Prof. Sumner's solution of the problem breaks down. You can not *buy* $2,600,000,000 worth of imports with $700,000,000 of exports. The foreign market does not want its pay in *our kind* of merchandise—food and raw materials. That market has other sources of supply, as we have found out to our discomfiture. We shall endeavor to analyze this more in detail in the chapter entitled "Schedule A."

The supplying of our "various needs"—the "various needs" of all of us—is the object of all our industrial efforts. The "maximum of material good" for "a given exertion and sacrifice" is a description of a case in which *a few men*, who had *appropriated natural agents*, might thrive best if they were allowed to maintain their advantage as monopolists.

We are now in a position to answer two of the questions propounded by Prof. Sumner.

"The *economic* question about the tariff is, Does it enable *the population* of the country to command *greater material good* for *a given effort?*" We answer distinctly, that it enables *all the population* to *command the greatest material good;* that is, *to supply all their various wants* at the *least possible effort.*

"The *scientific* question about protection is, Does it lessen *the ratio* of *effort* and *sacrifice* to *comfort* and *enjoyment?*" We answer distinctly, that protection—that is, the scheme of direct production—gives us the highest comfort and greatest enjoyment with the least effort. In other words, the ratio of effort to comfort and enjoyment —to the "satisfaction" of our "desires"—is less under a *régime* of the use of all our productive forces than under the theory of exchange values.

It is not only the *easiest*, it is the only way to procure satisfaction of our desires. When there is only *one* real route to a given result, it is idle to discuss its relative, advantages, or disadvantages, with respect to purely imaginary ones. When there is only one actual way to procure a thing, it is a useless waste of time to discuss the "*ratios*" of "effort" involved in exploring the impossible or the speculative.

Two railroads run from New York—one to Philadelphia, the other half-way, to Trenton. The rates to each place, we will suppose, are the lowest possible on each route. The fare to Philadelphia is two dollars and a half, the fare to Trenton is one dollar. To a man who desires to make the entire trip, the only resource is the through line. His maximum of material good for this effort is to get to Philadelphia. To him it is nothing that the fare to Trenton is at a lower rate: the cost is not the determining motive for him.

To a people who are desirous of consuming $2,600,000,000 worth of goods, information where they can get only $700,000,000 worth of them, even at a less rate, is of no particular use. In the case in hand, the $2,600,000,000 is the maximum of good we desire to reach, and we find it in the home market.

This is the terminus of the passage represented by the through-trip ticket. As it is the only route that takes us through, cost, again, is not the determining motive—especially as the whole trip is made at the least possible cost. The satisfaction of the desire can only thus be obtained.

CHAPTER X.

A STILL FURTHER ANALYSIS—"THE POLITICAL QUESTION"—"THE POPULAR QUESTION."

We have shown satisfactory reasons for believing that the greatest annual product of the industry of the people of the United States, as a whole, can be achieved under the subjection of our own natural resources to the operation of our own productive forces. No feasible scheme of entering upon all the industries natural to us has ever been indicated, except by restrictions imposed upon the foreign producer against his invading our domestic market with like commodities. For shortness, we call this scheme protection. Does a protective tariff—imposts levied for the sake of protection—bring about an unequal distribution of the rewards of our industry? As the total annual product of the industry and services of us all is finally distributed in wages, rent and interest to the owners of labor, land, and capital, does a protective tariff result in an unjust and inequitable division of the recompense among these three great factors of production? Or, to adopt the questions framed by Prof. Sumner, pregnant with his prejudgment, the inquiries may be thus stated:

"The *political* question about protection is: Does the statute enacted by the legislature *alter the distribution* of property so that *one man* enjoys *another man's earnings?* Has the State a law in operation which enables *one citizen to collect taxes of another?*

"The popular question about protection is, Does it prevent me from *supporting myself and my family* by my labor as well as I could if there were no *protective taxes?*"

Of course, every free-trade professor, every free-trade scribbler in the reviews, every free-trade speaker on the stump, and every free-trade statesman from his seat in Congress, triumphantly answers these questions affirmatively. He says "Yes," and complacently goes his way as if he had got to the bottom of the problem.

Let us start with a supposition, which, in fact, is not all a supposition. Let us assume that the 55,000,000 people in the United States, and the lands and minerals of the nation, were the only people and the only lands on the earth. Let us suppose these people to have discovered mutual wants to the aggregate of $10,000,000,000 annually, which is the fact. Let us suppose that they think it worth the while to go to the cost of supplying those wants by the exchange of services in procuring food, clothing, shelter, transportation, education, and religious appliances, indulgence in amusements, luxuries, and vices, just as we do think it worth while. Let us suppose that, having reached a certain stage of civilization, we think it worth while to *tax* ourselves with the physical and mental efforts necessary to satisfy our desires, which is just the tax we now do impose on ourselves. It is manifest that, under the operation of economic laws in this community, services would be exchanged as nearly as possible in a human society under the laws of demand and supply. Each laborer, each land-owner, each capitalist, would receive his true and exact proportion of the total annual product. So far as the operation of economic laws, scientific laws, were concerned, no "one man would enjoy another man's earnings," "no one citizen could collect taxes of another." Skill, efficiency, industry, thrift, intelligence, integrity, and persistence, would be in full exercise and receive just remuneration. All would be natural, straightforward, and equitable. Monopoly could not exist; a monopoly would be impossible in any business open to the competition of all the labor and capital of 55,000,000 people. If anything is settled in, around, or about the science of political economy, and is patent to observation, it is this, "that no industry can for any length of time obtain a higher rate of profit than that which is common in the community." And if monopolies did grow up, they would be domestic monopolies, subject to the regulative control of our own legislation, and not foreign monopolies against which we should be without remedy. The power of capital to grow and accumulate inheres in its nature, and is not a question of geography, or free trade, or protection.[1] So far as the science of political economy is able to predict anything, it would declare that in this community, so circumstanced, each member would take out of the annual products all which his services entitled him to—subject to the contingencies which crime and accident impose on any society of human beings.

Let us now, after the manner of the *a priori* economists, introduce the "disturbing elements" of *the other*

---

[1] Ordinarily accurate observation will show that the great fortunes made in this country were not made by the organizers of the protected industries. The average of the profits in iron, steel, the textile fabrics, and pottery, is the one usual in the country. Only when the patent laws gave a monopoly of process have there been undue earnings—and these conditions operated upon all patented processes, whether in protected or non-protected industries.

The great fortunes of the land have been made by sagacious capitalists, who seized upon valuable railroad routes ; took the ownership of large holdings of valuable mineral or timber lands ; discovered valuable mines of gold, silver, or copper ; or, more than all, appropriated the earnings of other people by speculation in the grain and stock markets.

nations with their industrial systems. In what way should we, for economic reasons, permit it to disturb our organization of industries? At what point would foreign nations, or any of them, possess superior productive efficiency? In soil? No. In skill? No. In industry? No. In machinery? No. In any natural gratuity? No, except certain tropical fruits. In raw materials? No. In motive power? No. In "cost of production" reckoned in actual effort and sacrifice? No. In "cost of production" reckoned in labor and abstinence? No. In what, then, will their "superiority" consist? In "cost of production" reckoned in the wages of labor and returns to capital. With this "advantage" they can undersell us in our own market, or compel us to produce under like rates of wages of labor and profit on capital. The disturbance they create destroys the just and natural equilibrium under which we had been working. The American labor thus displaced can find no "something else" to do here, and must stand idle or go to other countries.[1] This we have abundantly seen. We now apply protection. It restores the original, natural *status quo*. Everybody gets every commodity he needs as cheap as the richest natural resources, the best organized industry, and well-paid labor will permit. "Protective taxes," as they are called, introduce no inequality and work no injustice which did not exist in the isolated nation. The nation, as a whole, has become evolved into

---

[1] "No industry will ever be given up, except in order to take up a better one; and if, under free trade, any of our industries should perish, it would only be because the removal of restrictions enabled some other industry to offer so much better rewards, that labor and capital would seek the latter. It is plain that, if a man does not know of any better way to earn his living than the one which he is in, he must remain in that, or *move to some other place*."—SUMNER, "Protectionism."

Yes, it is very likely that free trade would drive the capital and labor out of the country.

a highly specialized organism, with differentiated organs and specialized functions. It *costs* more to be a vertebrate than to be a jelly-fish. The nation must submit to the *tax* —as the free-trader likes to play on words—of having higher and more numerous sensations at the cost of greater expenditure of vital force. But the object of all production is consumption; the end of all consumption is destruction. The motive of all effort is satisfaction of desires. The possession of these sensations, and the ability to gratify them, has been the object of its struggles, the test of its civilization, and end of its existence. In the environment in which it found itself, and with the capabilities locked up in its being, the jelly-fish must perish as such or pass into the perfected organism. The transformation doubtless cost something; its energies were taxed in the operation. But it "pays" to be a vertebrate.

Now, to say that in the United States, grown into a highly diversified organism, under the conditions of just and symmetrical development, one part is maintained at the expense of another; that "one man enjoys," or can, under any known economic laws, "enjoy another man's earnings," is a gross blunder which amounts to an absurdity. The whole nation, socially, politically, and industrially, is a growth. The society, as an organized unit, discharges functions *as a whole;* and these are other than, and in addition to, the functions discharged by its several parts.[1] The anatomist, by means of the dissecting-knife, or

---

[1] Prof. Sumner is constrained to admit something like this: "It" (the nation) "exists historically and traditionally, and as both it is handed down to us. It is an organized human society, whose limits are given historically, and are maintained for convenience, because they allow play to certain local interests, prejudices, traditions, habits, and customs. Whether it is formed by accident and immemorial tradition, or by colonization and legislative act, it develops an organic life. The society, as such, develops functions." ("Protection in the United States," p. 10.)

by chemical analysis, treats separately the different organs of the body, to see their mechanical structure, or to learn by observation what operations they actually perform. We thus speak of the gastric juices, the liver, the brains, the heart. Separated from the body, the parts become meaningless; and, while they continue to bear the name, they cease to be the thing they were when joined in the vital processes of life, and health, and growth. We speak of laborers, capitalists, landlords, producers, and consumers. There are no such people detached from society.

In a proper environment, no one part of a true organism grows at the expense of another part. The liver can not complain that it would have less work to do if the stomach did not *tax* it, nor could the brain exclaim that its efficiency is reduced by the necessity of sharing nutrition and nerve-force with the stomach, nor the stomach rebel and set up for itself, because it was compelled "to share its abundance" with the heart and the vascular system. All such attempted treatment of the separate parts of a distinct organism is not only negatively useless, but is positively vicious, in suggesting error, and leads to conclusions which must be undone and corrected. We fail to identify the real organism we have in hand, and we undertake to deal with the parts as if they were new wholes.

If the United States, under the supposition we have made, would have grown up into an orderly, symmetrical system, with co-ordinated structure and balanced functions, as must have been the case, then there is demonstrably nothing in the *foreign* environment which must necessarily have changed it. We have, by restrictions on foreign trade, preserved our original and natural condition. We are, at least, no worse off than if our territory constituted the planet, and we had it all to ourselves. Under such a form of growth, to talk about protection—under which we preserved this status—as altering the distribution of property so that one man enjoys another man's earnings, or as enabling one citizen to collect taxes of another, is a fallacy of the same kind as the idiotic system of accounts in which the brain should be charged with the earnings of the stomach, or the nervous system be treated as collecting a tax on the digestive organs. Unquestionably protection, as against free trade, altered the distribution and consumption of property; that is, we produced and consumed different kinds of commodities in a greater variety, and in different proportions; but that had no effect to transfer one man's earnings to another. It did not repeal or suspend the great overmastering law of competition.

Let us see about these first beginnings. The nation, if industrially fitted to exist, must be self-supporting. In the providence of God, populations have settled upon the districts of the habitable earth where they could live. The great migrations which have swept its surface from time to time have come to stay and not turn their faces backward. In some cases they have moved in a measured, orderly way, as the resources of field and forest and seas invited; in many instances, by great floods of conquest, as of the Huns and Vandals into southern Europe. And last came the European overflow into America—an overflow great enough even to relieve the workshops of England and Germany and give those who remained behind a new chance in the race for life—an overflow inspired as much by moral and political considerations as by motives terminating in mere bread and butter. Food was a primary want, but neither the natives nor these immigrants were all stomach, as is the jelly-fish which lives on sea-water. They not only had all the rudimentary organs of vertebrates, they were fully developed mammals. The demands of their stomachs were readily supplied. How should they go about to supply the demands of their hands, their eyes, their hearts, and their souls—the aggregate of sensations which constitute the pride of life—the real ends of existence? With the mere cravings of hunger appeased, were they now to sit down and estimate the relative profitableness, dignity, and importance of the functions of the farmer, the blacksmith, the carpenter, the mason, and the trader? Was there any right of priority in the order in which these classes were entitled to have their wants supplied? Any warrant for either class to say to the others: "I supply my wants here at a certain rate of effort, and can supply them at less effort if you will stay in Europe and work for me on European terms and not set yourself down here by my side. I am in possession of a fertile soil which gives me a great advantage over a farmer in Europe. If you accompany me and open your shop or your factory alongside of me, my very advantage operates as a premium against the pursuit of your calling, and unless I pay you more than I ought to, you will abandon your craft and pursue my industry. If you are here, you will want the same wages, the same returns for your labor which I receive from my land. To me, your industry is an unprofitable one—it *doesn't pay me* to have you make things in America which I can get done cheaper in Europe"? This is the line of argument which the free-trader puts into the mouth of the owner of the soil. If there is any set of theorems in morals or politics or political economy by which the owner of the soil can thus claim priority of right, there is an end of the case. The implication is that no handicraftsman or laborer, in any calling, which the land-owner is not compelled to have alongside of him, has any right, as an independent freeman, or as an individual soul, to be admitted as a member of that society, or to participate in the abundance of the fruits of the soil. And then he crowns his absurdity by inviting him to "take to the land" and assist him to increase that abundance to the point of valuelessness. Because, as owner of the soil, he has become the proprietor of all the most advantageous instruments of production, he warns off all new-comers, whether by birth or immigration, as trespassers. Their continued residence with him compels him to share the advantages of natural resources, whereas otherwise he might appropriate them all. So long as the land remains open, they all turn in on the land industries. Food is plenty enough, but they can not sell enough of it to foreign nations, three thousand miles away, to buy, with its proceeds, all the clothing and carpets and blankets and cutlery and chains and axes and anchors which their abundance suggests or their further conquest of the fields, forests, mines, and seas constantly tempts them to make or buy. So things happen exactly as they did in 1783–1789, and from 1789 to this hour. The purchasing powers of these "advantageous industries" failed—it was as if they were in possession of no natural resources. This early discovery of a want of vent for their raw materials was no ambitious conceit or self-imposed delusion. The discovery was made at the cost of a bitter and well-nigh fatal experience—so bitter that it threatened to ingulf all the results of seven years' war. England dumped cargo after cargo of just the goods the people needed, and they were cheap. The crisis of free-trade prosperity was reached, and we "were flooded with cheap foreign goods." England did not want our kind of "cheap products," and we were unable to flood them in return, and the colonists paid the balance against us, more than $20,000,000, in coin. Notwithstanding that Adam Smith had just demonstrated the fallacy of the "mercantile system," and that "wealth" did not consist of silver and gold, but of "commodities," the country was bankrupted. Sedition and rebellion rose against constituted authority in all the colonies. Insolvency and distress pervaded all occupations and all communities. The nation has never forgotten the crisis, and never ought to, as it never will. It was a powerful motive which could drive them from the natural, peaceful, profitable industry of agriculture. And yet Prof. Perry has said of this epoch: "No ill effects followed this general liberty to buy and sell with foreigners." [1]

As "the proof" of this page is being read, there has been placed in my hands Part I of a most admirable "Short Tariff History of the United States," by Mr. David H. Mason, of Chicago. He has portrayed by the clearest historical data the causes and consequences of the hard times suffered by the American people from 1783 to 1789. He has made good his claim "to have dug down to the original protecting power through nearly a century of eruptive overflow from the volcanic discussions of the tariff question, and to have laid bare the distinct outlines of that buried and forgotten Herculaneum of the Constitution, which was as familiar as their own door-steps to the first generation of American statesmen." We make two or three citations out of the hundred with which Mr. Mason fortifies his conclusions.

From Marshall's "Life of Washington": "On opening their ports, an immense quantity of foreign merchandise was introduced into the country, and they were tempted, *by the sudden cheapness of imported goods*, and *by their own wants*, to purchase beyond their capacities for payment. Into this indiscretion they were in some measure beguiled by their own sanguine calculations on the value which *a free trade* would bestow on the produce of their soil, and by a reliance on those evidences of the public debt which were in the hands of most of them. So extravagantly, too, did many estimate the temptation which equal liberty and vacant lands would hold out to emigrants from the Old World, as to entertain the opinion that Europe was about to empty itself into America, and that the United States would derive from that source such an increase of population as would enhance their lands to a price heretofore not even conjectured."

From Bancroft's "History of the Formation of the Constitution," Appendix: "There is no trade with any but the British, who alone give the credit they want and draw off all the bullion they can collect. They see no prospect of clothing themselves, unless they have the circuitous commerce they formerly enjoyed with Great Britain, which many think a vain expectation, now that they are no part of the empire. The scarcity of money makes the prod-

A STILL FURTHER ANALYSIS. 223

Prof. Sumner ("Protection in the United States") endeavors to shift the troubles to "currency errors." Doubtless, but as effect, not cause. He can not conceal the real causes and effects. He says: "The States, however, still

uce of the country cheap, to the disappointment of the farmers and the discouragement of husbandry. Thus the two classes of merchants and farmers, that nearly divide all America, are discontented and distressed. Some great change is approaching." (1785.)

From Hildreth's "History of the United States": "The farmers no longer found that market for their produce which the French, American, and British armies had furnished. The large importation of foreign goods, subject to little or no duty and sold at peace prices, was proving ruinous to all the domestic manufactures and mechanical employments which the non-consumption agreements and the war had created and fostered. Immediately after the peace, the country had been flooded with imported goods, and debts had been unwarily contracted for which there was no means to pay. The imports from Great Britain in the years 1784 and 1785 had amounted in value to thirty millions of dollars, while the exports thither had not exceeded nine millions. . . . The excessive importation of foreign goods had drained the country of specie. The excessive importation of foreign goods, and the consequent pressure upon domestic manufactures, had diminished a good deal of the old prejudice against customs duties. A party had sprung up in favor of raising a large part of the public revenue in that way. . . . This, however, was opposed by the merchants as injurious to their interests. They came forward as the champions of free trade, and insisted upon the old system of direct taxation."

Minot, "History of the Insurrections in Massachusetts": "Thus was the usual means of remittance by articles of the growth of the country almost annihilated, and little else than specie remained to answer the demands incurred by importations. The money, of course, was drawn off, and this being inadequate to the purpose of discharging the whole amount of foreign contracts, the residue was chiefly sunk by the bankruptcies of the importers."

Mr. Mason has produced the most abundant authority for his own digest of the facts of this era, which is in the words following: "Such were throughout the Confederation, and such have always been in other countries, the results of free-trade principles in the culminating stages of their operation. Step by step the movement of the country was constantly retrograde, proceeding through variously excessive importations to a pinching shrinkage of home industry and of employment for domestic labor, then to an exhaustive draining away of specie, until the people were almost entirely without a cir-

had vast quantities of paper afloat. As soon as the war ended, this specie was all exported and expended in the purchase of goods long missed. The export of specie in 1783 was ten millions. . . . This explains why the English were so well satisfied with the revival of trade. . . . During the war many industries had sprung up to supply the wants of the people for manufactures formerly imported. Whatever may have been the effect of peace to destroy the war mushrooms, we find that there were in 1784 manufactures of iron, glass, paper, and cloth here. . . . And propositions were made by competent capitalists for mining iron on a large scale in Pennsylvania, which fell only on account of *the turbulency of the inhabitants*

---

culating medium; then to sore and exasperating distress for lack of money, and to unendurable pressure in the relation of debtor and creditor, with widely extended impoverishment; then to resentful discontent, weakened respect for the law and its tribunals, decay of allegiance, loss of confidence between man and man, and an unloosening of societary ties; then to turbulence, open antagonism to the constituted authorities, insurrectionary commotions, and an appeal to armies in search of unattained redress. Had there been no free trade, there would have been no inundation of foreign goods; had there been no inundation of foreign goods, there would have been no distress for lack of circulating medium; had there been no such distress, there would have been no impulse toward insubordination to the State. The starting-point was free trade; the outcome was rebellion and an imperious necessity to resort for deliverance to the protective system. As this was the closest approach to absolute free trade ever tried by this country, so there was the largest harvest of calamities and dangers ever experienced by the American people. That awful crisis, at the outset of our career as an independent nation, should be regarded as a monument erected by the sufferings of our forefathers to warn posterity against the delusive and mischievous plausibilities of the free-trade policy. Nor is it now less needful to ponder those solemn teachings of our history, when Peter-the-Hermit *doctrinaires*, emerging from their retirement amid theoretic book-lore, are organizing a crusade to recover the desolate and accursed Jerusalem of unrestricted commerce. The sorrows drunk by our Revolutionary sires to the very dregs, under that system, should be to all following generations what the red signal-light is to a place of peril."

and *the insecurity of titles* (!) . . . Meanwhile the Government of the Confederation was falling to pieces, and was a pity and a laughing-stock. . . . Misery was great throughout the country, owing to paper money and debt, and the losses of the war. The people were discontented and rebellious." (Why should they be? They were "flooded with cheap foreign goods." Why did they not flood back foreign nations with their own abundance of cheap food and raw materials? The truth was, the whole societary movement was arrested by the export of all their coin to pay their debts contracted for foreign goods.) . . . "The question of import tax was, therefore, bound up with the question of civil order, protection to manufactures, foreign commercial relations, and the misery arising from bad currency at home. This led to the Congress of Annapolis in 1786, *which was only a commercial convention*, and which found no better way to discharge the task it had undertaken than to recommend Congress to call another convention in the following year to revise the Articles of Confederation, that is, to provide for a common revenue system and for 'the regulation of commerce,' by giving the General Government permanent power for those purposes."

It is not too much to conclude that the present Constitution grew out of the free-trade crisis under the Confederation. This was then the work of men who were looking upon the inmost nature of trade—at the very genesis of our commerce. It is no longer the mere power "to collect taxes," "to lay import duties" for revenue "only," or "for public purposes exclusively," but the true vital organic act of "regulating commerce."

The agriculturist, who, as possessor of the soil, furnished the exportables of those days, allowed the artisans who made his houses and barns, and repaired his clothes and shoes, to remain alongside of him at a high rate of wages, and accepted the reduced average returns of their joint industry. The farmer was compelled to submit to the tax of having houses, and barns, and wells, and harness, and the like. This was imposed on him by the nature of things—just as he is compelled to submit to the tax of a short crop, or the seed he sows—or *the tax* of a glut in the European market. The farmer himself would not either in 1784 or 1884 have thought of these results, in which the efficiency of his labor was reduced by the necessary cost of living, as a *tax*, but that is the way in which free-trade professors and stump-speakers in Congress put it in later days. It is the modern trick-word. His free-trade patronizer would persuade the American farmer that any commodity made here, when it might be made cheaper abroad, is made at his loss, and he is taxed to enable our artisans " to engage in a losing business." [1]

---

[1] Mr. Henry J. Philpot, representing the Iowa State Free-Trade League, addressed the Tariff Commission. (",Report," vol. i, p. 1107, etc.) The bucolic exegesis of this gentleman is one of the curiosities of economic literature. His whole address will be found entertaining, if not instructive—not for his logic, which is neither better nor worse than that of his more skillful coadjutors, the Professors—but for a certain exuberance of rhetoric under which he conceals his argument. He claims the credit of forbearance that certain classes of mechanics are allowed to live here and work without the aid of protection—that they are permitted to earn wages in certain callings. "I never knew a farmer who got his horse shod in England, or who had his house built there, or had it plastered or glazed there, or had his cellar dug there, or his cistern walled, or his well. I therefore consider that those classes of occupations can not possibly be protected by the tariff; that we would still need the wells without the tariff, still be *compelled* to get them dug as well as our cisterns and our cellars, and that we *could not* get it done abroad."

So that, logically, the only reason for having houses built and cellars dug and horses shod by American workmen is because the American food-raiser is compelled to live under such a dispensation. These are *taxes* which he does not see how to escape. They had to pay their neighbors to engage in

The farmers, in common with their fellow-citizens, need more than food and houses and cellars and cisterns. They need a given amount of iron, and the various tools and implements made of it, and cotton and woolen fabrics. These can be produced at home, or else the glowing inventories of our resources which free-traders always feel bound to offer us are a fraud.[1]

The yearly labor of the people working under just and tolerable conditions of competition will produce the yearly

---

a losing business to themselves—losing, because, if they could have imported houses and cisterns and cellars made cheaper abroad, it looks as if they would have been gainers.

Undoubtedly some kind of body politic might be built up under the auspices of the Iowa State Free-Trade League. Poland, Turkey, Ireland, Brazil, and Egypt are examples. Patagonians and Esquimaux come still nearer the type in which the exertions to maintain life are freed from such taxes. They are organisms with a single organ and a single function—the food-raiser—and they are almost exempt from the taxes which the tailor, the shoemaker, the school-teacher, the minister, and the doctor impose on men—they do not need them.

[1] Here is one from our bucolic friend of the Iowa State Free-Trade League: "But I think the sublimest cheat on record is the man who tries to cheat God Almighty out of the credit of making this a good country to live in, and who pretends that what God has done in the way of piling up mountains of iron, silver, and gold, filling the bowels of the earth with salt, copper, coal, and petroleum, and covering its surface for centuries with rich vegetable mold, and watering it with mighty lakes and rivers, and planting boundless forests—that all this would do the farmer and the working-man no good unless they were taxed with a tax such as no other people ever submitted to. I think brass ought to be placed on the free list."

Well, scarcely, while domestic supplies of this richness and purity hold out.

Does the author of this declamation conceive that this iron and coal will forge themselves into bars and rails and nails and machinery without the intervention of the American laborer? Or can he, while his constituents kick their heels into the counter of some store at the Iowa Cross-roads, devise a plan by which he can buy the bars and rails and nails and machinery in England with the Iowa corn which is consumed as fuel in the very stove which is warming them?

supply of all our wants, including our need of iron and textile fabrics, and add a thousand millions annually to our capital. The total product will be distributed necessarily and equitably in rent, wages, and profits. The farmer takes his share as land-owner and toiler; the workman takes his share as laborer for wages; the professor takes his share as the earner of his salary; the capitalist takes his share for interest and risk; and the *entrepreneur* takes his share as the wages of superintendence. Each takes all the share which the economic law of the society permits. The statute law makes no interference. The legislature stands neutral, with hands off. Producers are remanded to the law which the Almighty has imposed on the societary movement. The products and services of each in market are a market for the products and services of all. No one of the members of this industrial entity—this organism—had any possibility of increased earnings, or of making a product with a higher exchange value, out of which he has contributed or could contribute to "the protected industries." The farmer, for instance, put into his pocket all there was in the case for himself. Nobody has taxed him—nobody collects taxes of him—there is no taxation except the cost of satisfying the desires which he thinks it worth while to satisfy, and no mode has ever been pointed out in which he could satisfy them at less effort. Nobody has "robbed" him. Who has robbed him? The "protected industries"? They are an abstraction. Certain laborers in these protected industries earned wages which they expended in food, and clothes, and shelter, and the education of their children. Certain capitalists in the protected industries got their profits, which again got distributed principally to labor, in new tools, new houses, new family wants. Their profits were only such as were usual in the country. Certain organizers got the wages of management. These wages were only such as other persons, in Europe or America, in possession of equal skill and executive powers, can earn.[1]

Certain landlords received rent, which again is subject to the law of supply and demand. The fulcrum upon which the whole industrial superstructure was raised is the total of our resources and aptitudes, and no one has been raised at the depression of another. The point of reaction is not on one man or one group, but upon all.

And of the sums which went to capitalists and superintendents and landlords, the greater, by far the greater portion, went at the last into the hands of laborers in other departments, who were building houses, papering, painting, plumbing, making new stone foundations, and erecting new brick walls, and making new carriages and harness, and so forth, and so forth, new things, and render-

---

[1] To those who so flippantly discourse of "monopolists" and "robbers" in aid of free trade I commend these words, by the author of "What Social Classes owe to each other." Most of these careless thinkers seem to have no objections to the rise and success of great industrial establishments, only so that they are on foreign shores:

"The great gains of a great capitalist in a modern state must be put under the head of wages of superintendence. Any one who believes that any great enterprise of an industrial character can be started without labor must have little experience of life. Let any one try to get a railroad built, or to start a factory and win reputation for its products, or to start a school and win a reputation for it, or to found a newspaper and make it a success, or to start any other enterprise, and he will find what obstacles he must overcome, what risks must be taken, what perseverance and courage are required, what foresight and sagacity are necessary. Especially in a new country, where many tasks are waiting, where resources are strained to the utmost all the time, the judgment, courage, and perseverance required to organize new enterprises and carry them to success are sometimes heroic. Persons who possess the necessary qualifications obtain great rewards. They ought to do so. It is foolish to rail at them. Then, again, the ability to organize and conduct industrial, commercial, or financial enterprises is rare; the great captains of industry are as rare as great generals. They are paid in proportion to the supply and demand of them."

ing the thousand services which do not issue in commodities. The whole fund returns to the treasury of the society, to be distributed over and over again, as men discover new wants and find the power to render new services to each other, as members of *this industrial organism, the organic unit,* this *ensemble.*

All the wages and all the profits in the protected industries are paid out of the exchange values of the products of those industries. What is the gain to the nation, as a whole? The whole value of the articles produced by these industries, or rather the whole of the new articles themselves. The gain *to the nation*, then, is the total price or value of the exports now saved, which must otherwise be sent abroad to buy the same products which we could make in the protected industries. If a ton of iron in England cost fifteen bushels of wheat, and costs twenty bushels in America, we have not lost five dollars by purchasing it at home, but have gained the ton of iron.[1]

---

[1] I am not aware that any satisfactory reply has ever been made to the following argument of Sir John B. Byles in his "Sophistries of Free Trade":

"Suppose England to manufacture from English materials gloves to the amount of a million sterling a year.

"This million sterling does, as we have seen, two things: First, it affords net annual income to that amount, available (every farthing of it) for the support of the population. Secondly, this million sterling creates a market to that amount for other English products. The whole million is every year feeding, clothing, and lodging men, women, and children, and, at the same time, finding a market for cottons, woolens, hardware, corn, timber, silk. When an industrious population are employed, they not only enrich the whole community to the extent to which they themselves are enriched, but by the market which their prosperity affords to other industries. When Manchester is in full employment, what a market does Manchester itself afford, not only for other articles, but even for its own productions!

"Now change the supposition. Suppose that French gloves can be imported cheaper by five per cent than English gloves can be made. It is the immediate pecuniary interest of all consumers to buy French gloves instead of English ones, and they will be bought accordingly. We will even suppose

It is a ton of iron added to the annual product of American industry, to be distributed to rent, wages, and profits. But, says the free-trader, the labor spent in producing the iron might have been put upon some other industry at greater advantage. We have already seen that it

---

the French Government to allow the French gloves to be bought by the very same English cottons, woolens, hardware, corn, iron, and silk that bought the English gloves before; nay, we will go further, and admit the extravagant postulate that all these English products could, in exchange for the French gloves, find as good a market in France as they formerly did in England. Now take the account. Let us see what individual glove-consumers have gained, and what the English nation has lost.

"Gloves have in the aggregate cost those who wear them less money than before by five per cent on a million sterling, that is, by £50,000. Glove-consumers have gained by the change £50,000 in one year. But *the nation* has lost, in the same year, the million sterling which used to maintain Englishmen with their wives and children. Englishmen, *as a body*, have, by the change, lost a revenue of £950,000 a year.

"But this is only part of the mischief; for, though their revenue, their subsistence is gone, the English men, women, and children remain, and must be supported by public charity.

"But we have given the free-traders the benefit of three suppositions, no one of which is true. We have conceded, first, that the French Government would allow the free import of as much English produce as would entirely pay for the gloves; we have conceded, secondly, that all this English produce finds at once as ready and as good a market as it did at home; we have conceded, lastly, that there will be no exportation of the precious metals, depreciating prices, appreciating the currency, and augmenting the pressure, not only of taxes and public burdens, but of all debts and private obligations.

"But if these concessions are not true, then, in addition to a million a year lost as revenue, formerly supporting men, women, and children, you lost a market also for other productions to the extent of a million a year, and are subject to all those numerous evils that afflict industry, when there is a tendency to the export of the precious metals.

"Nor does the mischief stop here. Other commodities which have lost their market will to that extent cease to be produced. And by that cessation not only will the subsistence of the people to that extent disappear, but other markets will be injured, and so the mischief will go on and be felt through every grade of society and in every department of industry."

could not have made a product with any higher exchange value. We have already conclusively seen that the trade in a foreign market is forbidden, not by the high rate of wages, but for the want of a foreign market for the special product here in which the rate of wages is high. We do not know of any "something else" in which the labor could have been employed.

The addition to the total annual product of our industry, the gain to the nation, is the whole value of the cotton, tobacco, wheat, and provisions, which we should have been compelled to send abroad to pay for the products of our protected industries. They remained here, and constituted a demand for other American labor.

The loss is the difference in price between the domestic and foreign commodity, reckoned in present prices and on present exchange values. On no right use of the facts can this loss be made to equal any definite sum. Suppose it $100,000,000. A loss of only six per cent on the value of our exports and an increase of six per cent in the cost of imports alone would come to $100,000,000. It is as likely under free trade to be twenty-five per cent each way. If, now, the farmer says, I could have bought more iron for a given number of bushels of wheat; if the laboring-man says, I could have bought more muslin and blankets and dinner-pails for a given number of dollars received for wages; if the professor and the capitalist say they could have bought more yards of fine English broadcloth and decorated china and Axminster carpets with their salaries and dividends—it is pertinent to ask, What could the farmer, the laboring-man, the professor, and the capitalist, have bought them with? Exportables: what are they? Cotton, tobacco, wheat, and provisions; these are and have been the only purchase-money we had to offer.

Assuming, now, the possibility of selling enough of

those abroad to buy the manufactured articles which we consume, a moment's examination of the state of the case will demonstrate the ruinous terms on which we must effect the exchange. Our farmers raise annually, say, $3,600,000,000 worth of food and raw materials. Constituting somewhat less than half the population, they themselves consume probably $1,400,000,000 worth. They now export $700,000,000 worth, and sell $1,500,000,000 at home. We now buy abroad $350,000,000 worth of goods like those made in the protected industries, and a like amount—$350,000,000—which our climate is unfitted to produce. It is notable that our food exports do not go to the countries which furnish our tea, coffee, sugar, wines, fruits, and luxuries. We consume at a low estimate $2,500,000,000 of commodities made in our own protected industries. These we propose to abandon, and supply our needs from abroad. Our demand for foreign manufactured goods will now suddenly be increased to $2,850,000,000. Our surplus of raw materials and food, increased by the fourth of our people released from the protected industries and going into agriculture, will now be $1,600,000,000.[1] But the foreign market has never taken but $350,000,000 in exchange for manufactured commodities. Into that market you are now going to dump $1,600,000,000 food-products, or five times as much as before, and demand in return $2,850,000,000, or seven times as much as before. We want and must have these goods; they do not need, will not take, ours. Even if the trade could go forward at all, it would be at the loss of all exchange value and at the collapse of all purchas-

---

[1] The $700,000,000 + $900,000,000, the one fourth of $3,600,000,000. This fourth of the people either will or will not go into agriculture. If they "catch on" to the scientific game of the free-trader, they will. If they do not, they must stay in the protected industries and try to produce under European conditions. What else is there to do? Think of it, and answer.

ing power on our part. We should be hopelessly at the mercy of the foreign market. The absurdity of the proposal is fairly fantastic.

But the exchange could not go forward. We can not buy the "satisfaction of all our desires" in the world's market. For nine tenths of them we have no available or possible means of gratification except by the scheme of direct production.

No real scientific results can be attained by the atomistic view of the co-workers in a given society or nation. Unless burdened by inherited injustices and artificial antecedents, the laws of nature will work out just results among the competitions in the body of the nation. The attempt to deal with the individuals, as units, involves us in the vicious error to which Mr. Herbert Spencer has called our attention, that of "mistaking a part for a whole," and thus "its relations to existence in general will be misapprehended." By this discrete treatment the whole is completely lost sight of, and the aggregates which the whole involve disappear from our investigation. Men may be trusted to pursue the industry which seems to offer the best returns, and this is done by them as individuals. But when we come to the exchanges which are made in international commerce, we must view them from the outside. While, considered as individuals, men may be trusted to pursue the industry which seems to offer the best returns, when we come to international exchanges we must abandon this atomistic view of the co-workers in an organized nation. Our scientific standpoint must be at an elevation which places the given nation in proper perspective with all the other political and industrial units which compose the commercial nations of the world, who also have "desires" which they wish to gratify. The wants of the nation as a whole, and its powers of supplying them as a whole—

whether by domestic production or foreign exchange, or by their joint operation—are aggregates. The nature of our surplus production, and the relation of that surplus to the markets of the world, involve aggregate estimates. The wants of foreign nations are aggregates. The amount of foreign products needed, and the nature of the purchase-money which we carry in our hands, are to be treated as aggregates. Our wants are an aggregate, and the means of buying their gratification is an aggregate. It is the business of the legislator, who stands for all of us, to understand these details, however numerous and vexatious. The founding of a great commercial organization like A. T. Stewart's could not be brought about by the unregulated individualism of department superintendents, clerks, and porters. So some one, statesman or layman, must take the trouble to sum up the details of a nation's industrial resources and liabilities into the correct aggregate.[1]

The "equation of international demand" sets a distinct limit to foreign exchanges; the law of "reciprocal demand" hedges our power of "satisfying" our "desires" abroad. Recurring to Prof. Perry's equation, "the silks which England wants from France do not equal the cottons which France wants from England."

Now, what is the aggregate of the "desires" of the people of the United States, which they think it worth the while to make the necessary effort and sacrifice to gratify? The census of 1880 gave in round numbers the products of our agricultural and extractive industries at

---

[1] Says Prof. Denslow: "The man who says, 'I do not look upon the aggregate people of a country *en masse*, nor propose any paternal panacea for promoting the general welfare; I dissolve your so-called general welfare into 51,000,000 units, and propose to limit the function of government to keeping these units from breaking each other's heads'—such a man is not a political economist at all. His calling should be to put on a blue uniform and carry a policeman's club."

$2,200,000,000, and of our mechanical industries at $5,300,000,000. Revised and safe estimates put the former at $3,600,000,000 and the latter at $8,000,000,000. Here, then, is a gross annual productive capacity of $11,600,000,000. Of this we save annually the sum of $1,000,000,000, which is added to the capital of the country, to be employed for the purposes of future production. The "effective desire of accumulation" takes effect to the enormous amount of a thousand millions a year—about three millions a day surplus over expenses—one third of the savings of the whole human family are made in the United States.[1]

This leaves, in round numbers, $10,000,000,000 to be spent annually by the people of the United States for the "satisfaction of their desires" for the purchase of services, which issue in commodities—to say nothing of the vast number which do not thus issue. This is the *tax* which their natures and "historical antecedents" impose on them as *the cost* of the lives they see proper to lead. It is a very remarkable evidence of the productive powers of the universal activity which protection has stimulated, that we reproduce every five years the entire estimated value of all the goods, wares, and merchandise, lands, improvements, and money of the entire nation. That value is put at $53,000,000,000, greater by $10,000,000,000 than the value of all the property in England.

It is probably not possible to ascertain of this aggre-

---

[1] Mulhall, the statistician, says: "Every day that the sun rises upon the American people it sees an addition of two and a half millions of dollars to the accumulated wealth of the republic, which is equal to one third of the daily accumulation of mankind. These are as follows, viz.:

"United States	$825,000,000
France	375,000,000
Great Britain	325,000,000
Germany	200,000,000
All other countries	725,000,000."

gate the exact proportion in which satisfaction of these ten thousand million "desires" is furnished at home and abroad in what are known as "protected industries," that is, industries upon the like products of which made abroad we impose tariff duties for the sake of "protection" and not for "revenue only."

It has all along been assumed by free-traders that the cost of the domestic article has been increased over that of the like imported article by the amount of the duty imposed. It was then argued that the price of the entire volume of home manufactures was by the amount of the tariff rate increased to consumers, no part of which went into the Treasury of the United States, but all of which went into the pockets of the home manufacturer. And thus they conceived that they were entitled to an affirmative answer to "the political question about protection: Does the statute enacted by the legislature alter the distribution of property so that one man enjoys another man's earnings; has the State a law in operation which enables one citizen to collect taxes of another?"

Prof. Perry puts this tax, levied upon the people for the benefit of the protected industries, at $600,000,000 annually, reached, by dead-reckoning, thus: "If now we may fairly suppose that, on the average of each one foreign article paying a duty into the treasury, there were four domestic articles raised each in price as much as the foreign article paid in duty, then it follows that the people paid, in each of those years, under chiefly protective tariff taxes, $632,000,000, or $12,640,000,000 in all, no penny of which went to the Treasury of the United States; that this is a reasonable supposition appears partly from the known proportion between imported and domestic, as to several leading articles: for example, of steel rails in 1880 the domestic was twenty times the imported, and the people paid nineteen times more under the duty than the treasury got. On woolen blankets, in 1881, the treasury took in less than $2,000, while the people paid in the extra price of blankets more than a thousand times that sum that year. And, on iron goods of all kinds, we have seen that the average duty was about seventy-seven per cent, while the vast bulk of the iron consumed is known to be of domestic production; and that this is a reasonable supposition appears further, if we look at the annual average amount of domestic manufactured goods; the census of 1880 gave $5,232,000,000 as the value of home manufactures for that year, which we may fairly take as the average of the twenty years under consideration; and, if we throw off *one third of those as not affected by the tariff at all*, and consider that the rest were only raised in price twenty-two per cent—which is one half the average rate of duty on dutiable goods—then almost precisely the same results will follow as before, namely, an annual average of $632,000,000 paid by the people under the protective tariff, no cent of which reaches the national treasury. An acknowledged statistical expert, J. S. Moore, calculated, from data similar to our own, that the people paid $1,000,000,000, in 1882, extra to the sum reaching the treasury under protective tariff taxes." [1]

---

[1] This kind of reasoning exposes Perry to the criticism which Prof. Ely fairly makes on Ricardo and his "Political Economy." These deductionists are all alike: "No mention is made of a single event which ever occurred. It is really astounding when one thinks of it. The whole discourse is hypothetical. 'Suppose now a machine,' writes Ricardo in one place, 'which could, in any particular trade, be employed to do the work of one hundred men for a year, and that it would last only for one year. Suppose, too, the machine to cost £5,000, and the wages annually paid to one hundred men to be £5,000, it is evident that it would be a matter of indifference to the manufacturer whether he bought the machine or employed the men. But suppose labor to rise and consequently the wages of one hundred men for a

The "one third" indicated in italics is, then, the length and breadth of the field of employment, the "something else" which we can do, when we abandon protection and the protected industries. The Parsee merchant known by the words and figures "J. S. Moore," does not balk at all at putting this tax at $1,000,000,000. One would think that such a *reductio ad absurdum* would arouse suspicion, and lead to a recasting of calculations.

---

year to amount to £5,500, it is obvious the manufacturer would now no longer hesitate; it would be his interest to buy the machine, and get his work done for £5,000. But will not the machine rise in price? . . . It would rise in price, if there were no stock employed in its construction. . . . If, for example'—and, in this strain, which sufficiently illustrates his style and method, Ricardo continues indefinitely. Inside of two pages, he introduces no fewer than thirteen distinct suppositions, all of them purely imaginary."

CHAPTER XI.

SCHEDULE A—PRODUCTION UNDER FREEDOM.

DURING the recent tariff debate in Congress (1884), a dozen or more speakers produced "Schedule A," as they called it.[1] The schedule is as follows:

---

[1] This schedule was first propounded by Hon. William R. Springer, in an article entitled "Incidental Taxation," in the "North American Review" for June, 1883, which contains a very precise and detailed estimate, and which makes the amount of this *tax* very definitely, $556,939,637.

For the purposes of the argument in hand, it is not necessary to expose the fallacious method of manipulating these figures, some of which are official and some of which are "rigged" to suit the purposes of their compiler.

Especially it will be observed that the "estimated rate of increase *ad valorem*" is less in every instance than the rate of duty imposed. This is a concession which sustains the protectionist, and shows progress in the direction which the protectionist urges, that with increasing skill the domestic article can be produced as cheaply as the foreign. Everything on the list (as appears) can be produced and sold cheaper than the foreign article, *plus* the duty. It will inevitably result that they can all be sold at the cheapest rate which American skill and competition can achieve. The rates of increase given above are purely conjectural, and are vastly overstated.

The table makes the contribution of labor to the value of the finished fabrics less than 20 per cent, and rent and profits more than 80 per cent of the proceeds. This is a guess, and a palpable error. On these figures, the foreigner would sell the $2,440,502,649 for $1,883,564,012. Deducting wages at the American rate, this would leave for rent and profits to the foreign manufacturer, $1,506,851,210, which is again 80 per cent, or, if they had paid the total American wages, the profits would have been over 70 per cent, a rate not possible in Europe, as we have all been taught to believe.

Again, the number of hands employed in the protected industries is given as 1,327,881. If this is meant to include all who are directly and indirectly concerned in producing the finished fabric from the raw materials, and who

SCHEDULE A—PRODUCTION UNDER FREEDOM.

STATEMENT showing the amount of incidental taxes annually imposed on the people of the United States, in the increased cost of home products, by reason of discriminating duties on imported articles of like character, together with the value of such home products, the amount of wages paid and number of hands employed, and the imports and duties received thereon, for the year 1882.

ARTICLES AFFECTED BY THE TARIFF.	MERCHANDISE IMPORTED DURING THE FISCAL YEAR ENDED JUNE 30, 1882.			Value of home products, census year, 1880.	Average number of hands employed. Boys under 16 and girls under 15 counted as one half a hand.	Total amount in wages during the year.	Estimated rate of increase, ad valorem.	Incidental taxes—being the increased cost of home products by reason of the tariff.
	Values.	Duty received.	Average ad val. rate.				Per c.	
Chemical products	$21,517,169	$6,718,561	Per c. 31·32	$117,377,324	28,895	$11,840,704	20	$23,475,464
Earthenware and glassware	13,822,043	6,693,257	48·42	31,632,309	30,674	13,130,403	45	14,234,539
Metals—iron and steel, and all metal manufactures	74,427,988	30,358,936	40·79	604,553,460	290,000	122,648,191	20	120,910,692
Wood and wooden wares	6,654,327	1,589,851	18·37	311,928,884	185,426	47,817,199	15	46,789,382
Sugar and molasses	94,540,269	49,210,573	52·05	See note			40	4,846,714
Tobacco	8,216,132	6,000,961	73·03	118,665,366	81,609	25,041,257	25	29,666,341
Cotton and cotton goods	34,868,044	13,482,167	38·67	210,950,383	170,363	45,614,419	20	42,190,076
Hemp, jute, and flax goods	33,578,076	9,844,652	29·32	5,518,866	4,829	1,238,149	20	1,103,773
Wool and woolens	47,679,502	29,254,284	61·36	267,182,914	145,341	47,351,628	40	106,873,165
Silk and silk goods	39,535,475	22,832,490	58·73	41,033,045	28,554	9,146,705	50	20,516,622
Books, paper, etc	4,923,620	1,406,787	28·57	65,960,405	25,274	9,895,995	20	13,192,081
Sundries	62,410,690	17,272,269	27·63	665,699,693	337,216	129,881,399	20	133,139,938
Total	$433,173,335	$194,464,758		$2,440,502,649	1,327,881	$463,606,049		$556,938,637

NOTE.—Planters' product for 1880 was: Sugar, 196,759,230 pounds; molasses, 16,578,273 gallons. Number and wages of laborers not stated.

We deal with the figures as they are, and with the argument which they are intended, by implication, to support. They are intended to assert that, somewhere between the producer in the protected industry and the consumer of his product, productive forces are lost; and that the actual earnings of the latter are, by force of the protective statute, transferred to the former. The inference is meant to be drawn that every individual farmer got less iron for his wheat under this dispensation; that every individual laborer, every hedger or ditcher, with two dollars in his pocket, is compelled to spend them both, to procure at home what he could purchase abroad for one dollar; and that some receiver of fixed income, derived from American enterprise, could take the money which he received from American consumers of his services and buy two broadcloth coats in London, instead of one in New York.

Extract from Hon. Frank Hurd's[1] speech in Congress, April 29, 1884:

"If I have by a day's labor earned one dollar, it is my

---

are supported by the protected industries, the number is evidently below the fact. The number of men engaged in these industries and those necessarily related to them is nearly 5,000,000—considerably more than one fourth of the adult male population of the country.

"Sundries" may or may not conceal a large African. I do not know how it is arrived at.

[1] The depths of pathos which some gentlemen can reach by mere rhetoric are beyond the reach of any plumb line. When it comes to logic, these people strike their heads on hard facts before they get their bodies out of the range of unpleasant exposure. This kind of economics is illustrated by the story of Artemus Ward's first visit to Cleveland. Approaching a stranger, he asked:

"I beg your pardon, but could you tell a stranger where a dinner could be obtained for a quarter of a dollar?"

"Right over the way," was the reply.

"I beg pardon, but one question more. Could you inform me where a stranger could get the quarter of a dollar?"

We await Mr. Hurd's answer to this conundrum.

own. It represents the toil, the anxieties, the life of one day. It is all that I have in material product to represent that day. With that dollar I go to purchase from a Frenchman an article which I wish. The contract is about to be consummated. The Government of the United States steps in with its power and says, 'You shall not buy of this Frenchman; you must buy of an American'—a man, say, who manufactures this article at Providence, R. I. I go to him with my dollar, and propose to buy the article which for that sum I could have obtained from the Frenchman. 'No,' says the manufacturer, 'I charge more than a dollar for this article; you must pay me two dollars.'"

This is the old assumption that what is true of the individual, considered in his social group, is true of him apart from his social group. It is an assumption that a structural part in an organism could perform the same functions, as a separate whole, which it does when correlated with the other units in an organic whole. It is an assumption that what is true of hydrogen in a chemist's jar is true of the hydrogen in the Atlantic Ocean.

Manufactures are supported by agriculture and mining. But the manufacturer is not *supported* by the agriculturist and miner, in the sense of, at the expense of—by taxation levied upon one for the other. They are co-workers in one entity. We have the authority of Bastiat for their functions in a society: "Agriculture, manufactures, commerce, may be an excellent classification when the object is to describe the processes of art; but that description, however essential in technology, has little connection with social economy—I should even say that it was positively dangerous. When we have classed men as agriculturists, manufacturers, and merchants, of what can we speak but of their class interests, of those special interests to which competition is antagonistic, and which are placed in opposition to the general good? It is not for the sake of agriculturists that agriculture exists; of manufacturers that we have manufactures, or of merchants that we have exchanges, but in order that men should have at their disposal the greatest amount of commodities of every kind." ("Economic Harmonies.")

"The illusion which I am combating, that demand and supply are independent economic forces, sometimes assumes another form, in the notion that producers and consumers are distinct classes, and that production and consumption are acts which may go on irrespective of each other." (Prof. Cairnes.)

They are organs of one body.

Now, it was never true that any particular farmer in the United States, *in connection with all the other farmers*, could get more iron for his wheat in England than at home. It was never true that any particular laboring-man who had earned two dollars by rendering services to his fellow-citizens here, *in connection with all the other like laborers*, could buy abroad for one dollar what cost two here. If he spent two dollars in Providence, instead of one dollar in England, it was because the societary movement, of which Providence was a part, enabled him to have the two dollars in his pocket, where England would have put but one. He had the two dollars when he started for Providence. It was never true that any professor who receives his twenty-five hundred dollars from his fellow-citizens here, *in connection with all other salary-earners*, could get more broadcloth for the price of his services abroad than here. Any one of them, having got his wages under the present arrangement in his pocket, might buy a single ton of iron, a blanket, or a suit of clothes *provided the others did not*. The farmer wishes good prices for his wheat, the laborer high wages, and the professor a worthy salary—in return for the services which they render to their neighbors. If their neighbors, the rest of us, are given no chance to render services in return, how are we to pay their profits, their wages, and their salaries? Who is to pay them the means of purchasing the next ton of iron, the next blanket, and the next London suit? The farmer? Not he: we have seen that his raw products have lost their exchange value, and that free foreign trade has robbed him of all the gratuities of his rich soil. The laborer and the professor have nothing to export. If the return services are to come from abroad, the laborer and the professor, at least, had better live abroad.

Professors in colleges, the capitalists whose money is invested in banks, railroads, farms, and plantations worked by tenants, go abroad. In London, Paris, and Berlin they purchase many articles of *vertu*, household decoration, and personal adornment, which we either can not make at all or can not make as cheap as the foreign artisan. Our travelers soon acquire an air of condescension toward Americans and America's products; they are fond of reckoning the cost in " francs " or " pounds sterling." On their return they are landed at a custom-house, and the " wealth " they are bringing into the country in the shape of gloves, cravats, and the like, is intercepted long enough to enable the Government to collect the share of taxes which they ought to contribute to the common revenue. The professors and the capitalists are hurt as to their feelings, and proceed at once to join a free-trade club. They try to forget that their colleges, banks, railroads, and farms are on the Hudson, the Delaware, and Mississippi, and not on the Thames, the Seine, and the Congo. They try to ignore the great fact that the earning-power of their possessions is rooted in the American industrial organization. Most of us do not make voyages abroad, and do not encounter the custom-house officer. The expenditures of the American farmer and laborer, and of every average household, are met here, in our own market, on better terms, both as to abundance and cheapness, than in any market in the world. We have found no commodity which any foreign nation can furnish us at less cost in labor and abstinence.

The farmer, the laborer, and the manufacturer resume, then, on our own soil, the system of the division of functions which is natural to us. The industrial system is a social co-operation, working automatically. To quote our author of "Social Classes," who writes forcibly always, and most sensibly when out of range of free-trade prepossessions: "All this goes on so smoothly and accurately that we forget to notice it. We think that it costs nothing—does itself, as it were. The truth is, that this great co-operative effort is one of the great products of civilization—one of its costliest products and highest refinements." Our co-operative scheme can only be marred by trying to gear it into foreign machinery. It is ours, local and not cosmopolitan.[1]

---

[1] This industrial structure is not only local in its origin in that it could not be imported—it is also a growth on the soil.

"Even more important than the differences in the physical strength and vigor of laborers are the variations that we find in the skill and intelligence, their foresight, quickness, vigilance, and resource in availing themselves of advantages which forward production and in avoiding or removing all that impairs it. Superiority in these respects is partly, as I have said, congenital and transmitted through physical heredity; but to a great extent they are handed down from generation to generation by conscious training and learning; primarily by technical training and learning of special arts and processes, though the effort of general education in developing industrial intelligence must not be overlooked. We must also bear in mind the extent to which industrial efficiency is transmitted by association and unconscious imitation. 'The child,' says Prof. Walker, 'becomes a better workman simply by reason of being accustomed, through the years of his own inability to labor, to see tools used with address, and through watching the alert movements, the prompt co-operation, the precise manipulation of bodies of work-

Our author fitly characterizes the attempt of the atom —the unit—the individual, the organ, which endeavors to evade its share of the proper work of the organism and to do better for itself than the whole to which it belongs. "There is no man, from the tramp up to the President, the Pope, or the Czar, who can do as he has a mind to. There never has been any man, from the primitive barbarian up to a Humboldt or a Darwin, who could do as he had a mind to. The Bohemian who determines to realize some sort of liberty of this kind, accomplishes his purpose only by sacrificing most of the rights, and turning his back on most of the duties, of a civilized man, while filching as much as he can of the advantages of living in a civilized state."[1] Individualism is an impossibility in either a political or industrial organism.

---

men. This unconscious imitation operates powerfully in keeping up the habitual energy of individuals in a society where a high average standard of energetic work is maintained. The more prudence and self-control the laborer has, the more he will increase the wealth of the community; while, again, the more he is actuated by sense of duty and wide public spirit, the more productive his labor will be under circumstances in which the coincidence between his own interests and that of society is wanting or obscure.'" (Sidgwick, p. 104.)

Pascal says, "Humanity is like one man who lives and learns always."

[1] What Mr. Frederick Pollock ("History of the Science of Politics") says of men in their political relations is equally true of them in their industrial relations: "Man is born to be a citizen in that he comes into an existing social order, and is attached to it by duties of others to himself, and himself to others, which are not and can not be of his own making. He does not come into the world as an unrelated unit, and acquire by some convention a fantastic title to some hundred-thousandth undivided part of the indivisible sovereignty of the people."

"Man is born to be a citizen" is the underlying maxim of Aristotle. The "clanless and masterless man" is a kind of monster. The state is the highest unit yet evolved, and men are not yet citizens of an indefinite universe. A man is born a citizen of a definite state with a definite kind of social existence. The state is natural, first as imposed on man by the general and permanent conditions of life; and next, is the only form of life we as

So of certain economic Bohemians, they would turn their backs on most of their duties to their fellow-citizens, and, having filched all they can of the advantages of living in our great co-operative system, would sacrifice the right of the society which has placed in their hands the purchase-money by means of which they supply their wants.

But let us return to our aggregate. Some of us can satisfy some of our desires by exchanges abroad. Can all of us satisfy all our desires by purchase abroad? We shall see.

The satisfaction of the aggregate desires of the people of the United States requires an outlay of effort, and sacrifice embodied in services and commodities, which have the exchange value of $10,000,000,000 annually. It may be we were wrong a hundred years ago in laying grounds for having so many people here. It may be that these people are wrong in harboring these desires, the gratification of which subjects them to such an enormous tax. It may be that if they had kept their desires for the necessaries, conveniences, amusements, and luxuries of life within bounds, they would not have been put to so much trouble in supplying them. It may be that civilization and modern progress and great achievements "don't pay." It may be that the jelly-fish and the clam are better types of "living and being comfortable," and better illustrate the blessings of "leisure." But "inherited traits and historical traditions" are against us. If, after what "God had done in the way of piling up mountains of iron, silver, and gold, filling the bowels of the earth with salt, coal, and petroleum, and cov-

---

yet know of, in which man can do the best he is capable of. The substance of Burke's comment on Aristotle is that civil society will not come by counting of heads; it is a social organism and a social discipline. If it is artificial in its perfection, yet it is more truly a state of nature than a savage and incoherent mode of life, or rather it is this, because it is artificial; for "art is man's nature." "One man," says Aristotle, "is no man."

ering its surface for centuries with rich vegetable mold, and watering it with mighty lakes and rivers, and planting boundless forests," he also set fifty millions of Yankees down among them, with their illimitable capacities, and boundless aptitudes, and insatiable desires, we may reverently conclude that he designed the adjustment of the organism to its environment. These desires then are natural, legitimate, and necessary, and we have thought it worth while to gratify them. Either the nature of the organic being with which we are dealing must be changed, or we must change its environment.

Of this aggregate we satisfy them to the amount in round numbers of $6,700,000,000 by the direct application of our own energies to our own resources. The census shows that laborers on them embrace one hundred and thirty-five classes. Their labors include most articles of common use, and laborers get a larger share in making these commodities than in making luxuries. These result in productions against which no foreigner can compete— productions not in the "protected industries."

We import annually commodities which we can not pretend to produce (tea, coffee, fruits, etc.), which gratify other desires to the amount of $300,000,000.

According to "Schedule A" (which, for the purpose of this argument alone, we accept as correct), the remaining desires are for commodities, some of which are produced in the "protected industries" here, and others of like character by manufacturers abroad. They amount, in round numbers, to $3,000,000,000 (domestic, $2,440,502,649 + $433,173,335 foreign; total, $2,873,675,984).

That they are legitimate desires appears from the schedule. They are chemical products; earthenware and glassware; metals, iron and steel, and all metal manufactures; wood and wooden-wares; sugar and molasses; tobacco; cotton and cotton goods; hemp, jute, and flax goods; wool and woolen goods; silk and silk goods; books, paper, etc.; "sundries."

Now, the free-trade proposal is, in order to save $556,-938,637—which is *the tax* which the protective statute enables one group of citizens, the manufacturers, to collect of another group, the consumers—that we shall buy the goods in the foreign market.

It is a law of international trade that the *exports must pay for the imports;* commodities must be paid for by commodities. We then propose to import goods to the amount of $3,000,000,000 annually. With what do we propose to pay for them?—$800,000,000 of exports! Of these, $700,000,000 is in food and raw materials—all the foreign market will take—and $100,000,000 in manufactured goods, of the only kind with which, just now, we can beat our competitors. We propose to buy $3,000,000,000 with $800,000,000! The trade is impossible. We have been so often confronted with this dilemma, we have dealt with it so carefully, patiently, and even tediously, that it is time to be done with it. It is time to characterize this assumption of an illimitable foreign market, either as containing a surplus of commodities we would buy, or as adequate to take the proceeds of our "land industries" which we would sell, as it deserves. It is an unfortunate suggestion, a vain proposal, a pretentious lie, a stupendous fraud, a solemn humbug. We can not *buy more value than we can sell.* We can not *therefore buy* the "satisfaction" of all our "desires" for goods manufactured in the protected industries. Nor are they for sale in any market in the world except our own.

We now see the bog into which the professors and statesmen have floundered. The fallacy which they have played on themselves is an old one. It is the "fallacy of division." Surely these people must have run across it in Archbishop Whately's "Logic":

"This is a fallacy with which men are extremely apt to deceive themselves, for, when a multitude of particulars are presented to the mind, many are too weak, or too indolent, to *take a comprehensive view of them,* but confine their attention to a single point in turn, and then decide, infer, and act accordingly. For example, the imprudent spendthrift, finding that he is able to afford this *or* that, *or* the other expense, forgets that *all of them together* will ruin him."

It is the illogical attempt to draw a universal conclusion from a particular premise: "Some foreign exchanges are feasible and profitable, therefore *all* foreign exchanges are feasible and profitable." It is a *non sequitur.*

Now we see the trouble with the atomistic view of society, with this sending the individual all over the planet with a salable article in his peddler's pack to find a purchaser. If one man may peddle, all may peddle.

One man may draw a prize in a lottery, all can not.

One man may get rich smuggling, all can not.

Now we can answer the question why, if a man trades with profit between southern Vermont and northern Massachusetts, he should not be allowed to make equal profit by a free trade between northern Vermont and Canada. If one man may thus trade, all may.

The individual peddler and the individual free-trader may drive a profitable trade for a while. But, if we all trade, and all undertake to buy abroad the satisfaction of our desires, we discover that we can not do it.

The Minnesota farmer asks what difference does it make to him whether the thousand barrels of flour which he sells, at a price fixed in Mark Lane, is consumed in Lowell or Manchester, and why he can not freely import the things he needs for the flour he exports. There is no reason, if he were not an individual in a social group, and if the welfare of the group were not the proper end of government. If all the individuals in the group did the same, all would fail to get the import corresponding to the export; or, rather, the failure of the export would result in the failure of the import, and their desires would fail of gratification.

Now, take the nation at large—all-of-us—we can not by exports purchase all the commodities named in Schedule A if we connect them by the copulative "and."

We can buy $800,000,000 worth, or, under free trade, the foreign market might be slightly enlarged, though free trade would make no more mouths to feed in Europe, nor induce the cultivation of less acres there; their home production and our $300,000,000 food-exports seem to keep them alive.

The exports involved in the discussion are exports of food and raw materials. They are $700,000,000 annually, but one half of this amount goes to fruits, wines, tea, coffee, and leaving $350,000,000 with which we can buy just one eighth of the manufactured commodities we need. The other seven eighths we must manufacture for ourselves, or go without.

We may then buy abroad the commodities named in Schedule A to the amount of $700,000,000 if we go without tea, coffee, fruits, etc. We may combine them in any proportion we please, only so that no group exceeds that amount. We may buy, with or without a tariff, "metals," $678,981,448; *or*, "cotton and cotton goods," "wool and woolen goods," $560,680,843; *or*, "wood and woodenware," "sugar and molasses," "earthenware and tobacco," $597,459,340; *or*, "chemical products," "silk and silk goods," "books, papers," "hemp, jute, and flax goods," etc., $328,443,980; *or*, "sundries," $728,110,383; but we

SCHEDULE A—PRODUCTION UNDER FREEDOM.   253

can not buy them all. The rest we must make or go without. We prefer to make them.

We now come to see just the economic force of the following point put by Prof. Sumner in his lectures ("Protection in the United States"):

"By the census of 1870, the laborers engaged in manufacturing pig-iron numbered altogether 27,554, and their wages amounted to $12,400,000. The capital employed is returned at $56,100,000. We are pointed to this as a great industry—a grand thing to have. The duty was, when the census was taken, $9 per ton, and the market price of American over imported iron showed that this sum was directly added to the cost of all we used. The product of the home manufacture was 2,000,000 tons, on which the tariff cost us $18,000,000, of which the public treasury got not one cent. Seven per cent on the capital in pig-iron manufacture would be $3,900,000, which, with the wages paid to labor in that trade, would make $16,000,000. If, therefore, we had made a bargain with the pig-iron manufacturers to let their capital decay, paying them seven per cent on it and with the people employed to stay idle, while we paid them their full wages, provided that we might have our iron free, we should have made $2,000,000 per annum, to say nothing of the fact that, at the lower price, we might have afforded a larger consumption of iron. We should, moreover, have had 509 steam-engines to apply to other work. We should have saved $18,000,000 worth of coal, charcoal, and coke for other uses, and we should have left 4,000,000 tons of iron-ore in the ground for those who come after us to use when they can do it profitably."

Without stopping to note the minor suggestions of false inferences and assumptions which the extract contains, without pausing to be told to what "other work" the 509 steam-engines could be applied (for we never shall be told), for what "other uses" the coke and coal could be saved, and when and under what conditions the iron-ore could be "profitably" used—and how much longer the human family should leave all this treasure untouched —and the failure to credit the total annual product of the nation's industry with the total exchange value of the 2,000,000 tons of pig-iron (worth $40 per ton in 1869), $80,000,000!—all of which was distributed within the country to wages and capital—we remand the paragraph to the class of fallacies to which it belongs.

If there were no political, moral, governmental reasons compelling the independence of this nation of other nations, for the supply of a staple like iron, reasons of an industrial, educational, or military nature, and we proceeded on the mere economic notion to get the little iron a purely agricultural people required, we may admit that we should have got it cheaper abroad, temporarily at least. That is, if this want of iron, to be had in no other way, had induced us to import it to the exclusion of some other kind of commodities, we should have got it cheaper by exporting something in which we had greater advantages of production. But when the "desire" for iron takes its place in the catalogue of other "desires," which, in the aggregate, overmastered our purchasing power, we then proceed to procure it *and* them in the only way which will result in supplying them all. We produce the things we can, and import the things we must, according to the strength of our desires and needs.

Prof. Sumner has simply treated the group of iron-makers on the atomistic plan. Instead of the individual, he has taken a class. As the only class, and by itself, we should have got its products cheaper (at least temporarily), by importation. As a single desire, it was satisfied (temporarily, at least) at less effort by exchange. As one of the aggregate of desires amounting to $3,000,000,000, it could only be gratified at the expense of some other satisfaction, more or less urgent. The nation takes its choice of imported satisfactions up to $700,000,000. It can put iron among them if no other considerations prevail. If other considerations do intervene, it produces it under the best conditions available.

It remains to provide $2,200,000,000 for the satisfaction of desires for which we have no recourse but domestic resources and domestic labor. We have been driven to a rather laborious, but we think conclusive demonstration, that seven eighths of the goods made in what are called "protected industries" *must* be made in the United States. They must, of course, be made under the conditions of returns to American capital and labor. The *cost* of all to the consumer here will be the cost of making the most expensive portion. This is a law which it can not be possible that we ought to stop now to demonstrate, and human legislation is powerless to repeal it. It is the well-known and undisputed law on which rent arises. Nor is it necessary to hold with Ricardo that rent is the price paid for the "original and indestructible power of the soil"—it may well be due to the development of the human community inhabiting that soil—it is the price of so much "space," which is also an instrument of production, limited in extent and in exclusive ownership. It is a payment for "space," as Mr. Carey puts it, "because of its nearness to the societary movement." But the principle that when the whole of a given product is necessary to supply the demand, the price of the whole will be the cost of the most costly proportion, can not be denied. It will be found laid down in any text-book.[1] In the nature of things this must be so, oth-

---

[1] Commenting on Ricardo's law of rent, Prof. Perry says: "The Ricardo

erwise the most costly portion would not be produced. The producers of the least costly portion make a greater profit, and they may or may not reduce prices. The *cost*, then, to the consumer of goods made partly under American and partly under European conditions, would not, in the long run, be reduced by foreign trade. Either the importer does or does not reduce his prices. If he does not, the protective *tax costs* the consumer nothing. If he does, he drives the home manufacturer out of business and into something else. In the first case we get the whole supply on the American terms, which "freedom" will not make less onerous. In the second case we go without the goods. The problem is to get some one to make the seven eighths of the goods we must have, made at home. Prof. Sumner, David A. Wells, Henry J. Philpot, Frank Hurd, and Thomas G. Shearman, *et id omne*, need their share, but I see no

---

law of rent lost most of its significance and the simple truth remained, applicable to all products that have a market rate, *that the rate must be presupposed to be sufficient to meet the cost of that portion produced with the greatest difficulty, otherwise that portion would not be produced at all.*" ("Political Economy," p. 241.)

"In order to estimate the influence of this fact upon price, we must distinguish between those commodities, the cheapest manner of the production of which may be extended at pleasure, and those in the production of which it is necessary, *in order to satisfy the aggregate want of them*, to call in the dearest mode of production to aid the cheapest. In the former instance the price of commodities is naturally regulated by the least cost of production. . . .

"If the same laws were applicable in the latter case, producers placed in a less favorable situation" (and high wages puts the American producer in a less favorable situation) "would be compelled to immediately abandon the market. The market, in consequence, would no longer be able *to provide for the aggregate need;* and the price of the commodity would continue to rise until the producers who had been driven from the market returned to it again. Hence, here, *the price in the long run is determined by the cost of production of the commodity, produced under the least advantageous conditions, while such production is necessary in order to satisfy the aggregate need.*" (Roscher, "Politcal Economy," sec. 110.) In other words, we here must depend on our own conditions of production for the greater portion of our aggregate needs.

proposal on their part to undertake their manufacture on European terms, or "under freedom." In truth, we are simply back to Mr. Mill's proposal of the protective tax as the easiest way out of it. What has occurred, and what will occur, is the uncertainty, fluctuations, and ruin which periodically overtake the American labor and capital which is subject to such competition, and the consequent failure to get the goods at all. We can not escape "competition," for we are making the same goods for the same market. If, then, at last, the far greater portion of the manufactured goods we consume must be made at home under our conditions, and the laws of cost of production here, the whole market may as well be given at once to our own workmen. To the whole consumption the American production must contribute the larger portion. "Inundations of cheap goods," "bankruptcy," and "fire-damaged bargains," are not a normal or reliable source, either of supply or cheapness. It would not seem possible that any elaborations of argument or illustrations are needed to strengthen this statement. The whole significance of the situation, and the whole philosophy of protection as well, was summed up by John C. Calhoun in his speech on our second tariff act of 1816: "The cotton and woolen manufactures are not to be introduced, they are already introduced to a great extent, freeing us entirely from the hazards and, in a great measure, the sacrifices experienced in giving the capital of the country a new direction. The restrictive measures and the war, though not intended for that purpose, have, *by the necessary operation of things*, turned a large amount of capital to these new branches of industry. But it will no doubt be said, if they are so far established, and if the situation of the country is so favorable to their growth, where is the necessity of affording them protection? *It is to put them beyond the reach of contingency.*"

Since the Revolutionary War there has been no day when the people of the United States have not stood in need of the domestic manufacture for the greater proportion of the supply of its manufactured goods. They have always been under the necessity of using an aggregate, the greater portion of which was supplied under our own conditions of remuneration to labor and capital. This has been "the necessary operation of things here," and manufactures were *natural* to us. It was as well to put them "beyond the reach of contingency" first as last; otherwise their introduction must depend, as John Rae says, "on the miscarriage of early projectors," or, as Mr. Mill puts it: "But it can not be expected that individuals should *at their own risk*, or rather, *to their certain loss*, introduce a new manufacture, and bear the burden of carrying it on, until the producers have been educated up to the level of those with whom the processes are traditional. A protective duty, continued for a reasonable time, will sometimes be the least inconvenient mode in which a nation can tax itself for the support of such an experiment."

And this, without adverting to the powerful operation of the *vis inertia* of custom, which, as Prof. Sidgwick remarks, "is no less liable to maintain the importation from abroad of goods which might be advantageously produced in the proximity of their market, than it is to keep any other part of the process of production in an economically backward condition." [1]

---

[1] In this connection it may be interesting to note what "an instructor in political economy in Harvard College" says: "There are two sets of conditions under which it is supposable that advantages not natural or inherent may be found in one country as compared with another, under which merely temporary and accidental causes may permit the use of certain branches of industry in the second country, and under which, therefore, there may be room for the application of protection. These are, first, the state of things in a new country which is rapidly growing in population, and in which, as

And it is a *tax* only when prices are considered in the period when we are undersold by the foreign maker, for the sake of the destruction of the domestic industry, with the expectation of making good losses by subsequent control of the market and advance of prices. The truth is, no human being knows what foreign goods would cost under free trade and with no manufactures here.

Mr. Sumner thinks the forces of labor and capital committed to an industry are like the water in the reservoir which supplies the city. It may be turned on and turned off at pleasure—now here, now there—or need not be used at all, at your option. But capital and labor are not aggregates of pure force in any such sense.[1] Hence the Professor, in dealing with our epoch of 1816, says ("Protection in the United States," p. 39): "Evidently we can not understand these things without taking into

---

population becomes more dense, there is a natural change from exclusive devotion to the extractive industries toward greater attention to those branches of production classed as manufactures. The transition from a purely agricultural state to a more diversified system of industry may, in a complete absence of other occupations than agriculture, be retarded beyond the time when it might advantageously take place. Secondly, when great improvements take place in some of the arts of production, it is possible that the new processes may be retained in the country in which they originate, and may fail to be applied in another country, through ignorance, the inertia of habit, and perhaps in consequence of restrictive legislation at the seat of the new methods." (F. W. Taussig, in "Protection to Young Industries," p. 11.)

[1] This is adverted to by Prof. Ely: "A further hypothesis was the absolute lack of friction in economic movements. Not only do capital and labor move with perfect ease from place to place and from employment to employment, but this, it was implicitly maintained, is accomplished without the slightest loss. The silk manufacturer diverts his capital into another employment, like the construction of locomotives, with precisely the same facility with which he turns his family carriage-horse from an avenue into a cross-street, while the Manchester laborer, on a moment's warning, finds a suitable purchaser for his immovable effects, and, without expense or loss of time, transfers himself to London, where employment is at once offered him at the rate of wages there current."

account the movements which were going on in other industrial nations, but the popular opinion here was that the English had set out, by a sacrifice of some millions' worth of goods, to destroy American manufactures. This belief had deep root, and perhaps has only lately died out, since we have ceased to hear cries of 'British gold,' whenever any one spoke of free trade. The notion I have referred to received strong re-enforcement from a remark of Brougham's which you may find quoted in the first popular protectionist's work you choose to take up, in which he recommended his countrymen to *reconquer the American market*. If he meant to propose to them to sacrifice their capital in giving several millions' worth of goods to the Americans in order to *destroy factories which would spring up again* the moment they tried to reimburse themselves, they would have been the first to laugh at him."

The historical fact is that *destroyed factories* do not thus spring up again, without defensive duties. And English human nature, or rather the human nature of Manchester capital, is in pretty effective action yet. Here is a citation from an official report on strikes, of a Committee appointed by Parliament and made to Parliament in 1854. This will also probably continue to appear in any " popular protectionist's work ":

"I believe that the laboring classes generally in the manufacturing districts of this country, and especially in the iron and coal districts, are very little aware of the extent to which they are often indebted for *their being employed at all*, to the immense *losses* which their employers voluntarily incur in bad times in order to destroy foreign competition, and to gain and keep possession of foreign markets. Authentic instances are well known of employers" (the report is, of course, dealing with English employers) " having in such times carried on their works at a loss amounting in the aggregate to three or four hundred thousand pounds in as many years. If the efforts of those who encourage the combination *to restrict* the amount of labor and to produce strikes were to be successful for any length of time, the *great accumulations of capital* could no longer be made which enable a few of the most wealthy capitalists to *overwhelm all foreign competitors in times of great depression*, and thus *to clear the way* for the whole *trade to step in* when prices rise, and to carry on *a great business* before foreign capital can again accumulate *to establish a competition* in prices with any chance of success. The *large capitals of this country* are *the great instruments of warfare* against the competing capitals of other countries, and are *the most* essential instruments now remaining by which our manufacturing supremacy can be maintained; the other elements—cheap labor, abundance of raw materials, means of communication, and skilled labor—being rapidly in progress of being equalized."

Why will not the scientists who hold that "an economic investigation may be carried on independently" take scientific notice of the sociological forces which wield the economic ones?

This theory takes no account of the organization through which the productive forces must operate. When the flow is from the foreign reservoirs through the channel of foreign trade, the flow from the domestic reservoirs must cease. Bear in mind we are dealing with competitive industries. "Springing up again" is a very good thing, but it is not met with in practice. Henry Clay impatiently disposed of it as a patent fact (speech, House, March, 1821): "Now I contend that this proposition" (that manufactures will in due time spring up) "is refuted by all experience, ancient and modern, in all countries. If I am asked why unprotected industry should not succeed in a struggle with protected industry, I answer, the fact has ever been so, and that is sufficient. I reply that uniform experience evinces that it can not succeed in such a struggle, and that is sufficient. If we speculate on the causes of this universal truth, we may differ about them. Still, the undeniable fact remains."

But it is easily accounted for. The assumption overlooks *in toto* the organization by means of which modern industries are carried on. It overlooks the structure through which functions are discharged. If the function ceases (as it does when the foreign supply is on), the structure degenerates. It simply becomes atrophied in accordance with well-known laws in organic life. The structure is the joint adjustment of capital and labor co-ordinated to a common end. When then the function ceases—that is, when the work stops—labor must disband and go elsewhere. Labor must take itself to a market at once, or perish; a day's work to it lost now is lost forever. Capital necessarily follows. If not destroyed, it is paralyzed in rust, friction, and disuse.

The aggregate consumption is a reservoir holding 2,800,000,000 gallons. Certain pipes can deliver 350,000,000 gallons, and certain others 2,400,000,000. The mechanism is such that when the 350,000,000 run freely, the 2,400,000,000 stop. If either is to stop, which one do our interest and welfare dictate we shall prefer? To ask this question is to answer it.

We see, then, upon what an utter perversion of the facts " Schedule A " is based. The protective *tax* does not add a *sou marqué* to the cost of the $2,440,502,647 worth of goods made at home. They are a necessary part of the whole supply, and must cost the price of producing the most expensive portion. The protective *tax* partly raises the price of the imported commodity, but not to the full

SCHEDULE A—PRODUCTION UNDER FREEDOM. 263

amount of the tax, and in many articles it adds nothing. A *protective tax* simply covers the difference in cost of production, but the whole tax on the foreign commodity goes into the public treasury, and besides saves the domestic industry; the final result of which is the whole supply of our whole natural demand at the lowest cost to our people—the lowest cost which our relations to the world permit.

The *abundance* of commodities which Americans are to consume lies spread before us in the richness and prodigality of nature in field, forest, mines, rivers, and seas.

Their *cheapness* depends on the skill and fidelity with which we overcome the obstacles which nature alone offers to us. We have no false starts to recover, no false traditions to reverse, no false institutions to overthrow. The safe, independent, manly, and heroic course is to accept the challenge nature offers. We formulate our demands on nature, and ask nothing of government but that it keep foreign product off our backs, that it applies *laissez faire* to ourselves, and "hands off" to all other nations. Nature's returns are unfailing, her markets are never in a state of glut; we need never depend for "bargains" on "bankruptcy" or "some fire-damaged goods."

Their *distribution* depends on the just and fair rewards for services rendered, under Nature's own law of supply and demand, superintended and re-enforced by the decrees of a strong, highly civilized, and well-governed state. The state is not something external to the worker, with a purpose foreign or hostile to him. The individual is not the creature of *status*, but lives under a dispensation of free contract. Human laws do not infringe on his freedom. His only constraint comes from the finer and wider instincts of humanity imposed by the social movement, unfolded under the laws of its divine evolution and progress.

There is crime and overreaching, and the exploitation of labor inseparable from human society, under free trade as well as under protection. But each man has a chance to win "wealth" or the "satisfaction of desires."[1]

He wins it by the application of his own faculties to American physical, political, and moral conditions. He does not "make it out of anybody else."

It results, then, that the achievements and satisfactions of so highly differentiated a nation as the United States must be won by its own people on its own soil. They cost effort, but the effort is reduced to a minimum. *Under free trade, we could not win from nature, here, anything at a less cost in labor and abstinence;* and it is settled that we can not *buy* our satisfactions.

To call this cost a *tax* may please an economist fond of antitheses. But it is hardly worth while to carry on a controversy with any one who seriously insists on the identity of such antipodal things.

It appears, then, that some of us, a number whose desires, when taken individually or in groups, did not cost in satisfaction more than $700,000,000, could buy their satisfaction by exchanges in a foreign market, provided always that the whole number could be fully employed in the most advantageous industries, and provided the foreign market continued to take the surplus we offer for sale and the surplus we wish to buy. The trouble is, that our desires increase faster than the capacity of the foreign market. It appears also that when all of us, just as we are, undertake to satisfy our desires by exchanges in the foreign

---

[1] It sounds harsh, but the author of "What Social Classes owe to each other" says truly: "We each owe it to the other to guarantee rights. Rights do not appertain to *results*, but only to *chances*. They pertain to the *conditions* of the struggle for existence, not to any of the results of it; to the *pursuit* of happiness, not to the *possession* of it."

SCHEDULE A—PRODUCTION UNDER FREEDOM. 265

market, we fall $2,200,000,000 short annually. We fall back then on the domestic production, in which no owner of labor or capital hands over to another anything over and above that which that other's services are entitled to, under the laws of supply and demand, operating equably, fully, and fairly throughout the entire field of industries.

The Government here has never constrained the citizen to do that which even might have been better for him. It has never invaded the liberty of any citizen to buy what he pleased and sell where he pleased.[1] And so it has resulted that, according to our respective desires, we go on and import iron and sugar, steel and velvets, figs and India shawls, china-ware and Persian dates, silks and seltzer-water, wines and nutmegs, wool and coffee, tea and London-made hats, raw-hides and salicylic acid, until the aggregate reaches the $700,000,000. The trade then stops, or ought to stop. If we go further, we export our bullion. If we still go on we get hopelessly in debt, and bankruptcy ensues upon inactivity thus enforced. What stops the trade? Protective taxes? No. The trade ceases because we have exhausted our salable exports. We are locked up in the equation of international demand. "Every transaction in commerce is an independent transaction." The traders who send out the exports are not the ones who bring in the imports, but in due time, each going his own way, they are both brought to bay by the balance of trade—the par of exchange is against us, specie goes out, and we can only resume the operation when commodities may again be paid for by commodities. Two very promising apothegms of Prof. Perry disappear in the test: "Man is man, motive is motive, and exchange is exchange." "Free trade does not compel anybody to trade, does not even recommend

---

[1] The only exception is the purchase of ships abroad.

anybody to trade, it merely allows those to trade who think it for their advantage."

Man, motive, and exchange are all submerged in the law of international balances—the antecedent law of supply and demand. As things are, we stop on the exchange of the $700,000,000. "Free trade" does not even allow the trade except in strict subordination to that law: nor is this the old *bête noir* of "the mercantile system."[1]

What "Schedule A" tends to prove, if its figures were correct, is this: *If* we could buy and import the whole $433,173,335 + $2,440,502,647 = $2,873,675,984 worth of foreign goods, and *provided* our exports exchanged at present prices and the imports cost no more than now, we should save $556,938,637, and, *economically*, it would be a judicious operation. We concede nothing of its moral and physical effects. But we have seen how the "if" stands for an impossibility in the trade, and the "provided" represents an adverse change in values, ruinous and fatal to us.

What "Schedule A" actually makes clear and evident is the impossibility of procuring the commodities in any mode except by direct production. There is no other way to get them, and we can not do without them. The cost of their use and consumption is *the tax* imposed on us for being a highly differentiated organism, a highly civilized

---

[1] "In this manner new light has been thrown upon our studies, and we learn that our fathers have been wiser than we have been inclined to think, and that it has not been reserved for our day to discover all that is good and true in the economic life of nations. A concrete example of the fruits of this new method is found in the almost complete reversal of opinion concerning the policy advocated by those we call Mercantilists. It is now acknowledged that they were, on the whole, very shrewd, sensible men, whereas, not long since, doctrines and measures were attributed to them which would lead one to suppose it necessary to go back only two hundred years to discover man with a caudal appendage."—Prof. Ely.

people—the tax is the penalty of being a vertebrate instead of a mollusk. That is all there is of it. I think protectionists ought to thank Mr. Springer for "Schedule A."

If any farmer or manufacturer or transporter is appropriating more than his share of the $556,938,637, it is not in pursuance of any human statute. If one citizen is collecting taxes of another citizen, under this state of the facts, it must be in accordance with the divine ordinance under which society is moving to its fulfillment.

We are, therefore, entitled to answer "the political question about protection: Does the statute enacted by the legislature alter the *distribution* of *property* so that *one man* enjoys *another man's earnings?* Has the state a law in operation which enables *one citizen* to *collect taxes of another?*" with a clear and demonstrated negative.

And we can answer "the popular question about protection: Does it prevent me from supporting myself and *my family* by my labor *as well as I could* if there were no *protective* tax?" with an equally emphatic negative. You are supporting yourself and your family, with your standard of life, by less exertion than in any other country, and you could not increase the ratio of your comfort and happiness to your labor and sacrifice by exchanges made in any market on the face of the earth. You can go without the satisfaction of your desires, but you can not buy them outside of the United States.

And, now, inasmuch as it is natural to have the men who work for us, work on this side of the Atlantic, especially as they work on the same materials, with the same tools, and with the same skill, let the free-trader give us the reasons for having our workshops on the other side of the ocean. The burden of proof is on him, if he changes this natural order, to establish these three propositions: First, that free trade would increase the total annual product of the nation's industry; second, that it would more equitably distribute the total product; third, that a decreased total product would exchange for a total of commodities equal to and as equitably distributed as the total product under protection.

There are four alternative conditions under which we may attempt to procure the consumable goods indispensable and desirable to us, or rather in which we may adjust the supply of them to our demand for them—in which we may bring our desires and their satisfaction into conformity to each other. We can not buy them to the amount of $3,000,000,000. We can, then, first lessen the demand—the "desires." We can do this either—

1. By exterminating the people who entertain these various and costly desires, and the human beings who are living under their dominion.

This will scarcely be regarded as feasible, in view of the progress we have made in Christian civilization.

2. By eliminating the desires themselves.

This has been done successfully in Tyre, and Sidon, and Carthage, and Ireland, and Spain, and Egypt, and Poland. Great people have lost their energy by their failure to reap returns for its exercise. The pressure of external social and commercial systems has produced despair, and they have disappeared from the arena of human contentions. They work no effective demand for commodities, for they bring no purchase-money in their hands. The hungry boy gazing in the pastry-cook's window makes no demand for tarts without the penny in his hands. If the struggle to procure the penny becomes hopeless, he will in time lose his hankering after tarts, and his desire for tarts will be diminished. He is then rid of that source of *taxation*.

Second: We can procure the supply, the "satisfaction," either—

SCHEDULE A—PRODUCTION UNDER FREEDOM.

1. By the process of direct production, under a protective or prohibitory tariff, as we have had experience in the United States for a hundred years; or,

2. By the process of indirect production, through exchanges made abroad under free foreign trade.

The latter is the scheme commended to us by the advocates of theoretical, scientific, orthodox, Manchesterian free trade.

It remains to examine its practical application to the actual facts as they exist in the United States.

We are now to produce "under freedom"—freedom not only between the 50,000,000 of us who have accepted the duties and burdens, along with the privileges of American citizenship, but freedom for all the world to come and go from our harbors and docks. We are to breathe that metaphysical entity which is longingly spoken of as "the air of commercial freedom." Let us analyze it, and see whether it will exhilarate us or asphyxiate us.

We are supposed to have completed the exchanges of the $700,000,000 of products in which we are not in competition—products of dissimilar kinds; we have put off upon the foreigner all the products in the production of which wages are high—either all we have to spare, or all he cares to take. We now accept the competition which is forced upon us and which we can not evade, in the joint effort with all the world, to produce $2,200,000,000 of similar products, to be sold in the same market, to wit, our own domestic market.

The conditions of production are not materially different on the two sides of the Atlantic, except in the wages of labor.

A reasonably fair estimate of the advantages and disadvantages under which we work will be found in the "Contemporary Review" for October, 1878, by Mr. Henderson,

"America as a Manufacturing Competitor." They are stated as follows:

ADVANTAGES.—1. More convenient access to raw materials.

2. Important natural advantages in the shape of water-power.

3. A better educated and superior class of work-people.

DISADVANTAGES, compared with England, in the—

1. Lower rates of interest upon capital.
2. Lower cost of building materials.
3. Lower wages.
4. Sounder system of finances and taxation.
5. Lower rates of fuel and light.
6. More convenient and ready access to the markets of consumers.

It will be noted that our "advantages" are all of a permanent nature. Of the "disadvantages," "1" is rapidly disappearing; "2" and "5" are questions of amount of labor involved in which we constantly approach equality; "3" is a "disadvantage" under which we propose to continue to labor; "4" is doubtful and temporary, at best; "6" is not true of our home market, which embraces the "consumers" we are primarily struggling to supply. It resolves itself, at last, mainly into a question of the cost of labor. All the other conditions are equalized or rapidly becoming equalized.

There is a well-known and recognized law of political economy, as well as of common observation—the law of indifference—that there can not be two prices for the same commodity in the same market. It is thus expressed by Prof. Jevons: "In the same open market, at any one moment, there can not be two prices for the same kind of article." We are now beyond the region of Reciprocal Demand, where one gives cotton cloth for tobacco—or oatmeal for bananas—where the trade depends merely on strength of desire and not upon cost of production. We are now in the presence of a fair, stand-up bargain, made in the same market, in which cost of production in money-wages settles the advantage of the parties to it. All other conditions of production being equalized, one of three things must take place—one of three possible adjustments must ensue:

1. Wages of laborers in the United States, engaged in these industries (and the same rate must soon follow in all others), must sink to the level paid to workers in Europe on the same industries.

2. Wages in Europe will be raised to the level of the American rate—which will readily be conceded to be impossible. We are rich, but our riches are not great enough to "go around" on this scale.

3. Wages here and abroad will meet on a common level at some intermediate point.

In either the first or last event we should have lowered the wages of our own workmen: we meet the foreign laborer on a level lower than ours. The result of Bastiat's exposition of human destiny was this: "*The constant approximation of all men toward a level which is always rising*—in other terms, *improvement and equalization;* in a single word, *harmony.*" I believe it. The epoch in which it will be true is commonly known as the millennium. Then, and not until then, will universal free trade be a good theory and good practice. We shall approach it by gradual steps, and not by a catastrophe. The United States might bring about a cataclysmic ruin of itself by decreeing free trade in the last quarter of the nineteenth century, but it could not bring on the millennium for its own citizens. For the present, its economic salvation depends on its holding to the high level which Providence and Nature allow it to maintain in the interest of "all men" who choose to come here, labor, save, and enjoy here. It will thus best exercise its natural liberty and right to pursue and secure the welfare of its people.

Prof. Cairnes, when asked how we can compete in the same industry against European labor (I will not say "pauper labor," for the skilled industrious mechanic in England or on the Continent is not a pauper), with our higher-priced labor, frankly says, in effect, we can not. Let the American workman be content with the wages of the hedger and ditcher, and he can compete, etc. His words are: "But, secondly, I beg the reader to consider what is meant by the alleged inability of New England and Pennsylvania to compete, let us say, with Manchester and Sheffield, in the manufacture of calico and cutlery. What it means, and what it only can mean, is that they are unable to do so consistently with obtaining that rate of remuneration on their industry which is current in the United States. *If only American laborers and capitalists would be content with the wages and profits current in Great Britain, there is nothing that I know of to prevent them holding their own in any markets to which Manchester and Sheffield send their wares.*"[1]

Mr. John Stuart Mill's account of the economic phenomena which would attend the experiment would be this: "If American producers generally should be unable to compete with English producers at the present rate of wages, a flow of gold (wages being regarded as measured in gold) from America would set in, by which, ultimately, a general fall in the price of labor and commodities would be effected, until American producers gained possession of the market with regard to the commodities in the produc-

---

[1] "Some Principles of Political Economy newly expounded," p. 386.

tion of which they are at the greatest advantage or at the least disadvantage."

That is, the coin goes out and gold becomes dear. Prices, reckoned in gold, fall, values depreciate, and goods get so cheap that the process of exportation is resumed, and, in the end, things come around to an equilibrium. Exportation which is brought about by the necessity of *paying debts* incurred by excessive importation is uniformly made at a sacrifice. It is *the getting in debt* by overtrading, and the necessity of paying debts, which distresses nations as well as individuals when pay-day comes. When the man of business checks out his bank-balances in the course of his business, he suffers no disadvantage; but when he checks them out to pay debts incurred in business—while it is the best thing he can do with his money, pay his debts—yet his business stops. It is so with the nation. It is better to pay in bullion than not to pay at all, but there is no option about it. The coin goes out and *the trade stops.* We are thrown back on the domestic commerce.

Mr. Carey has well expressed the law and necessary sequence of the events:

"All the facts presented by the history of the United States may be adduced in proof of the assertion that *a country which maintains a policy tending to promote the export of raw materials must have against it a balance of trade requiring the export of the precious metals, and must dispense with their services as measure of value.*"

These facts may be briefly stated thus:

"Protection ceased in 1818, bequeathing to free trade a commerce that gave an excess *import* of specie, a people among whom existed great prosperity, a large public revenue, and a rapidly diminishing public debt.

" Free trade ceased in 1824, bequeathing to protection

a commerce that gave an excess *export* of specie, an impoverished people, a declining public revenue, and an increasing public debt.

"Protection ceased in 1834–'35; bequeathing to free trade a commerce that gave an excess *import* of specie, a people more prosperous than any that had ever then been known, a revenue so great that it had been rendered necessary to emancipate tea, coffee, and many other commodities from duty, and a treasury free from all charge on account of public debt.

"Free trade ceased in 1842, bequeathing to protection a commerce that gave an excess *export* of specie, a people ruined and their government in a state of repudiation, a public treasury bankrupt, and begging everywhere for loans at the highest rate of interest, a revenue collected and disbursed in irredeemable paper money, and a very large foreign debt.

"Protection ceased in 1847, bequeathing to free trade a commerce that gave an excess *import* of specie, a highly prosperous people, State governments restored to credit, a rapidly growing commerce, a large public revenue, and a declining foreign debt.

"In 1857, with all the hundreds of millions of dollars of gold supplied by California exported or locked up by want of credit, commerce was paralyzed; the price of money in commercial cities ranged from ten to thirty per cent, and indebtedness to foreign nations increased to such an amount that the payment of interest alone required a sum equal to all our food-export."

If the United States should try this experiment, the next thing to be done would be to endeavor to extricate themselves from the predicament in which free trade had placed them, and restore the home market to our own producers by restrictions, as they did in 1789, 1816, 1842, and

1861. There are no indications in history, present experience, or prophecy, by which the United States can secure, by the export of food and raw materials, any greater conquest of the foreign market than she has already made. She will master the commerce of the world, so far as it will be useful to her, by the export of her food, raw materials, and manufactures, founded and maintained by protection. And she will maintain the protection of her "infant industries" until this dominion is secured, if it takes a century. What is a hundred years in the life of a great people?

Those revenue reformers who would reach this triumph of our commerce through manufactures rather than through agriculture and the extractive industries are on the right track. But the way to raise manufactures to this height of achievement is not to begin by razing them to their foundations. No man who does not assent to the economic value of protection as a scientific doctrine ought to be allowed to tinker with the tariff.

It is not worth while to pursue the consequences which would attend free trade; no real authority will dispute them. First, the impact of the foreign competition, the filling of our warehouses with the cargoes of foreign fabrics, the abandonment of the struggle by the domestic producer. Then the disbandment of workmen out of employment, or "squeezing," as Mill says, "by their competition, their food and necessaries from the shares of other laborers," the destruction of the capital invested in buildings and machinery, crumbling to ruin under idleness and rust; the absolute dissipation of the existing industrial organization. Then the loss of our gold and silver, which loosens, cripples, and destroys our whole existing association; the people to be left, at the last, in a condition of hopeless indebtedness, constantly increasing to foreign nations, and consequent condition of permanent bankruptcy. When the situation became intolerable, we should be poor enough to enter upon the unprofitable industries, and the time would have arrived when, according to Prof. Sumner, we could use the coal and coke and iron-ore which we had been saving for future generations, and when we could find a use for those "509 steam-engines," for we should have come to that ideal "something else" to do. We have reached the promised land, and the "something else" is done under European conditions of wages, under the European standard of living, comfort, and enjoyment.

This is exactly what will happen under the attempt to procure $2,200,000,000 in the necessaries, conveniences, and luxuries of life "under freedom." The wickedness of the proposal is more manifest in that the professors, at least, know that these results must flow from the action of economic forces which are acknowledged elements in the science which they teach.

We dismiss it as the "paradise of fools."

CHAPTER XII.

COST OF PRODUCTION—A PARADOX.

A VERY formidable attempt has been made by English and American free-traders to solve this question on a consideration of "cost of production."

Prof. Perry, in agreement with them, attempts to offset the cost of labor in the United States by depreciating the proportion of labor to the other elements of the cost of production. With him "cost of production" is made up of "wages" and "profits." In the proportion in which he could eliminate the labor which enters into a product, he would be enabled to claim that some other reasons than a high rate of wages should be assigned to account for our inability to compete with the foreign manufacturer. This seems to give him a motive for unworthily disparaging the contribution which "labor" makes to our aggregate industrial results. It is paid with higher wages by the day, but it is more efficient—the American laborer works more hours per day, and loses a less number of Mondays, because he drinks less beer on Sundays—and, at last, gives only twenty per cent increased value to the materials his labor enters into.

So, to avoid the argument that we can not compete with the foreign manufacturer, because wages are high in this country, it is necessary to neutralize their effect in some way, either by reducing the proportion which labor bears to the whole cost of the product—saying that our labor is more efficient—or that other elements of "cost of production" are higher, such as taxation, raw materials, etc. But after excluding all these items of cost, there still remained the "high rate of wages" to contend with. Mr. David A. Wells, in his report for 1868 (as Commissioner of Revenue), set off against our rate of wages the higher efficiency of our laborers. He argued that wages were higher, but that our laborers earned more. While the American workman was earning a higher pay *per diem*, he put by so much a higher effort into his work; and so it resulted that, effort for effort, the American got no more remuneration than the European. In that way he supposed he had answered the protectionist's argument that we could not compete because of high wages. His proposition was that the same amount of money purchased no more *labor*, in the sense of effort, efficiency, here than it did abroad; and that the English operative received as high a compensation for what he actually did as the American operative. It was Mr. Brassey's argument over again, probably in his lifetime the greatest employer of labor in the world. The moral he endeavored constantly to enforce was the heavy detriment which Great Britain suffered from her dear labor—a detriment so heavy, an economical drawback so serious, that only her great resources in other respects enabled her to bear up under it against the stream of *Continental* competition.[1]

---

[1] And right here let us ask why Great Britain, whose "advantageous industries" are mining coal and iron-ore, does not exclusively pursue them, and turn them over to the cheaper labor of the Continent, to be wrought up into the commodities she needs by the *cheaper labor* there. Englishmen have "historical antecedents," and it is not in their nature, morally, industrially, or historically, to "fall in" in the march of the family and stand at the point of their most "advantageous industries"—coal and iron. Coal and iron would not employ all their labor and capital. English statesmen rightfully think it their duty to provide for the welfare of Englishmen who are on

So Mr. Brassey was gotten rid of by calling him a "commercial writer" instead of an "economist." What he said was this: "It is the opinion of Mr. Lothian Bell, one of our highest authorities, that after all the efforts of our iron-masters to contend with the difficulties of high-paid labor by the improvement of machinery, labor costs fifteen per cent more in England than on the Continent." (Prof. Perry figures out the disadvantages of America as against England, by reason of higher wages, at only *four* per cent.) "And this disadvantage, in his opinion, entirely neutralizes the advantages we derive from our great facilities in the proximity of our iron-mines to our coal-beds. Our workmen are not sufficiently alive to the necessity for the exercise of the utmost efforts of ingenuity in order to enable capital invested in England to hold its own in the industrial campaign."

This position could not be logically assumed by the scientific free-traders. "What," they said, "is now the grand argument with the people of the United States for the maintenance of protection?" "Why, the high *cost of production* in that country." "And what is the evidence of this high cost of production?" "Simply, the high rate of wages which prevails." "How," they ask, "can we, with our high-priced labor, compete with the pauper labor of Europe?"

"I must frankly own," says Prof. Cairnes, "accepting the point of view of the current *theory of cost*, I can find no satisfactory reply to this question, and I am quite sure that Mr. Wells, who implicitly adopts this point of view" (in one of his Cobden Club essays), "*has wholly failed to furnish one.* . . . What he shows is, that labor in England, though much higher-priced than in most European

---

English soil. An Englishman has resources enough to go to the front, and to the front he goes.

countries, and in particular than in Russia, is still so much more efficient here than there, that the high English rates are practically cheaper for the English capitalist than the lower Continental rates for the capitalists of the Continent. What is the bearing of this upon the *American* demand for protection against *England?* Will Mr. Wells maintain that, as the efficiency of English labor is to that of Russian, so is the efficiency of American labor to that of English? If not, how does his objection to the protectionist's criterion of cost, founded on the different degrees of industrial efficiency, affect the argument? And as little does he seem to me to make good the pertinency of his objection to the other ground taken." (The other ground taken was "the varying purchasing power of money in relation to the laborers' requirements." Mr. Wells, like all others who labor to minimize the difference in wages in the United States and England, takes the ground that the workman in the latter can purchase as much by the wages of a day's labor as in the former.) He continues: "It is possible that in a few manufacturing districts in the United States *the rent* of an artisan's dwelling is higher than in some manufacturing districts in England, but in *the most important articles* of the laborer's consumption—in the whole list of "provisions," for example—the advantage in respect to price is unquestionably with the American consumer." (See Carroll D. Wright's "Generalizations," Chapter XVIII, *infra*, page 409.)

The free-trader, then, is headed off as he attempts to proceed according to "the current theory of cost." We retrace our steps, and try a new route. We must start with a different conception of the "cost of production."

The words "cost of production" are not, they say, now to be interpreted from the capitalist's point of view. They do not represent the *expenses* which the manufacturer has been put to in order to produce the finished commodity. They do not stand for the outlay in wages and interest—the money which the capitalist has advanced to pay "wages," and that which he will retain as "profits." These words are to be understood as representing the "actual difficulties of production as measured by the sacrifices which production requires; not the amount of wages and profits, whether measured in money or produce, comprised in the capitalist's outlay and return." They stand for the actual labor and abstinence. The *sacrifice* which is taken into the account is *labor*, not the *price* of labor, the physical or mental effort, expended to produce the given commodity. This is reckoned as the *cost*, and it is estimated in so many days' labor of so many men. In this point of view, a ton of iron *costs* no more in America than in England; and in this point of view wages and profits are not elements of *cost*. "Indeed," says Prof. Cairnes, "it may be doubted if the theory of comparative cost of production as the ruling principle of international trade could ever have been worked out from the point of view which regards cost as consisting in wages and profits; and, however this may be, it is at least quite certain that the theory of international values, adopted alike by Mill and Ricardo, is absolutely irreconcilable with that view."

Prof. Cairnes then administers the *coup de grace* to Mr. David A. Wells, and the protectionists as well, who think that our high rate of wages handicaps us in the industrial race: "The rate of wages, whether measured in money or in the real remuneration of the laborer, affords an approximate criterion of the cost of production, either of money or of the commodities that enter into the laborer's real remuneration, *but in a sense the inverse of that in which it is understood in the argument under consideration.* In other words, a high rate of wages indicates not a high but a low cost of production for all commodities measured in which the rate of wages is high, as, on the other hand, a low rate of wages indicates a high cost for all measured in which the rate is low. Thus, in the United States the rate of wages is high, whether measured in gold or in the most important articles of the laborer's consumption, a fact which proves that the *cost* of producing gold, as well as that of producing those other commodities, is low in the United States. On the other hand, the rate of wages in Europe, measured by the same standards, is, at least, as compared with the rates in the United States, low, which again merely proves that the cost of producing the commodities constituting those standards is high in Europe as compared with their cost in the United States. This elementary truth is so far from being generally appreciated, that I should not be surprised if its simple statement should appear to some persons, and possibly even to some economists, as *paradoxical*."

Mr. Wells had been set down with considerable vigor, because he, in common with protectionists, had indicated, as the disadvantage under which American industry labored, the high money-price of labor. His criterion was the "cost of production," as measured by the high rate of wages paid in the manufacture of the articles claiming protection. Mr. Wells had innocently supposed that a high rate of wages meant, in the protected industries—competing industries—a high cost of labor; and that the "cost of production" would be greater or less, according to the cost of the labor which entered into the production. The elementary truth, which Prof. Cairnes thought would appear to be "paradoxical" to some persons, and possibly even to some economists, was this: that in the United States a "high rate of wages" proved that the "cost of production" was low. Of course there was a dialectic artifice in this. It was a case of juggling with the words "cost of production," sometimes meaning the *money-price of labor;* sometimes meaning *the sacrifice, the physical efforts* expended to produce the given commodity. To the same effect Prof. Sumner, in his tariff commission address: "If it is alleged, as it constantly is in this controversy, in a sweeping way, that American industries need protection, because American wages are higher than foreign wages, it is a case of joining a very wide inference to very inadequate premises. What are the comparative conditions of industry in America and elsewhere, as regards convenience and cost of raw materials, quality and cost of machinery, rent of land used, character of the climate as affecting the requirements of various industries, national character as respects industry, diligence, sobriety, intelligence, etc., of laborers, distance from the market, or convenience and cost of transportation, convenience and cost of natural agents (coal or water), taxes and tax system, the security afforded by the excellence or otherwise of the government, etc.? Surely it is plain that these things are the conditions of production, and the comparative rates of wages, taken apart from the purchasing power of money or the efficiency of labor, to say nothing of all the other conditions enumerated, are by no means a criterion for a decision whether an industry can be carried on successfully or not. *The lists of comparative wages* which have been made and which are relied upon by protectionists, and are often accepted by free-traders as pertinent to the issue, and perhaps as decisive of it, *have no value at all for the purpose.*[1] The em-

---

[1] Prof. Perry ("Political Economy," edition 1873, chapter on "Foreign Trade"), contending that high wages or low wages, high interest or low interest, have little or nothing to do with the profitable exchange of commodities, does say:

"To this law of foreign trade there is, however, a single not unimportant

ployer alleges that he can make no profits because he pays high wages. He assumes, apparently, that wages and profits displace each other. It is certain that they do nothing of the kind." Now, the protectionist assumes nothing of

---

exception. When two nations go into the market of the world with the same commodity, to buy gold and silver, then the absolute money-cost of that commodity is, as between the two, an important question. That one of the two nations, whose wages are lower and whose rate of interest is less, in the manufacture of the common commodity, will, *in a trade for gold*, undersell the other. . . . This is clear, and it is the only case where foreign trade is determined by the absolute *cost of production.* But our objector gets no crumb of comfort here; for, in the first place, the commerce of the world is not a commerce for gold and silver, but a commerce of commodities, in the exchange of which *relative* cost is the only principle. And, in the second place, when two nations go into the market of the world for gold, they rarely carry the same commodity. . . . And, in the third place, if two nations do carry the same commodity into the same market, to buy the same gold, and the nation whose wages and profits are higher is thereby at a disadvantage in the trade, how is a restrictive tariff at home to help that matter? The true remedy is to cultivate our own peculiar advantages to the highest point, and carry those commodities abroad to buy our gold, and not endeavor to compete with our neighbor in the same commodity."

This attempt of Prof. Perry to smother the truth in mere verbiage is positively misleading. Let us take a short cut through all this circumlocution. The United States is a gold-producing country. When any foreign manufacturer offers in this market the same goods offered by the American manufacturer, they are both equally engaged in "a trade for gold." The foreigner, then, by reason of lower wages and less interest, *undersells* the domestic manufacturer. What is the logical remedy proposed by the Professor? Abandon the *competing* industry in which we are beaten. We have seen often enough why we must summon the *restrictive tariff* if we are to have our wants supplied. The *protected* industries are these same *competing* industries.

The great trades of the world are carried on between countries widely removed from each other in the scale of civilization and in respect to their natural resources and productions. Between such countries "cost of production" is of no account. Their industries are non-competing. It is a case of reciprocal demand. We do not know and do not care what it costs to produce tea, coffee, Apollinaris water, Smyrna figs, and the like. If we want them "bad enough," and can pay for them, we *buy* them, otherwise go with-the kind. It is not they who say with the professors, that "wages and profits are the leavings of each other." Prof. Sumner then goes on to allege, what no one, no protectionist at least, is interested to deny, that "profits and wages may both be high or both low at the same time, or one may be high and the other low. The fact is, that instead of one being displaced by the other, they most always go together, both high or both low at the same time."

Without stopping now to vindicate the American manufacturer, as having the common sense to equalize the other conditions enumerated, we are simply to inquire whether, inasmuch as the wages of labor are higher in America than in Europe, that fact *pro tanto* increases the cost of production to the American manufacturer. The point is distinctly raised by Prof. Sumner: "Let us look now at the other dogma, high wages make protective taxes necessary. It is the very opposite of the truth. If wages are high, that is the reason why no protection taxes are needed, even if they might be in some other case. In Germany, the protectionists generally allege that lower wages in Germany than in England are a proof that Germany is industrially inferior, and needs protection against England. The protectionist's argument never flags on account of any little variation in the facts."

Prof. Cairnes takes a further step: "It is strange that those who employ this argument" (that the cost of producing commodities is higher in America than in Europe, because the rates of wages measured in money are higher here than there) "should not perceive that it proves too

---

out them. In the *competing* industries it is a question of cost of production. We can't buy *all*, and therefore must make some. I commend the reader to the clear and intelligent discussion of this distinction between international trade based on cost of production and reciprocal demand, in "Some Leading Principles of Political Economy, Newly Expounded," by Prof. Cairnes, Part III, chap. iii (Harper's edition).

much. The high rates of wages in the United States are not peculiar to any branch of industry, but are universal throughout its whole range. If, therefore, a high rate of wages proves a high cost of production, and a high cost of production proves a need for protection, it follows that the farmers of Illinois and the cotton-planters of the Southern States stand in as much need of fostering legislation as the cotton-spinners of New England or the iron-masters of Pennsylvania. . . . If American protectionists are not prepared to demand protective duties in favor of the Illinois farmer against the competition of his English rival, they are bound to admit either that a *high cost of production is not incompatible with effective competition, or else that a high rate of wages does not prove a high cost of production:* and if this is not so in Illinois, then I wish to know why the case should be different in Pennsylvania or New England. If a high rate of wages in the first of these States be consistent with a low cost of producing corn, why may not a high rate of wages in Pennsylvania be consistent with a low cost of producing coal and iron?—or a high rate of wages in New England be consistent with a low cost of producing calico?"

Now we have had a long chase after this subtle paradox, but we are in a situation to take it firmly in our grasp, as also to see just what it is fitted to prove. An Illinois farmer, on his fertile prairie-land, gathers a large crop of corn, say, with a comparatively small amount of labor—that is, at a small physical effort. *Measured in corn*, which is *his wages*, he gets *a high rate* of wages; *the cost of production*, measured in sacrifice—muscular effort—is low. But it is low only by comparison with the amount of corn which a like effort would produce, say, in England. There is no natural absolute standard uniformly regulating the proportion between corn and effort; that depends on the fertility of different soils—the advantages of one instrument of production over another. In England, the farmer expends the same effort and gets less corn. The "cost of production," measured in sacrifice, in effort, is high. Measured in corn, which is his wages, he gets a low rate of wages. What, exactly, does this difference represent? Not, at all, the difference of *labor*. In the case of the Illinois farmer, it represents the increased quantity of corn—wages measured in corn—which the land, the natural instrument of production, had added to his labor. His product is now what labor *plus* "the gratuitous forces of nature" creates, or, if you dislike that phrase, a natural instrument of high productive power. The Illinois farmer has, with the consent of the Government under which he lives, been allowed, for reasons touching the general welfare, to appropriate a natural instrument of production. His labor alone would, for example, produce fifteen bushels of wheat, as would the labor of an English farmer. The fertile soil adds ten bushels as a *gratuity*—to somebody. The English farmer is using a less productive natural instrument, its cost has been increased by the necessary repairs, fertilizing, underdraining, etc., which have been going on for centuries. Labor for labor, the American labor is no more productive than English labor. The superior product comes from a better instrument of production, placed in the hands of the American laborer by the consent of the society in which he lives. Even though the owner paid full value for it, its use costs the *nation* at large nothing.

"If," then asks the Professor, "a high rate of wages in the first of these States be consistent with a *low cost of producing corn*, why may not a high rate of wages in Pennsylvania be consistent with *a low cost of producing iron?*" As before, there is no natural absolute standard uniformly regulating the proportion between effort and iron. The rate of wages, measured in iron, may be as high as when measured in corn—it certainly would be if there were no other nations, comparison in which disturbed relative standards. It is money-prices which confuse us. In the limits of the same country, effort for effort, the farmer and furnace-man would reap proportional rewards, under the laws of competition. In the limits of two countries, say England and the United States, with similar conditions of production—the same chemical equivalents in ores, coal, lime, steam, and the same general physical power in their workmen—effort for effort, thew for thew, sinew for sinew—the Englishman and the American would produce, for a given exertion, equal quantities of iron. The "cost of production," estimated in sacrifice, physical labor, would be the same in the two countries. The two quantities of iron would represent equal effort; for in the example, the forces of nature had contributed equal gratuities to the respective workmen—they are using equally efficient natural instruments of production.

Why, then, in America, should not equal efforts embodied in Illinois wheat and in Pennsylvania iron exchange for each other? They should. It is the aim of protection to cause them to exchange one for the other, not by the force of the statute, but by the decree of Nature; to equalize the natural facilities of production, to pool the resources of the land, and to enable each American to receive his pay for his onerous contribution to the gross annual product.

Why does not the Pennsylvania iron-master's product exchange, ton for ton, for that made in England, or, in other words, bear the same value in a neutral market? Because the iron-worker in England is compelled to sell the sacrifice, the physical effort, embodied in his product at a lower rate in money than his American brother. There is no difference in "cost of production" in these cases, measured in sacrifice; measured in "wages," there is a vast difference. The American workman is fatally undersold, and so we are around to our starting-point. Our new criterion of cost of production has not availed us. What we have discovered is, that when capital and labor in America have possession of superior instruments of production, there are high returns for labor, considered as effort, and high wages in some industries, reckoned in the products of the industries. What the market value of these products is or will be, we are furnished with no data for determination.

Logically, we have reached the end of our abstract reasoning; but the mere speculation has given us no sense of security for practical action. The whole question is resolved at last into one of *fact*, not of science. I state it in the words of Prof. Cairnes, whom we have so pleasantly followed around this Robin Hood's barn: "I must, therefore, contend that the high scale of industrial remuneration in America, instead of being evidence of a high cost of production in that country, is distinctly evidence of a low cost of production—of a low cost of production, that is to say, *in the first place, of gold*" (this being a gold-producing country), "*and, in the next, of the commodities which mainly constitute the real wages of labor*—a description which embraces at once the most important of *raw materials of industry and the most important articles of general consumption.*"

That is, the group of industries which his economy prescribes that we should pursue are the ones in which *land, as a natural instrument of production*, adds that increment to the product which marks the distinction between a low "cost of production" and a high "cost of production," in the Professor's sense of the words.

"As regards commodities not included in this description, the criterion stands in no constant relation of any kind to their cost, and is, therefore, simply irrelevant to the point at issue."

On the contrary—for here the Professor is guilty of a singular slip—"the commodities not included in this description" are the very ones to the production of which *protection* does apply, and for the reason that the criterion of wages does stand in such a constant relation to their cost as to keep our products out of our own or a neutral market. Unquestionably there is a vast expanse of neutral territory, in which we efficiently supply our own wants. Lumber, stone, building materials, household goods, carriages, sewing-machines, guns, clocks, and professorships in colleges, are examples of commodities in which we ask no odds of outsiders. Of the ten thousand millions of our annual consumption, these industries supply six thousand seven hundred millions of commodities in which no people can successfully compete with us, and we need no *protection*. For the three hundred and fifty millions of foreign fruits, raw materials, and so on, we can not *compete*, and *protection* is useless. For the three remaining thousand millions we consume, we are in *competition* in production. And it is in all these most important articles that *protection* does protect.

"And now we may see what this claim for protection to American industry, founded on the high scale of American remuneration, really comes to: it is a demand for *special legislation*, and, in consideration of the possession of *special industrial facilities*—a complaint against *the exceptional bounty of nature*."

But the *exceptional bounty of nature* does not furnish us the *exportables* with which we can buy the satisfaction of our desires. How next shall we proceed?

Bastiat has himself furnished a perfect answer, even though he did not intend it:

"*A man who has in his hands the tools necessary for labor, the materials to work upon, and the provisions for his subsistence during the operation, is in a situation to determine his own remuneration.*"

The whole case lies in that nutshell. The nation has the tools of every possible kind known to nature's bounty or to human invention; perfect stores of force, skill, industry, effective desires of accumulation; every known motor ever suggested by an *a priori* economist; and " the provisions for subsistence" during the operation. The operation in our case has consisted in the building up of the most complete industrial organization in the world. We have, by the confession of the free-trader, "accumulated capital far more rapidly than any other people in the world." Our own production has determined our own remuneration. Our annual production in manufactures is greater than that of England; and the inventory of the wealth of the United States is to-day greater by ten thousand millions of dollars than that of Great Britain, built up by centuries of war, diplomacy, colonial conquest, protection, and free trade. How could a greater absurdity be conceived than to treat the "provisions for subsistence," which we had in our hands, as the be-all and end-all of our efforts, if they failed to furnish the purchase-money for the gratification of our other wants, and we had at last to resort to home manufactures? We had only to reach out and gather food from our boundless acres, and then, because it costs us little, call off the people and their masterful energies from "the operation" of the subjugation of a continent which, in the fullness of time, the God of nations had ordained the nation to undertake!

This was not the destiny which our "historical antecedents" forced upon us. It accorded alike with the divine ordering of events, with the ideals of the people, with the demands and exigencies of the great movement for political and commercial freedom, with the maxims of common sense, and with the canons of sound political economy, upon which alone we were enabled to lead the kind of lives we were fitted to live. The American people were neither tricked into this order of development by monopolists, betrayed into it by corruption, nor duped into it by greedy manufacturers. It was the natural order of conducting this mighty " operation," which was made possible *because* food was plenty, and " cost of production " was low. It was the only method by which the vast resources of the land could be made contributory to the welfare of the people possessing them. We are engaged in a common cause—farmer, manufacturer, and laborer—of supplying the " necessities, conveniences, and amusements " of each other. It is not money values we ask; it is the commodities themselves we make and divide, to each his share in the production. The land-owner, as such, has no distinct right nor distinct interest in any different proportion of distribution. In his behalf, it is urged that " we can not afford to compete in any industry which will not pay here as well as those which have special advantages here. If we can not compete, it is because we can not afford to compete. *We are too well off*." This would be like the workman who dropped his tools and quit work, for the reason that he has " provisions for his subsistence," without the ability to buy and enjoy anything else. When we steadily contemplate the full meaning of the proposition that the United States are to drop their tools and quit all work for the reason that food is cheap, we may thank the Providence which has superintended us that the free-trade *doctrinaire* is a recent product; and we may rely on the sturdy common sense of the people that they will never accept his teaching.

The early statesmen looked out upon the dimensions of the republic, and took an inventory of its effects. I know of no better summary of them than I find in the rhapsody of Prof. Perry. The Professor endeavors to break the force of the facts by thrusting between them his irrelevant suggestions: "The idea that the United States, with a greater variety and abundance of natural resources than any other country on the globe, with an industrious, enterprising, and skillful people, with mountain-streams which leap to the wheels of industry with a song, with forests and coal-fields and mines, with marts and markets and navigable rivers, with a genius for traffic and a keen eye to profit, the idea that the United States is to be reduced to a mere farming country, unless Government can be coaxed to tax foreigners and citizens in behalf of some branches of manufacture, which are asserted to be otherwise unprofitable, is too ridiculous for serious repetition. Why? *No nation of the earth has such facilities for manufacturing; the raw materials are here, the food is here in abounding measure; the instruments are here in water, wood, and coal; cattle and horses and pastures are here;* everything is here which a nation can ask for with which to produce either directly what is wanted, or indirectly that with which to purchase at the cheapest rates what is wanted abroad; and if God shall give us grace to mind our own business, to avoid entangling alliances and wars, to get and keep a sound money, and to rise above the silly jealousies which have hitherto restricted trade— we shall yet be the bee-hive of the nations, the chosen home of the industrial and civilizing arts."

My good Professor, there is something yet lacking in your inventory. You omit the only factor which, *on your philosophy*, can start this vast complexity of industry. We want men who will consent to labor on the terms of the

European laborer—men who will consent to lower the standard of their lives to that of the European, reduced to the hopeless and helpless slavery of industrial systems.

By the terms of your argument you make the returns for rude labor spent on the soil operate as a premium against industries involving skill and capital. The very exigencies of your logic compel you to waste intelligence, energy, inventive talent, educational power, in vocations where they are useless. You want us to raise *exportables*, in which "cost of production" is low. Why have not the kind of people you describe entered upon the possessions you so glowingly catalogue? What *is* the economic reason why we never started on our career, until *restrictions* of some sort gave us "a lift"? Do you know of anybody who will or can enter upon them "under freedom"? You think we can, now. Prof. Sumner thinks we can not, and *ought not to;* we are too rich to do so now; we must wait until we can afford to take hold of our resources.

What are "industrious and enterprising and skillful people" without a field of employment? What are "our mountain-streams" without an industry to which they can leap? What are "our forests," if we are to get our lumber from Canada? What are "coal-fields," if we are to get our coal from Nova Scotia? What is the use of "mines," if we are to get our metal fabrics from England? What are our "raw materials," if we are to get our woolen goods from Germany, our cotton goods from Manchester, and our hemp from Russia? What are "cattle and pastures," if we are to get our wool from Australia and our tallow from the Baltic? What are "marts and markets" without products in them? What boots it that we have a "genius for traffic and a keen eye for profit," if they are to be wasted in "the clash of chaotic cupidities" which marks the world's market? What is the good of all these resources, if we are not to enter upon their enjoyment? Why have we not entered upon their enjoyment except under restrictions? You have denounced through six hundred pages of your book on "Political Economy" the men who have endeavored to appropriate these bounties, as robbers, monopolists, lobbyists, parasites, thieves. You know there is not an item in your list which your theory of "advantageous industries" allows us to touch, except agricultural products. You have emptied the nation of the power to apply its labor to any occupation, except the soil, in which the forces of nature supplement its returns, and in which you pride yourself that you have shown that the "cost of production" is low. These are the products which you say should constitute the outgoing cargoes for which in return we are to receive the cotton and metal fabrics of England, the china of France, the woolen goods of Germany, the coal of Nova Scotia, the hemp and tallow of Russia, the wool of Australia, and the lumber of Canada. In these products of the industry of America, according to the census of 1880, our own laborers added $1,200,000,000 to our stock, which products in market were a market for other $1,200,000,000 worth of other American labor—*American* labor, mind you. There is not a single one of these industries which you do not denounce as "unproductive," as "an abomination" when carried on under "protective taxes" —for so you prefer to denominate the scheme of direct, home production. You say they do not pay. You cram a transparent fallacy into that use of the word "pay." Your inventory is at last a humbug, and your radiant picture is a deceitful mirage.

You shut the American people up to the choice between the horns of a dilemma. They will never become *profitable*, in your sense of the word, until we can *compete in the markets of the world* with them. This can come about on one of two conditions: Either our workmen must consent to reduce their share of the "cost of production," reckoned in wages, or they must by increased skill render the "cost of their labor" less. They must become more expert and efficient in proportion to their higher wages. On the latter condition, without *restriction*, we never should have entered upon these forms of industry. Achilles himself can not overtake the tortoise unless he starts. Industrial skill and efficiency are only attained by practice, generations after generations—years after years. Our present industrial scheme is a process of education; and its full effects, as an educational process, are daily required to enable us to "keep up"—to hold our own in the race. That we could rise *per saltum* under the philosophy of *laissez faire* from an agricultural state to a highly organized, industrial state, is impossible. As is said by Robert Scott Moffat: "It is impossible for an unorganized industry, at any point of its progress, to attack an organized one without entailing loss and submitting to temporary disadvantage; and if *immediate advantage* alone is to be consulted, *the industry of such a country must forever remain unorganized.*" ("Economics of Consumption.") Mr. Mill has said as much.

On the former condition—reduced wages—we do not want them on any terms.

Many excellent people have denounced Dr. Malthus for enunciating his law of population, as if he had enacted it. I commend his words to free-trade promoters: "If a country had no other means of growing rich, except by seeking success in the struggle with other countries at the cost of the reduction of the wages of labor, I would unhesitatingly say, 'Away with such riches.' It is much to be desired that the working-classes should be well remunerated, and this, for a reason much more important than all the considerations relating to wealth—that is, the happiness of the great mass of society. Nothing is more detestable than the idea of knowingly condemning the laboring-classes to cover themselves with rags, to lodge in wretched huts, to enable us to sell a few raw stuffs and calicoes to foreign countries."

Rather let us rejoice that God has given us grace to mind our own business, has enabled us to avoid entangling alliances and wars, and has kept us out of the maelstrom of foreign industrial machinery which would have ingulfed our capital and labor.

The assumption is that under free trade we shall not abandon any group of industries worth pursuing. Prof. Cairnes thinks we could rely on the "exceptional bounty of nature," and worry along with the industries to which his economic paradox, that a high rate of industrial remuneration was only evidence of a low cost of production, was applicable. "Perhaps I shall here be asked how, if the case be so, the fact is to be explained, since fact it undoubtedly is, that the people of the United States are *unable to compete in neutral markets*, in the sale of *certain important* wares,[1] with England and other European countries. No one will say that the people of New England, New York, and Pennsylvania are deficient in any industrial qualities possessed by the workmen of any country in the world. How happens it then, that, enjoying industrial advantages superior to other countries, they are yet unable to hold their own against them in the general markets of commerce? I shall endeavor to meet this objection fairly, and, in the first place, let me state what my contention is with regard to the cost of production in America. I do not contend that it is low in the case of all commodities

---

[1] According to "Schedule A," the consumption of these "important wares" in the United States amounts to $3,000,000,000 annually.

capable of being produced in the country, but only in that of a *large, very important,* but *still limited, group.*"

Here we are back again to the agricultural group. All the industries outside of this group, he takes the trouble to say in words, would not be extinguished by free trade. Great Britain would still continue to produce *some* corn, and the United States *some coal* and *iron,* and *some* textile fabrics. Transportation over great distances to some of the inland markets of the United States might operate *as a tariff.* "It is probable that the abolition of the high import duties now imposed by the latter country would lead to some *more or less* considerable readjustments of the proportions in which the industries they occasion are carried on; but this is a very different thing from the extinction of those industries. . . . The capital now employed in the United States in developing resources which would *be better reserved for another day,* would not be slow in finding employment in *more profitable* channels. . . . It can not, therefore, be denied that under free trade American manufacturers would not improbably have to undergo the patriotic anguish of finding themselves undersold in some kinds of goods by foreign merchants in their own markets. But there would be no need, therefore, for them to despair."

This is very kind in the Professor. Somehow the philosophers in their study-chambers never tell us what these more profitable channels are. What are we to do, Messrs. Professors? Answer in facts, and not in rhetorical vagueness and audacious guess-work. The business men of America have been fretting on the edges of all their resources for a century. It is probable they have discovered all there is to discover. *There is nothing to do except to go on and continue to produce the things we must and will have,* and produce them under the American conditions, under *protection*. This gives us access to the grand inventory of resources so eloquently set out by Prof. Perry. We either are or are not worthy of them.

Our old critical friend Prof. Leslie (who was a free-trader all the time we have been reading his criticism) is as dogmatic as any other professor when he gives us an Englishman's advice as to what Americans ought to do: "The best economy, of course, would have been for American capital to confine itself to the fields in which it had superior productiveness, *awaiting a rise of wages*, and *in the cost of coal-mining in England*, for competition in others." ("Fortnightly Review," October, 1881.) This lets the whole free-trade cat out of the bag. Rates of wages will rise in England, the productiveness of our fields will constantly diminish, our wages will come down, we shall be on equality with England. Then we shall be so poor that we can afford to compete with England—we are too rich to do it now. It is Prof. Sumner's old proposition: "If we can not compete, it is because we can not afford to compete. We are too well off." Most practical business men, foreseeing the time when they must build an extension to their works, would do it when and while they were well enough off to afford it, and not wait until forced by their necessities to go into a new enterprise, under compulsion of poverty—especially as in either event it must be done at their own cost, and under the conditions of the average efficiency of the people as a whole. And Mr. Mill is on record as agreeing with the practical business men.

Few will have had the patience to follow this ingenious and subtle argument, by which free trade was going to determine for us what to do—under the notion of "cost of production." It has landed us in the old bog. Having consciously failed to enlighten us, in this regard, we are exhorted by Prof. Cairnes to abandon protection and go into the general business of *civilization*. "As a scheme for promoting civilization, protection amounts to a plan for putting an end to international trade—putting an end to the chief occasion and most enduring motive for the intercourse of mankind, . . . free trade being one of the principal and most powerful of civilizing agencies." What it really puts "an end" to, what it is "the chief occasion and most enduring motive" to, is the occasion and motive to have the manufactures of the world carried on in the island of Great Britain, and to have Americans truck-farm it for them. No American will have any doubt that when it comes to international trade in civilization, our exports will largely exceed the imports. I have seen a calculation made that, for every missionary England has sent to foreign lands, she has opened a market for English goods to the amount of fifty thousand pounds. And the London "Times" has given expression to the "patriotic anguish" which Englishmen underwent when, in the Russian war, English troops were compelled to "kill a customer or a debtor of England." At the same time English gunsmiths sold guns to kill English soldiers, because there must be no interference with trade. Americans are asked to furnish the ammunition with which they may be themselves slaughtered.

Prof. Cairnes advises thus: "If they" (the Americans) "desire to command a market for their products in all quarters of the world, they must be prepared to admit the products of other countries freely to their own markets, and must learn to seek the benefits of international trade, not in the vain ambition of underselling other countries, and so making them pay tribute in gold and silver to the United States, but in that which constitutes its proper end and only national purpose—the greater cheapening of its commodities, and the increased abundance and comfort which result *to the whole family of mankind.*" This last enterprise seems rather an indefinite one for American statesmen to enter upon, charged, as they are especially, with the welfare of the people of the United States. Our present mission is to make commodities cheap and abundant for ourselves, and we have been fairly successful so far.

CHAPTER XIII.

A CASE IN POINT—THE AUSTRALIA EPISODE.

THIS business of "advantageous industries" and "cost of production" has received recent illustration in actual history. Gold was discovered in Australia in 1851. Let us look at the course of development there, in the light of its economic and social growth. It sheds light on very many phases of economic problems. At the time of the discovery of gold in Australia in 1851 it was a grazing country, with extensive areas of rich, fertile lands. Wool and tallow were its principal exports. The wages of common labor were about one dollar and a quarter per day. Upon the gold discoveries, a common laborer could earn at the mines, by simple processes of labor involving little capital and moderate skill, five dollars per day; that is, he could produce, by washing the sand, enough gold to be of that worth—say, one quarter of an ounce. The cost of producing gold thus became, then and there, low. Wages reckoned in gold were high, so long as *gold in the outside world held its exchange value.* Immediately the rate of wages in the whole country rose to the rate of earnings in the gold-fields. An employer was compelled to pay quadruple wages; the price of all *Australian productions* rose in the same proportion. In the course of two or three years the more accessible and richer mines became exhausted; processes became more expensive. The rate of earnings in gold-digging were reduced to about two dollars and a half per day, and this for some years was the cost of labor there. The returns to labor in the most "advantageous industry" and in ordinary callings met at the average about midway between the ante-gold rates and the highest rates under their most efficient conditions. The gold-digger was compelled to share his abundance with the laborers who prosecuted the unprofitable industries. He could not have them serving him in Australia without parting with a share of his earnings at the point of his superiority; and the people of Australia, *as a whole*, took the advantage of the gold discoveries at an averaged rate. These people were *a tax* on him. If the miner could have gotten along without neighbors and helpers, he would have realized the whole of the fruits of his most advantageous industry; but, under an irrepealable law of society, he was compelled to divide. Whoever was allowed to go to Australia and to work, was necessarily permitted to share in the averaged results.

Inasmuch as the population, in the main, took to the gold-diggings, and inasmuch as they could not subsist on the gold itself, *they were compelled to part with it.* So far as they could not supply their wants by Australian productions, they were *compelled to export it* as the only and best means of payment for imports. The wages of shepherds and ranchmen had doubled, and the cost of raising wool doubled also. The market for wool was in Europe, and the price of wool there had not doubled; and as Europe was not dependent on Australia for its supplies, wool and tallow could be no longer exported. An unexpected consequence saved the industry. Previously, butcher's-meat had had no market at home, and grazing had been carried on principally for the products in wool and tallow. The great influx of population now gave them a sale for their meats, and they were then enabled to continue the exportation of their old products at old prices; but this was merely an incident, or rather an accident. The great industry was gold-mining. So long as it remained the most advantageous industry, all the others were merely ancillary to it —mere instruments to supply food and clothing to those actually employed in it. How did it affect them in relation to other nations?

Whereas the colony formerly supplied her own wants by her own productions of butter and lumber, she now imported her supplies of the former from Ireland and the latter from the Baltic. Her facilities in raising gold were so far superior to the facilities of Ireland and Russia, that it was her interest to turn her labor and capital to gold-mining rather than to farming. Her fields were fertile, but they could not hold their own in competition with gold-mines. It resulted that nothing which could be imported was now made in the colony. The price of labor was so high that she could not afford to compete with foreign countries. *But that price was high because the cost of gold was low*—that is, the returns for labor, *reckoned in its product, gold*, were high. Reckoned in the commodity which that labor brought forth—gold—these were high returns. *Gold in Australia was cheap*, measured in the effort, sacrifice, which procured it. In Australia, prices were high, commodities were high. In other countries *gold maintained its exchange value*, its purchasing power over other commodities. In Australia there was a rise in prices corresponding to the fall in the cost of gold. If the supply of gold under its lessened cost could have been kept up long enough and in sufficient volume, prices, reckoned in gold, all over the world would have risen, and the equilibrium would have been restored *by a fall in the price of gold*. But, as it was, the volume of gold currencies throughout the world was too large to be sensibly affected in value by the reduced cost of it in Australia and California; and, further, in due course of time the increased cost of procuring gold from the mines of both countries had so far destroyed their special advantages in its production that commerce has returned to its normal relations. Both manufacturing and agricultural pursuits have been resumed. In both countries the actual wealth is increasing, and the decrease in the productiveness of gold-mining has removed an actual barrier to their social and economic progress. The special industry had drawn all labor and capital to it; but the wealth of the country had been only such as could be effected by exchanges. They did not import capital, but consumable goods.

If studied in detail, the Australian episode furnishes a study of many sides of the problem of international trade.

It shows in what manner the existence of a specially advantageous industry operates as a barrier to the prosecution of the less advantageous ones, or rather, how, if open to all, it raises wages in all departments to an equality with those to be won in it. It explains what the free-trader means when he says we "can not afford to compete" with other nations where wages are less. He means to say that we ought to stay in the advantageous pursuit and not try to compete in the others. He argues that present current prices are the criterion upon which we ought to conduct our exchanges. What he *overlooks* is his own error in assuming that because we might advantageously effect *some* exchanges—procure a *limited* amount of foreign manufactured commodities in that way—we might with equal advantage effect *all our* exchanges and obtain *all the supplies we required* in like manner. This is the old fallacy of division with which we have already dealt.

Let us now substitute *food* in the United States for *gold* in Australia, and see how the analogies hold out:

Gold is an article in universal demand, and an overproduction is a danger which no pains need be taken to prevent. No gold-miner need anticipate a glut in the gold market. At all events, prices throughout the world have not risen at all in the proportion in which the cost of gold in Australia and California has been reduced.

Wheat is a product annually renewed, and the history of prices shows the wide and violent fluctuations of its value in the world's market. Especially are the foreign markets accessible to the American surplus characterized by great uncertainties in value and requirements.

Gold was of no value in Australia, except as it was used for the purposes of foreign trade. The miners and the people there could derive no benefit from it except so far as they parted with it. If it could have been consumed or used for purposes of further production *in Australia*, can any one doubt that its wealth, as a colony, would have been doubled in virtue of the double production it could have provoked by expending it on new creations?

Wheat in the United States has the function of being directly applied to the subsistence of laborers while entering upon operations directed to further production. The closer the supply was held to the domestic demand, the less would be the loss in its purchasing power, and the greater the gross annual product of the industry of the nation of native-born laborers, supplemented by immigration which supplied all deficiencies.

In Australia, the disadvantages which the producers of commodities other than gold labored under were too great and exceptional to enable them to enter into competition with the gold-miners in articles for export. In proportion as the cost of procuring gold rose, they were enabled to resume the production of other merchandise for exports.

In the United States the difference between advantages

of raising wheat and manufacturing commodities was never so wide and exceptional. The constantly increasing proportion in which we are exporting manufactured goods shows a constant tendency to the equalizing the facilities of production between manufacture and agriculture. One is tempted to wonder—if the lamentations of the free-trader, that we do not export more manufactured goods, should be hushed, and if we should export food, raw materials, *and* the products of our mills—how foreigners are to pay us; what are they to do for us; what imports are to pay for all these exports. The truth is, when we get to supplying all our own wants, foreign trade will cease, as it ought to. Nobody wants foreign trade for itself. All the high-sounding talk about our sails whitening all the seas is nonsense and buncombe.

The highest *taxes* any nation pays are the taxes levied under the form of transportation, especially in the carriage of merchandise which can be produced where it is consumed. Commerce is the penalty of making things, or of having things made, in the wrong place.

We are all familiar with the habit of free-traders, and other loose thinkers, to measure the prosperity of a nation by the amount of its foreign commerce. The true measure is in its domestic exchanges. The total amount of British exports, with its boasted mastery of the world's commerce, was in 1880, $1,400,000,000. For the same year the people of the United States made exchanges among themselves, through the agencies of railroads alone, and exclusive of all other instrumentalities of trade, such as ships, wagons, boats, and animals, to the extent of over $12,000,000,000: or, in other words, each four millions of our fifty millions exchanged commodities among themselves, each year, to the extent of more than $1,000,000,000—nearly equal to the entire export trade of Great Britain.

Prof. Cairnes has remarked of the phenomena in Australia: "The foreign trade of Victoria presents the singular and almost unique spectacle of *a steady decline in its amount* over a period marked by an extraordinarily *rapid growth of population* and *general wealth*. I have no returns of the population of that colony for 1856, but it was probably between 300,000 and 400,000; in 1861 it was 541,000, and in 1870 729,000. In other words, the population must have nearly doubled itself in these sixteen years; the general prosperity of the country during the same time being almost unexampled. But *the noteworthy circumstance is, that while the country was then prospering, its external trade was undergoing constant contraction*, falling from a total of $77,445,000 in 1856, to $62,350,000 in 1870. *The fact, I may mention in passing, shows how little the foreign trade of a country, as measured by its exports and imports, furnishes a correct criterion of its industrial progress or growth in real wealth.* . . . The result has been, that from being a large importer of breadstuffs, butter, beer, boots and shoes, provisions, spirits, etc., Victoria has either discontinued altogether, or greatly curtailed her importation of all these commodities, which she now produces from her own internal resources. *Is this course of development for the advantage of Victoria? Plainly, I think, if we have regard of her general interests, social and political, as well as pecuniary, we must answer in the affirmative.*" Then, as if remembering that he was a professor of the science of orthodox English political economy, he feels constrained to add: "Though, as economists, we must also recognize that, looking at the question from a purely material stand-point, this affirmation can not be made good, since it certainly is a fact that the diminishing returns of her gold-mines have deprived her of that command of foreign markets which she formerly possessed; while the resort to her own fields of production in lieu of foreign markets, being as it is a *dernier ressort*, can not but indicate a diminishing productiveness of her general industry." America never had the command of foreign markets with her wheat as Australia had with her gold, for many and obvious reasons.

The whole case of protection might be risked on this concession: "The general interests, social and political, as well as pecuniary," of Australia have been advanced by a resort to her own fields of production, after her people had come to them over the failure of a specially advantageous industry, the pursuit of which alone had retarded her progress and her wealth, even though *it had given her command* of the foreign markets; and that an industry which yielded the precious metals themselves, for which there was an unlimited demand in the markets of the world.

California presents precisely similar conditions of development—so that it might almost be said that her special industry had been a curse to her in retarding all other industry.

We see now what the free-trader means by "advantageous industry" and "cost of production." If our advantage consists in the lower cost of production reckoned in labor and sacrifice, the actual difficulties of production, we can get no benefit from it except as we part with the commodity produced under these conditions. The farmer himself must part with his surplus either at home or abroad, but the nation *as a whole* is not under that necessity. It may provide, by a protective tariff for example, for its consumption at home. If it must be exported in order to evolve its purchasing power, this purchasing power may be lost, either by the competitions of international trade which squeezes out all the value except what is conferred by the contributions of our labor estimated on the Russian and Indian basis, and eliminate all the value conferred, as a gratuity, by nature: or it may be lost by the breaking down and failure of the foreign market to take it off our hands, in which event the product itself perishes.

In the former case, we can only receive remuneration for labor, which must issue eventually in European rates, and so lose our only superiority in production; in the latter case, we can not part at all with our product, and are forced back to domestic markets and domestic manufacturing, which we can have only on the condition of restricting the import of foreign goods.

There is no other escape from the dilemma. All which only shows that a mere bucolic America is not as rich as we assume it to be. We must resort to our other fields of production. We long ago reached our *dernier ressort*.

CHAPTER XIV.

COMPETITION IN A FOREIGN MARKET COMPELS US TO EXPORT OUR GRATUITIES.

THE analysis which we have been making under the head of "cost of production" has brought us to a crucial test. We are now face to face with another awkward question. Its proper solution will negative the whole series of propositions not proved, and assumptions not warranted, which so abound in the writings of Profs. Perry and Sumner, Mr. David A. Wells, and the propagandists of the Cobden Club.

The people of the United States, by virtue of their soil, climate, rivers, mines, and forests, have a superiority over other nations in "cost of production" in a certain group of industries.

We have seen that the result of competition is to eliminate all the elements of value except the onerous contributions of man. The *tendency* of economic laws set into operation by competition is to equalize values with the labor and abstinence incorporated in commodities. International commerce now takes the place of competition—sets it in operation rather. The nature, capacity, and occupations of an Englishman, a German, a Frenchman, and an American are not so dissimilar that they might not compete on equal terms, and, in the long run, with equal outcome. Their labor, their skill, and their endurance would be equal factors in a given product. But to the labor, skill, and endurance of the American are added the natural resources of a new continent. *Each nation, as a whole, has the use of its land for nothing.* In the case of the United States, this possession gives them a vast and incalculable advantage in our case, not in the *selling* but in the *consuming* of its products. How far will free foreign trade—international commerce—render that which is a *gratuity* to us, a *common possession* to other nations? We are monopolists to the full extent of the superior productive powers of the soil of our great territory. The monopoly does not belong to the land-owner as such—it does not run with the land into the usufruct of the citizen alone, in whom, as an economic and political expedient, we have vested private title. To what extent will the operations of foreign commerce level us down? How far shall we be ingulfed if we enter the vortex of free international exchanges?

It seems to me that, if we are allowed to discuss this question from the stand-point of American nationality, as a question of the wealth and welfare of the citizens of this nation, it is capable of a definite answer. But it is a topic for a man who stands, open-eyed, in the daylight, gazing on actual facts, and not for a dreamer, with his impalpable vision of universal brotherhood, or the blind votary seeking national suicide in the cause of universal free trade. It may be that, in the final *status* of nations and humanity, we shall all ride upon some Mediterranean Sea, and that we shall meet our brethren of other races and climates and civilizations upon some average level. In the mean time, as a nation, we shall best pursue Adam Smith's system of natural liberty by doing the best we can for ourselves.

An evident economic proposition is this: that by the direct, domestic production of the commodities that we need, if not interdicted by "the nature of things," we retain for the citizens of the nation, as a whole, all the gratuities which nature has conferred upon us.

A clearly scientific proposition is this : that in the effort to obtain them by free foreign exchanges we shall part with these gratuities—shall surrender our position as proprietors, as against the other nations of the world, of a monopoly of cheap food and raw materials; and that the food and raw materials which we export will bear no exchange value over and above the *actual* labor, sacrifice, effort, which we have expended in their production.

A further proposition, true alike in morals, justice, and economics, is this : that a commodity which is *cheap*, by reason, not of an effort embodying less relative skill or labor in its production, but of less highly remunerated labor, is not therefore a *gratuity*. To us, *as a people*, the cost of our products is measured by the effort required to overcome the obstacles nature presents, and not the money-price. In the long run, no prosperity can be built up on the unrequited toil of others.

To establish the first two propositions, I quote at length some paragraphs from Frédéric Bastiat's chapter on Competition. I trust the reader will patiently go over them :

"The gift of God" (say in our fertile fields) "has become common—and the reader will observe that I avail myself here of a special fact to elucidate a phenomenon which is universal—this gift, I say, has become common to all. This is not declamation, but the expression of a truth which is demonstrable. Why has this beautiful phenomenon been misunderstood ? Because community" (commonness) "is realized under the form of value annihilated, and the mind with difficulty lays hold of negations. But I ask, is it not true that when, in order to obtain a certain quantity of sugar or cotton, I give only one tenth of the labor which I should find it necessary to expend in producing the commodity myself, and this because the Brazilian sun performs the other nine tenths of the work—is it not true, I say, that in that case I still exchange labor for labor, and really and truly obtain, over and above the Brazilian labor, and *into the bargain*, the co-operation of the climate of the tropics? Can I not affirm with rigorous exactitude that I have become, that all men have become, in the same way as the Indians and Americans, that is to say, *gratuitously*, participators in the liberality of nature, so far as the commodities in question are concerned? . . .

"England possesses productive coal-mines. That is no doubt a great local advantage, more especially if we suppose, as I shall do for the sake of argument, that the Continent possesses no coal-mines. Apart from the consideration of exchange, the advantage which this gives to the people of England is, the possession of fuel in greater abundance than other nations—fuel obtained with less labor, and at less expense of useful time. As soon as exchange comes into operation—keeping out of view competition—the exclusive possession of these mines enables the people of England to demand a considerable remuneration, and to set a high price upon their labor. Not being in a situation to perform this labor ourselves, or procure what we want from another quarter, we have no alternative but to submit. English labor devoted to this description of work will be well remunerated; in other words, *coal will be dear*" (that is, to a Frenchman), "*and the bounty of nature may be considered as conferred on the people of one nation, and not on mankind at large.*

"But this state of things can not last, for a great natural and social law is opposed to it—competition. For the very reason that this species of labor is largely remunerated in England, it will be in great demand there, for men are always in quest of high remuneration. The number of miners will increase, both in consequence of the sons of miners devoting themselves to their fathers' trade, and in consequence of men transferring their industry to mining from other departments. They will offer to work for a smaller recompense, and their remuneration will go on diminishing until it reach the *normal rate*, or *the rate generally given in the country for analogous work*. This means that *the price of English coal will fall in France;* that *a given amount of French labor will procure a greater and greater quantity of English coal*, or, rather, of English labor incorporated and worked up in coal; and, finally (and this is what I pray you to remark), that *the gift which nature would appear to have bestowed upon England has in reality been conferred on the whole human race*. The coal of Newcastle is brought within the reach of all men *gratuitously*, as far as the mere material is concerned. This is neither a paradox nor an exaggeration—it is brought within their reach like the water of the brook, on the single condition of going to fetch it, or remunerating those who undertake that labor for us. When we purchase coal, it is not the coal that we pay for, but the labor necessary to extract it and transport it. All that we do is to give a corresponding amount of labor which we have worked up or incorporated in wine or in silk. So true is it, that the liberality of nature has been extended to France, that the labor which we refund is not greater than that which it would have been necessary to undergo had the deposit of coal been in France. Competition has established equality between the two nations as far as coal is concerned, except as regards the inevitable and inconsiderable difference resulting from distance and carriage.

"From what has been said, we may deduce the solution of one of the problems which have been most keenly controverted, namely, that of free trade as between nation and nation. If it be true, as seems to me incontestable, that *competition leads the various countries of the globe to exchange with one another nothing else than labor*, exertion more and more equalized, and to transfer at the same time reciprocally, and *into the bargain*, the natural advantages that each possesses, how blind and absurd must those men be who exclude foreign products by legislative measures, under the pretext that they are cheap, and have little value in proportion to their aggregate utility; that is to say, precisely because they include a large proportion of gratuitous utility!

"In fact, were it possible for *an individual, a family, a class, a nation, possessed of certain natural advantages,* of an important discovery in manufactures, or of the instruments of production in the shape of accumulated capital, *to be set permanently free from the law of competition*, it is evident that this individual, this family, *this nation,* would have forever *the monopoly of an exceptionally high remuneration,* at the expense of mankind at large.

"Seeing that the advantages which appear at first to be the property of certain individuals, become, by an admirable law of divine beneficence, the common patrimony of all; seeing that the *natural advantages* of situation, of fertility, of temperature, of mineral riches, and even of manufacturing aptitude, slip in a short time from the hands of producers, by reason of their competition with each other, and turn exclusively to the profit of consumers, it follows that there is no country which is not interested in the advancement and prosperity of all other countries. Every step of progress made in the East is wealth in prospective for the West. Fuel discovered in the South warms the men of the North. Great Britain makes progress in her spinning-mills; *but her capitalists do not alone reap the profit, for the interest of money does not rise; nor do her operatives, for the wages of labor remain the same.* In the long run, it is the Russian, the Frenchman, the Spaniard; in a word, it is the human race, who obtain equal satisfactions at a less expense of labor, or, what comes to the same thing, superior satisfactions with equal labor."

This exposition rests upon the undeniable economic results of competition. Bastiat's logic, in this paragraph, is unimpeachable—his rhetoric is sound and the consequences he traces are inexorable. The American farmers are asked to work upon a competition among themselves so intense as to compel them to *export all their gratuities.*

I have said that a commodity which was cheap solely by reason of ill-requited labor put into it was not a *gratuity*. We have now left the region of natural agents or tools, and have reached the human being.

It is easy enough to justify the attempt by one nation to appropriate the natural advantage of situation, of fertility, of temperature, of mineral riches, and of manufacturing aptitude in another. These may be made to slip out of the hands of their possessors by their competition with each other. The gains thus achieved are real and advantageous. It is giving something for something. The value of the trade depends on the relative situation of the parties to it. But one nation could not long successfully grow rich at the cost of the prosperity of another—no more than an individual. A country in which labor was oppressed and inadequately rewarded, could not justly be said to be in a state of advancement and prosperity. Labor in such a country is in a state of quasi-bankruptcy. It possesses no essential purchasing power. Unless it is in possession of one of the commercial advantages just referred to, it can have nothing to offer to us which possesses any *gratuitous* element—at least nothing upon which a great people, who can give that same labor employment as part of themselves, could afford to rely upon as a permanent source of supply. "Cheapness" is a fetich which will cheat its worshipers. It has no more efficacy than the cucumber which the Congo African carries about with him as his god. It is idle to offer a man an article at a low price if he has nothing to buy it with. To a purchaser with the means of payment in his hands, price is of little account. A consumer in this attitude is strong. The producer can not continue, as such, to deal with a consumer, on terms of bankruptcy, whether he offers commodities or labor for sale.

I read in Prof. Sumner's tariff commission address these words: "If there is anything cheap anywhere, the protectionists spring into activity to keep the American people from getting it. If there is an abundance of food, clothing, furniture, and other supplies which is offered to the American people on easy terms, the protectionists call it an inundation and run to set a barrier against it. A few weeks ago I saw a hundred women waiting for hours on the sidewalk for the opening of a store at which some fire-damaged goods were to be sold cheap. A protectionist must hold that these women were insane, or that they were selfishly ruining the country."

A protectionist would undoubtedly say that any political economist who recommended the people of any city or nation to depend, habitually and on system, for the supply of the commodities they need, "on some fire-damaged goods which were to be sold cheap," was in an acute stage of insanity, and that such a case could never become chronic, for the patient must either get well or die *instanter*.

To await the prosperity which may come from this source is to await the bargains which come from bankruptcy and commercial disaster. The American workmen stand here idle to wring *gratuities* from laborers, pauperized, brutalized, bankrupt in industrial, social, and domestic resources! A man or a nation which did either—wait on bankruptcy or fire-damaged goods—with productive forces in its own hands, would reap the punishment inflicted by outraged nature, by witnessing the disappearance of all producers as well as of all products in market. There can be no ordination of justice in heaven or on earth which can make such a scheme operate to confer a *gratuity* on us. It is a scheme of commerce based on bankruptcy, financially, industrially, and morally, whose fruits, if such it had, we could not appropriate. Moral law and economic law alike remand us to our own fields of labor, under our own natural conditions of sacrifice and abstinence. The God of nations has put it in the power of the people of the United States to redeem the promises we have held out to all the world, to come here and participate in the labor and remuneration which America offers. We can ameliorate the laborer's life if he lives here—our resources will not hold out if we undertake to distribute them, through the machinery of foreign commerce, to all the non-resident population of the earth.

What confers value is the removal of obstacles. The labor of removing the obstacle is what constitutes cost. The expense to the people of the United States, as a whole, is the food eaten and clothing worn out in the process of production. The better clothes and more food put into the laborer's consumption is not to be regarded as the more fuel put into a worse machine or a machine working under disadvantages. It is not cutting with a duller axe. It is using a higher-priced human instrument, capable of the sensation of happiness and a sharer in the actual entity which we call "the general welfare." [1]

---

[1] "We are thus led to notice an ambiguity that is latent in our ordinary

This is attained distinctly, *as an end*, by having the laborer here, and is attained directly by employing him here on work which otherwise would not be done here. The sum of the happiness of the human family is increased, but the increase is mainly enjoyed by the American laborer. We can not cheat Providence by the trick of employing the starving laborer abroad—appropriating his labor, and then sit down, do nothing ourselves, and call it a gratuity. The gratuity belongs to those who are on the ground, in possession of the natural advantages which Providence has conferred on us, on condition of their use

---

vague estimates of the productive efficiency of human beings; it is not quite clear whether we are to measure it by the total value of the commodities produced, or by the excess of this value over the value of what is necessarily consumed. The latter measurement is suggested by the analogy of the instruments, especially the living instruments employed by the laborers, since in measuring the productiveness of useful animals we should always consider not their *gross* produce, but their *net* produce after subtracting the value of the food, etc., consumed by them. The analogy is too obvious and irresistible to be ignored; and we must admit this measurement of the productive efficiency of laborers as valid for some purposes: for instance, any employer who undertook to feed his laborers would rightly use this measurement in reckonings of his private business. But, for the reason given incidentally in the preceding chapter, it is not, I conceive, the measurement normally applicable in our present consideration of the matter from *the point of view of the community;* so far, that is, as the additional consumption which causes the additional efficiency is held to be desirable, in itself, or in its use of bodily or mental vigor, *as an amelioration of the laborer's life*, and, therefore, an element of *the ultimate end to which the whole process of production is a means.*"—H. Sidgwick, "Principles of Political Economy," p. 144.

Says M. Wolowski: "The abstract deductions of pure science do not leave us without disquietude, since they treat man much more like a material than like a moral force. Under the vigorous procedure of speculation, man becomes a constant quantity for all times and all countries, whereas he is in reality a variable quantity. Man is something different from the sum of the services he may be made to render, and from the sum of enjoyments which may be procured for him. We must not run the risk of lowering him to the level of a living tool; and from the moment that we are required to take his moral destiny into account, what becomes of abstract calculation?"

in productive toil, and does not consist in the power to extort exchange value from unrequited toil and sorrow. If we are to divide with other people, it ought to be, as it must be, on condition of their coming here and casting in their contribution to the common glory and happiness of the citizens of the nation, by helping to swell the annual product, the national income—for the economist and statesman measure success by that income.

There need be no doubt that, in virtue of the operation of competition, as put by *Bastiat*, if we enter into it by way of the world's commerce, we could be made to exchange the products of our labor, and throw the gratuities which nature has conferred on us "into the bargain."

In the first place, free trade recommends that we all enter into land industries. Our entire population is then in competition, one with another, in the production of exportables. When we go to our markets we find we encounter the strong competition of all the world which is self-feeding, excepting only England and small tracts of Western Europe. We have drained Europe of its artisans and located them upon our lands, with the twofold result, first, of lessening the competition abroad of workmen in the manufacturing industries there, and diminishing the supply in the market of the goods which we buy; and second, heightening the competition of laborers in agriculture here, and reducing the demand for its products which we must sell. This may be a beneficent work. It may help "the constant approximation of all men toward a level which is always rising," but we must descend to reach it. The wealth of nations may be increased, but it is at our expense.

Accordingly, with strict scientific precision, Prof. Cairnes says that while the steam-engine, the spinning-jenny, and the mule cheapen manufactures, "the superior agricultural resources of foreign countries, made available through free trade, keep down the price of our agricultural products"; and Prof. Bonamy Price, speaking of our prairie farms, observes, "I call these emphatically English fields, because political economy knows nothing about political divisions." Free trade enables an Englishman to say that. Americans wish to know how it affects the "political division" we call the United States. He adds: "Political economy asks no questions about the origin of the bread which it finds on English tables. The Australian and American corn are as much English corn as that grown in Lincolnshire or Sussex. Of these superlatively rich lands, many *pay no rent*, and the reason presents itself at once. The *cost of carriage eats up that part of the produce which could generate rent.*" The American farmer may well ask some questions about this, and inquire whether the bread on English tables originates solely in his labor and toil, and whether he has exported his superlatively rich lands with it as a gratuity into the bargain. Herein, also, distinctly appears the truth of Mr. Carey's maxim that "whoever is compelled to seek a market must pay the cost of getting to that market." Does anybody suppose that Englishmen preach free trade for the purpose of enhancing the price of American food—England, whose population has outrun its native food capacity? If American food is to be cheapened, let us feed it to American workmen.

The free-trader professedly puts the American farmer in competition with the farmers of Europe, Asia, and Africa, and confidently counts upon our underselling them in a very limited market. Luckily for him and his case, the cost, or rather impossibility, of transportation from some of the rich and undeveloped food-centers of those countries has disguised his weakness. The Slavs of Russia and the Ryots of India now loom up with threatening import.

"Pauper labor" seems about to try its hand in competition with the American agriculturist. Free trade must, as it is intended to, tend to put an equality of price on all the labor employed in the raising of portable food over the entire portion of the earth which lies in the area of cheap and close commercial intercourse. It may turn out that the ill-timed sneer of the representative of the "Iowa State Free-Trade League," who addressed the tariff commission, that "the American farmer used more wheat in seeding his lands than all the protected industries furnished consumption for," may result in a different form of irony.

Any merchant's clerk who had never ventured across the threshold of a free-trade professor's lecture-room could tell where this kind of trading must end. He could instinctively point out two considerations which would forbid the extension of a series of such exchanges.

CHAPTER XV.

GENERAL THEORY OF WAGES—HIGH RATE OF WAGES IN THE UNITED STATES.

As yet, political economy has failed to furnish any answer to the question, why the remuneration of industry, as a whole, is such as we find it to be in the various countries of the earth; why the "rate of wages" or "value of labor" and the "rate of profit" or "value of abstinence" are such as they are in different nations.

If the labor and capital which enter into the production of a given commodity are in effective competition, about all we can answer is, that the wages of the laborer will be determined by the competition of the laborers contending for employment in it, and the profit on capital by the competition of capital seeking that industry. That is, we can thus get partially at the relative remuneration of the laborers among themselves and of the capitalists among themselves. We know of no principle on which the share of labor, as a whole, and of capital, as a whole, can be determined. It does not yet appear that "wages are the leavings of profits."[1]

---

[1] A tentative formula as to the result of the competition between capital and labor is the one suggested by Ricardo, Prof. Senior, and others, and may be thus stated: "In proportion to the increase of capital the *absolute* share of the total product falling to the capitalist is augmented, and his *relative* share is diminished; while, on the contrary, the laborer's share is increased both *absolutely* and *relatively*." That is, in other words, the *rate of interest* is de-

There is no single formula which can settle the exchange relations of commodities, and, at the same time, the exchange relations of labor and the exchange relation of abstinence or profits. They are incommensurable with each other. "Some such aim," says Prof. Cairnes, "seems to have guided the speculations of Bastiat, whose work on the "Harmonies of Political Economy" is, in effect, an essay toward the determination of the required formula; but the result of Bastiat's attempt is not encouraging to those who would essay the same path. He produces, indeed, generalizations which seem to satisfy the needed conditions, but, closely examined, they either collapse into identical propositions, or are found to contain some flagrant *petitio principii*.

The economist treats the dealer while offering his commodity in terms of value, as expressed in price, and the laborer, while offering his services in terms of value, as expressed in wages, as if the commodity and the laborer were equally created in view of an industrial "demand," and they were simply the "supply" to answer it. It is assumed that the forces—labor and capital—are operative under the same conditions of impersonality, and that each only exists for the sake of exchange. "And yet," says Prof. Francis A. Walker, "there is complaint that statesmen and the mass of the people entertain such slight regard for political economy, whose professors, in the interest of the purity and simplicity of their science, discard from the premises of their reasoning all the 'sympathies, apathies, and antipathies' of mankind, and insist upon treating a Manchester spinner, with a wife and six children —ignorant, fearful, and poor, in debt to his landlord and grocer—as possessing the same mobility, economically, and

---

creasing, the *rate of wages* is increasing. But the formula seems to leave out of consideration the increasing number of laborers who compete.

under the same subjection to the impulses of pecuniary interest, as a bale of Manchester cottons on the wharf, free to go to India or to Iceland as the difference of a penny in the price may determine."

Adam Smith's contribution to the discussion was the terms "supply and demand." This is, in truth, nothing but a statement of the "conditions" of the problem, and furnishes no law for its solution. Mr. Mill is supposed to have demonstrated the inadequacy of that formula. His own doctrine has been successfully challenged by Mr. Thornton and Prof. Cairnes, who agree that the doctrine of the equality of supply and demand, as the condition of market prices, becomes a mere identical proposition.

This is manifestly a method of generalizing names instead of things. "Nothing is easier," is the criticism of Prof. Cairnes, "than to say that the value of labor, like the value of other things, depends upon supply and demand. We may find the formula in any newspaper we take up, but what light does that throw on the causes which govern the values either of labor or commodities? Simply none at all, or next to none at all. What we want to know is, not whether an increase of supply will cheapen a commodity or will cheapen labor, and an increase of demand raise the price of each. Every costermonger will tell you this, but what is it that governs supply and demand in each case? Now, we can not take a step toward dealing with this question without being brought face to face with the fact that the motives which influence human beings in the production and supply of commodities are not those which influence them in the production and supply of labor; in other words, that the conditions operative in the two cases are distinct.[1]

---

[1] The futility of treating laborers and commodities as equally objects of sale in the market inheres in the nature of things, and I adopt Prof. Cairnes's

The discussion is an illustration of the vice of attributing reality to the economists' abstraction—the abortiveness of contemplating a society of human beings in its simple aspect as an arena for "buying and selling." And so political economy fails to reach any solution of the "burning question" of wages. We turn, then, to the

---

language in showing why it must be so. "The production of 'commodities' is an onerous act, which will only be undertaken in the prospect of reward, whence it follows that the supply of commodities will only be secured on the condition of this prospect presenting itself. On the other hand, the production of labor which, in other words, is the production of human beings, is not an onerous act, but a consequence of complying with one of the strongest instincts of humanity—an instinct which, so far from needing the stimulus of reward, can only be kept in due control by powerful restraints. The cost in the production of a commodity is undergone deliberately, and with a distinct view to industrial ends. In the preparation of human beings for a career in life, I will not say that industrial ends have no place at all in the calculation, but I will assert this, that except in the case of professional or technical education—a mere *bagatelle* in the general expense of rearing a laborer—industrial considerations are entirely subordinate to considerations of a wider and altogether different character. . . . A man, whatever be his rank of life, brings up his children—I speak of the common case—as far as he is able, according to the ideas prevailing in that rank of life. He does so mainly because he feels certain obligations of morality and affection toward them, and because it would be shameful to do otherwise. His children once arrived at maturity, no doubt his views and theirs will take a direction more distinctly governed by industrial consideration, or at least consideration bearing on success in life; but at this point *the supply of labor has been already determined*. It is now in existence, and the industrial motive, now that it comes into play, operates not upon the aggregate supply of labor, but merely upon the mode of its distribution. The adaptation of the supply of commodities to the demand is determined by strictly commercial motives; the adaptation of the supply of labor to the demand is not so determined. Human beings, at least out of slave countries, are not produced to meet the requirements of the market. Now, this being so—the conditions determining the phenomena in the two cases being essentially different—what can come of forcing the solution, by dint of verbal refinements, into a single formula? Simply this: either our theory will be flagrantly untrue, or it will not go more than word-deep, and our show of explanation will merely seem to obscure the essential facts of the problem."

mechanism of production in America for the reasons of the high rate of wages and the high rate of profits which have rewarded our exertions here in the United States.

Here we shall find a *consensus*, among free-trade writers, that the productiveness of our labor, and consequently the high rate of wages here, come from agriculture. And on this is based the logical sequence that we ought all to take to that pursuit, at least until it breaks down. In fact, it has broken down already.

"The endless opportunities of agriculture in this land are the steady force that lifts our wages and keeps them to their actual height. Cheap and fertile farms, to be had almost for the asking, are open to all laborers and all immigrants; . . . and this, on the one hand, reduces the supply of laborers in the mills and factories, and on the other keeps up the rates of wages there to a point marked by *the average success* of labor in agriculture." (Prof. Perry, "Political Economy," p. 498.)

"No one will be willing to turn away from the industries for which the country offers the best advantages, to take up those in which other countries have the best advantage, unless the difference can be made up to him in some way. Hence, manufacturing industry here has always had to contend with the profits possible in agricultural pursuits. Wages, so far as any wages-class has ever yet been developed here, must be high enough to give the *same scale of comfort* as can be won in using land. The *high wages* and *general high average of comfort* are, therefore, plainly *the same thing*, and both proceed together out of the actual *physical circumstances* of the people." (Prof. Sumner, "Princeton Review" essay.)

"No wonder the protectionists are enraged at the economists who are still stupidly teaching that we can produce nothing except by applying labor and capital to land. . . .

"In a new country in which there is an immense amount of unoccupied land, and in which the amount of capital required for tilling the soil is small, any man who has a pair of stout hands, although he has no skill and very little capital, may become a land-owner and agriculturist. . . . Every man of the unskilled labor class, therefore, has an alternative offered to him. . . . He owns a thing (his labor) for which there is a high demand in the market. *The comfort* he could win on the land fixes *a minimum* below which wages can not fall. If they do temporarily fall below that minimum, the laborers take to the land, as they did in the hard times a few years ago. . . .

"In the second place, all the protected industries of this country are now parasites on the naturally strong industries. Agriculture now supports itself, and all the rest and their losses; therefore, even if it were true that all the population would, under free trade, take to agriculture, it is mathematically certain that agriculture could support them all better than under the present arrangements." (Prof. Sumner, Tariff Commission address.)

Prof. Walker, in a very neat piece of analytic work, under the head of "The Competition of the Farm with the Shop" ("Political Economy," edition 1885, p. 396), has shown how, by virtue of the protective statute, laborers in the protected industries, as well as carpenters, blacksmiths, and masons, domestic servants, physicians, lawyers, and schoolmasters, may be let into "a participation in the abundance enjoyed by the agricultural population," as he chooses to express it. And he concludes thus:

"But while the law may thus create high rates of wages in factory industries, it does not and can not create the wealth out of which that excess of manufacturing wages over those of older countries is paid. *That wealth is cre-*

ated by the labor and capital employed in the cultivation of the soil." [1]

---

[1] "THE COMPETITION OF THE FARM WITH THE SHOP.—It has been the competition of the farm with the shop which has from the first most effectually retarded the growth of manufactures in the United States. A population which is privileged to live upon a virgin soil, cultivating only the choicest fields, and cropping these through a succession of years without returning anything to the land, can live in plenty, if not fare sumptuously, every day. . . . Now, the mode of living on the part of the agricultural population has necessarily set a minimum standard of wages for mechanical labor. With an abundance of cheap land, with a population facile to the last degree in making change of avocation and residence, very few native-born Americans, and comparatively few immigrants, are likely to be drawn into factories and shops on terms which imply a meaner subsistence than that secured in the cultivation of the soil.

"THE HAND-TRADES.—There are certain classes of mechanical pursuits, however, which by their nature secure to those who follow them a minimum remuneration fully up to the standard of the agricultural wages of the region. Such, for instance, are the trades of the carpenter, blacksmith, and mason, in which the work is of a kind which *can only be done upon the spot.* The house can not be built abroad and imported for the farmer's use; the wagon must be mended near the place where it broke down; the horse must be shod, the tools sharpened, by the artisans of the neighborhood. If, then, the farmer will have such services performed, he must admit those who perform them to share of his own abundance. . . .

"PERSONAL AND PROFESSIONAL SERVICES.—But, again, there are certain classes of services of a personal or professional nature which have also secured for those rendering them a participation in the abundance enjoyed by the tillers of the soil in the same region. The remuneration received by the members of these classes, whether called the wages of domestic servants, or the fees of physicians and lawyers, or the salaries of schoolmasters and clergymen, or the profits of retail trade, has been out of all relation to the remuneration of similar services in other countries, and has amounted to just what I have termed it—*a participation in the abundance enjoyed by the agricultural population.* Since *these services could only be performed upon the spot*, the agriculturists have been *obliged*, if they would have the services rendered, to pay for them out of the large surplus of their own products. . . .

"THE FACTORY INDUSTRIES.—But, now, we note that there are still other important classes of service to be rendered, respecting which the rules change. The remuneration of the persons rendering these services no longer

It is evident that the artisans who make all that portion of the "sundry articles" which we are "*compelled*" to

has reference to the abundance of agricultural production in the several sections of the United States, is no longer irrespective of the remuneration of such similar classes elsewhere. These persons are not, necessarily, admitted to a participation in the fruits of American agriculture.

" The services referred to are such as can be performed *without respect to the location of the consumer of the product.* They are nearly identical with what we call, in the technical sense of the term, manufactures.

" Whenever an American farmer wants a pane of glass set, or a pair of boots mended, or a horse shod, he must pay some one of his neighbors enough for doing the job to keep him in his trade, and to keep him out of agriculture, in the face of the great advantages of tilling the soil in New York, or Ohio, or Dakota, or wherever else the farmer in question may live; but how much he shall pay the man who makes the pane of glass, or the pair of boots, or the set of horseshoes, will depend upon the advantages of tilling the soil, not where he himself lives, *but where the maker of horseshoes, of boots, or of glass, may live.*

" If he will have the work done, he must pay some one somewhere enough to keep him in his trade and out of agriculture, but not necessarily out of New York agriculture, or Ohio agriculture, or Dakota agriculture; but, perhaps, out of English agriculture, or French agriculture, or Norwegian agriculture, such as that may be, with the advantages no less and no more there enjoyed by the cultivators of the soil under the requirement of constant fertilization, deep plowing, and thorough drainage, and subject to that stringent necessity which economists express by the term, 'the law of diminishing returns.' . . .

" Now, to offset and overcome the inducements to engage in agriculture, even in merry England, is a different thing from keeping a man in his trade and out of agriculture in the United States. . . .

" The American agriculturist, having large quantities of grain and meat, of cotton and tobacco, left on his hands, after providing ample subsistence for his family, and even after hiring the carpenter, mason, and blacksmith, the schoolmaster, lawyer, and doctor, for as much time as he requires their respective services, and still further, after putting a good deal into farm-implements and increase of stock, is desirous of obtaining with the remainder *sundry articles* more or less necessary to health, comfort, and decency. To him, consulting his personal interests, which is all the average man can be expected to do in a bargain, it makes no difference whether the articles he requires are made on *one side of the Atlantic* or *on the other;* but it makes a great difference to him what he is obliged to pay for them; how much of

have made on this side of the Atlantic are entitled to participate in the abundance enjoyed by the agricultural population, *by the ordinance of nature,* and *not by the ordinance of the statute.*

---

his surplus grain and meat, tobacco and cotton, must go to secure a certain definite satisfaction of his urgent and oft-recurring wants. If he must needs pay some one to stay out of American agriculture and do this work, his surplus will not go so far as if he were allowed to pay some one to stay out of English agriculture to do it.

"WHAT THE STATE CAN DO.—But here the state enters and declares that it is socially or politically necessary that these articles, these nails, these horseshoes, this cotton or woolen cloth, or what not, *shall be made on this side of the Atlantic,* and not on the other. That *necessity* the agriculturist, as consumer, can not be expected to feel: *he does not care where the things were made;* he only wants them to use. He does not care who makes them; he does not even care whether they are made at all; they would answer his purpose just as well were they the gratuitous gifts of nature, spontaneous fruits of the soil, or the sea, or the sky. Whatever his own economical theories may be, he will, as purchaser, every time select the cheapest article which will precisely answer his need. He will not, of his own motion, *pay more for an article because it is made on his side of the Atlantic* than he could get an equally good article for, bearing the brand of Sheffield, or Birmingham, or Manchester. But if *the state says he must,* he must; and consequently the American maker of this article is, by *force of law,* admitted to a participation in the abundance enjoyed by the American agricultural class. The tiller of the soil is now *compelled, by the ordinance of the state,* to share his bread and meat with the maker of nails or of horseshoes, of cotton or of woolen cloth, just as he was before *compelled, by the ordinance of nature,* to share his bread and meat with the blacksmith, carpenter, and mason, the schoolmaster, lawyer, and doctor.

"It is perfectly true, therefore, as the protectionist asserts, that a tariff of customs duties upon foreign goods imported into new countries tends *to create and maintain high rates of wages in the factory industries.* But for *protective duties,* those articles which, in their nature, can be readily and cheaply transported, will be *produced predominantly* in countries where the minimum standard of mechanical wages is set by agricultural conditions far less favorable than those which obtain in the United States, in Canada, or Australia.

"But while the law thus can and does *create high rates* of wages in factory industries, it does not and it can not *create the wealth* out of which that excess of manufacturing wages, over those of older countries, is paid. *That wealth is created by the labor and capital employed in the cultivation of the soil."*

We have seen that this will include the producers of about nine tenths of the "sundry articles" made in what is called the "protected industries."

The extracts selected contain the argument in its full force, and the free-trade economist is entitled to the just force of them. They, nevertheless, do not contain the truth of the matter. They do not give a true analysis of the mechanism of the society, as a whole. They proceed on fallacious assumptions which it is possible to trace up and expose.

First, then, it is not true that "we can produce nothing except by applying labor and capital to land."

This was the doctrine of the Physiocrates of France, and is now exploded.[1]

---

[1] Their doctrine was this: All national wealth is derived from the soil; agriculture is the only productive occupation; the production of raw material is the only calling in which the value of the product exceeds the cost of production. The labor of the farmer produces not only enough to support him while engaged in the labor, but a surplus over and above this, which may be called the net product. This net product generally falls to the landlord under the form of rent, and is the fund from which all expenditures of a public nature must be defrayed. The landlords, since they live without labor, are called the *classe disponible*, and they may devote themselves to the service of the public. *Manufacturers and artisans* are *unproductive*. They add value, it is true, to the raw material which they work over, but only as much as is equivalent to the cost of their support while engaged in their work. If they are able to save anything from their income, they do it either by limiting their consumption within too narrow bounds, or by some favoritism of government, or of chance, which secures them against competition. Although unproductive, these classes are by no means useless, since by their labor they give permanence to the utility embodied in raw material, and by their improvements they lessen the cost at which the agricultural classes can supply themselves with the needed manufactures, and so, by diminishing the cost of living of the farmers, they render possible the increase of the ground-rent, that is, of the "net national revenue." The system was refuted by Adam Smith, with partial success ("Wealth of Nations," IV, chap. ix, sec. 28), and since by John Stuart Mill completely. Of course, the materials of all industries, in one sense, come from the earth. Any increase of value conferred

Second. "All the protected industries of this country are now parasites on the naturally strong industries."

This is a glaring *petitio principii*. Agricultural industries here or elsewhere are "naturally strong" in the sense that using natural instruments of production they yield large returns in kind, for labor expended. What the economist wants to know is, Are they strong in the sense that these large returns have a high exchange value? To assume, as he does, that ours would exchange in the markets of the world at the same rates that they do now under a system of free foreign trade, with a vastly larger supply, is to settle in advance the very question of fact, which is the essence of the controversy.

Third. "Agriculture now supports itself and all the rest, and all their losses."

If this simply means that agriculture supplies its want of food to the people, furnishes *the means of subsistence*, it is true. If it means that the exchange values of the products of the manufacturing industries which supply our other wants—*the means of existence*—are conferred at the expense of agriculture, it is not true. By the census of 1880 the value of the products of the manufacturing industries was $5,369,579,191; of farm products, $2,213,402,564.[1]

If it is meant that agriculture (in case all the population took to it) would furnish them a living amount of

---

upon a material thing by actual human service is an act of production, and every man who confers that value is a producer; and it is further true, and has been so recognized since the days of Adam Smith, that less value is conferred by labor as such in agriculture than in most other departments of production.

[1] The capital employed in manufactures, $2,790,272,606; net value given to materials used, $2,000,000,000—71 per cent; value of farms, $10,197,096,776; value of productions (revised estimate), $3,600,000,000—35 per cent. It may be noted that the value of the product of English manufactures for the same year was $4,000,000,000.

food, and thus *support* them, no one is interested to question it. If it means that, under these circumstances, agriculture would furnish all the population with the abundance they now have at the same price, the Professor again makes an unjustifiable assumption of a conclusion for which he has furnished no premises in the facts, and one which the facts fatally negative. Agriculture could furnish the same supply of goods made abroad, on one set of conditions:-that the laborers abroad who make the goods, and all the workmen who make goods for them, consume the same quantity of American food, vegetable and animal, exportable and perishable, which the same workmen here would; that the exports continue to bear the same prices, and that the foreigners pay the cost of freight both ways, and the commissions, insurance, and profits of the middlemen. Why don't they buy ours? They have other sources of supply.

Fourth. We now come to "the competition of the farm with the shop."[1]

We begin with the agriculturist as the sole occupant of a virgin soil, and the abundance of food and other necessaries of life which follow its cultivation. The services of the carpenter, blacksmith, and mason are at once necessary to the satisfaction of his desires, and he employs them. What he pays them is not *taxation*, nor does he pay them out of *his* abundance. He simply finds himself in the category of Aristotle—" One man is no man." His wants exceed his powers. Then come the schoolmaster, the doctor, and the parson. It is physically possible that *they* might go on the land, but not morally possible. If they did, and

---

[1] The writer has often wondered why Prof. Francis A. Walker (who made the clear analysis given above) seemed to close his eyes to the consequences which his analysis led up to; or, rather, why he did not carry it a step further, which would have brought him into the clear light of *protection*.

the carpenter, blacksmith, and mason followed suit, they would only have created a duplicate demand for *other* carpenters, blacksmiths, and masons, and other schoolmasters, doctors, and parsons. The process would never end, and we should never reach an organism with co-ordinated structure and functions. And so they simply surrender to their humanness and make common cause, supplying their wants in the order of strict necessity. The necessity for food happening to lie at the bottom, they all share whatever abundance their physical surroundings afford. Which shall satisfy the desire and necessity for food, and which shall satisfy the desire and necessity for houses, and wells, and education, and religious teaching, is a mere matter of expediency in the "division of labor." This community, now, *as a whole*, need alike, whether farmer or parson, "sundry articles" more or less necessary to health, comfort, and decency. Inasmuch as agricultural conditions in foreign countries set a less favorable *minimum* of comfort on a farm there, the standard of mechanical wages there is lower, and there men can be found to produce these "sundry articles" at less wages, and they can in consequence be bought for less price. (This is Prof. Walker's argument, not mine.) The conclusion is, that our community should buy these "sundry articles" in the foreign countries. Well, if they could, there would be no economic objection. Can they? The moment the surplus of grain and meat, of cotton and tobacco, which our community produces, fails to buy the whole supply of "sundry articles" which the whole society needs, a portion *must* be made by themselves. This portion, now a "necessity," must be produced upon the same conditions under which all the other members of the society are operating. When this portion becomes the larger part of the supply, its producers stand in the same relation to the farmer which the carpenter and schoolmaster did—they *share the abundance,* not of *the farmer,* but of *the resources of the society. The society as a whole has the use of the land for nothing.* They confer a private title to his land upon the farmer, but that is not in the interest of the farmer, as such. It is found the most expedient way to secure the largest production from the soil, and is a mere form of the division of labor. This will be more clearly seen if we take an advantageous industry of some other form—if the farmer produced oil, say, instead of wheat. Title to the oil-well might be conferred on the individual producer. If the number of producers was limited, he and his necessary neighbors might buy abroad all the "sundry articles." The moment their purchase-money—oil—failed for all their supply, and home production became a necessity for a part, we at once see the right of the society, as a whole, to share *the abundance* of the *oil industry* in working for each other, *not the abundance* of *oil-well owners.* The oil-well never was and never can be absolutely private property; it must, in the nature of things, subserve the public purpose.

Or suppose the first comers had found ready-made looms, limited in number, and gave them out in the "division of labor," and in the interest of the best care and highest production, to individual ownership. Up to a certain point, the use of the looms would be the most advantageous industry. If, however, the product of the looms failed to buy in the foreign market the food of the whole society, and the society was driven to raise a portion of the food-supply on its own fields, it is evident enough that, in that event, it could not be said that *the farmer shared the abundance* of the *loom-owner;* he simply shared the abundance which belonged to the society as a whole.[1]

---

[1] England must buy half its food and most of its raw materials by working its looms.

16

These natural looms cost the society, as a whole, nothing; and weaver and farmer are simply different organs of one body. It matters not under what disadvantage the home production of the food is carried on, if it is a necessary part of the whole supply. It could not, then, be said that the high wages received by the farmer under these circumstances—the same wages the weaver got—were created by the labor and capital employed on the looms.

In the cases put, the land-owner, the oil-producer, and the loom-proprietor are the owners of monopolies. The monopolies must, in the very nature of the case, pass to the people at large. Their owners are trustees for the public.[1]

If we may believe Alexander Hamilton on a question of fact, this was the condition of things, historically, in the United States in 1791. In his report we find this remarkable testimony:

"A constant and increasing *necessity* on their part" (the people of the United States) " for the commodities of

---

[1] "In the first place, *land is a monopoly*, not by the act of man but of nature; it exists in limited quantity, not susceptible of increase. Now, it is an acknowledged principle that when the state permits a monopoly, either natural or artificial, to fall into private hands, it retains the right, and can not divest itself of the duty, to place the exercise of the monopoly under any degree of control which is requisite for the public good. The self-interest of the owners of land, under perfect freedom, coincides with the general interest of the community up to a certain point, but not wholly; there are cases in which it draws in a totally opposite direction."—JOHN STUART MILL, "Fortnightly Review," 1870, p. 642.

Exactly. When the products of the industry carried on by the owners of a monopoly fail to supply, by exchanges, the wants of a given community of which they are part, when the industrial entity composed of the monopolists fails to supply the wants of the political entity on the same arena, we have reached the point when the self-interests of the monopolists cease to coincide with the general interests of the community. Natural laws and human laws alike, then, operate to compel the monopolists to share their abundance with the whole society.

Europe, and only a partial and occasional demand for their own in return, could not but expose them to a state of impoverishment compared with *the opulence* to which *their political and natural advantages authorize them to aspire.*"

Whose opulence? Manifestly that of the whole society; not that merely of the land-owners.

To the same effect is the resolution of the General Assembly of Pennsylvania, cited in the Preface of this book.

In other words, as a matter of fact, more than a hundred years ago we in this country found that a portion, more or less, of the " sundry articles " must be made here, on our soil, and that it was just as necessary that makers of that portion should be here, alongside of us, as it was that the carpenter, blacksmith and mason, the schoolmaster, the doctor and parson, should live in our midst. The vice of the whole analysis is, that it assumes that the farmer would have none of them around him, unless he was compelled to, whereas the farmer, *as such*, has no more right to have his say about it than the hod-carrier. None of the vast number of artisans engaged in the great production, of which we are all consumers, " participates in the abundance enjoyed by the agricultural population." They participate in the abundance of the society to which they belong, though each must work for his own share. Without the one hundred and fifty classes of workmen, co-operating in our industrial system, *the agricultural population would have no abundance.* They might have enough of mere food—so has the Esquimau and the Patagonian. Every workman, farmer, oil-producer, weaver, artisan, pastor or pedagogue, whose mission here is necessary to supply the home demand, is entitled to share in the abundance which *our* resources, the *nation's*, make possible.

If we operated under free trade, and supplied our wants from surplus agricultural products sold abroad, the surplus would not come out of the farmer, it would not be the abundance, even, of agriculture—it would simply be the form of the surplus which our productive industry, as a whole, realized. The power of that surplus to satisfy our wants is the very question of fact to be settled. It is the same as if we expended our energies in producing gold, or silver, or coal; we convert our labor into that commodity. The size of the surplus and its salableness depend on the wants of buyers abroad; and the advantages to be derived from the exchange depend upon the further circumstance, whether their market contains what we want. The moment we are compelled to make a part of the same kind of goods at home, the abundance has failed us for exchange purposes. The home producers of that part must then share this abundance, and as the whole production, domestic and foreign, must be sold under like conditions of price, the foreign product, be it more or less, is handicapped by a duty, to bring the cost to home prices. "But this in no way proves the inexpediency of the duties in question, since they may very well give adequate encouragement to native industry, without completely excluding the foreign products, and it can not be an objection to them from a purely national point of view, that a part of their effect is merely to levy a tribute on foreigners, for the national exchequer." (Sidgwick, p. 449.)

The moment this community were compelled to make any part of the "sundry articles" at home, their abundance failed them for exchange purposes abroad. For this portion *there were no foreign exchanges to restrict.* If, then, the *indispensable* services of the artisans, in non-protected industries, are in no true sense *a tax*, so neither are the *indispensable* services of those in the protected industries *a tax*. They have *necessary* relations to the society, and *have a right* to share in the abundance of that society. They do not *tax* it.

Having got rid of these fallacious views of the correlation of the producers in a society, let us see how *the high wages* in the United States do arise.[1]

In America, wages of common labor have always been high; not only money-wages, but the real wages, reckoned in the commodities received. It is generally assumed that the *minimum* of wages here was high, for the reason that the laborer was sure of a certain amount of comfort if he went on the land; and this is, too, the *minimum*, which itself implies that there is some *higher* rate. But this would be true only in the case he became a land-owner, the proprietor of a natural agent. In such event, too, there was always held out to him the rise in the value of his estate by reason of the general advance in society; he would reap in the end the benefits of the settlement of others around and near him. The labors of other people expended on roads, highways, telegraphs, would confer great value upon him arising out of mere societary growth. In point of fact, the increase of value in agricultural lands has amounted to many thousand millions of dollars over and above the capital and labor spent upon the land—"the unearned increment" of Mr. Mill.

---

[1] Mr. David A. Wells, in addressing the Free-Trade Convention which met in Chicago in November, 1885, uses this language: "But whatever may have been the case in former days—whether it be true or not that certain branches of industry have been more rapidly developed than they would otherwise have been by this method—yet, now we affirm that protection has ceased to protect. We affirm that neither the profits nor the wages in the protected industries are any higher, if as high, as they are in the great body of our industries which are absolutely free from the possibility of foreign competition."

No one ever pretended or desired that protection could or did raise the wages or profits in the protected industries above the rates current in the country. Labor and capital, in protected employments, simply shared in the abundance of the land, on the principle, to each according to its share in the common product of industry.

The wages, however, of the mere agricultural laborer have never been the criterion of wages paid to artisans and members of the different trades. It is true that every man could go upon the land without capital so long as the lands were in effect sold by the General Government for a nominal sum, or really given away under the homestead acts. It can scarcely be said that the economic instinct was the operative cause in these cases. Many reasons combine to take people to the land. Adam Smith had pointed out some of them; but they were operative under widely different conditions from those which swept so tremendous a wave of immigration over our Western prairies, and which has now reached the passes of the Rocky Mountains, lost in the returning wave from the Pacific coast.

"The beauty of the country, besides the pleasure of country life, the tranquillity of mind which it promises, and, wherever the influence of human laws does not distract it, the independence which it really affords, are charms that more or less attract everybody, and in every stage of his existence man seems to retain his predilection for this primitive employment." Again, he says: "From artificer a man becomes a planter, and neither large wages nor the easy subsistence which the country affords" (he is speaking of the American colonies) "can bribe him to rather work for other people than himself. He feels that an artificer is the servant of his customers, from whom he derives his subsistence; but that a planter who cultivates *his own land*, and derives his necessary subsistence from the labor of his own family, is really a master, and independent of all the world."

But in the very act of indulging in these sentiments, he secures their gratification at the loss of productive returns for labor as such. As an industry it is less profitable than mechanical or manufacturing pursuits, except under conditions never realized. He has more leisure, experiences a sense of independence; but these are secured at the cost of pursuing a less remunerative industry. He enjoys a high sense of security in the nature of his possessions, and a feeling of safety for the future of himself and his family. These induce him to expect and accept smaller pecuniary returns. This very tendency to agriculture may be so disproportionate as to result in an economic loss to the community as a whole. Labor which results in an agricultural glut produces nothing, or worse. England itself has passed from the condition of a people unduly agricultural to one unduly mechanical. We tried the experiment, and did not find it profitable or enjoyable. The American farmer himself is also the owner of American railroads, bank-stocks, factory-stocks, and all other forms of capital.

The temperament which moves him, characterizes, however, a very considerable number of men, and is sufficient to drive a palpably undue proportion of our population into the "most advantageous" industry. In an economical point of view, the differences in the purposes and results of the agriculturists must be distinguished from those of the adventurers who seek the gold and silver regions. There is, again, a very important distinction between a capitalist looking to the most remunerative investment for his savings and the laborer seeking a vocation which affords the most comfort and independence for himself and family.

In truth, we should not need *capitalists*, as such, in the United States. Until all the lands were taken up, the capitalist could not find laborers for his operations—the laborers would be *land-owners*. Only *as owner* of the soil could he get the returns from the soil, the cultivation of which was the most advantageous industry. There has always been a normal rate of wages in the United States above that paid to agricultural labor. The high returns did not come from agricultural labor, but from agricultural ownership. The draft in this direction lessened competition, and prevented wages going down.

It is a question of some bearing on the general discussion, to ascertain precisely what it is which has kept up the high rate of wages in the United States, but it can not be settled out of hand, as we have seen it attempted. The underlying reason seems unquestionably to be found in the character and aims of the men who settled the colonies, under whose dignity of character, and fidelity to their own rights as citizens and freedmen, their industries were begun and developed. With them, life had a serious and energetic aspect. They possessed the high spirit and mettle of a race who had the interests of a remote future as well as the present in view.[1] Self-respecting as they were, they could accept no condition of living which was not befitting themselves. There might be lack of means and power to gratify all the wants of men, with their desires and aspirations, but there was no abatement in their standards. Their surroundings were primitive, but lowly conditions of life were not incompatible with the purity, decency, and heroism of their lives. In the course of his eulogy on President Garfield, Mr. Blaine gets to the root of the matter: "The poverty of the frontier, where all were engaged in a common struggle, and where a common sympathy and hearty co-operation lighten the burdens of each, is a very different poverty, different in kind, differ-

---

[1] "In what way," asks Adam Smith, "has Europe contributed to the grandeur of the colonies of America? In one way, and in one way only, she has contributed a great deal. *Magna virum mater*. She bred and formed the men who were capable of achieving such great actions, and for laying the foundations of so great an empire. The colonies owe to Europe the *education* and *great views* of their active and enterprising founders, and some of the greatest and most important of them owe to her scarce anything else."

ent in influence and effect, from that conscious and humiliating indigence which is every day forced to contrast itself with neighboring wealth on which it feels a grinding dependence. The poverty of the frontier is, indeed, no poverty. It is but the beginning of wealth, and has the boundless possibilities of the future always opening before it."

Energetic efforts and temporary sacrifice give the hope of permanent achievement, of a secured status as men and self-respecting citizens.

Labor was their religion. The circumstances which surrounded them enabled them to reap its whole reward. Nothing went to the landlord for "rent," nothing to the capitalist for "profits." In truth, they were under economic conditions which were entirely anomalous. A people imbued with the knowledge, and practically realizing the scope of civilization, were face to face with a continent boundless in extent and resources to subjugate it to their uses. In the United States the working-classes were not compelled to carry their whole labor-power to market; indeed, there were no working-classes, as commonly understood. Wages were above the height of urgent necessity. A higher standard of living was attained; necessary wants of the workmen being easily satisfied, their need of decencies increased. And, above all, they were under the general stimulus of a good prospect for the future, by which an honorable artisan is distinguished from the proletariat. They were, moreover, possessed of that degree of intelligence and self-restraint which prevented an increase in wages from producing an oppressive increase in the number of children.

Their "isolation" from European systems was complete. The rewards of labor were distributed to them in the exceptional manner that their circumstances allowed

—a division to each according to his labor. The rewards of labor are distributed now to their descendants in like manner, so far as we have been enabled to retain their economic condition. It is the explanation of their and our high rate of wages, still maintained in the face of the greatest influx of laborers which the world has ever seen. Prof. Senior had commented on the causes which diverted the proceeds of labor from the laborer, and which fixed the laborer's share: "If all the laborers were employed in the production, direct or indirect, of commodities for their own use, the rate of wages would depend solely on the productiveness of their labor. But it is obvious that this could never be the case unless the laborers themselves were the owners of all the capital and all the natural agents of the country; a state of existence so utterly barbarous as to be without distinction of ranks or division of labor." (It must be borne in mind that the Professor wrote as an Englishman.) "A great portion of the labor employed in a civilized community is employed in the production of things in the use of which the laborer is not to participate. In a civilized community, therefore, the extent of the fund for the maintenance of labor depends not only on the productiveness of labor, but also on the number of persons employed in the production of things for the use of laborers, compared with the whole number of laboring families. . . . If all workmen were employed in nothing but the production of articles consumed by workmen, the rate of wages would be determined almost exclusively by the ratio between the number of the working population and the amount of their products. The effect must be much the same when the wealthy are exceedingly frugal and employ their savings as fully as possible in the employment of common home labor, while, on the other hand, the exportation of wheat and other articles which the working classes consume, in exchange for diamonds, lace, champagne, diminishes the demand for common labor in a country." To the extent, then, to which labor is employed in the production of things which laborers use, will their share of the product be large. There is more for the laborers to divide; their wages, measured in the commodities produced, will be larger. And labor in America has, in the main, been expended in the production of the very commodities which the laborer consumed. It left large dividends—high wages—for them.

There is nothing in the mere complexity of industry to change the operation of this principle. We have had occasion to urge that, by retaining the production of the commodities in use to our own labor in the United States, we provoke a double production and a double consumption—that there is so much more to divide among producers in their capacity as consumers.

The power of a people who grow into a higher class of wants to enforce the means of gratifying them even in an old society, has been illustrated in the rise of wages which has taken place in most parts of Europe within the last twenty years. Improved civilization has produced greater demands and requirements in the class of laboring-men; all authorities agree that they live, as a whole, better than they used to, and they *insist on getting better paid*. This is true in England, Germany, Belgium, and France. It may be that "where the skies are brightest, the air most genial, the work of husbandry pleasantest, life in every way most agreeable, the price of *farm-labor* is highest"; but that does not account for the higher wages of the other labor-classes in all these countries.

There is a general consensus of opinion among economists as to the causes of this phenomenon. In these causes really lie the only hopeful outlook which we get for the race of wage-earners. They result from the access given to all the workmen of a society to the productive occupations. They do not result from agricultural conditions nor the opportunity to enter upon agricultural pursuits. *When the people of a country co-operate in production, much is produced*, and, there is *much to divide*. In an article on "The Movements of Agricultural Wages in Europe," in the "Fortnightly Review" for June, 1874, will be found a careful statement, founded on official reports, of the causes co-operating to make wages high; not merely a high rate of money-wages, but a high purchasing power in them. Of Germany it is said: "Speaking generally, the southwestern region, whose boundary has just been roughly sketched, is the main region of industrial and commercial enterprise, communication by steam, general activity, intelligence, and wealth. Vicinity to the chief countries and markets of western Europe, numerous lines of railway, a river crowded with steamers, coal, iron, and their products, cause a greater abundance and more rapid circulation of currency, a greater demand and competition for labor of all kinds, and a generally higher price for agricultural, as well as town or mechanical labor, than is to be found in the northeast of the empire, which lies remote from the traffic, civilization, and progress of the Western world, is much less completely provided with railways, and is in a more primitive condition as regards customs, ideas, and industrial life.

"In Belgium, again, although the principal cause (as in every progressive country in Europe) of diversity in the local rates of *agricultural* wages is the presence or absence of mines, manufactures, or commerce on a great scale, other causes are at work.

"In France, as in Germany, the chief causes of high agricultural wages are—proximity to great industrial centers or easy communication with great markets. In Normandy the rate of wages is as two to one compared with the rate throughout a great part of Brittany, and there are several reasons for the difference: Normandy is much nearer to the market and Paris; it has great manufacturing towns, and Brittany none.

"Thus there are various causes in each country for great diversities of agricultural wages, but the most powerful and the most general cause is the unequal distribution of advantages for manufactures and commerce and of good markets. The currency of all Europe has been vastly augmented by new mines and instruments of credit; the rapidity, also, of the circulation of money has multiplied, and the prices of all things, labor included, which have not increased in proportion, have by consequence risen. Secondly, money has increased most, and the price of labor has risen most, in the districts whose money-getting powers have increased most through industrial development and rapid communication with the best markets.

"Thirdly, our Continental neighbors have acquired in recent years those new avenues of industry and commerce, iron, coal, the steam-engine, steam locomotion, which England possessed a generation earlier; prices, consequently, have risen in many parts of the Continent to the English scale from a much lower line."

The writer of this essay, Prof. Leslie, summarizes the results as follows: "Capital, money and its representatives, and the demand for labor, have increased most where the means of production and the means of communication with the best markets have improved most; where coal, iron, and mechanical power have multiplied the product of the human hand, and where railways and other modes of communication have made rapidest progress. Broad exemplifications of the influence of these two sets of conditions (which are closely related to superior natural advantages and the means of development) are to be seen on every side at home and abroad."

The American farmer has never had any market so good for himself as the home market. Now, when railways have put him in communication with all parts of it, the free trader asks him to abandon it for the imposing, wide-sounding "world's market." The condition of things digested in the abstract, as here quoted, is a demonstration from the facts of actual experience of the power of society association, which Mr. Carey indicated as the central fact in the progress of civilization, the divinely appointed lever with which man moves the universe. The rate of wages in America has no real relation to the amount of comfort which a man gets by working the soil. The early settler in the country was a man with his wants awakened, wants not only of food and clothing and shelter, which political economy conceives him as mainly striving to supply, but wants of his moral, political, and industrial nature. "The whole boundless continent" was for his appropriation to uses which would not contract his powers. There were inducements to all the industries open to human skill and persistence. His labor could be profitably employed upon the soil; it would not be unprofitable to employ it upon coal and iron and textile fabrics. The whole tone of things generally about him was energetic. He would not, it is true, starve upon the land, but the steam-engine and the locomotive would add a thousandfold to the efficiency of any labor he could combine with them; the mountain-streams would leap with a song to turn his wheels. It had not occurred to him to wait until the higher wages of labor in Europe had made agriculture in America less profitable, and that he was so well off that he could not afford to use the bounties which lay at his feet. The rate of wages in America was higher than the *minimum* which the alternative of taking to the land afforded, because the American was the kind of man he was, and because the physical conditions of things were such as they were. He could satisfy all the wants of his nature by the application of his energies to the materials about himself—fields, mines, forests, treasures in earth and air and water—at a less cost of effort than the inhabitant of any other country in the world. It comported with his tastes, his aims, his aspirations, his safety, and his independence to produce them directly. With his farm, and with his own workshop in co-operation, he could make the greatest annual product of his industry, and sound political economy justified his methods. And that is the way in which wages came to be high, and these the reasons why they continue to be high.

"A permanently high rate of wages, both as cause and effect, is very intimately connected with a flourishing condition of national life. It proves, on the one hand, great productiveness of the public economy of the people generally, prudence, self-respect, and control, even of the lowest classes; virtues which, however, are found, on the whole, only where political liberty exists, and where the lowest classes are rightly valued by the higher. On the other hand, it produces a condition of the great majority of that portion of the population who have to support themselves on the wages they receive, worthy of human beings, a condition in which they can educate their children, enjoy the present, and provide for the future." (Prof. Roscher.)

Only the free man cares for the future. The distribution of the aggregate wages earned by American labor did not depend on differences in their social positions. Political institutions made them equals. American society early became definitely industrial. No social discredit attached to labor as such. Since the close of the rebellion in 1865 it seems certain that no such exhibition of devotion to useful labor of hand and brain has ever been seen in the whole history of the race as has been offered by the citizens of a restored country competing with each other for the fruits of a high civilization. It has been the policy of this country to have free trade in laborers, although just at present the immigration of laborers from China is restricted. Prof. Perry remarks, "If China should precipitate itself upon the United States, or India upon England, as the mere *economical* impulse might indicate, it would be disastrous to the Western nations." The disaster would consist in the economic and social degradation of labor, denoted by the low standard of living which the Mongolian adopts. The competition of "cheap Chinese labor" menaces the English race in America and Australia in only one respect, the smaller necessary consumption of the Chinese as compared with the Englishman. The latter makes a smaller total net produce of a day's labor because his consumption by so much more exceeds that of the former, whose gross earnings are much less. The American or English workman considers himself a man and not a mere tool. The same general protest takes effect against the cheap laborer, as well as the cheap labor, of any other people, if it be manifested in a lowered standard of life. In America, witness the uprising against the squalid Hungarian now seen in the anthracite coal regions of Pennsylvania. We can not insist, too frequently and too urgently, on the necessity of maintaining a high rate of wages in the United States.

Whether men or society, as a whole, have any real control over the distribution of the joint produce of land, capital, and labor, is the one valuable problem of political economy. In the United States, so far, the facts are that an equitable relation has been established and maintained between rent, interest, and wages. So far as this relation has been realized, it gives satisfaction to every right-minded man. This feeling of satisfaction is one of the principal conditions precedent to the highest prosperity of production, inasmuch as upon it depends the participation of all owners of funds, lands, and forces.

Every deviation from this relation or proportion is a misfortune, but never so great as when it takes place at the expense of the wages of labor. "It should never be forgotten," says Prof. Roscher, "that rent is an appropriation of the gifts of nature, and that interest is a further fruit obtained by frugality from older labor already remunerated. Besides, the rate of wages, when high generally, adds to the efficiency of labor, which can not be claimed for interest or rent. The best means to preserve the harmony of the three branches of income is, however, *universal activity.* . . . Rich or poor, strong or weak, the idler is the knave."

From whatever point of view we approach the industrial organism, it is seen that every new thing which is added to the national income comes from labor, which is repaid by wages. The best distribution of the national income will result from that condition of things which enables them to produce real goods in an increasing quantity and variety. Neither rent, interest, nor wages, as such, are any addition to a nation's income. The only true increment possible is *the new things, new commodities,* which her workmen can be induced to make and add to the inventory of her national possessions.

The high rate of wages, then, is the product of several forces. A principal one is the varied standard of living which has become a national habit. If the power to live up to that standard resides entirely in the returns which the laborer may get from going upon the land, it introduces a disquieting conception of society, and one which must be looked into in the further discussion. What we have been calling "wages" is, then, in essence, seen to be "rent." It accrues to the *land-owner* as such. The consequences and the responsibilities attaching thus to the owner of a natural instrument of production become more and more serious as we approach the time, now nearly reached in the United States, when all the land has been appropriated and has passed into private ownership. The option, then, of going upon the land will have ceased, and the laborer must be something of a capitalist, more or less, before he can buy lands, which now will stand him in considerable of an investment. It is manifest that the high returns to labor, as such, expended on the soil, depend on several conditions: First, that the laborer on the land is the owner of the land; second, that his wages, measured in the products which he raises, are subject to the law of diminishing returns; third, so long as he can not retard the operation of that law, his returns *in kind* will continue less—that is, the bushels of wheat or corn, the bales of cotton, or the pounds of tobacco per acre as a return for a day's work; but, fourth, the exchange value of his crops, as measured by the quantity of foreign products which he can buy with them, is subject to conditions imposed on him by facts in foreign markets over which he has no control, and which are incapable of prevision by any laws of the game of "catalactics." And the facts in the foreign market are of three descriptions—whether there is a demand for all his surplus, the market value of that surplus, and whether it offers him a full supply in return.

The proposition, then, that the high rate of wages has grown out of the refuge which the laborer has heretofore had in taking to the land, leads us to rather startling prospects. Adam Smith had said: "The cheapness and plenty of good land encourage improvement and enable the *proprietor* to pay these high wages. In those wages consist almost the whole price of the land, and, though they are high considered as the *wages of labor*, they are low considered as the price of *what is so very valuable.*"

As between us and the rest of the world, our advantages consist in something in the nature of *rent.* "Whole countries may, because of their great natural advantages, possess—*so far as the commerce of the entire world is concerned*—something analogous to rent: thus, for instance, North America, although there that world-rent finds expression in the natural height of the wages of labor and rate of interest." That is, the apparent wages of agricultural labor is made up partly of rent.

In connection with the accepted fact that most articles of consumption which the laboring-man makes by the aid of machinery (and Mill thinks machinery has not relieved the working-man of an hour's labor) have been cheapened some hundreds and some thousands of fold in the last century, and that the price of food has not decreased at all, the following observations by Prof. Cairnes do not bear an optimistic import. They are somewhat suggestive of "Progress and Poverty." They hint at some further analysis of the relations of men and things in the social state, some such analysis as Mr. Gladstone has been compelled to essay in the recent Irish land acts:

"*The productiveness of industry only affects the rate of wages and profits in so far as it results in a cheapening of the commodities which enter into the consumption of the laborer.*

"Not, indeed, that the introduction of improved processes into agriculture has been for naught; it has resulted in a large augmentation of the aggregate returns obtained from the soil, but without permanently lowering its price, and therefore without permanent advantage to either capitalist, or laborer, or to other consumers. The large addition to the wealth of the country has been neither to profits nor to wages, nor yet to the public at large, but to swell a fund ever growing, even while its proprietors sleep—*the rent-roll of the owners of the soil*. Accordingly, we find that, notwithstanding the best progress of agricultural industry effected within a century, there is scarcely an important agricultural product that is not as dear now as it was a hundred years ago; as dear, not merely in money-price, but in real cost. The aggregate return from the land has immensely increased, but the cost of the costliest portion of the product, which is that which determines the whole, remains pretty nearly as it was."

If the rate of wages in the United States was fixed by *the wages* which a man might earn as *a laborer* in agriculture, not as *a land-owner*, there might be logical force in the constant injunction by all free-traders to "take to the land." Professors Perry and Sumner iterate it, times without number : "*The comfort* the laborer could win on the land fixes a *minimum* below which wages can not fall. If they do temporarily fall below that minimum, the laborers take to the land, as they did in the hard times a few years ago. Since *the comfort* obtainable from an abundance of cheap and fertile land is high, the *minimum* of wages is high."

It is submitted, that this does not meet the exigencies of the argument. We are seeking the causes of the average rate of wages, which must be above the minimum. " The comfort " a laborer wins on the land is not a matter of which market values can be predicated, and a foreign commerce must be based on exportable values. If "hard times" drive the laborer to the land, it is a temporary expedient. There is no occasion to have any confusion of ideas on this subject. If high wages grow out of agricultural pursuits, the argument is, it is because agriculture gives high returns for labor, and we should buy abroad our other commodities with the products of this most efficient labor. The food and raw materials which can be raised by a great nation of fifty millions of people, great as they are in volume, are not great enough to override the law of supply and demand, and the consequences of a loss of purchasing power. The proprietors of this vast aggregate of industries are as amenable to market values as the single owner of the Apollinaris Spring, the group of individuals who own the oil-wells, and the corporations that control the anthracite coal fields of Pennsylvania. In each case they own efficient instruments of production, but their efficiency consists only in a precise adjustment of production to consumption. A monopoly of ownership in the wells, or a limitation in the area of coal, makes this possible. If the number of farms, or the agricultural area, were limited, the American farmers might use the leverage such a situation would give them; they might keep within the demands of the outside world, and assert their superiority against the world. But the fathers of the republic threw open a domain almost without limit, and invited mankind to come and subdivide it into farms almost beyond enumeration. It resulted in a great surplus of food, which the farmer did not need, and which he, at least, must part with to enjoy all his advantages, but which the outside world could not take off his hands. "Man does not live by bread alone." His wants of shelter, mental and moral culture, and his social ambitions, are just as urgent in demanding gratification. He will make as much effort, pay as much, for one as the other. Whoever renders the services which terminate in the satisfaction of these various desires will receive his wages. Whoever makes the things needed, whether food, clothing, colleges, churches, or theatres, will get his pay according to his work, provided the work is necessarily done in this political entity. Prof. Sumner, therefore, improves his own statement, which we have just quoted, when he adds: "*High wages*, therefore, simply mean that *the soil* of this continent *is rich, the climate is excellent and well varied, the rivers are large and convenient, the mountains are full of metal and coal,* the *people* are *industrious* and *energetic,* and are *eager to accumulate,* the *public order is fairly secure,* and *the general intelligence is good.* The *conditions of production* are therefore *good,* and we *produce a great deal. We accumulate capital far more rapidly than any other people in the world.*"

Undoubtedly. But all this production does not come from cultivating the land, nor are the values of products conferred by agriculture, nor on the basis of agricultural *labor*. We do not share the abundance of the owner of the soil.

To recall what Bastiat says: "*A man who has in his hands the tools necessary for labor, the materials to work upon, and the provisions for his subsistence during the operation, is in a situation to determine his own remuneration.*" This has been our situation.

This is the state of our industry under the facts as they are, and under a protective tariff. In his address before the Tariff Commission (and it is a very energetic address) Prof. Sumner undertakes to demonstrate that a protective tariff lowers wages. I give a paragraph of it, and the reply of Mr. George Basil Dixwell, and submit to the practical judgment and common sense of the reader which is the natural version of the facts. No *demonstration* is possible, because of the absence of any second term with which comparison can be made.

GENERAL THEORY OF WAGES.

Prof. Sumner: "Let us next look at the effect of protective taxes on the alternative which is open to the American laborer to go upon the land. The protective taxes enhance the cost of all articles of clothing, furniture, crockery, utensils, tools, and machinery. They also increase the cost of fuel and transportation. They, therefore, reduce the amount of all the commodities mentioned, which a farmer can get for a certain amount of farm products. They, therefore, lessen the profits of agriculture in all its forms, and lessen the attractiveness of the land. Whatever lessens the attractiveness of the land lowers the minimum gain of all manual laborers, increases the number of competitors in the labor market, and reduces the amount which the employer needs to bid in order to counteract the advantages of the land. Protective taxes, therefore, take away from the laborer the advantage which he has by nature in this country; that is to say, they take away from him part of his advantage in the labor market. *Consequently*, they lower wages."

Mr. Dixwell: "The truth is as follows: Protection prevents a vast number of people from flying to the land, and makes them consumers instead of producers of raw materials. It diminishes the aggregate of the farmer's products and increases the demand. It, therefore, increases the profits of agriculture in all its forms, and increases the attractiveness of the land. Whatever increases this, increases the minimum gain of all manual laborers, and increases the number of competitors for labor, and increases the amount which the employer needs to bid in order to counteract the advantages of the land. Protection, therefore, secures to the laborer the advantage which he has by nature in this country, and increases it by diversifying employments. Consequently, it raises wages above what they would be under foreign competition. At the same time, it hastens the moment when increasing skill may compensate for the higher moneyed cost of labor."

Prof. Sumner unquestionably undertook a very difficult piece of inductive reasoning. Even with the *assumptions* of an illimitable foreign market, and the ability of a limited number of farmers to maintain a monopoly of production, only a moderate success attends his effort. "Protective taxes" have not enhanced the cost of the farmer's living in any different proportion from what they have that of all the other co-workers, members of the same society. It is one of the attempts of which Mr. Mill has said, "no one could have looked closely into the sources of fallacious thinking without beeing deeply conscious that the coherence and neat concatenation of one's philosophic systems is more apt than we are commonly aware to pass with us as evidence of their truth."

One ought to be cautious in very positive assertion in a case where absolute knowledge is out of the question, but one may be allowed to suggest that the Professor's "*consequently*" bears a very suspicious resemblance to the "argal" of the clown in the grave-digging scene in "Hamlet."

CHAPTER XVI.

WHY INDUSTRIAL ENTITIES SHOULD CORRESPOND WITH POLITICAL ENTITIES.[1]

PROF. WALKER remarks: "It is, of course, possible that some new analysis of the conditions of production may yet disclose the law which thus makes trade within the lines of sovereignty beneficial, and trade across the boundaries of separate states deleterious to one or both parties; but, thus far, assertion, coupled with vituperation, has taken the place of the analysis required."

We venture to submit one form of analysis, and it does not seem necessary to accompany it with vituperation.

It is indispensable, if a given nation is to live on a given area, that opportunity should be afforded them to render mutual services to each other, or to somebody somewhere else. Otherwise there would be no nation on such a portion of the planet. If there were no such opportunity, the nation would be non-existent. There is no existing or historical nation in which the vast mass of services by which men satisfy each other's desires have not been rendered within the lines of the political entity. To that extent the political entity and the industrial entity, as mat-

---

[1] In plain English, this inquiry means, why should the people of a given nation (a political entity) endeavor so to arrange matters that the capital and labor of its people (the industrial entity) should in the main be employed in rendering services to one another, within the geographical limits which the given people inhabit?

ter of fact, do correspond. There are, however, in the ordinary case left outstanding, certain needs which are to be supplied by international exchanges. If the given nation was the product of purely economic forces—was composed of "economic men," and became one of a group of industrial countries constituting a larger industrial society, *formed by free trading*, the group, as a whole, would continue to subserve its purposes by free trade.

This is not an identical proposition, but it is so nearly such as to reduce the question at the head of this chapter to a mere abstract inquiry: for there is no such industrial group as yet on the earth.

"The most that can be said, at present, so far as an economy of mankind, or a world-economy is concerned, is that it may be shown that important preparations have been made for it. We are approaching more nearly to it, by the ways of the more and more cosmopolitan character of science, the increasing international co-operation of labor, the improvement in the means of transportation, growing emigration, the greater love of peace, and the greater toleration of nations, etc." (Roscher, "Political Economy," sec. 12.)[1]

The industrial group so formed would in no wise correspond with the actual political groups as we now see them on our political maps. The external relations of the nations not having grown out of economic movements, there is no *a priori* certainty, or even likelihood, that the "services" of the individuals in them would or could be so rendered to each other, as if the aggregate of the nations, constituting the industrial society, had been evolved

---

[1] "The hypothesis, in accordance with which this science should discard all consideration of the state, or should refuse to presuppose its formation, would lead us into an ideal region, difficult to define, probably entirely impossible, and inaccessible to experience." (Roscher, sec. 17.)

under the action of steady, uninterrupted economic forces alone. A nation is the resultant of many forces, of which the economic is not the strongest. The people of a nation, if the nation is to exist, may be compelled to exchange services with each other on the soil of the nation. Such we have seen to be the case in the United States, where in any event the people must produce at home about seven eighths of their consumption of commodities in which other nations have been unable to help them out. The other nations do not need our services to the extent of more than one fourth part in the exchanges which involve an expenditure, at home and abroad, of $2,800,000,000. If, now, free trade breaks up our power to render these services to each other here, we at once come to a reason why *our* industrial entity should correspond with *our* political entity. The United States, in truth, is the best, as it is the only, type of a nation which has been generated by the harmonious co-operation of moral, social, political, and economic forces. Here the political and industrial entity substantially do correspond. Certainly, the nearer the correspondence, the stronger the nation.

The people of a nation are bound together by sentiments different in degree, not in kind, from those which bind together the members of a household. In the nation, as in the family, there is a vast multitude of services exchanged between its members which are not economic. The economic and non-economic services are grounded in the same substratum of humanity, and the effort to separate them and render one here and the other with people in another family, simply means disintegration. It is the union and mutual exchange of these two kinds of services which result in our welfare and create the sentiment known as patriotism. It is a genuine emotion, and is a true economic force. It reconciles us, also, to accept the averaged results of our efficiency expended on our own physical conditions. It engenders that sense of community which operates with such force in family and nation. "Thanks to this feeling for the common weal, the eternal and destructive war—the *bellum omnium contra omnes*—which an unscrupulous self-interest would not fail to generate among men engaged in the isolated prosecution of their own economic interests, ceases in the higher, well-ordered organization of society. On it are based the various forms of economy in common—family economy, corporation or association economy, municipal economy, and national economy. And these forces of economy in common are so essentially the condition and complement of industrial economy that the latter without them could either not be maintained at all, or, at least, only in the very lowest stage of civilization." (Roscher, "Political Economy," section 12.) If that nation must be the richest in which each individual is most completely left to himself, savage nations would be the richest.

Every independent household management, then, contains the germ of all politico-economic activity.

Bear in mind we are dealing with a national family, thus predisposed by various considerations to satisfy their desires by exchanges of services, primarily, with each other when they can; with strangers, foreigners, when they must; and further willing and desirous that the family may be as large and prosperous as possible. A group of economic nations, *formed by free trade*, might do well to continue to exchange freely with each other. They have reached an adjustment, and no *redistribution* of its labor or its capital will take place. They go on and grow, or decline together. If the United States belonged from the start with such a group, we might go on and continue to enjoy the average prosperity or adversity of *the group*.

But we have reached a development very different from that which these conditions imply. It is confessed by all candid economists that a *redistribution of labor and capital* must take place if a country passes, for instance, from protection to free trade. "There are men, however, who live solely by their labor, and then if labor is suppressed they have no alternative but extinction. Like machines, then, free trade may oblige workmen to remove from one place to another. . . . When such displacement is accomplished, men will everywhere be better off by reason of the greater productiveness of their labor, but they will perhaps be differently distributed" (among the nations of the earth, he means), "and this can not be effected without suffering" (and capital must follow labor). "The practical conclusion is, that we should create no fresh legal monopolies by means of which *workmen are settled where nature can not yield them a large recompense*" (the italics are mine), "but that when such monopolies already exist, the tariffs which maintain them must be reformed with prudence and circumspection." (Dr. de Laveleye, "Elements of Political Economy," p. 238.)

"A similar injurious effect might result in this country from the sudden introduction of free trade, or even from a sudden great diminution of protection. . . . But it may be for a while harmful to the labor and capital which have been employed in the protected industries. This labor and capital may not be able to withdraw with ease from their existing occupation to the more productive industries which need no protection." (Prof. Taussig, De Laveleye, *supra*, p. 277.)

The point of the citations is to call attention to the *redistribution* which must take place in capital and labor. Of course, there can be no assurance that it might not be redistributed *entirely out of the United States*.

We take the case put by Prof. Sidgwick in his "Political Economy," at page 494:

"Suppose a country (A) so thickly populated that additional agricultural produce could not be obtained from the soil except at a rapidly increasing expense, and suppose that one third of its actual produce of this kind—say, for brevity, corn—is now consumed by the persons engaged in its chief branches of manufacture. Suppose that the country, having been strictly protected, adopts free trade, and that consequently the manufactures in question are obtained at half the price from another country (B) in exchange for corn. And for simplicity let us assume that the result of the fall in price is that the *same total price* is paid for the manufactures annually consumed." (Observe that Mr. Sidgwick puts his supposition in terms which could never be so favorably realized in this country.) "What, then, are the manufacturing laborers, thrown out of work by the change, to do? The course most obviously suggested by the circumstances is that they should emigrate and supply the labor required in the extended manufactures of B, or in the newly developed trade between A and B. If they do not do this, there seems to be *no general ground for assuming* that they will be *able to find employment* in A as remunerative as that withdrawn from them. ... And if they could not be profitably employed in agriculture, it is theoretically possible that they could not be employed at all, so that the natural result of free trade may be that A will only support a *smaller though wealthier population*—the economic gain resulting from it to the community, as a whole, being a gain which it would require *violent governmental interference to distribute*, so as to retain the laborers thrown out of work."[1]

---

[1] If we accept the dolorous pictures of Hon. Frank Hurd, David A. Wells, and others, they could not profitably be employed in *our* agriculture, for

A redistribution would then take place between the United States and the other political entities composing the international group of free-trading communities—that is, the United States would witness the migration of many laborers and the transfer of much capital to other fields of employment. That would result, obviously, in a less gross annual product of this nation's industry. If free trade, under the laws of economy, would depopulate the country, and decapitalize it, I suppose it is one of the functions of American statesmen to erect barriers to that sort of exodus. Whether those who remained would be better off is not the question. The welfare and happiness of those driven away are equally objects of concern with those whom fortune or accident may place it in their power to remain.

If, we repeat, the nations of the earth, and their political and industrial relations, had been evolved from a common economic center, and had widened out on economic motives alone, no *economic* reason could be given, of course, why the industrial entity should correspond to the political entity, for the whole would then constitute one industrial group. Having been thus generated, the whole, in fact, is one industrial entity, and political lines are of no moment. In the group thus generated, the introduction of *protection* would produce a redistribution and probably a very serious disturbance of labor and capital. Concerning an aggregate of trading nations thus formed, the question is about as pertinent as if we were to ask why a curve equally distant at all its points from the center should correspond to a circle. It would, for that is the law of its

---

food, they say, is already "rotting on the ground"; and if we accept the pictures English statesmen, like Lord Salisbury and the Earl Dunraven, give us, free trade in England has distributed the labor and capital employed on iron ship-plates from England to Belgium, and has left the laborers in its silk manufactures stranded in idleness. They are too poor to emigrate.

case. But from the equation of a circle you can not generate an ellipse. Whether the curve might not under other conditions have been better as an ellipse would be an inquiry more germain, in the facts of the actual world. The question, then, we are discussing assumes the existence of certain facts to which it is applicable. And the statesmen of a country (whatever the economists may propose) do not deliberately incline to destroy the political entity in their charge, that, with its fragments, they may piece out some new industrial whole. It is certainly conceivable that the economic services which Germans on German soil, or Frenchmen on French soil, could render to citizens of other nations, might, so to speak, give out, and they yet retain the capacity to serve each other. It is conceivable that there might be nothing which they could do so much better than the workmen of other nations, that with the surplus they could buy what they wanted of them—nor is it inconceivable that the surplus of the other nations should happen to be in the very commodities which the Germans and Frenchmen could make for themselves. The motive to foreign trade ceases. In that case German and French statesmen provide for keeping their workmen employed on services to be exchanged at home. Were it otherwise, the German and French laborers, acting on economic considerations alone, might be driven from their native land. There might be nothing else for them to do. But they are held (the great majority are) to the fatherland and to *la belle* France by social and political motives, overruling the economic motives. The one tends to take them out of the country, the other tends to keep them in. And so Bismarck and Thiers, in patriotic co-operation with their people, provide by defensive duties that all their population may mutually serve each other on their native soil. They do not presume to "enlighten their desire for profit "—that takes care of itself. The problem is simply to provide the opportunity of economic labor, for a population born or thrown together on a given geographical area, on which area there are overruling political motives for maintaining a political entity. The industrial entity must then be made to conform to the political entity, or both perish. Drop all considerations of patriotism, social ties, kindred, politics, and submit to the economic forces alone, and I grant there would be no economic reason for any correspondence of the industrial and political entities, in the case of these two nations. But, then, there might be no economic reason for the existence of Germany or France. The people and statesmen alike of these nations would hardly consent to follow this abstraction, pretty as it is, to the point of their self-annihilation. We have at last, come to one economic problem which can not " be solved independently" of sociological considerations.

The protective tax may operate to shield the low-priced labor (the "weak") against the high-priced labor (the "strong"), or to defend the high-priced labor against the low-priced labor, the "strong" against the "weak." It has exactly the advantage which Prof. Sumner states, in order to ridicule it, that "it goes as well one end foremost as the other." Why? Because it is all the while nothing but a proposal to enable the inhabitants of a given political entity to wage their war for subsistence against nature, on their own soil, on which, we assume, they do not attempt anything which is forbidden by the nature of things —the nature of their things. Common products may be obtained equally well in any properly developed country. In this connection, the words "strong" and "weak" have no relevancy. If they had, all economic men ought to, and would, live in the *strong* nation. But, as there are valid reasons why all men do not and can not, the inhabitants of *weak* nations must continue to provide material services which they may render each other—the fruitful employment of the forms of labor which mutually replace each other.

It is not denied that great migrations are constantly taking place on the face of the earth. The expulsion of the Huguenots from France, in consequence of the revocation of the Edict of Nantes, transferred bodily to Holland and England certain great industries, much to the loss of France. This was expulsion by force, but free trade might do the same.

These are, it seems to me, valid reasons why statesmen do not submit to the *redistribution* of *capital* and *labor* which free trade must bring about between the group of freely trading nations. It is the old judgment of Napoleon, that the economists would grind the empire to powder, even though it was made of adamant. These considerations, it seems to me, show the expediency, and indeed "the necessity of drawing the lines of industrial circumvallation along the boundaries of empire."

But now we take the reverse problem. Take the United States, for example. "Here," says the free-trader, "are thirty-eight States, trading among themselves with the utmost activity, the exchange of commodities and services being free as the movements of the air, and in this freedom all good citizens rejoice. But this condition of things is made, by the doctrine under examination, to be dependent entirely upon the political relations of these States. Were they under *different governments*, the exchange of commodities and services which now promotes the *general wealth* and the *general welfare* would be fraught with mischief and possible ruin."

The United States are an industrial entity, as they are a political entity. The industrial entity took the form it did for the reason, and the only reason, that the exchanges of commodities and services were as "free as the movements of the air." The exchanges were thus free because it was a political entity. Living under the same laws, customs, language, traditions, religion, and ideals, the competition of different capitals was absolutely effective, and the competition of labor effective over large areas. This resulted, in the industrial entity submitted to these conditions, in as exact a correspondence of remuneration, in all employments, with the sacrifice undergone, as is possible under existing human progress. The conditions resulted from the uniformity compelled by the political entity.[1] We are what we are because, while under the same moral, social, and political forces, we developed also under the free play, between the States, of economic forces, pulling with them. We pooled our issues; we submitted to that community of results which community of interest dictated. It is not supposed that an American economist or an American statesman cares in which State, or in what part of the political unit, the greatest prosperity is achieved—on what points its capital and labor are concentrated. The migration of the instruments of production takes the place of a trade in products. That is, capital and labor are perfectly mobile within the limits of the nation. If a man doesn't like things in one State, he goes to another, without leaving his political habitat. An American will neither go to Mexico nor send his money to Peru, as he would migrate to Colo-

---

[1] "One of the principal conditions determining the relative profitableness of particular occupations and the terms on which their products are exchanged consists in the degree of facility which happens to exist for moving capital and labor from one to the other. Now, this facility is very different in the case of occupations carried on within the limits of a single country and those carried on in different countries; and in *this difference* is to be found the chief fact discriminating *the phenomena of international from those of domestic trade.*"—PROF. CAIRNES, "Political Economy," p. 302.

rado or make his investments in California. But, subject Mexico and Peru to American civilization, laws, customs, and society, incorporate them in our political entity, and the economic and social objections to the transfer would begin to disappear.[1] The greatest total annual product of the nation's industry is the object of concern. Nobody, under these circumstances, cares whether the yard of calico is made in Lowell or Raleigh; whether the ton of iron is made in Johnstown or Birmingham; whether the locomotive is made in Paterson or Atlanta. The outcome is the common possession, and contributes to the common glory and happiness of one people—one political entity. We get the best effects, because the economic, social, and political forces are all in operation at once, supplementing each other. Those who take the atomistic view of our structure do not thus think. The gentleman before referred to, as representing the Iowa State Free-Trade League, says: "It does not matter to us whether our tribute goes to Pennsylvania or to Europe. So far as we" (Iowa free-traders) "are concerned, I will say it is better to have manufactures at home" (in Iowa), "but it does not concern us a particle to have them in Pennsylvania or Massachusetts." A little matter like that never concerns an American free-trader any more than it does a member of the Cobden Club. This, for illustration only, but it is not a true view of an *organism*. There is a sense in which the Iowa farmer need not care, *as a farmer*, whether his wheat is consumed in New York or Liverpool. The market which New York affords is, *pro tanto*, as valuable as that of Liverpool. If market prices are fixed at Liverpool, it is because free trade has brought the whole earth into competition with him. If the price in Liverpool is less than the price in New

---

[1] The last census shows that there are seven millions of our inhabitants living in States other than those of their birth.

York, *plus* the cost of carriage (which it sometimes is), the "Pennsylvania" or "Massachusetts" market may be indispensable to him, *as a farmer*. But this is collateral.

If we treat the States of the Union as nations constituting a larger *national* entity, we may freely grant that the permanent stoppage of a channel of trade which free competition would open could not, in the words of Prof. Sidgwick, "tend to increase the wealth of *the industrial society formed by the aggregate of nations* whose trade is thus restricted—supposing such nations to be composed of economic men."

But while political motives *and* social motives have constrained the States to form the political aggregate, it by no means as yet appears that any given member of the aggregate *may* not have sacrificed mere economic progress in joining the Union. The group, *as a whole*, may be better off, but one or more members of it *may* be the worse off by reason of the unrestricted trade. That is, upon the geographical area which some one State occupies, there might, to-day, have been more men and money, more population and wealth, if it had remained a distinct political and industrial entity; and have enlarged its domestic exchanges by restrictions upon its foreign exchanges. For example, Michigan, by means of protection, *might have* drawn to itself manufactures of iron, cotton and woolen goods which now swell the inventory of wealth in Pennsylvania and Massachusetts.

It might not be difficult to prove that "the South," as a geographical section, with her special cotton product, has been a loser by virtue of her membership in this group of free-trading States. Her failure early in the century to turn her labor upon the manufacture of her own cotton into the fabrics which her laborers consumed, was an economic blunder. For such industries, aside from slavery, the only disadvantage the South labored under was that the North began hers sooner. As an independent entity, and with restrictions, she, *as a section, might* have been wealthier than she is. If, now, the South persists in the line of development upon which she has started, she will cause a *redistribution* of the labor and capital of *the nation,* which will enrich her as a *section.* The citizen of the denuded section may go with the new tide if he choose. He may remain and continue as a patriot to rejoice in the aggregate prosperity of the country.[1]

We may find other illustrations of the reasons why free trading between industrial entities may profitably stop

---

[1] The following curious dialogue took place before the Tariff Commission, Prof. Sumner being on the "witness"-stand ("Report," vol. ii, p. 2331):

"Commissioner Kenner: 'That is the doctrine' (referring to Prof. Sumner's previous free-trade discourse) 'that has been advocated in the South for the last fifty or sixty years.'

"The witness: 'And I hope they will stick to it.'

"Commissioner Kenner: 'They will not stick to it; they have seen the folly of it.'

"The witness: 'They are going to begin to manufacture there, to their very great loss.'

"Commissioner Oliver: 'To their loss or New England's loss?'

"The witness: 'New England can stand it. I do not think it would be any loss to the country if there was no New England.'

"Commissioner Kenner: 'I agree with you in that last remark, that it would be no loss to the country.'

"The witness: 'And it would be no harm to the country if there was no Louisiana.'

"Commissioner Kenner: 'Yes, there would be. I wish you would prove that proposition. We tried to leave the country and you would not let us, and yet you say it would be no loss. That is a *non sequitur* which I do not understand.'

"The witness: 'We should all live here and be happy, and get our living, even if there wasn't any New England, any Louisiana, or any Pennsylvania, I suppose.'"

The Professor is evidently willing to take his chances against all catastrophes—as a "clanless, masterless man."

at the lines of a political entity, and open and close with the shifting lines of nationality.

Napoleon found France, Italy, Belgium, and Austria independent kingdoms, with custom-houses on their outposts. When they became component parts of his empire, he abolished these obstacles to internal commerce and introduced free trade throughout its limits. Now, the inquiry of the free-trader is, how can the advantage, the gain of exchanges, depend upon the accident whether the parties to it are or are not citizens of the same political entity? The answer to the question is tolerably obvious. On the supposition that France, Italy, Belgium, and Austria could become a homogeneous people, with common laws, language, institutions, and aspirations, the only true marks of nationality (and which, of course, were not realized, but which Napoleon affected to assume would be realized, in order to give his conquest the appearance of rational statesmanship), there would then have been the economic conditions under which competition becomes effective, and labor and capital perfectly mobile. In all the empire the laborer moves freely to his work, and his migration takes the place of an exchange of products. The parties to the exchange may move out of the lines of the old political entity. By the assumption, both labor and capital would be transferred to the localities and the industries within the empire—the new industrial entity—which would have rendered them most efficient. There would, in due time, have been a *redistribution* of the population and a reorganization of industry. Taking the empire *as a whole*, there would have been the greatest annual product of the industry of its people. Without undertaking to forecast the changes in detail, it is evident that one or more of these states would have suffered a drainage of population and a diminution of capital which, *as a state*, might have crippled it and reduced its relative importance, but which, as a component part of the empire, was of no sort of consequence. These changes, when become permanent, would have given great and powerful strength to the empire. If, now, it is again broken up into separate kingdoms, it will be seen that this *régime* of free trade within the limits of the empire has degraded or ruined some of them. In rearranging, for the best advantages, the industrial forces of the empire on new lines, some of the areas of territory which constituted the original states would have been denuded of portions of their money and men, drawn off into new fields. As parts of the empire, such inhabitants as remained in these areas of reduced production could recoup themselves by sentiments of pride and patriotism which terminated in the national prosperity. If they expected to reap economic results, they would have to move into some other part of the empire. When the geographical subdivision again became a separate political entity, and the old political lines were restored, it might simply find itself hopelessly poor, and, to recover its *status quo*, be compelled to recall its men and money by imposing the old duties and setting up the old line of custom-houses. All which shows that free trade may be good policy between the members of certain kinds of industrial groups, and bad policy between other kinds. The *group* may *gain*, but *a specific member* may *lose*. The very fact that the nations of the earth are of all sizes, shapes, physical resources, and ethnical characteristics, shows that they were not formed by economical or industrial but by political and social motives. Political motives dam up productive forces in certain pools; free trade, operating on industrial motives, draws them down to a certain water-level. It is manifest that the drainage may uncover one or more of them. The political motive fills them with men—the industrial motive may empty them. Non-competing nations will gain, because they need not occupy the same level; competing nations may be drained to the bottom and emptied of productive agencies—labor and capital, men and money.

We can see, at least, the final conditions under which the industrial entity need not correspond with the political entity—the terms on which alone universal free trade is possible. It will not come, and it can not come, until the final *status* of the industry of each political entity has been fixed, when all "natural" advantages have been explored, when "acquired" advantages have asserted their mastery in the great and deadly competition of races and ideals, and when men have discarded all patriotic pride in the nation, and sunk their allegiance to their proper political entity into the vague worship of some abstract industrial entity. When their relative "advantages" have come to be recognized by the nations, and each accepts its place in the hierarchy of industry, then, and only then, can free trade be true in theory as it will be in practice. Then the economic man will correspond with the historical and moral man. Nationality will give place to cosmopolitanism, labor and capital will have undergone their final redistribution over the surface of the globe. Then the "seller, as such," may shoulder his peddler's pack and seek the "buyer as such," at the farthest end of the earth, and make that "swap" which has been the "reason of his being"; and no man shall say, "Tariff!"

In the mean time the American statesman will continue to busy himself with the original question, *How can the people of his country create the greatest annual product of their combined industry*, and prevent that product from being *distributed out* of the hands of its true owners in this political entity—the workmen of THE REPUBLIC?

CHAPTER XVII.

A FALLACY WHICH FREE-TRADERS PUT IN THE MOUTHS OF PROTECTIONISTS—CREATING INDUSTRY.

IT remains to dispose of one other fallacy which free-traders are apt to indulge in; or, rather, to unload the fallacious assumptions which free-traders put into the mouth of the protectionist. The purpose to confuse the argument is manifest from the very way in which they set about to state their questions.

"How can anybody then intelligently suppose that *a body of taxes*, which somebody must pay, can be so cunningly adjusted as to become a *positively productive agent*, a spur to the progress of society? Taxes of some kind are, indeed, necessary, but how they can be made a blessing to the payers and enrich the whole society, *they* must explain who suppose that possible, provided they *can* explain it." (Perry, "Political Economy," p. 480.)[1]

---

[1] Prof. Robert Ellis Thompson, in his "Political Economy," pp. 243–428, had maintained that "protection to industry gives the farmer an abundant and steady market for his breadstuffs, and creates a market for crops more remunerative than grain." Perry, in his work at page 504, replies; the underscored passages in the reply, on careful study, will be found, I submit, to render the answer a palpable failure: "A *bigger home market* consists in *more domestic buyers* than before, all ready with *acceptable pay* in their hands. If protection can *enlarge the home market*, it must be by either *increasing the number of births* or *diminishing the number of deaths* in a given time in a given country.(!) Precisely how a *big bundle of taxes*, which the whole population must pay in one form or another, may be made to *stimulate births* or *prolong lives*, no reasonable man can see, though a protectionist may see it. If he can see

"It is evident that a protective tariff can not render any *foreign capital* or *labor* available to help the nation which lays the tariff. If a nation lays import duties for revenue, some part of them may fall on the foreigner; but if it lays such duties for protection, it keeps foreign goods out. If, then, the foreigner *stays at home*, and is forced to keep his goods at home, the protecting country can not make use of him or his goods in any way whatever to suit its ends or avert its misfortunes. Whatever effect the protective taxes exert, must be exerted in the protecting country, on its own labor and capital. Any favor or encouragement which the protective system exerts on one group of its population must be won by an equivalent oppression exerted on some other group. To suppose the contrary, is to deny the most obvious application of the conservation of energy to economic forces. If the legislature did not *simply transfer* capital, it would have to *make capital out of nothing*. We can not collect taxes and redistribute them without loss, much less can we produce forced monopolies and distorted industrial relations without loss." (Prof. Sumner, "Princeton Review.") Whether the words "forced monopolies" and "distorted industrial relations" are truly descriptive of our industrial organization is exactly the question at issue.

---

it and show it, his task is then but half done, for he must see and show how these same men's *taxes* may multiply *return services* in the hands of this increased population. If he try to get out of this snug place by claiming that the better 'home market' is made by new immigrants with *values* in their hands, he can not escape by this route, because he must first see and show what there is in *big taxes* to *invite immigrants* at all; and besides, he is scared even by the handiwork of 'pauper labor,' and, of course, he is not *prepared to welcome* the 'pauper laborers themselves!'"

The political policies of the country invited immigrants which even "big taxes" did not repel. The economic policy which increased the number of those, whether natives or immigrants, who are not engaged in farming, but must live on its products and pay for them, did "multiply" the "return services" and enlarged *the farmer's* "home market."

"There is not, and there never can be, any positive virtue in *restraint*," is the language of Prof. Walker. "Its only office for good is to prevent waste, and save the misdirection of energy. There can be no life in it, and no force can come out of it. That which is called 'protection' operates only by restraint; it has, and can have, neither *creative power* nor healing efficacy. All the energy that is to produce wealth, *exists before it* and *without respect to it*, and, just to the extent to which protection operates at all, it operates by impairing that energy, and reducing the sum of wealth that *might* be produced if protection did not exist."

Now it is manifest that the foregoing propositions of Profs. Perry, Sumner, and Walker are based on the assumption that, without protection, all the productive energies of a given people are already devoted to the most productive employments, that they are all fully employed, and that there is "nothing else" to which they might be directed with equal efficiency, and without "waste" and "loss."

It would be difficult in the same number of words to state more misconceptions of the attitude of protectionists; more perversions of the application of words to things; a more glaring example of the *ignoratio elenchi*, as the logicians call it. It is an attempt to transfer to the region of mental dynamics the notion of "the conservation and correlation of forces," as understood in respect to the material world. The man who applies a match to a powder-magazine *creates* nothing. But the motive which induces him to apply the match is *the occasion* of an explosion, and operates to produce rather striking results.

The protectionist proposes to create nothing. He can create neither matter nor material forces. The energy he proposes to set free is already in the men and things he deals with. He finds abundant stores of it in the human agencies and the matter about him. When the engineer subjects coal to the process of combustion, under the boiler of an engine, he sets in motion mighty machinery. He creates nothing. He only correlates results—he sends them through a structural organization. He sets free the forces in the coal, and he loosens the spring under which his own energies had been coiled. The protective statute furnishes the motive for his exploding the powder-magazine. New productive agencies are released; the protective statute has removed the restriction which had rendered both productive tools, the man and machine, inert and useless. The American man and the American coal were as if they were non-existent, so long as we substituted the foreign man and the foreign coal for him and it. It may be that we could produce, with their joint effort, "something else," and use both the domestic and foreign combination, but that is a distinct issue. If the two schemes will not work together —and, as we have seen, we must use the one *or* the other— which scheme results in the greatest annual product of the nation's industry? Which method of procedure results in the satisfaction of the greatest number of the desires of the people of the country? These questions raise the true issue.

Prof. Sumner takes some pains to disprove the idea that a new country might need "a lift" (as he calls it) to move it on in the way of growth. John Rae, in his "Political Economy" (page 56 *et seq.*), had very dispassionately proved this. And this is the case to which Mr. Mill had made decided concessions. It seems a work of supererogation to adduce "authority" to establish a proposition which lies so open to observation and common sense.

Prof. Roscher, not an unqualified protectionist ("Political Economy," Appendix III, sec. 1), agrees: "Directly, therefore, these hindrances to importation produce no increase, but only a change in the direction of the national forces of capital and labor" (assuming that every man capable of working always busies himself, producing for a remunerative market), "an increase only in case that *foreign producers are thereby caused to transfer their productive forces within our limits;* which may certainly be considered the greatest triumph of the protective system."

And then he adds (sec. 4), as to the educational and economic effects of the industrial protective system:

"The sacrifices which the protective system directly imposes on the national wealth consist in products, fewer of which, with an equal straining of the productive forces of the country, are produced and enjoyed than free trade would procure" (temporarily). "But it is possible by its means to *build up new productive forces*, to *awaken slumbering ones from their sleep*, which, in the long run, may be of much greater value than those sacrifices. Who would say that the cheapest education was the most advantageous? Only by the development of industry does a nation's economy become mature. The merely agricultural state can attain neither to *the same population*, nor the *same energy of capital*, to say nothing of the skillfulness of labor, as the mixed agricultural state, nor can it employ its *natural forces* so completely to advantage. How many beds of coal, waterfalls, hours of leisure, and how much aptitude for the arts of industry can be turned to scarcely any account in a merely agricultural state? If, therefore, the protective system could materially promote a national industry, or *if it made such industry possible for the first time*, the sacrifice connected therewith in the beginning should be considered like the sacrifice of seed made by the sower. But this can be justified only on the three following conditions: *That the seed is capable of germinating;* that *the soil be fertile* and properly cultivated, and that *the season is favorable.*" All which conditions are fairly met in the American industrial protective system.

The protective statute renders possible the formation of the structural organization, peculiar to a given country, through which the productive forces take effect. Prof. Walker, in the citation made, intimated that "protection reduced the sum of wealth that *might* be produced if protection did not exist." He felt constrained to add:

"I say that *might* be produced, not that *would be* produced. The latter point may fairly be disputed between the free-trader—who should rather be called the free-producer—and the advocate of the system of restricted production. The channel of the river adds nothing to the force with which the water within its banks tends to its level. On the contrary, that force is reduced by the friction between the flowing water and the sides of the channel. Yet it is the water confined in rivers, and not water spreading widely over the fields, which yields power to manufacturing industry. The force of the steam at the piston-head is less than the force of the steam in the boiler, less by all that is necessary to conduct it thither from the boiler; yet it is the force of the steam at the piston-head, and not where it is generated, which moves the engine."[1]

---

[1] How production (*not* creation) ensues upon bringing the right men into contact with right conditions is shown by Prof. Senior ("Political Economy," p. 134). Free trade for Ireland separated the productive forces in Ireland.

"The climate, the soil, and the situation of Ireland have been described as superior, and certainly are not inferior, to our own. Her poverty has been attributed to the want of material capital, but were Ireland now to exchange her native population for seven millions of our English north-country men, they would quickly *create* the capital that is wanted. And were England, north of Trent, to be peopled exclusively by a million of families from the west of Ireland, Lancashire and Yorkshire would still more rapidly resemble Connaught. Knowledge has been called power—it is far more certainly

But we have a most notable example of the *productive* effects of *restrictions*. The restrictive statute in this case became the banks which confined the water in its channel—it became the means of conveying the force of the steam at the boilers to the piston-head. This is the English Navigation Act. Enacted in the time of Cromwell, re-enacted and extended three times in the reign of Charles II, it remained on the statute-book for two hundred years, and was only repealed after it had wrought its full effects as the scaffolding for English commercial and marine supremacy. Adam Smith, "the free-trader," the apostle of "natural liberty," called it "that great *prohibitive* and *protective law, intended* to advance the merchant marine, the wisest of all English commercial regulations."

John Adams says of it ("Life and Works," vol. x, p. 330): "Earth, air, sea, all colonies and all weaker nations were to be made subservient to the growth of the British navy and marine, which in turn were to be the instruments for the enlargement of British wealth, British commerce, British power, and British domination, as much so as all nations and things were, in times past, to be sacrificed to the grandeur of Rome."

It resulted, as intended, in making Englishmen the sole manufacturers, the sole carriers, and the sole middle-men for all the colonies, and for most of the nations of the earth, until her supremacy was threatened by the great rival built up out of her own colonies here under the American protective system. The preamble to the act was in these words:

---

wealth. Asia Minor, Syria, Egypt, and the northern coast of Africa were once among the richest, and are now among the most miserable, countries in the world, simply because they have fallen into the hands of a people without a sufficiency of the *immaterial sources* of wealth to *keep up the material ones*."

"In regard his Majesty's plantation beyond seas are inhabited and peopled by his subjects of this, his kingdom of England, for the maintaining a greater correspondence and kindness between them, and *keeping them in a firmer dependence upon it,* and *rendering them* yet *more beneficial* and advantageous to *it,* in *further employment* and *increase of English shipping and seamen,* vent of *English woolens* and *other manufactures and commodities,* rendering the navigation to and from the same more safe and cheap, and making *this kingdom a staple,* not only of the commodities of these plantations, but also of the commodities of other countries and places for the supplying of them."

The following striking summary of its results is given by Mr. Eben Greenough Scott ("The Development of Constitutional Liberty in the English Colonies of America," p. 188):

"At last, when England was rent by cruel strife, and in a predicament so sorry as to render her an object of insult to the domineering Dutch, just at the time when it could be least expected of her to rise and resent affront, and when, perhaps, she herself did not seriously contemplate such an act, just at that time she took the step which henceforth wrought such a wonderful change in the destiny of herself and of her rival. In a few years the carrying-trade of Holland declined, her magnificent fleet was brought to its destruction, the commerce of the world was transferred from the Dutch to the English shipping, the supremacy of the ocean was shifted from the decks of Van Tromp to those of Blake, and England was *started* upon a career of prosperity which at last made her mistress of the seas. All this was accomplished by an act of Parliament in 1651, in the time of Cromwell. It provided simply that thenceforward no goods—the product of Asia, Africa, or America—should be imported into England or exported out of it but in vessels belonging to the people of England, and that no goods, the produce or manufacture of any part of Europe, should be imported unless in English ships, or the ships of the country where such goods were produced or manufactured; and that of these English ships the master, and three fourths of the marines, should be English. . . . Its results far transcended the wildest dreams of Lombard and Venetian avarice, or the grandest schemes of Spanish and Portuguese conquest. It not only secured to the people who enacted it the greatest share of the world's carrying-trade—Trade knew its master, and followed at once with becoming servility."

At this time the aristocracy in England held monopolies in the trade in hides, wool, salt, gold thread, flax, hemp, and many other commodities. All the guilds were monopolists.

There was one vast scheme of monopolies, the results of royal grants for the purposes of royal revenue. There was no competition in the internal trade and manufactures of the country. Under the Navigation Act these monopolies passed from individuals to the people at large. Henceforth the colonies were regarded mainly as feeders to England's carrying-trade, or consumers of her manufactures, or factories for the distribution of its capital, and, in a word, as mere commercial appendages of a great commercial power.

Adam Smith summarized results in these words: "A great empire" (the American colonies) "has been established for the sole purpose of raising up a nation of consumers, who should be obliged to buy from the shops of our different producers all the goods with which they could supply them." The idea of "a lift" is not so grotesque after all. The Navigation Act lay exactly athwart the path which the *natural liberty* of the individual dictated that he had a right to enjoy, both in offering his labor and commodities in any market in the world he might choose.

The view we have been combating is the modern form of the old argument of Adam Smith and John Stuart Mill—the only solid argument either ever offered against governmental interference in a nation's industries. It is in substance this. Adam Smith says:

"If a foreign country can supply us with an article cheaper than we can make it ourselves, we had better buy it with some part of the product of our own industry, employed in a way in which we have some advantage." (We have seen that we can not buy our supply of the large number of articles we need.) "The general industry of the country, being always in proportion to the capital which employs it, will not thereby be diminished, no more than that of the above-mentioned artificers, but only left *to find out the way* in which it can be employed to the greatest advantage. In every period, its revenue *might have been* the greatest which its *capital could* afford."

Here we are back to the wages-fund theory, which is no longer considered tenable. Doubtless, "to find out the way" is the burden of the problem we are trying to solve. The argument proceeds on the assumption that labor is all the while working as hard as it can on the most profitable employment, and that a definite limited fund of capital only is at its disposal. This is more exactly expressed by Mr. Mill:

"Yet in disregard of a fact so evident" (that a part only of the capital of a country is allotted to the support of productive labor, and there will not and can not be more of that labor than the portion so allotted will feed and provide with the materials to work on), "it long continued to be believed that laws and government, without *creating capital,* could *create industry,* not by making the people more laborious or increasing the efficiency of their labor—these are objects to which the government can in some degree contribute—but when the people already worked *as hard and skillfully as they could be made to,* it was still thought that the government, without providing additional funds could create additional employment."

It is incredible that any sane economist ever thought that a man " could work harder or more skillfully than he could," capital or no capital. A protectionist has no need of an identical proposition like that.

The syllogism of Adam Smith and Mr. Mill, when put in form, is this:

Major Premise.—Industry can be increased only by the increase of capital.

Minor Premise.—Laws and government can not increase capital.

Conclusion.—Therefore, laws and government can not increase industry.

As Judge Phillips says in his " Proposition concerning Protection and Free Trade ": " This is very transparent logic; the sophism is glaring. The major is what old Robert Burton would designate 'a stupend fallacy.'"

Mr. George Basil Dixwell, in his " Premises of Free Trade examined," has dragged the fallacy into the open day, and the series of propositions is seen to turn on a question of fact, and not on a process of deductive reasoning.

" But to make the latter proposition flow from the first, a vast gap has to be filled. It requires to be proved that, in a normal condition of things, there is no unemployed capital, and no funds which, although intended for unproductive consumption, are capable of being instantly turned to the support of production the moment that a new industry introduced by a protective law presents a profitable field of employment. This is a question of fact, and the moment we inquire into the facts we find that the unemployed capital in the United States is vast, probably much exceeding $1,000,000,000, and that the ability to re-enforce this out of the funds intended for unproductive consumption within the year is also most probably a good deal over $700,000,000. Before these facts the whole argument falls to pieces."

It ought not to be necessary to cite "authority" for an obvious fact, but we venture a citation from a modern English economist: "Even on extraordinary occasions, when unlooked-for events in the political or commercial world disturb ordinary calculations and give enormous advantage to particular industries—such occasions, for example, as occurred in the early years of railway enterprise, or again in the linen trades on the breaking out of the American War—even on such occasions the equilibrium of remuneration and cost can always be restored, not, indeed, in a moment, but after no long delay, through the action of labor and capital *still uncommitted to actual industrial employment, and without any sensible encroachment on the stock already actively employed. The existence of a large amount of capital* in commercial countries in disposable form, or, to speak less equivocally, in the form of money or other purchasing power capable of being turned to any purpose required, *is a patent and undeniable fact.* Nor is it less certain that this capital is constantly seeking the best investments, and rapidly moves toward any branch of industry that happens at the moment to offer special attentions." (Cairnes, "Some Leading Principles," etc., p. 63.)

No. The protective statute does not *create* energy. It releases the productive forces which await the joint action of the human agent and the material instrument. This action the protective statute induces. It never was a question of the "conservation and correlation of forces," but a simple question of commercial fact.

"Do the restraints imposed by law have the effect to direct the productive force generated by human wants, setting in motion human labor, to act upon the natural agents of production with a better actual result than under the rule of freedom? "If the protectionist can show this," says Prof. Walker, "*he will make his case.*"

We feel entirely confident that this question has been affirmatively answered in the discussion of facts in foregoing chapters.

CHAPTER XVIII.

INDUSTRIAL RESULTS ACHIEVED—SOME PRACTICAL MAXIMS OF TARIFF REFORM.

WE have endeavored to conduct this inquiry on the sole consideration of economic results—that is, results terminating in the greatest product of industry, realized in wages, profits, and rents, and ultimately in consumable commodities and desirable services. The only use made of *social* considerations has been to account for the common aims which inspire us; of *political* considerations, has been that they furnish the common legal conditions under which we work; of *moral* considerations, as indicating the nature and amount of the things our inherited traits lead us to desire. These, together, account for the aggregation on our soil of the people who, among themselves, own all the instruments of production—land, labor, and capital. The motive-power of it all has been the satisfaction of desires.

The answer to our inquiry required neither learning nor philosophy. The only question was, which was the best way for these men to act under certain motives? The reply was simply an account of what they did, and the reasons why they acted as they did. If resort has been made to the technical language of the political economist, it has been because the common unfamiliarity with it has engendered the idea that there was some occult explanation not accessible to mere business-men. We need take no account of any *theory*, which, we may agree, is only " a rational description of a group of co-ordinated facts in their sequence and relations."

What were our facts? According to Franklin and Hamilton, the opinion of the whole people of Pennsylvania, as expressed in their act of September 20, 1785, and of the people of all the colonies—according to the testimony of Bancroft, Hildreth, Minot, and other historians, cited in the foregoing pages, and many others who might be cited, the facts were: the farmers, the lumbermen, the carpenters, the masons and day-laborers, the schoolmasters, parsons, and doctors found themselves unable to procure the supplies of manufactured goods which their "opulence" entitled them to enjoy. They could not trade off their kind of "abundance" for these "sundry articles." Without consulting Adam Smith or Jean Jacques Rousseau, by common consent they said to certain of their neighbors: "You can make just the things we need—our cotton, woolen, and iron fabrics. You make them for us, and we will agree to buy them of you. We will patronize you. Invest your money in the requisite 'plant,' and we will see that you are remunerated for your capital and labor on the common terms which our joint resources will allow. We will trust your skill and industry for results in cheapness. We will go further. So that neither party may back out, we will put this agreement in the Constitution, authorizing Congress to 'regulate commerce' to this end. Of course, with the understanding that if the results do not turn out best for a majority of us, we may annul this arrangement and buy anywhere in the world—have free trade. Certain *doctrinaires* are abroad who want these goods as well as we, but they preach '*liberty*' and their 'inalienable rights' of 'exchange'—they prefer these abstractions to the commodities which satisfy our and their desires. We prefer the commodities. Nevertheless, you take your chances, that we may repudiate the present understanding, for the majority must rule."

This is all there ever was in protection, in fact or in law. It was a balancing of the expedients open to them —to enjoy the goods or go without them. They knew, then, for they said so in terms, that the price of the domestic goods was higher for the moment than the price of such foreign goods as they could buy.

Nor did they trust the skill and industry of their manufacturing neighbors in vain, for the domestic goods, if the whole supply be taken into the account, are cheaper now than the foreign. The results have turned out so well for all of us that the compact is still adhered to.

And the *doctrinaire* is still abroad, insisting on *free trade* as a *mode of his liberty*—still talking about "robbery" and "spoliation," and the "subtle and unjust invasion of his rights," growing out of this agreement of the vast majority of his neighbors. The "force" he denounces is the legitimate force of the societary compact. The compact will be promptly abrogated when it ceases to work the results intended. But our *doctrinaire* cares nothing about economic results. He risks his all on the transcendental "liberty" he claims he is entitled to. Let that have full play, and he cares not whether he has prosperity or adversity—satisfaction of desires or not—*liberty* is the desire he wishes to gratify, the rest will regulate itself. "*Hence*," he concludes, "*either prosperity in a free-trade country, or distress in a protectionist country, is fatal to protectionism, while distress in a free-trade country or prosperity in a protectionist country proves nothing* against free trade." Why? Because the economic results of "liberty" are to be accepted, whether good, bad, or indifferent. The results of "protection" are to be rejected, even though they are the best attainable, because, forsooth, they are "adventitious." "Liberty" is the panacea for all ills—just as "liberty" was the idol enthroned by the French Revolutionists. "Man," they cried, "is naturally a *perfect and solitary whole—the will of the lawgiver* has transformed him into *a fraction* of a greater *whole*." Unregulated liberty is license, violence, disintegration.

The argument we have essayed has not been conducted on this view of the individual and of the society with which he has *necessary* relations. We started out with a study of the scientific validity and economic operation of defensive duties in the United States. We have traced them, and are willing to submit the necessity of their imposition and results to the test of observation and experience. Abstract rights are not within the field of discussion; the concrete judgment of the majority of American citizens on a question affecting their general welfare is final and conclusive before any tribunal to which an appeal can be made.

We have said nothing of the moral and educational effects of protection, or the economic advantages coming from density of population, and its relation to the creation of fresh desires, calling for fresh efforts to their satisfaction. Nor have we discoursed on the utter helplessness of agriculture itself, when unattended with the other arts and sciences. We have only taken the free-trader's premises, the power of agriculture to effect the exchanges needed. We have discussed it from the low elevation of the exchange of material commodities, and that on the sole consideration of their accessibility and cheapness—cheapness, both in the sense of the expenditure of labor and effort upon it, and the money price—accessibility, on the contemplation of other sources of supply. The free-trade view intrinsically contains in itself the idea that what we want is "*leisure*," and the temperament which prescribes that we save labor by having fewer desires and consequent release of effort to gratify them. It is unnecessary to encumber our discourse with abstruse speculation on the subject. We are not the kind of people which that philosophy contemplates. We do not lead fixed, stationary lives, which run in rigid grooves. We are a progressive race—with convolutions in our brains which expand, and sutures in our skulls which allow expansion. We have never ventured to try the experiment of returning to fewer and coarser desires, but our whole effort has been to render our organization more sensitive, our pains and pleasures more acute, and our lives more energetic in the pursuit of means by which we might secure the one and avoid the other. We have simply surrendered to the law of our nature under the stimulation of our proper environment. The great facts of our environment are all contained within the geographical area which bounds the nation. The actions and reactions which we undergo are the actions and reactions between the men and the things which are common to us as the inhabitants of a given territorial area; the social forces which move us are the forces of *the society* of which we are component parts, and not a society in Europe or Asia; the functions which we discharge are the functions of the *organic unit* to which we belong, and not of an organism of which we are not members, on some other continent; the whole of which we are parts is the *American Nation*, and not the abstract humanity which cosmopolitanism contemplates. We are a great, healthy, independent entity, with our own co-ordinated nervous system, subject to the reflex action of the external world which surrounds us, amenable to the sensations which our adjustment to our own conditions of existence has generated. We have no conceivable calculus by which we could estimate the loss which would accrue to us—*the cost*—of being an Esquimau, and subsisting on whale-oil, or a Bornean, living on bread-fruit. We, therefore, furnish no data by which the free-trader can use us as mere counters in the reckoning of the gains and losses of the unworthy and insignificant game which he conceives us as playing. And thus it happens that when the free-trader has fenced us in by his definitions, he blurts out his protest the moment the true inquiry lands us outside his inclosure—the moment you trace the roots of his science to the true undergound of human nature, he cries, "Halt!"

Prof. Sumner says an economic problem may be worked out by itself.[1] He leads us up to the border-land where the problem begins to take hold of vital factors, and then wishes us to solve it with the aid of the few tokens he has been pleased to place in our hands. With a given lot of commodities made and in hand, ready for sale by all the individuals and all the nations of the earth, he wants the trade made, the swap instantly accomplished, on the market prices current in the world at the moment. He wants the books instantly balanced all over the world on a given day. Each man trades what he has for what he wants, on a given signal, with no thought for the morrow. When presented in that form, it is soluble "by itself." Even then, we, in the United States, would be left with a large surplus of unsalable food and raw materials on our hands, and consequently would not get what we wanted. But, when we contemplate the morrow, with its development of new desires and new forms of consumption, with new products and new forms of production, and that these are the desires of Americans and the products of Americans, we see that it is a question of sociology, and a question of social science—of science in that society which we call the United States. To deal with the situation as a purely economic one, to stop and palter with the feeble waves which break

---

[1] See page 74, *supra*.

along the beach, is to ignore the massive power of the great ocean itself.

The problem which is presented is, therefore, as we have seen, over and over again, a political, social, moral, religious, as well as an economical one.

If we had confined our exertions to the raising of food and raw materials, with the needed mechanism of such pursuits, would we have accumulated the material, tools, and instruments, including land and houses, which we now have? Manifestly not. Should we have made the progress we now have, even in agriculture? Probably not. Would a McCormick have been developed, and his reaper, without the skill and genius which comes of the attrition of a race of trained artisans? We do not, of course, know, but probably not. The South previous to the war has shown us what the rude labor needed in cotton-raising can do, and what it can accomplish in the way of progress and achievement. It is no answer to say that they were subject to the conditions of slavery. The real question is, what is the nature of the requirements needed in the raising of cotton? A gold-mining country has the machinery, and the machinery only, required in that business. A coal-mining country, when that business is the main occupation, needs only the machinery appropriate to that business, and the labor peculiar to it; an agricultural people will come to no implements not indispensable to the working of the soil. In the presence of a race who refuse to limit their labors to that pursuit, we have developed much labor-saving machinery for the farmer; by himself, would he have done it? None of us can do more than guess—probably not. What we are, we see and know; what we might have been under free trade, even as cotton and food raisers, is a matter of idle conjecture and poor guess-work. The free-trader may fairly be called upon to construct his landscape under a *régime* of free foreign trade. He may be fairly challenged to estimate, under the demands of a foreign market alone for our surplus, how far he thinks the area of arable land would now extend westward from the Alleghanies; how he imagines the sites of the cities of Lowell, Troy, Philadelphia, Trenton, Johnstown, Pittsburg, Cleveland, Wheeling, and Chicago would look. How his landscape would hold out in churches, and school-houses, and hospitals, and places of amusement; and how meager and thin would the census be. And whether, in fact, he does not know that, as a whole, the country would not only now be better off, but would be industrially more healthy and more "wealthy," if under wise guidance we had never raised a dollar's worth of surplus food and raw material? Whether a sagacious manager would not have done better, treating the land as a food-factory, to have produced supply according to demand. Whether, in fact, he does not know that the loss in exchange value which has accrued from the vast overproduction engendered under liberty would not have paid the cost of all the machinery which protective tariffs have enabled our people to erect. Whether he does not know that we should have made the best use of our resources, and should have shared our prosperity on a higher level with each other, if we could have managed to conduct our industries so that there would be no surplus— no overproduction anywhere. These propositions are, of course, purely speculative, but the burden is upon the advocate of free foreign trade to answer them. He complains of existing things; let him put his science to some constructive work, and exhibit demonstrable results.[1]

---

[1] These suggestions are put interrogatively. What the true development of the subject-matter of them demands is a chapter devoted to the explicit proof, which is possible, that without manufactures we should have had no agriculture. As it has been, our agriculture was wasteful, and *extensive* rather

So intent has the philosophical free-trader been to preserve the *status* by which he could reach up and pluck his bread-fruit without effort or sacrifice—so anxious for the "leisure" which he thought he had the capacity to enjoy, but had not—so persuaded that he could lead the life and experience the sensuous impressions of the vertebrate, consistently with the faculties and habits and "cost of living" of the mollusk, that he really overlooked his humanness— the imperiousness of his desires and his marvelous ability to work their satisfaction. The mandate of the Almighty, to subdue the earth, reached the ears of the men in America— an old family in a new home. They had all the accumulated experience and all the inherited traditions of the race. You might attempt to expel their American human nature with a pitchfork, but it would return. The mandate meant more

than *intensive*. We should have encountered, without the domestic manufacture, the danger of degeneration in our whole nature, wants, desires, and aspirations, and of the total collapse of our career, with the loss of hope and power to recover the lost ground. It would be idle to attempt any real picture of the American people as mere farmers—food-raisers for foreign capitalists. The free-trader is prompt to present a mere dogmatic denial that they would accept the *rôle*, but certainly his philosophy prescribes that they should have accepted it, and he fails to show how it is to be escaped.

The American farmers would probably present a new type; their inherent characteristics, energy of soul, intelligence, and manly virtue, would have prevented their degeneration to the level of producers of raw materials elsewhere. These are the same characteristics which have prevented their acceptance of that *status* in the world's economy, and which have insisted on nobility of industry and pursuits, under the machinery of protective tariffs. They would constrain them to do the same thing over again, if their history was to be repeated. They had strong arms to do the rude labor required in the cultivation of their fields. But their historical traditions were such as to make *social considerations* an ingredient in their nature, and compel them to a higher education, which, as rude laborers, would not have paid them. One of Bishop Berkeley's "Queries" was, "whether the awaking of wants is not the most probable way to lead a people to industry." Our ancestors were born with these various wants, masterful and unappeasable, except by complete satisfaction.

to them than to run plow-marks across their fields and to resume the pastoral life which their predecessors had followed on the plains of Asia. Subtlety of brain furnished free play for deftness of finger. Their divine commission extended to earth, and air, and sea. Elasticity of steam stood for human muscles, electricity did human errands under great oceans, and man's audacious invention dissolved the stable chemical compounds which had locked up the treasures he sought in dead matter. The Promethean fire had been wrested from the sky. Alone, "the wants of man exceeded his powers"; aggregated in society, "man's powers exceeded his wants." Contemporaneous with the origin of the nation, began the triumphant siege which the human family laid against the obstacles interposed between nature and the gratification of human wants. Engine after engine was wrested from nature, and turned into mechanism which carried the conquest into new regions. The actual achievements of the past have only raised us into the view of the illimitable spaces yet before us. The satisfaction of lower wants has only brought us into the presence of unmeasured higher wants which come trooping in upon us.

But, in the mean time, and as the result of the process, vast tracts of nature lay subdued at man's feet. The production of given commodities, under the progressive efficiency of human skill, called for a less and less onerous contribution of human labor. *Utilities* increased and *values* diminished. Values diminished, because less human effort was expended in surmounting the obstacles which Nature presented, and with which she resisted man's advances. Nature herself thwarted his purpose to be a jelly-fish, by inflaming him with new desires at the moment when, having planted his feet on the means of satiating old desires, he proposed to sit down for "*leisure*"—for a regular free-trade *dolce far niente*—for a good old Patagonian industrial *nihilism*.[1] Nature flanked us at last; her old edict still operates: by the sweat of his brow shall man eat his bread; but she has made man of more account and greater than the bread he eats.

In all this process, then, commodities have become cheaper to the human family—not cheaper to some, by the temporary and fortuitous circumstances that a portion of the children of Adam labor and strive on a remuneration which barely supports the human being as a tool, and that some are able, for a few weeks or a few years, to exchange a few gratuities of nature with their overburdened and overworked fellows, and thus make good economic bargains out of them, swap a little rude labor of the hands for much travail of the soul—but cheaper for all mankind, by virtue of the mighty and successful assault which our humanity has inspired and enabled us to make against the material universe. Shall the American, with the divine equipment with which he is invested, remain behind in this assault? Armed alike in body and soul, shall he shirk heroic duty and fail of heroic rewards by staying at the

---

[1] "There is immense force, apparently, in the fallacy that we want 'industries,' when in fact we want goods to supply our needs; in the idea that we want work, when in fact we want leisure. We are trying to sustain life on the face of the earth, and we find it hard work. All our discoveries and inventions have for their object to make it easier; that is, to get more goods for the same labor, and to sustain more and more highly developed men. For this we want leisure from drudgery as the first and most imperative requisite. Therefore, everything which *gets the goods* and *lessens labor* is an advance in civilization; and everything which makes more labor necessary to get the goods tends to barbarism. Labor for a material good is simply a gross necessity, which we are all the time trying to conquer in order to get leisure for pleasanter and higher occupation; and, above all else, it follows that those whose lives are all spent in drudgery over material needs are most clogged in their efforts for emancipation by everything which increases labor. Hence *this aim, with which the early American statesmen set out*, has proved a chimera. The further we follow it, the further it leads on. We get more industry and less good."—SUMNER, "Protection in the United States," p. 61.

rear and playing "sutler," or be content to furnish "commissary supplies"? We may thank God that our "historical traditions" prevented us from being that sort of men.

Can any theologian measure the gravity of our sin, had we rejected the divine message to subdue the earth, and undertaken to evade that responsibility to a Creator which attaches to highly endowed creatures?

Is there any judicial tribunal, in which honor or fair play sat as umpire, which would withhold condemnation of the act of a people whom *inertia* or cowardice inspired to vacate their place in the history of the race, which this century is writing?

Or, on the low level of the free-trader, is there any professor who can reckon up the immeasurable economic gains which the people of the United States have reaped by virtue of the entrance of American artisans upon this great warfare against nature? Can he estimate the *cheapness* which has resulted from this assault and conquest—cheapness to ourselves and to all the world? Will he attempt to deny that portion of man's power over nature, which the efforts of the American skilled laborer and inventor have conferred, in the act of adding their exertions to those of their worse-rewarded but struggling brethren in Europe? Hour by hour and day by day, the price of commodities has been reduced by the mighty co-operation of all men everywhere. The momentum of the attack made on our soil, and with our natural forces, has been felt along the whole line. The whole world has had cheaper iron and steel, cotton and woolen, because the builders of American furnaces and factories have achieved distinct improvements in machinery and processes, because the products of American furnaces and factories have been thrown into the markets of the world—been made available for the consumption of large divisions of the human family. This is America's contribution to the *civilization* of the world. It matters not that the effort has been to supply the American demand by America's production. The efforts have been expended here on the best natural conditions. The demands we should have made on England, for instance, for iron, have been withdrawn to the advantage of the rest of the world. The American supply now equals the American demand. Manufacturers have as much interest in making cheap things as in making dear things, as much interest in making cheap things as the people have in consuming cheap things. The price is an index of our power over nature. What the world wanted was the new thing, and an easy way to get it; and not the price of it—that depends on the hardness of the way to get it. The discovery of the new want of railroads has called upon the labor and capital of the world in the last forty years to a degree incapable of estimation. A decided proportion of the efforts of us all has been withdrawn from overcrowded pursuits, and has been directed to the satisfaction of this new and pervading desire for cheap transportation.[1] Does the free-trader argue for an instant that rails, steel or iron, would have been as cheap as they are now, unless American brains and muscle and money had co-operated in the stupendous and eager effort to build railroads? Is there use in any debate as to the *money price* which rails would have borne, if the demands of all the world had been made upon a limited group of producers, say, in Great Britain? Is it not manifest that every pound of iron or steel, and every yard of cotton or woolen goods, produced under natural conditions in America, has operated to reduce the price in all the markets of the world—the price in the United

---

[1] It is believed that the stoppage of work on the railroad system of the world—now aggregating 350,000 miles—will account of itself for the depression now existing in all industrial nations.

States as well as elsewhere? Is it not evident that the protective policy which induced this domestic production was a wise and beneficent scheme—in the interest of *cheapness;* and an unavoidable procedure, if on American soil, rather than foreign soil, the activities of our own people were to be diverted into this channel, and swell the volume of commodities which the family would have, available for division among themselves? What is the sense in postponing the achievement to a future time? Does the free-trader fear there are no more worlds to conquer? Doubtless, if we had not done it this century, we might have done it the next century; but we wanted the railroads *now*, and we wanted them with sufficient intensity to turn to and make them now. We wanted those "509 steam-engines" now. Stop and look deliberately in the face the proposition that America was to buy abroad—import her railroad system of 125,000 miles, and its equipment of iron and steel machinery! If it was worth while for the world to have the railroad system, it was worth while for us to make our share of it. Why not? And make it here, at home. Why not? We could not have imported it if we had tried. The welfare of that portion of the human family which was here was greatly increased, and it greatly increased the numbers who came here to participate. Future generations must discover for themselves enough of "something else" to do. Doubtless, by the same token, if the colonists had kept away from this continent a century or two longer, future generations would have all the magnificent forests along the Atlantic seaboard still for future use. Does not the free-trader regret the economic loss which we have suffered in cutting down and burning up, in order that we might make arable new ground, the millions and millions of pine and oak trees which the woodmen of America have sacrificed to premature cultivation? Or, rather, ought he not see and regret that, by our insane haste to overproduce for the foreign market, we have been guilty of the earth-butchery which has made a sterile waste of the Atlantic States south of the Potomac—has robbed the Genesee Valley of its eminence, and reduced the prairie-farms of Illinois to an average wheat-crop of about ten bushels to the acre? Was not this an economic blunder—to destroy so ruthlessly all these natural instruments of production? The result of all which was to skim our lands of riches and bring ourselves earlier under the unmitigated dominion of the "law of diminishing returns," to which all agriculture is subject. Desiring to know why the inhabitants of Virginia and North Carolina may now be found in Texas or Arkansas, the answer is, "They borrowed from the earth, but they did not repay, and she expelled them."

Or, on another line of considerations, ought he not to see and rejoice that the protective economy has enabled Prof. Sumner, for instance, to escape *competition* with "the hedger and the ditcher," because it has created a society in which his "services" as *a teacher*[1] were in demand, and allowed him the full use of his natural advantages? An economy which gave the society the "services" of "the late Mr. Scott in running a railroad" instead of keeping him in *competition* with "an Irish laborer in

---

[1] If we should take Prof. Sumner at his word, he is engaged in an industry which does "not pay." Forgetting his economics, and speaking as a sociologist, he says ("What Social Classes owe Each Other"): "There is a great continent to be subdued, and there is a fertile soil available to labor, with scarcely any need of capital. Hence the people who have strong arms have what is most needed, and, *if it were not for social considerations*, higher education would *not pay*."

While saving Prof. Sumner and the late Mr. Scott, we have also saved millions of other workmen who had not strong arms, but did have inspired aptitudes. Fortunately for the Professor, one of the ingredients in the "historical traditions" of the people he is dealing with, made "social considerations" one of the desires to be satisfied. And this is outside of his science.

digging a ditch"? We may be sure that the society of which they are members were the gainers in utilizing, in appropriate callings, the superiority of the Professor and the organizer. Imagine the wasteful picture of Prof. Sumner devoting his skill to driving a four-horse team hitched to a McCormick reaper on a wheat-factory like the Dalrymple farm in Dakota; and Mr. Scott, seated on a broncho pony, frittering away his marvelous energies on the "round-up" of a herd of Texas steers, for export to meet the foreign demand for beef![1]

The time had come when the *human family* needed this continent—and they needed it all—forests, soil, ores, textiles, cattle, steam, electricity. The development required the skill, effort, and sacrifice of the men who were on the soil, and not of men three thousand miles away. The society was to be built up here. This particular army corps was encamped on the arena of its struggles. It assailed the obstacles on its own front. The assault involved all arms of the service. Its impetus would have been weakened, and its final triumph delayed, had it made any detachments in aid of the struggles going on elsewhere, or

---

[1] " If it is said that we can not compete, what is meant? These phrases are allowed to pass without due examination. I can not compete with my inferiors or with my superiors. I can not compete with an Irish laborer at digging a ditch, and I could not compete with the late Mr. Scott in running a railroad. Could any taxes enable me to run a railroad as Mr. Scott did, and to earn such remuneration as he earned? Certainly not. No taxes can possibly enable a man to compete with a superior. Could any taxes enable me to compete with an Irish laborer at digging a ditch? Indeed they could. They might interfere between me and the laborer and *prevent me from getting his services*, and *I might be forced to dig my own ditch*, turning away from other and better paid occupations to give my time to an inferior occupation. That would impoverish me. Such is the only way in which protective taxes can make competition possible. They drive us down to compete with those who are far worse off than we, instead of allowing us the full use of *our natural advantages*"!—SUMNER, "Tariff Commission Report," vol. ii, p. 10.

left behind important numbers to struggle with harder obstacles to no purpose. The ramparts have been carried, its great labors have been done. It can turn and look at the field of the conflict. The conflict is past—it has been waged " once for all "—the actual problem now is to find new wants in order to absorb its efforts. We turn, then, to new conquests. We no longer ransack our resources in exchange values, to contrive how we can pay for an importation of twenty-four thousand tons of iron, as in 1824, at eighty dollars per ton. We need about five million tons annually, and can make it ourselves for from twelve to fifteen dollars per ton. We are no longer compelled to ease off a too sudden desire for steel rails to be supplied from England at a cost of one hundred and sixty dollars per ton. We can produce all we need at twenty-six dollars per ton. Of course, English and German and French skill has helped cheapen production, but American skill has been an equal factor, and present prices are the resultant of adding the competition of American labor and capital to the existing industrial organization which the human family had set up. Free-traders are quite apt to speak of American skill as bungling—of American commercial instincts as dishonest [1]—of American industrial attempts as

---

[1] One scarcely knows whether to hold the master or the pupil responsible for the bad morality exhibited in the following passage, taken from Prof. Perry's "Political Economy," at page 514: "While this knit-goods bill was pending (in Congress, in 1882), *the writer met an old pupil*, a manufacturer, and asked him, 'What are you running on now?' 'On these knit goods they are making such a fuss about at Washington.' 'I thought you spun and wove cotton.' 'I do.' 'Are not knit goods woolen?' 'No.' 'Is there no wool in what you are making?' '*Not a shred.*' 'I thought this bill was to protect woolen manufactures.' '*Oh, we are obliged to print the figure of a sheep on every piece we make, but every fiber of it is cotton.*' "

Now, however valuable this incident might be as the basis of a discourse in criminal jurisprudence, it is rather narrow as the foundation of an argument against protection.

if they were an "abomination"—of American products as if they were coarse, valueless, worthless, and the whole capital and labor put into them as "wasted" and "frittered away." There is no end of praise for the "cheap and nasty" products of foreign shops. A man who continues to sit on the top rail of "leisure," in the Sleepy Hollow of cheapness, and takes no note of this grand conflict between human forces and physical conditions on the plains above, is an economic idiot. He misconceives the real scope of the problem of human society—the real motives of the mundane struggles of humanity—the real outcome of our earthly efforts and sacrifices, the subjection of Nature by turning against her her own enginery—the true, final issue, cheapness and abundance.

The distributive justice which is realized in the rewards and remunerations between man and man, between group and group, is administered by a higher power.

In what degree have we ourselves profited by the cheapness which we have helped to bring about? Every commodity made by the average American workman, for consumption in the average American household, is as cheap, in money price, as anywhere else in the world. The cotton and woolen goods the average American citizen wears, the shoes on his feet, the food that he eats, the ordinary crockery on his table, the carpets on his floors, the utensils used in the kitchen, and the chains and plows and tools used on the farm, the fuel that warms his house and cooks his food, the fare on the railroad which bears him on the pleasure excursion or to distant friends, are cheapened American products, and could not be imported, tariff or no tariff. Some exceedingly fine prints, some silks and velvets, some decorated china, some wines, some *bric-à-brac*, are imported for the rich or fashionable or luxurious, and they properly furnish revenue until our own production can take these forms. A visit to any large dry-goods store will show many articles upon the manufacture of which Americans are as yet unwilling to bestow the requisite time, or unable to expend the requisite skill, on terms of European compensation. *I desire to repeat it, however, that all the commodities which enter into the consumption of the ordinary well-to-do American family are produced here at no greater cost in labor, and no greater average price in money, than anywhere else in the world.*[1] In all the great

---

[1] The most complete attainable statistics of wages of labor and cost of living, and a comparative statement of these as between Massachusetts and Great Britain, will be found in the "Fifteenth Annual Report of the Bureau of Statistics of Labor," page 469, issued in 1884 by the Massachusetts Bureau of Labor, and compiled by Carroll D. Wright, Esq., chief of the bureau.

The report states: "In the ninety industries in Massachusetts and Great Britain, supplying statistics of average weekly wages for the period between the years 1840 and 1883, the wages of at least one and a quarter million (1,250,000) of employés are represented."

The grand comparison gives this result, as to wages:

"*That the general average weekly wage of the employés in the industries considered was 77·49 per cent higher in Massachusetts than in Great Britain.*"

As to cost of living:

"*That, on any basis of expenditure, the prices of articles entering into the cost of living were on the average 17·29 per cent higher in Massachusetts, in 1883, than in Great Britain; that of this figure 11·49 per cent was due to higher* RENTS *in Massachusetts, leaving 5·80 per cent as indicative of the higher cost of living in Massachusetts, as compared with Great Britain, as regards the remaining elements of expense.*

"The Massachusetts working-man expends 48·41 per cent *more* on his family than the working-man in Great Britain. Of this 48·41 per cent, 5·80 per cent is paid extra for articles which could be purchased 5·80 per cent cheaper in Great Britain; 11·49 per cent is paid extra to secure more and larger rooms and more air-space than the working-man in Great Britain enjoys; the remainder, 31·12 per cent, indicates also an extra amount expended by the Massachusetts working-man to secure better home surroundings," the better and more furniture, the better and more food, the better and more clothing, etc., which constitute the higher standard of living he indulges, compared with the working-man in Great Britain.

These figures lead to this grand result:

"*That the* HIGHER PRICES *in Massachusetts are represented by 5·80 per*

fields of consumption the domestic supply is nearly equal to the domestic demand. In these departments the American struggle, under defensive duties, has worked its full results. In others, success is just in view. And all along the line definite progress is being made in the direction of cheapness, and the full supply of all our domestic wants by the direct act of domestic production.[1] That is all there is

---

cent; *that* INCREASED ACCOMMODATIONS *in housing* (11·49) *and* THE GENERAL HIGHER STANDARD OF LIVING (31·12) *maintained by Massachusetts working-men as compared with the standard of living of working-men in Great Britain is represented by* 42·61 (11·49 + 31·12) per cent of the total GREATER COST (NOT HIGHER) *of 48·41 per cent*, or, stated as a *direct ratio*, the STANDARD OF LIVING OF MASSACHUSETTS WORKING-MEN IS TO THAT OF THE WORKING-MEN OF GREAT BRITAIN AS 1·42 TO 1."

[1] "There are named, in a late report ('Annual Statements, Treasury Department, by Counties and by Customs Districts, of Imports and Exports of the United States, for the Fiscal Year ending January 30, 1883') by the Bureau of Statistics, 112 classes of manufactured products that are imported. But many of them are more largely exported, showing that other countries depend on us for such products more than we depend on other countries. In less than one fifth of these classes does the excess of imports over exports exceed one twentieth part of the home consumption. The excess in cutlery, for instance, is only 4 per cent of the consumption, in 'other manufactures' of iron only 3 per cent, in lead and paints each 3 per cent, and in carpets only 4 per cent. Practically the home manufacture supplies the whole demand in 90 out of the 112 classes. We import over one twentieth of the entire consumption in only 22 classes, viz.: cotton goods, lime, and glue, each 5 per cent; steel ingots, and ground coffee and spices, each 8 per cent; hair, 9 per cent; sauces and pickles, 10 per cent; woolen goods, 11 per cent; drugs and dyes, 12 per cent; zinc and books, each 14 per cent; glass and fancy goods, each 15 per cent; combs, 20 per cent; salt, 25 per cent; earthen and stone ware, 40 per cent; silk goods, 43 per cent; miscellaneous forms of steel, 46 per cent; buttons, 46 per cent; flax and hemp goods, 55 per cent; sheet-iron, 86 per cent, and tin, 97 per cent. Only three out of the 112 classes are supplied more largely by foreign than by home production. This serves to show how few branches of manufacture there are that do not closely approach ability to supply the entire home demand. With a little more growth, if undisturbed, nearly all will command the home market entirely, and by competition at home secure as low prices as consumers can reasonably desire."—W. M. GROSVENOR.

of it. That was the end proposed, and the only end proposed. Abundance and cheapness are the only economic ends conceivable to which human exertions can legitimately be directed. There have been blunders, there have been miscalculations, there has been immaturity, there has been vacillation, there have been ambitious attempts to scale inaccessible heights, but, on the whole, it may be affirmed, without the introduction of speculative conjectures, that all this has been achieved here at less waste, at less friction, at less miscarriage of effort, at less misdirection of energy, at fewer false steps, at lower outlay of capital, at less expenditure of hard work, than the industrial system of any other people.[1] It is the best, as it is the latest, product of human genius, care, adaptation of means to ends, co-operation, courage, and foresight. The faculty of invention by which we turned material forces to our use, we have seen successfully exercised in the field of social forces, through the intervention of the Government, which has formulated the corporate resolution of the people to supply their wants from their own resources. When the people resolved that they could and would do all these things for themselves, they, at that moment, imposed a protective tariff on themselves. So favorable were the social, political, and physical conditions in the United States that they reacted on the economic conditions. Our industries built themselves, just as the Pacific Railroad was carried across the continent on itself. The true source of our effective progress was, of course, the material conditions which surrounded us, and in the nature of the human agency which moved us; but the true results were possible

---

[1] In the midst of these congratulations it is only proper to drop a note of sympathy for the anguish of certain free-traders who are persuaded that somehow protection broke down in the presence of the problems of *emery, copper, nickel,* and *spool-thread!*

only by the access which the one had to the other; were accomplished only by the actual application of the one to the other. It looks like a truism to say that our resources could only become utilized on the condition that we used them; but the free-trader, by implication, denies it. The human agent was drawn to this field of employment from the four ends of the earth. He came under the multiplied attractions of moral, political, material, and economic advantages. The supply of labor was thus secured. The only capital required was the subsistence in food and clothing, consumed by labor, while the great operation was being carried forward. To these premises, our unquestioned successful career of achievement stood in the relation of a true *propter hoc*, and no cheap fortuitous *post hoc*. The conclusion was contained in the premises, and necessarily flowed from them.

Nor was the local prosperity of the workers in this geographical theatre of the division of human labor the only beneficent result of American endeavor. The Western republic became a vent for the overcrowded labor of all Europe, and our wages withstood the terrible influx; we assimilated even the garbage dumped upon our shores. The workshops of England, Germany, Russia, and France felt the relief which our great draft made upon them. The demand we made for labor here thinned the ranks of competing hands and brains there. Their wages and standards of living rose responsive to the removal of repressive burdens there. The general level of welfare was raised through all the world. When the founders of the nation invited the human instruments of production to our own soil, they entered into an implied contract to provide opportunity to render material services here—one to the other. The transfer of the laborer himself took the place of a trade in the products of his labor. Glad and prosperous as things became here, they led also to gladness and prosperity elsewhere. The places in Europe made vacant by the seven million immigrants, who have reached us since 1860, have widened the margin of comfort and enjoyment of every laboring-man and his family in every country in Europe. The human family has been the gainer in a large sense, but it was also true, all this time, that we kept our higher rate of progress by entering into possession of all our own resources, moral, mental, and material. We divided on a higher level by dividing with each other. We reaped greater economic gains by plowing our fields, rather than by plowing the ocean. We pocketed all the profits by the domestic exchanges, rather than export all our *gratuities* in the illusive rewards of foreign commerce. We have retarded our descent to the common level of rewards for labor and abstinence—wages and profits—which seems to be the admitted outcome of our struggles, and must flow from the improved appliances which render labor and capital mobile over large areas of the earth.

The American experiment has added incalculably, directly and indirectly, to the welfare and civilization of the whole race—resulting from our joint contest over nature: for the others, by draining them of surplus laborers, working at disadvantage, under unproductive conditions—by giving them a chance to recover their courage, their *esprit de corps*, their social integrity—by affording them an example of the worth of man and the dignity of labor; for ourselves, by dividing among ourselves the remunerations for hard and skillful toil on the maxims of justice and equity, and foregoing the silly ambition of sending our products in ships all over the world, in the idle expectation that we could find better bargains among foreigners than among ourselves.

So signal has been our own success in supplying our

own wants that a class of theoretical free-traders have changed their whole premises and their whole line of argument within the last few years. We were first told by the professors that a new country had neither the labor nor the capital to carry on great organized industries; that we must wait until one accumulated and the other multiplied, and that, "when competition had become as severe here as abroad, industries would come in naturally and of their own accord"; "that we had not the arts and sciences and the skill of older nations; that we had not their misery and their want, and that the advantages and disadvantages of those states were about equally divided," and that in consequence we must "take to the land." Protectionists have thought that if we could get Nature on our side, and get her to take a hand in our interest, the sooner we appropriated her services the better.

Now we are told that we have too much labor and capital, and that we must reverse the currents of our commerce. Let us see how this school go about it. Mr. David A. Wells, in the "North American Review" for September, 1884, says, *inter alia:*

"It is clear that there is no need whatever, at present, for any more furnaces or factories to supply any domestic or home demand, and that, if even the existing furnaces and factories are to be kept fully employed, and any construction of new ones entered upon, a larger market, or a market outside of the country, must in some way be obtained." Then he deduces certain conclusions which he calls "axioms":

"*First.* There is no sufficient market for our surplus agricultural products except a foreign market, and, in default of this, such surplus will either be not raised, or, if raised, will rot on the ground."[1]

---

[1] Mr. Wells has a formidable rival in rhetoric and a dangerous competitor

"*Second.* The domestic demand for the products of our existing furnaces and factories is very far short of the capacity of such furnaces and factories to supply, and until

in logic in the Hon. Frank Hurd. In the speech by the last-named gentleman in Congress, before referred to, he says:

"It must not be forgotten, as I said a while ago, this wheat finds its market in Liverpool in competition with all the wheat of the world. The price of the wheat there is determined by the competition. This competition not only fixes the price of the wheat sold there, but of every bushel sold at home. It is the Liverpool market which determines the price of wheat which may be sold at Chicago, Toledo, Milwaukee, or any of the great grain centers of the West.

"I say to the farmer of America that the prospect for him is by no means encouraging. With elevators, granaries, and warehouses all filled to overflowing, with the old crop still unsold, with the vast fields of the great West greening to the coming harvests, with *crops unexcelled in India*, almost ready for the market, with splendid promise among almost all *the wheat-growing nations of the earth*, and with the price of wheat less than eighty cents in Chicago, I predict that before January next the price of wheat will be so low that it will not *pay the cost of production*, and the corn raised on the Western prairies will be *burned again for fuel*, as was the case several years ago. When that time arrives *the farmers will be beggars in the midst of their own plenty, and paupers by the side of their own golden gathered sheaves.* [Applause.] There is absolutely no relief to the American farmer except in the making of foreign markets for him"!

That is to say, forsooth, *videlicet*—i. e., the non food-producers of the world take a certain amount of food, the market price of which is fixed at Mark Lane, London. The American farmers, in competition with the farmers of all the world, have this market *plus* the home market to the non-food-raisers here. Taken as a whole, the price of wheat is so low "that it will not pay the cost of production." Mr. Hurd's remedy: abandon the exchanges between the American farmer and the American manufacturer; abandon the capital and labor in American protected industries, and turn them upon the land.

One may try a long time without seeing the force of this logic. The American artisan will be glad to make common cause with the farmer, and their *joint labors* will supply all their wants. In that event, it is not apparent how either can be beggars in the midst of their own plenty, and paupers by the side of their own golden gathered sheaves. Mr. Hurd's "logic" fairly rises into the region of humor.

larger and more extended markets are attainable, domestic competition, while not preventing large sales (for a nation of fifty-six millions requires a large amount of commodities), will nevertheless continue, as now, to reduce profits to a minimum" (as protectionists have always contended it would), "and greatly restrict the extension of the so-called manufacturing industries.

"*Third.* With restricted opportunities for labor and the profitable employment of capital, the continual addition to our population from natural increase or immigration will inevitably tend, through increased competition, to reduce the wages of labor and promote social discontent and antagonisms between employers and employés."

Concluding, however, from a general review of our situation:

"But, in our case, whatever has happened has, as yet, occasioned no scarcity of capital for every fairly promising investment."

From all which it is proposed to deduce the logical conclusions—abolish all protective tariffs, raise more food "to rot on the ground"—supplement our existing furnaces and factories, and relieve the increasing competition of laborers *here*, by availing ourselves of the "services" of all the laborers of *Europe*, embodied in imported commodities made in the furnaces and factories there.

Indeed—

"Here *is* a pretty mess,
Here is a state of things,"

revealed by this Ko-ko of political economy.

At first blush it would seem, admitting Mr. Wells's axioms, that we had really, through the contemned and derided protective economy, reached the opportunity for the "leisure" so eloquently pleaded for by Prof. Sumner, only he wanted to enjoy the leisure before we had laid grounds for indulging in it—he proposed *leisure* at the beginning, instead of at the end of an industrial career.

Mr. Wells proposes to reverse matters, and export manufactured commodities. We then find ourselves confronted by a state of facts the operation of which has been indicated among the primary laws of political economy. We are remanded to the fundamental difficulty pointed out by Alexander Hamilton (whose writings, by-the-way, betray his intimate acquaintance with Adam Smith's "Wealth of Nations"), to wit, "The vain project of selling everything and buying nothing." We are called upon to answer Prof. Sumner's query, embodying his objection to starting in, on the protective system at all: "What, then, I ask, is the rest of the world to do for us? If we take all the industries, how will they pay us for what we do for them?"[1]

---

[1] We here, again, encounter the eloquence of our friend Hon. Frank Hurd:

"Last year England sold abroad one billion five hundred million dollars' worth of manufactured goods, and America, exclusive of the manufactured products of agriculture, sold abroad barely seventy million dollars' worth. Fifteen hundred millions of dollars for that little stormy island, and seventy million dollars for this continent! Yet we have opportunities and advantages vastly superior to hers. She has to go thousands of feet under the land and under the sea to get her iron and her coal, and go thousands of miles over the land and the sea to get her cotton and her wool. We find here our iron and coal close to the surface, on the mountains and hill-sides, and can tumble them together into the furnaces. We have the vast cotton-fields of the sunny South and the wide pasture-fields of the West for sheep to give us abundance of cheap cotton and cheap wool. It is an ineffaceable stain on the American name that the markets of the world have thus been surrendered to Great Britain, our great rival. Think you that if we could have sold abroad of our manufactured goods one billion dollars' worth last year, there would have been this stagnation, overproduction, and depression?

"If I could burn into the brains of the manufacturers of America one sentence, it would be this: 'Turn from this constant introspection, to the nations of the earth; down with the walls, out to the sea.' There are 2,000,000,000 people in the world who want to buy what you make."

Shutting our eyes to the beauties of this burst of rhetoric, let us submit

We are brought face to face with the formulated judgment of approved economists: "The great trades of the world are carried on between countries pretty widely removed from each other, either in the scale of civilization, or in respect to their natural resources and productions: *while, in proportion as countries approximate each other in natural resources, or in the industrial qualities of their inhabitants, the scope for international trade is narrowed;* it is even possible that it should fail altogether. The reason of this is by no means mysterious. The advantages to be derived from the separation of employments are, in countries in which industry has made any considerable progress, *in general realized to their full extent by the separation which takes place within the limits of these countries.*" (Cairnes, "Political Economy," p. 300.)

"It will also be apparent, *that nations possessing exactly similar powers of production can not gain by mutual commerce, and consequently will not have any such commerce, however free from artificial restrictions.*" (Jevons, "Theory of Political Economy," p. 210.)

"This is so strikingly the case, that the growth of a nation's foreign trade is sometimes vaguely spoken of as though it constituted absolute and unquestioned evidence of advance in industrial prosperity. It may, therefore, be useful to point out—what might otherwise seem too obvious to be worth stating—that it is, *cæteris paribus*, an economic disadvantage that any commodity should be produced at a distance from the market in which it is nomi-

---

it to a little logic. Mr. Hurd, with our full home supply of food, cotton, wool, coal, iron, silver, gold, copper, and most raw materials, in what will the 2,000,000,000 (!) people of the world, who want "of our manufactured goods *one billion* dollars' worth," pay us ? Suppose you take the trouble to think this over, and be ready with a specific answer. Really, now, what do you seriously consider to be the reason why we don't and never can reach them ? Have you ever heard of "the vain project of selling everything and buying nothing" ?

nally sold; and that if, in any case, this disadvantage can be got rid of—without creating an equally serious drawback—through the production at home of some commodity hitherto imported from abroad, *the resulting diminution of trade would obviously be a mark of industrial improvement and not of retrogression.*" (Sidgwick, "Principles of Political Economy," p. 214.)

"The noteworthy circumstance is, that while the country was then prospering" (he is speaking of Australia) " its external trade was undergoing constant contraction. The fact, I may mention in passing, *shows how little the foreign trade of a country, as measured by its exports and imports, furnishes a correct criterion of its industrial progress or growth in real worth.*" (Cairnes's Essays: "The Australian Episode." [1])

Let us see. Here in the United States is a people with an abundant supply of appropriated capital, with an adequate number of furnaces and factories, with a surplus of food and raw materials, with all the cotton and woolen goods they need, with all the houses to cover their workmen, their wives and children, with the blankets on their beds, with the carpets on their floors, and furniture, with the crockery on their tables, with the cooking utensils in their kitchen, with all the iron and steel they can use, with railroads to carry them to distant fields of business or pleasure, with literature, with churches, with places of amusement; over and above all these, capital as yet uncommitted to any enterprise, becoming cheaper and cheaper, and only seeking a " field of employment "; labor to use this capital, with constantly increasing productive power to make the more and multiplying new things, which will eventually

---

[1] Every economist who attempts to demonstrate the commercial prosperity of England or Holland under free trade, does it by manipulation of her custom-house returns. May be, for British progress, this is the test. Certainly, we in the United States can better measure our wealth by our census returns.

be divided among the laborers. All this is going along peacefully under the law, or rather the tendency, which Prof. Senior more fully pointed out, that, under the increasing efficiency of the co-operation between capital and labor, capital is getting a less and less *proportionate* share of the product, and labor is getting a constantly increasing *proportionate* share of the joint product. Really, this is quite as optimistic a result as Carey and Bastiat ever anticipated. It is a fair inquiry, what more a people so situated can enjoy? Any foreign commerce which they need can only be for the products of other climates, and for commodities the product of *non-competing* groups of industries. And it is this commerce with *non-competing* industries which it is our true policy to build up, whether with South America, Asia, Africa, or Europe.

On such a commerce there will be no *restrictions*, nor have we ever imposed any. We shall have time and money, also, to devote to the one outstanding conquest which free trade has prevented us as yet from essaying. I say free trade has prevented us from essaying, because in *the carrying-trade* there has been no attempt to impose restrictions, except as to our coasting-trade. There has been absolute free trade in freighting. Whatever may have happened to our ship-owners, by reason of the limitations imposed on buying ships abroad, our ports have been as free, in *ocean carrying-trade*, to all the world as they have been to ourselves. We have been driven off the seas, not by the tariff on ships, but by *foreign competition*, "under freedom." Doubtless we have been able to do better with our capital and labor in providing for our internal communications, by means of railroads and the commerce on our rivers and lakes. If we had bought the ships we could not have sailed them. The president[1] of the only American

---

[1] Mr. Henry D. Welsh, of Philadelphia.

company operating a line of steamers, carrying the American flag, running from Philadelphia, will tell you that, if their steamers were presented to the company as a gift, they could not be profitably employed in foreign trade in competition with the salaries and wages and expenses of English officers and seamen. "At the time of the repeal of the navigation laws all the best judges thought that the carrying-trade of the world must pass into the hands of the Americans. It has passed into our own. There are probably several causes for this; but the most important, to my mind, is that America has found in her internal development—in her farming, and in the railways which farming creates and sustains—an industry more profitable to herself and to the world than the ocean carrying-trade." (T. H. Farrar, "Free Trade *vs.* Fair Trade.") Free trade in freighting has driven us out of that industry. But we have about finished our system of internal communications. No people can do everything at once. Under proper defensive duties we are again about to enter this great field of employment, at present unoccupied by American labor and capital. We shall wrest from England a portion of the $500,000,000 annually charged the nations of the earth by her for carrying their products on the ocean. We shall at least rid ourselves of *the tax* which this operation imposes on us. The issue of that struggle is plainly foreshadowed in the generous words of Mr. Gladstone, in his article "Kin beyond Sea," "North American Review," September, 1878:

"I do not speak of political controversies between them" (the thirty-eight States of the Union) "and us, which are happily, as I trust, at an end. I do not speak of the vast contribution which from year to year, through the operations of a colossal trade, each makes to the wealth and comfort of the other, nor of the friendly controversy which in its own place it might be well to raise between the leanings of America to protectionism, and the more daring reliance of the old country upon free and unrestricted intercourse with all the world. Nor of the menace which in the prospective development of her resources America offers to the commercial pre-eminence of England. On this subject, I will only say it is she alone who, at a coming time, can, and probably will, wrest from us that commercial supremacy. We have no title, I have no inclination, to murmur at the prospect. If she acquires it, she will make the acquisition by the right of the strongest, but in this instance the strongest means the best. She will probably become what we are now, the head servant in the great household of the world, the employer of all employed, because her service will be the most and ablest. We have no more title against her than Venice or Genoa or Holland has had against us. One great duty is entailed upon us, which we, unfortunately, neglect, the duty of preparing, by a resolute and sturdy effort, to reduce our public burdens, in preparation for a day when we shall probably have less capacity than we have now to bear them."

I hope the most inveterate and obstinate *doctrinaire* in America will not object to this coming era of universal free trade, based on the United States as the economic center of the world, and can contemplate, with complacent satisfaction, the commerce of the world growing by concentric layers from the industrial *point d'appui* which our protectionism has established here; and may take pure scientific comfort in the fact that then our industrial entity and our political entity may be separated without the redistribution of our capital and labor throughout the planet. We are to become the center of gravity for terrestrial exchanges.

It is tolerably obvious that this grand plan of exporting manufactured goods, which free-trade economists now hint at, can not be carried out if we destroy the manufactories themselves. It therefore becomes us, in view of present revenue reform schemes, to explore the methods proposed. Our present industries have been organized on the basis of protection in the past, and these can only be kept in prosperity by judicious application of like principles in the future. Even if the present distribution of labor and capital is an artificial one, it may be fatal to change it. If, on the contrary, it has been made as the result of sound economic doctrines, any changes and adjustments ought to be made by statesmen who believe in the validity of the protective idea. Mere "tinkering" with the tariff by *doctrinaires* would be intolerable. And surely the system ought not to be overthrown unless it has failed.

Now the logical scientific free-trader will be found at least consistent. Rejecting *in toto* the validity of *protection* in the past, or prospectively, he would at once proceed with the "reform" in the direction of free trade—or, at least, for a "tariff for revenue only," "adjusted to the needs of the government economically administered." It is evident enough that such a tariff may have no relation whatever to *protection*. If for "revenue only," duties should be levied on the imports of commodities which we *do not* produce—a "protective" tariff is necessarily levied upon commodities which we *do* produce.[1]

Therefore it is that the *a priori* free-traders make their attack direct, and they do not flinch from the consequences of their doctrines. Says Prof. Perry ("Political Economy," page 510):

---

[1] "These three, then, are the vital principles of a revenue tariff, namely, *low duties on few articles*, and *these wholly foreign*, . . . and, therefore, the three vital principles of protection must be conceded to be *high duties on many kinds of goods, the counterparts of which are made or grown at home.*"—PERRY, pp. 481–484.

"The suppressed argumentation is something like this: Certain tariff-taxes are now a part of the law of the land. Property has been invested in virtue of this tariff law; therefore the tax must be touched gingerly, if at all. The just argument would take this form: All laws hostile to the public welfare are in their nature *void*, and should be *at once* repealed. Protective tariff-taxes are radically in conflict with the general interests of the people; therefore such taxes should be *at once repealed.*"

Prof. Sumner is uncertain whether a repeal of the tariff laws will produce any inconvenience at all, but says with confidence:

"It is generally assumed that it will be wise to do away with the system gradually and slowly. It is said that industries will receive a shock or be destroyed by any sudden action. No reason for these assumptions has ever been given, and they are not found in any facts or sound reasoning. On the contrary, delay in the process of reform would produce evils that would be avoided if the change could all be made in a day. The period of transition is the one of hardship, so far as there would be any hardship; therefore it is wise policy to shorten the period of transition as much as possible."[1]

If the principle of *protection*, of *defensive duties*, is to be abandoned, these gentlemen are right. There is no

---

[1] Henry J. Philpot, of Des Moines, Iowa, an amateur economist, was before the Tariff Commission, before which he made an address. He represented the "Iowa State Free-Trade League." In the course of his examination by the commission, this question was asked and this answer given:

"*Q*. Why do you not adopt a policy, then, of letting them" (the protected industries) "down at once?"

A. "We do not want to tear them down. If we can not live in an atmosphere of commercial freedom, then I say for myself, and I know that I represent the sentiments of thousands of people in Iowa, let them come down, and the quicker the better."

use in delaying with "horizontal" scaling. Whatever in this line is to be done by the tariff reformers had better be done at once; and whatever the manufacturers must do, in the readjustment they will undergo, they had better do at once. There is no use in waiting to see if our silk-factories can be converted into rag-carpet mills, plenty as rags will be, or if our iron-furnaces may not be changed into creameries. If it is true that the protected industries are "unprofitable" and "sink the money of other groups of industries," they ought to be stopped at once. If their machinery is "unproductive," it is not "valuable" property, and should be abandoned. If the capital invested in them is "worse than idle," it should be withdrawn. The whole inventory of wealth invested in them is worthless, is naught, and may as well be wiped off the national ledger, charged to "profit and loss," first as last.

We venture to assert that no statesman will be found, with sufficient confidence in the abstract deductions of the free-trade economist, to thus cavalierly wipe out the machinery, the capital, and the laborers, in the industries which supply $2,400,000,000 worth of the commodities annually consumed by the people, until somebody points out some other source of supply on equally advantageous terms.

The case is in a nut-shell; first, to determine upon the end sought, then the appropriate means to it. The social (or, if you please, the self-seeking) instincts of a people determine what line of commercial policies is best; having determined that, the public opinion, embodied in legislation, consolidates the forces and sends them through a definite structural organization, the form of which is given by the statutory enactment. Otherwise we fall back on the inane doctrine of *laissez faire*. This, as we have seen, involves an oversight of the distinctions between different forms of social development under the operation of the inward forces of society, and the direction which may be given them by the intervention of the governmental decree —according as that government is internal, "in and of the people," embodying their judgment, or is imposed by some external power. In the one case, the interest and views of the supreme dynastic political power may not be coincident with the real interests and views of the people; in the other, the social development is free, natural, and as the people wish and decree it. In the one case, will be evolved the history of the kings of England or France, for instance; in the other, the history of the people of the United States. In the one case, the proverbial sentiment is "*après nous le déluge*"; in the other, the struggle is for the earthly immortality of the nation, and it is in consequence "frequently compelled to make immediate sacrifices for the sake of a distant future, a thing which can never be to the private interest of the mortal individuals who compose it." (Roscher.)

The social forces which issue in growth of an indefinite form may be made to assume definite form by human control. Every law for establishing common schools illustrates this. Men can exercise their teleological faculties as well in the control of the social forces as in the control of the forces of the material world. Prevision and design are as available in the one case as the other. We make gravity, steam, and electricity operate on artificial lines, and take them off the lines they would *naturally have* taken. Our success depends on our knowledge of the powers we are dealing with, the wisdom of the end we seek, and the sagacity of our application of means to an end. The end must be definitely apprehended, wise, and attainable. Under these conditions, invention is as useful and applicable in human society and government as in the outer physical world.[1]

---

[1] "Society is simply a compound organism, whose acts exhibit the result-

The man who asserts that the American people do not clearly apprehend what they want, are incapable of adjusting means to the end, and that the national legislature is wanting in the wisdom, sagacity, and honesty to provide the necessary statute, assumes the burden of a very mighty responsibility. The only other alternative is to fall back on *laissez faire*, a barren conservatism which can only result, in our case, in a stationary existence and arrested development.

The true principles of *protection* were applied in the Tariff Act of 1816. It was drawn by A. J. Dallas, of Pennsylvania, then Secretary of the Treasury. He divided the importables into three classes:

First. Those of which a full domestic supply could be produced.

Second. Those of which only a partial domestic supply could be afforded.

Third. Those produced at home very slightly or not at all.

---

ant of all the individual forces which its members exert. Those acts, whether individual or collective, obey fixed laws. Objectively viewed, society is a natural object, presenting a variety of complicated movements produced by a particular class of natural forces. The question simply is, Can man ever control these forces to his advantage, as he controls other and some very complicated natural forces? Is it true that man shall ultimately obtain the dominion of the whole world except himself? I regard society and the social forces as constituting just as much a legitimate field for the exercise of human ingenuity as do the various material substances and physical forces. The former have been investigated and subjugated. The latter are still pursuing their wild, unbridled course. The former still exist, still exhibit their indestructible dynamic tendencies, still obey the laws of motion, still operate along the lines of least resistance. But man, by teleological foresight, has succeeded in harmonizing these lines of least resistance with those of greatest advantage to himself. . . . Legislation (I use the term in its most general sense) is nothing else but invention. It is an effort so to control the forces of a state as to secure the greatest benefits to its people."—WARD, "Dynamic Sociology," vol. i, p. 35.

This classification is a good and safe one yet, because it scientifically reaches the end proposed.

On the first class, duties should be laid heavy enough to secure the market to the home manufacturer, leaving it to domestic competition to keep down the price.

On the second class, the duties should be laid so as to leave the door open to foreign competitors and yet afford a fair protection to the domestic producers. Wise statesmanship and familiarity with our resources will enable any intelligent statesman to adjust the duties in this class so as to afford "revenue" *and* "incidental protection."

On the third class the duties, so far as *protection* is concerned, will be nothing unless revenue considerations intervene; the protectionist would put them all on the free list. Whatever duties are put on them will result in "revenue only."

It is not to be disguised that, in practice, it may be difficult to find the wisdom, strength, and singleness of aim to introduce protection only so far as it is advantageous to the community. But the problem is no more insoluble than any other one involving intelligence and honesty. Bearing in mind that the purpose of protection is to enable domestic producers to supply the domestic demand, protection should not cease until that end is reached. When it is reached, the protective statute is inoperative, whether repealed or not. The only practical purpose of a repeal in terms would be to shut the mouths of tricky economists and to silence noisy demagogues.

Sec. Consumers may rely upon two sources of supply:

First. Upon the foreign maker and foreign market for cheapness.

Second. Upon a second and independent market at home. We have made our choice of the latter, by nearly a hundred years of legislation.

Two distinct modes of levying duties arise:

In the first case, if the duty does not give the home producer a chance, if *it does not operate to create a second supply for the consumer*, it does *not protect*, and has no business to exist, except for *revenue*.

In the second case, if *the duty does operate to give the home producer a living chance*, in spite of foreign competition, the duty, be it high or low, is *protective*.

Mr. William M. Grosvenor has condensed these considerations into two sentences:

"I. The consumer suffers if *a revenue duty* is not *as low as possible*, to yield needed revenue.

"II. The consumer suffers if *a protective duty* is *not high enough to build up a home supply* and secure ultimate cheapness."

A horizontal reduction all around, as proposed in the Morrison bill, for example, has no justification, whether *revenue* or *protection* be the end sought. For *revenue only*, it imposes a higher duty than is needed. For *protection*, it is not high enough to save the home producer. The dikes which the Hollanders have built to keep out the sea must be high enough to exclude the sea at the highest as well as at the lowest tides.

Our present tariff is levied on only fifteen schedules or classes. In 1880 the imports, both dutiable and free, were $650,619,979. Of this amount, $202,557,411 came in free of duty. The total amount of the duty collected on the remainder was $193,800,897.[1]

---

[1] In 1882 the net income of Great Britain was £71,945,000. Of this amount—

Customs duties amounted to	£19,287,000
Composed of duties on tobacco	£8,800,000
Wine and spirits	5,500,000
Tea	4,000,000
Currants, raisins, and fruits	500,000

The census of 1880 gave the total product of our manufactures at $5,369,667,706, but it is believed to be nearer $8,000,000,000. In that year our total imports were, in round numbers, $600,000,000, as against a home product of $8,000,000,000, more than thirteen times as much. But taking the census figures, the home product under each schedule, according to which duties are levied, is as follows:[1]

In the process of mining anthracite coal, very considerable quantities of the strata are left in, in the form of pillars, for the support of the surface, and the towns and cities that often cover it. The coal thus necessarily left is part of the cost of mining the balance. Occasionally some reckless operators, thinking the coal left in is of more value

Coffee, cocoa, and chiccory..........	£300,000
Beer............................	6,000
All other articles.................	14,000

These "customs duties" on imported articles are offset by certain "excise taxes" on like articles made in England. These excise taxes amounted in 1882, on spirits produced, £14,300,000; beer, £8,500,000; wine and spirit licenses, £1,800,000. This is mainly a tariff for revenue only. It is easy enough to see that all these taxes fall on the laboring-man.

		Home product in 1880.
[1] Schedule A,	chemicals...................	$117,407,054
"	B, earthen and glass ware..........	28,956,693
"	C, metals.....................	604,553,460
"	D, woods.....................	509,485,611
"	E, sugars.	181,404,520
"	F, tobacco....................	118,665,366
"	G, provisions.	1,036,572,580
"	H, liquors.....................	142,122,048
"	I, cottons.	210,950,383
"	J, flax........................	5,518,866
"	K, woolens....................	267,182,914
"	L, silk.......................	41,033,045
"	M and N, sundries—paper, etc......	1,159,989,916
	Remainder....................	945,825,550
		$5,369,667,706

than the surface and the buildings upon it, proceed to remove so many of the pillars as they dare. This process is called "robbing the mine." The tariff reformers, who really hate the industrial system reposing on tariffs, now propose to remove the supports and let it down. They are proceeding to "rob the mine." Statesmen and economists who believe the system can be vindicated, at the cost even of the supports, will be in no hurry to ingulf the vast wealth thus supported—especially as in a short time it is manifest that it will be self-supporting. Except as a matter of form, it will then be immaterial whether they are left in or not. "Robbing the mine" will then be harmless. In the mean time it is unwise as it is unnecessary to remove the pillars.

We have encountered no practical disappointment as yet with our national legislature. A Commission of judicious, honest, and pure men, having a permanent existence, with no private purpose in view, dealing only with the economic forces in play, with power to act, would be a rational tribunal, to whose decision might be committed the commercial considerations involved. It is not necessary that Congress should undertake to enlighten anybody's desire for profit. Congress itself is enlightened by the national instinct for profit. At any rate, a protectionist will be satisfied if Secretary Dallas's plan is honestly carried out.

This is not exactly the place to suggest a tariff bill. When Prof. Sumner was before the Tariff Commission ("Report," vol. ii, p. 2325) he was asked this question: "Suppose the present tariff was wiped out, and we were to follow your theory of letting labor seek its own market, and letting the products of labor be sold wherever they can be sold at the highest price, regardless of a tariff or any outside consideration, what system would you advise us to adopt?"

The answer was:

"I am not a statesman at all; I can not formulate a revenue system for the country. I have never taken such a matter upon me; it is quite out of my line."

Illustrations may, nevertheless, be given of the application of the principles our discussion has led up to.[1]

---

[1] Van Buren Denslow, LL. D., of Chicago, has submitted the laws of the incidence of customs duties as follows. These laws are correctly deduced from observation:

"1. No duty can be protective unless there is some domestic production of the commodity on which it rests, nor unless the domestic supply is inadequate to fill the domestic demand. For instance, a duty on coffee would not be protective, because there is no domestic production of it. The duty on cotton or wheat is not protective, because the domestic production is more than adequate to supply the demand.

"2. In the case of every really protective duty, therefore, there is a domestic production which the duty is constantly stimulating into a condition more nearly approximating to that of fully supplying the demand. Hence, in the case of every really protective duty, the foreign price, with duty added, ceases to be the criterion for fixing the American price, for the latter is being constantly more and more determined by a new factor, viz., the competition and cost of production among American producers. Thus, for several years the American demand for steel rails was so great that America developed a capacity of production greater than that of England before the price began to fall under the influence of American competition between producers; but America reached a capacity of producing 1,500,000 tons, and our demand was only 1,100,000 tons; the price fell to $40, though the foreign price, with freight and duty added, would have been $52.

"3. In the ratio that American production becomes competent to supply the American demand, the price ceases to be in any manner affected by the duty. It depends on American cost of production only. For instance, there are cotton prints now selling in America for four and a half cents a yard, and which we export to China and all African and South American ports in competition with English prints selling at the same price. On the importation of these cotton prints there is a duty of five cents per yard. They are, therefore, not importable. But the duty forms no element whatever in the price, because American competition produces the prints as cheaply as English competition.

"4. Hence, the improbability that the price of an American manufacture is affected by the duty at all increases as the American supply becomes ade-

Raw materials of manufactures for which there is only partial domestic supply may be free. If we had, for instance, no iron-ores in this country, or not sufficient to supply the demand of "Bessemer" steel-works, such a raw

quate to fill the American demand, and when we see the American article going abroad as an export, that fact becomes conclusive proof that, whether a duty rests on the article or not, its price is as low in America as in England or any other part of the world. Yet Prof. Perry, in addressing an Iowa audience, told them that a returned missionary had told him that paper was cheaper in Natal, South Africa, than in the United States, and he argued, of course, that the dearness was caused by the duty. Had he looked at our commerce reports, he would have seen that we ship paper to South Africa, and that the missionary was as likely to have used American as English paper while at Natal.

"5. In strange obliviousness of all these principles concerning prices, it is the constant habit of free-trade theorists to charge that the greater the domestic production on any protected article the greater the 'tax' upon the people, since in all cases the whole amount of the domestic product is, they say, raised in price by the amount of the tax, whereas the fact is that the greater the domestic production the more difficult it is to raise the price in the least degree by any duty that can be laid upon it; because at the least rise in price, though it be by only one tenth of the duty, the domestic production expands in quantity, and so prevents absolutely a further rise in price. Thus, in my judgment, the wool that was protected by a duty of thirteen cents a pound can be demonstrated to have sold during three years past at not more than three cents a pound higher than the foreign price of wools of similar quality, because American wool-growers, producing nine tenths of the American supply (and those of them who produced it in Texas and the Territories, produced it nearly as cheaply as it could be produced in Australia), had too much to sell to admit of the American price rising to the foreign price with duty added.

"6. When the American supply is wholly or nearly adequate to the American demand, it may, nevertheless, happen that the article will be imported, notwithstanding the American price is no higher than the foreign. In every such case the foreigner either divides the duty with the American consumer or pays it all. I hold it to be demonstrable that about $35,000,000 of our customs revenue are in this manner paid by foreigners, and are not a tax on the American consumer at all.

"Such are the duties on wool and a share of those on woolen goods, the whole duty on lumber, coal, wheat, barley, rye, and other agricultural products, including rice, part of the duties on cottons, and lately on silks, much

material, though technically iron-ore, should be duty free, for it is really a distinct kind of commodity. If any one knows a "raw material" not now on the free list, let him name it and put it on the free list.

If the demand of the country for sugar were to be supplied from the cane, a duty on cane-sugar could not be *protective*—that is, it is a semi-tropical product, and the domestic demand could not be supplied from the home product. Sugar, therefore, should be on the free list, unless it was decreed a proper subject of taxation for "revenue only."

If the entire demand for wool could be supplied at home, it affords a subject for the application of a protective tax. If there are special kinds of wool of which there is no expectation of full home supply, that is a distinct commodity and is a proper subject for the free list.

A duty on wheat, or coal,[1] or iron-ore, or lumber, or cotton, or watches, would not be protective, because the domestic production supplies the domestic demand. The price is made here, and the duty imposed would fall on the importer and not on the consumer.

---

of the duties on cultery, iron-ore, crude iron, earthenware, and nearly every competing article.

"Briefly stated, then, the most important law concerning the incidence of a customs duty is that no duty can enhance the price of any article of which the country is producing an adequate supply; nor can any duty raise the price in favor of producers without setting producers into competition with each other, which competition constantly tends to reduce the price to the lowest one at which its production can be maintained. Hence a protective duty, once properly and wisely laid, never needs repeal any more than a fort once wisely built needs tearing down. Its only effective repeal, considered as a tax, is the reduction in prices effected by its operation. The repeal of the duty after this reduction in prices is effected is an idle and needless ceremony. The repeal of the duty before this reduction in prices ensues is a war upon the domestic production before it is ripe for the foreign competition."

[1] For a very satisfactory demonstration of this, see a monograph, "The Duty on Coal," by Israel W. Morris, Esq., Philadelphia, 1872.

A duty on tea or coffee or tropical fruits would not be *protective*, because there is no domestic production, and the duty is for revenue only.

A duty on the products of *competing* industries abroad operates partly for revenue and partly as protection. In the majority of instances the price of the foreign commodity is not increased by the full amount of the protective duty, because American competition reduces the home cost.

Whenever the American production in such industries reaches the American demand, the price ceases in any manner to be affected by the protective duty, for the reason that the cost of production under American conditions settles the market price. In the latter case, if the article is imported, the foreign producer pays the whole duty, or at best divides it with the home consumer, and the tax goes into the national Treasury. Prof. Henry Sidgwick, in his "Principles of Political Economy," at page 491, very neatly demonstrates this with the remark that "a simple case will show how a duty may at once protect the native manufacturer adequately and recoup the country for the expense of protecting him."

These illustrations exhibit the interplay of the forces involved. If we may rely with any confidence on the common sense, skill, honesty, and productive energies of the American people, in the future as we have in the past, to make what they can and buy what they must, we may safely leave the whole case in their hands under the fostering care and protective shield of defensive duties.

Our original problem in this essay was: *Given the population of the United States, with their various needs and powers of production, in possession of certain lands and other sources of materials; required the mode of employing their labor which will maximize the utility of their produce.*

We have explored our relations to the other nations of the earth. We have discovered that we are essentially thrown back on the proposition that, at last, *all "Americans" must support all Americans.* The external world can do very few things better for us than we can do them for ourselves. We are seeking the greatest annual product of our combined industry. Adam Smith says, "The annual revenue of every society is always precisely equal to the exchangeable value of the whole annual product of the country, or rather, is precisely the same thing as that exchangeable value."

"It is the accomplishment of a positive duty," says M. Chevalier, "so to act at each epoch in the progress of a nation as to favor *the taking possession of all the branches of industry whose acquisition is authorized by the nature of things.*" This Defensive Duties enable us to do.

Discarding, then, the atomistic view of the nation, and bearing in mind the true destination of wealth for the maintenance and *evolution of the society* to which we belong, we shall commit no serious mistake if we summarize our conclusion thus: *The nearer we come to organizing and conducting our* COMPETING INDUSTRIES *as if we were the only nation on the planet, the more we shall make, and the more we shall have, to divide among the makers. Let us, at least, enter upon all the industries authorized by the nature of* OUR *things.* Thus shall we reach the greatest annual product of the industry of the society we call the United States.

INDEX.

Abstinence, definition of, 19.
Agriculture, subject to law of diminishing returns, 20, 39; the advantageous industry contemplated by free trade, 131, 176, 233, 297–299; foreign markets for, fail, 136, 298; who may share abundance of, 330–339; useless without manufactures, 397; wasteful, 205, 405.
Alternatives presented by free trade, 131.
America, her final industrial triumph, 421.
American farmer, 341, 398.
American skill, 406.
Argument in epitome, preface, 391.
Argyll, Duke of, restrictions upon labor, 104.
Association in society, 41.
Assumptions made by free-trader, preface, 131, 153.
Atomistic view of society, unscientific, 217, 234.
Australian episode, illustrates economic forces, 302; gold-mining as an advantageous industry, 304; command of foreign commerce, 308; the *dernier ressort*, 309.

Bagehot, Walter, one-sided view of economists, 55; of wealth, 55; boundaries of political economy arbitrary, 56; English, only applicable to grown-up commerce, 68; no universal reasons can be given, 69; criticism on Adam Smith, 84–86.
Balance of trade, United States, with each nation, 1883, 161, 162; when disturbed, foreign trade stops, 265, 273.

Bastiat, Frédéric, definition of political economy, 10; of economic man, 40, 44; failure of mere liberty, 99; optimistic conclusion, 271; remuneration of labor, 358; effects of competition, 313.
Bonaparte, antipathy to the economists, 72; opinion of free trade, 80; Europe under, economically, 375.
Bowen, Prof., definition of political economy, 11; can not buy more value than we can sell, 127.
Byles, Sir John Barnard, sophistries of free trade, 230, note.

Cairnes, Prof., definition of political economy, 12; criticism on Bastiat's Harmonies, 101; cost, 152, 280; our inability to compete, 272; cost of produciton, 280; his paradox, 281; fallacy of his argument, 290; his advice to America, 298, 300; foreign trade no criterion of industrial growth, 418.
Calhoun, John C., market for farmer's surplus, 141; advocates tariff of 1816, 184; reason for protection, 257.
Capital, definitions, 16–19; foreign, as instrument of warfare, 260; free trade will redistribute it, 365; accumulation in United States, 358.
Carey, Henry C., definition of political economy, 10; of capital, 16; of money, 28; power of association, 42; criticism on economic man, 44; of wealth, 44; export of precious metals, 273; cost of getting to market, 322.

Carlyle, Thomas, the dismal science, 81.
Carrying-trade, destroyed by free trade, 420.
Cheapness, on what it depends, 263; according to Prof. Sumner, 318; result of protection, 401; to what extent effected, 408.
Chevalier, M., diversification of industry, legitimate, 152.
Chinamen, why offensive to other laborers, 352.
Choate, Rufus, protective duties constitutional, preface.
Clay, Henry, unprotected industries perish, 261.
Colonial system, Adam Smith's attack on, 83; free trade restricts with same effect, 84; England's purposes in, 384–386.
Colwell, Stephen, criticism on current political economy, 71.
Commerce, American, driven off the seas by free trade in freights, 420.
Commerce, international, based on division of labor, 22; regulation of, distinguished from taxation, 115, 225; penalty of having things made in the wrong place, 307.
Commodities must be paid for with commodities, 134, 250.
Comparison, wages of labor and cost of living in United States and England, 409.
Competition, eliminates gratuities, 26; forces protected industries on us, 188; foreign, wherein not efficient against us, 197, 216; Prof. Cairnes and Mr. Mill on, 272; compels us to export our gratuities, 311; proof by Bastiat, 313; cheapens our exportables, 317, 322; of farm with shop, 330; Sumner on, 405.
Comte, M., controversy with Mr. Mill, 70.
Conflict of humanity with nature, 407.
Constitution of United States authorizes protective duties, 115, 225; grew out of commercial crisis, preface, 225.
Consumers, not a class apart from producers, 243; may rely on two sources of supply, 428; what they are entitled to, 429; Mr. Grosvenor on, 429.
Consumption, correct theory of vital, 53; Prof. Walker on, 54; of goods made in protected industries, 165, 210; sources which supply, 290; extent of, in United States, 408.
Cost, in what it consists, 152, 280.
Cost of production, its elements, 277; wages most important element, 279; Prof. Cairnes on, 280; Prof. Perry, 283; Prof. Sumner, 283; argument from, not valid, 286.
Cotton, manufacturers of, 183–188.
Credit, what, 18; creates exchanges, 18.
Crisis—free-trade crisis of 1783–'89, 221; causes of, 222; Constitution grew out of, 225; Perry on, 222; Sumner on, 223.

Dallas, A. J., Secretary of the Treasury—Tariff Act of 1816, 427; his three classes of importables, 427; a scientific classification, 428.
Dalrymple farm as a food-factory, 406.
Defensive duties, compulsory, 195; results achieved, 391, 410, 411; how to be imposed, 423, 432.
Demand, not independent of supply, 244; and supply, 326; domestic, met by supply, 410.
Denslow, Prof., the Duke of Argyll's economic discoveries, 104; the atomistic view of society, 235; incidence of customs duties, 432.
Desires, their satisfaction, end of economic effort, 25; of wealth, not the central agent, 96.
Dillon, William, mobility of labor, 179.
Distribution, how equably effected, 263, 408.
Division of labor, theory of free trade based on, 22; limited by extent of market, 23; prescribes certain industries, 131; the assumptions involved, 131; the assumptions are wrong, 134; free trade pushes it to point of uselessness, 149, 171; Adam Smith on, 175.

INDEX.   439

Dixwell, George Basil, protection raises wages, 359; industry not limited by capital, 388.

Domestic industry supports two capitals, foreign only one, Adam Smith, 172.

Duties, minimum, 184; how laid for revenue, 423, 429; how for protection, 423, 429; in United States, 429; laws of incidence of, 432.

Economic man, definitions of, 36, 40, 43, 44: an arbitrary abstraction, lacks applicability to facts, 52, 57.

Economic problem, involves social, political, and moral considerations, 74, 79, 391, 396; Prof. Sumner, *contra*, 74.

Ely, Prof. R. T., the new political economy, 87; rejects *laissez faire*, 103–105; social considerations a factor, 96; criticism on the deductionists, 238.

England, free trade in, not result of deductive reasoning, 78; other causes of her prosperity, 78.

Equation of international demand, stated, 134, 176, 265.

Exchanges, grow out of association, 42; advantages of domestic, 172; restricting foreign, enlarges domestic, 207; extent of domestic in United States, 307; in British commerce, 307.

Exertion, and sacrifice, yield maximum of material good under protection, 198, 201, 209.

Exports, as yet, are cotton, tobacco, food, precious metals, and petroleum, 131; paid for by imports, 134; large exportation of bullion stops trade, 135; for United States in 1883, 159; of specie, paralyzes trade, 273; exports and imports no test of prosperity, 418, 419.

Factory legislation, violates *laissez faire*, 104.

Fallacy, assumption of adequate foreign market for food and raw materials, 131, 136, 250.

Fallacy of division; the free-trader must employ it, 251.

Farmer, American, 136, 341, 398.

Field of employment, industry in America awaits, 167, 389.

Food, value in foreign commerce, 306; fails in foreign market, 309.

Foreigners, if they will not buy of us, we can not buy of them, 130, 135.

Foreign market, can not take surplus of our land industries, 136; this drove early statesmen to protective system, 136; testimony of the fathers of the country, 136–143; compelled competing industries, 146; and led to crisis of 1783, 222.

Foreign trade, analysis of, 112; six questions and answers, 124–129; when and why it stops, 265, 273; most advantages between non-competing nations on, 377, 420.

France, under Colbert, 97; reasons for protection in, 368; expulsion of Huguenots, 374.

Franklin, Benjamin, inadequacy of foreign markets, 137.

Free trade, based on division of labor, 21; and *laissez faire*, 91; Napoleon on, 80; scientific premises, 22, 89; as laid by Adam Smith, 90, 91; ideal conditions of, in United States, 122; Prof. Perry's impregnable position, 127; compels us to buy more value than we can sell, 127, 130; not a natural right, 129; involves four false assumptions of fact, 133; pushes division of labor to point of uselessness, 149; prescribes an impossible series of exchanges, 210, 233, 250; involves "fallacy of division," 251; can not make American conditions of production less onerous, 256; production under freedom, 269, 272, 273; consequences, 275; fallacy of argument from cost of production, 290; puts the farmer in fatal competition with all the world, 321; preparations for, universal, 362; when it will be good in theory and practice, 377; in carrying-trade, has driven us off the seas, 420.

Free-trade crisis, of 1783–1789, 222; of 1816, 184.

440 INDEX.

Free-trader, burden on him to prove three propositions, 267; his test of prosperity and adversity, 393; proposal to reverse currents of commerce, 414; Mr. Wells, 414; Mr. Hurd, 415; favors repeal of protective statutes at once, 423.

Germany, reasons for protection in, 268.
Gladstone, William E., prophecy of American commercial supremacy, 421.
Gold, trade for, 284; in Australia, 302; its command of the world's market, 306.
Gratuities, utilities of nature, 20, 26; free trade compels us to export ours, 211; cheap foreign labor not a gratuity, 317.
Great Britain, annual savings, 236; export trade of, 307; annual value of manufactures in, 334; imports half her food, 337; customs duties in, 429.
Grosvenor, William M., domestic supply of manufactured goods nearly equals demand, 410; rights of consumers, 428; how duties for protection or revenue should be laid, 429.

Hamilton, Alexander, Treasury report of 1791. 136; on the mercantile theory, 137; inadequacy of foreign markets, 138.
Harrison, Frederic, criticism on current political economy, 71.
Home market, for agricultural products, 164, 378; for products of protected industries, 165; supports two distinct capitals, 172.
Horizontal tariffs, have no justification, 429.
Human family, needed this continent now, 406.
Hurd, Hon. Frank, his economics, 242, 414, 417.

Imports, must be paid for with exports, 134; into United States, 1883, 160; of specie, 273; free of duty, 429; dutiable, 429.
Independence, American, had its origin in English Navigation Act, 84; industrial as well as political, 84.
Individualism, impossible in an industrial or political entity, 247.
Industrial entity, distribution of proceeds of labor in, 227; must correspond with political entity, 361.
Industrial system, a social co-operation, 246; must be local, 246; individualism impossible in, 247; American the best product of human genius, 411.
Industries, foreign capital, instrument of warfare against, 261; need structural form, 262; proportionate supply furnished by each, 235, 290; unorganized can not attack organized, 261, 296; advantageous, 294; not limited by capital, 387.
Industries, competing or "protected," we are driven to them, 130, 145, 148; are not unprofitable, 158; natural industries, 152, 155; which do "not pay," 156; advantageous, Adam Smith on, 171; annual product of, in United States, 165, 248; demand for, 255; seven eighths of our goods must be made in them, 255; free trade could not reduce their cost, 256; when destroyed, do not spring up, 261; are an organization, 262, 383.
Ingram, Dr. John K., criticism on methods of economists, 76.
International trade, based on division of labor, 22; when it must stop, 273, 418; no criterion of industrial growth, 418; most profitable between non-competing nations, 377, 420.
Inventory, of American resources, 293.
Iowa State Free-Trade League, 226, 227, 372, 424.
Irish Land Act, violates *laissez faire*, 100.
Iron, history of, 181, 186; cheap and abundant, 407.

Jackson, Andrew, want of foreign market for agricultural products, 141.
Jevons, Prof., capital, 18; wages-fund theory, 31; noxious influence of

INDEX.   441

authority, 65; rejects *laissez faire,* 102; statement of the problem of economics, 194; law of indifference, 270.

Labor, its kinds, 15, 16; productiveness of, 23; distribution of proceeds of, 32; mobility of, 179, 325, 371; wages of, 341, 409.
Laissez faire, origin of, 97; ignores authority, 98; M. Wolowski on, 98; fallacy of, 99; Prof. Perry on, 98; rejected by Prof. Cairnes, 101; Prof. Jevons, 102; Prof. Walker, 103; by English statesmen, 103; American statesmen, Prof. Ely, 103–105; John Rae, 106; Mr. Mill, 109; Judge Phillips, James Madison, 111; not a scientific dogma, 88, 111.
Land, an instrument of production, 20; private title to, a mere expedient in division of labor, 192, 287, 337, 338.
Landscape, American, under free trade, 397.
Laveleye, M. de, definition of political economy, 12; redistribution of capital and labor, 365.
Law of diminishing returns, 20, 39.
Law of indifference, 270.
Laws, of the incidence of protective duties, 432.
Legislator, not bound by reasoning of economists, 60; when he may interfere to advantage, 108; protective problem not insoluble, 428.
Leisure, 394, 400, 401, 416.
Leslie, Prof. Cliffe, kinds of wealth, 55; mercantile system misrepresented, 56; destructive criticism on political economy, 73; *laissez faire* a fiction, 106; advice to Americans, 299.
Liberty, as a premise of free trade, 208, 393.
Living, standard of, in America and England, 409.
Lowe, M., political economy is of no country, 69.

Madison, James, promotion of manufactures, 140.
Malthus, Dr., theory of population, 29.

Manufactures, in 1791, 180; in 1815, 182; built on restrictions, 183; cotton and woolen, 184; iron, 186; Americans dependent on domestic production for seven eighths of the goods made in protected industries, 165, 177, 240, 255; must be made under American conditions, 255; which free trade will not make less onerous, 256; annual product of, 248, 334, 430.
Market, which the cheapest, which the dearest, 48; political economy can not tell us, 49; home market, Adam Smith on, 172. (See World's Market.)
Mason, David H., free-trade crisis of 1783 to 1789, 222.
Maximum of material good, 194; how attainable, 209.
McCulloch, Mr., definition of political economy, 9; general reasoning not sufficient, 60.
Mercantile system, misrepresentation of it, 54, 266; what it is, 83, note; no part of the protectionist's political economy, 83, 135, 273.
Milan Decree, as a restriction, 182.
Mill, John Stuart, definition of political economy, 10; capital, 17; political economy as an abstract science, 36, 62; not the science of exchanges, 80; social considerations, 93; concession to protective duties, 110; protest by Profs. Rogers and Price, 110; industry limited by capital, 387; fallacy of this, 388; operation of free trade in the United States, 272.
Minnesota farmer, case of, 251.
Money, medium of exchange, 27; kinds and functions, 28; Mr. Carey's philosophy of, 28; the instrument of association, 29.
Monopoly, impossible in United States, 215, 229.
Morality and religion, inseparable from economic forces, 94.
Mulhall, Mr., statistics of savings by nations, 236.

Nation, economy of each must be different, 9; economic problem must be stated in terms of nationality, 79; annual revenue of, 89; not result of economic forces alone, 79, 178, 363, 376; a true organism, an entity, 217, 227; atomistic treatment of, useless, 234, 244; highest unit yet evolved, 247, note.

Nature, our warfare against, constitutes cost, 152; results of our industrial warfare, 400.

Navigation Act, English, protective law, 384; a wise regulation, says Adam Smith, 384; its effects on English commerce, 385.

Non sequitur, an example of, 251.

Overproduction, not an explanation of commercial crisis, 28; of food and raw materials, fatal to exchange values, 147, 157, 175.

Pennsylvania, her "notion" embodied in her Tariff Act of 1785, preface

Perry, Prof., definition of political economy, 12; capital, 17; rent, 20; exposition of motives to foreign trade, 21, 22; effects of competition, 26; field of the science, 46; general good, 99; analysis of foreign trade, 124–129; free trade an inalienable right, 129; not proved, 129; his economic arch inverted, 130, 135; industries which do "not pay," 155, 295; cost of production, 283; trade for gold, 284; inventory of national resources, 293; what it lacks, 293; high wages in United States, 328; dishonest commercial instincts, 407; repeal of protective statutes, 424.

Phillips, Judge, on *laissez faire*, 111.

Physiocrates, their doctrine, 333.

Political economy, unsettled state of, 1–4; definitions, 8–12; desires, efforts, satisfactions, 24; Mill's abstract theory, 34, 62; Prof. Senior's four propositions, 38, 39; Bastiat's limitations, 44; Mr. Carey's criticism, 44; field circumscribed by Prof. Perry, 45–48; defects of his exposition, 50–53; unreal nature of the science, 60; its general reasoning not binding on legislators, 60; noxious influence of authority, 65; English economy, 67; universal reasons not assignable, 68; belongs to no nation, 69; destructive criticism by M. Comte, 71; Frederic Harrison, 71; Stephen Colwell, 71; Prof. Rickards, 71; Bonaparte, 72; Prof. Leslie, 73; Dr. Ingram, 76; experience and observation the only guide, 78; not the science of exchanges, 80.

Political entity, must be discussed as an industrial entity, 79; must correspond with industrial, 361; reasons for maintaining not economic, 178, 368, 376.

Population, theory of, 29.

Price, Prof. Bonamy, protest against Mill's concession to protection, 110; free trade makes American prairie-lands English fields, 322.

Production, instruments of land, labor, capital, 14; "under freedom," 240; in America and England, 269; forces of, conform to political lines, 376.

Products of labor, in United States, from what employments, 290; value of, 334.

Protection, not a question of taxation, but of restrictions on foreign exchanges, 113; its constitutionality, 115, 225; distorted definitions by the professors, 117; Prof. Sumner's four legitimate inquiries, 120; a question of fact, not of theory, 121; capable of analysis, 121; impregnable position claimed for free trade, 128; its weakness, 128; concessions to protection by Mr. Mill, 109; Prof. Taussig, 187, 258; the economic question, 120, 189, 211; the scientific question, 120, 189, 211; the political question, 120, 213, 267; the popular question, 120, 214, 267; to be defended on its own philosophy, 197; only mode of satisfying all our desires, 211; urged by Mr. Calhoun, 257; vindicated in Australia, 308; the strong against the weak, 369; all it is, in fact and in law, 373; a national question, 391–395; true subjects for its application, 427; does not present an insoluble problem, 425–429.

Protective duties, not a tax, 216, 240, 264, 335, 340; upon what classes of goods to be laid, 423; illustrations of their operation, 432.

Protective taxes, cost the consumer nothing, 256, 264; fallacy attributed to protectionists, 378; create nothing, 381; remove restrictions on home production, 381; as explained by Dr. Roscher, 381; John Rae, 381; Mr. Mill, 109, 381; Mr. Moffat, 296; render possible the industrial structure, 383; accumulate productive energies, 384; release productive forces, 389.

Rae, John, individual and national interests not identical, 106; when the state may interfere to advantage, 108.

Railroads, American system could not have been imported, 404.

Redistribution of capital and labor which free trade would bring about, 365.

Rent, definitions of, 20–21; our natural advantages give us a world-rent, 355.

Restrictions, protection a question of, 113; on foreign exchanges, effect of, 183, 187; Jefferson Davis on, 183; may result from war or legislation, 195; on foreign, enlarge domestic exchanges, 207.

Ricardo, David, definition of political economy, 14; capital, 17; rent, 20; strictures on his methods, 238, note.

Robbing a mine, 430.

Rogers, Prof. Thorold, protest against Mill's concession to protection, 110.

Roscher, Dr. William, protective system does not proceed from error and deception, preface; definition of political economy, 10; its greatest triumph, 382; protection, what it may do, 382; conditions which justify it, 382.

Rossi, M., grouping of our motive forces, 35.

Ruskin, John, the abstract man of the economists, 57.

Satisfaction of desires, true end of economic efforts, 12, 41; aggregate of, 234; cost of, for people of United States, 235, 248; requires products of protected industries, 249, 264, 298; must be won on our own soil, 264; can not be bought abroad, 264; how attained, 268; whence they come, 290.

Say, M., definition of political economy, 9.

Scott, E. G., results of English Navigation Act, 385.

Scott, Thomas A., driven to compete, 405.

"Schedule A," submitted by Mr. Springer, 240; exposure of its fallacies, 240; involves fallacy of division, 251; the peddler, the Minnesota farmer, 251; Prof. Sumner and pig-iron, 253; what it might prove, 252; what it does prove, 252, 266.

Sidgwick, Prof., definition of political economy, 11; capital, 17; economic man, 40; *vis inertia* keeps production backward, 258; protective taxes not inexpedient, 340; how repeal might operate, 366; foreign commerce no criterion of industrial growth, 418.

Sismondi, M., definition of political economy, 9.

Selfishness, assumed by Adam Smith as motive to production, 35.

"Selling everything," "and buying nothing," impossible, 417.

Senior, Prof., definition of political economy, 10; of abstinence, 19; causes of productiveness of labor, 23; his four general propositions in political economy, 39; legislator not bound by economist's reasoning, 60.

Shipping, American, broken down by free trade in freights, 420.

Smith, Adam, definition of political economy, 8; of capital, 17; division of labor, 23; motives to production, 35; *laissez faire*, 35; selfishness, 35; table of contents, "Wealth of Nations," 82; attack on colonial system of England, 83;

Mr. Bagehot's criticism on "Wealth of Nations," 85; what annual revenue of a nation consists of, 89; premises of free trade, 90, 91; exchange values in foreign markets, 165; what makes a state, 169; industrial freedom of the colonies, 170; advantageous industries, 171; domestic trade supports two distinct capitals, foreign only one, 172; division of labor limited by extent of market, 23, 175; protected industries forced on United States, 177; industry limited by capital, 387; fallacy of, 388.

Social considerations, an economic force, 96, 405.

Social forces, legitimate field for legislation, 426.

Society, atomistic view of, unscientific, 217, 234.

"Something else" to do, 232, 276, 299.

Sophistries of free trade, Sir John Barnard Byles, 230.

Specie, effect of export of, 273.

Springer, Hon. William R., "Schedule A," 240.

Steuart, Sir James, definition of political economy, 9; economy of every nation necessarily different, 9.

Summary, final, 436.

Sumner, Prof., his four questions about protection, 120, 189, 211, 214, 267; industries which do not pay, 156; effect of restrictions, 182; statement of the problem, 194; his solution inadequate, 210; destroyed factories springing up, 259; high wages no justification for protection, 283; reason of high wages in the United States, 328, 358; protection reduces wages, 357; Mr. Dixwell's reply, 359; test of economic prosperity and adversity, 208, 393; leisure, 401, 416; competition with the hedger and ditcher, 405; protective statutes should be repealed at once, 424.

Tariffs, of 1816, 184; of 1789, 222; what they involve, 425; Secretary Dallas's scheme of, 427; on what classes of goods to be levied, 430.

Tariff commission, a permanent one, a rational tribunal, 431.

Taussig, Prof., restrictions, effect of, 183-185, 187; protection, when it may be justified, 258, note.

Thompson, Prof. R. E., Mr. Mill reaffirms his concession to protection, 110; natural industries, 155; the home market, 378.

Traits and traditions, 123, 399.

Trade, foreign, can only supply some of our wants, 193, 199, 249, 264, 298; no criterion of industrial growth, 418.

Taxation, no scientific laws of taxation, 113; protection not a question of, 113. (See Protective Duties and Protective Taxes.)

United States, economic problem in, 190; two modes of its solution, 194; its resources, 42, 299; resultant of many forces besides economic, 363; is a free-trade group, 364; redistribution of its capital and labor, 365; an industrial entity, 370; how formed, 371; the group, as a whole, prosperous, 373; how a particular member may have suffered, 373; the South as a section, 373; cost of living in, 407; wages of labor in, 341, 358, 407; accumulation of capital in, 358; annual saving in, 236; annual expenditures in, 236.

Utility, to be distinguished from value, 25; comes from two sources, 26; increase of, in United States, 400.

Value, exposition of, by Mr. Carey, 24; by Bastiat, 25; to be distinguished from utility, 25; how notions of value and utility arise, 25, 26; can not buy in foreign markets more value than we can sell, 127, 130; this fatal to free trade, 127, 130; what confers value, 15, 319, 400.

Vis inertia, delays introduction of manufactures, unduly, without protective duties, Sidgwick, 258; Taussig, 258, 259, note.

Wages, how affected by free trade, 271; high wages no justification for protection, Prof. Sumner, 283; general theory of, 324; in United States, according to Prof. Perry, 328; Prof. Sumner, 328; Prof. Walker, 329; real origin, 341; do not come from agriculture alone, 341, 358; where highest, 349; depend on universal activity, 353; effect on, by industrial movements in United States, 412; comparative rate of, 409.

Wages-fund theory, statement of, 30, 31.

Walker, Prof. F. A., definition of political economy, 10; of economic man, 43; correct theory of consumption important, 54; rejects *laissez faire*, 103; theory of wages in protected industries, 329; competition of the farm with the shop, 330; should carry his analysis a step further, 335; do protective taxes create energy? 380, 383.

Wants. (See Satisfaction of Desires.)

Ward, Lester F., social forces, 426.

Wealth, corner-stone of political economy, 39; a generalization of various impulses, 39; the term discarded by Prof. Perry as useless, 41; defined by Carey and Perry, 44; abstract view of, 55; does not consist solely in money, 85; not central agent in human nature, 96; inventory of, in United States, 195.

Webster, Daniel, protective tariff constitutional, preface; speech on tariff of 1824, 142; in 1846, 142; failure of agricultural exports, 143.

Welfare: general welfare limits each man's right of freedom, 99; ultimate end of government, 319; Sidgwick on, 320; Wolowski, 320; of us all best secured by efforts on our own resources, 208, 408, 413.

Wells, David A., definition of protection, 117; wages in protected industries, 341; proposal to reverse currents of commerce, 414; why impracticable, 417.

Wolowski, M., on *laissez faire*, 98.

World's market, neither gives nor takes according to the requirements of the people of the United States, 128, 130, 134-144, 159, 177, 193, 202, 210, 232, 244, 250, 252, 265, 290, 338, 392.

Wright, Carroll D., comparative wages of labor and cost of living, 409; his grand generalizations, 409, 410.

THE END.

D. APPLETON & CO.'S PUBLICATIONS.

THE HISTORY OF BIMETALLISM IN THE UNITED STATES. By J. LAURENCE LAUGHLIN, Ph. D., Assistant Professor of Political Economy in Harvard University; author of "The Study of Political Economy," etc. With Sixteen Charts and numerous Tables. One volume. 8vo. Cloth, $2.25.

"Although the plan of this book was conceived with the view of presenting simply a history of bimetallism in the United States, it has been necessary, in the nature of the subject, to make it something more than that. And yet it was my hope that the effect of an historical inquiry in suppressing some of the theoretical vagaries of the day might be realized by showing what our actual experience with bimetallism has been in contrast with the assertions of some writers as to what it may be."—*From Preface.*

THE STUDY OF POLITICAL ECONOMY. HINTS TO STUDENTS AND TEACHERS. By J. LAURENCE LAUGHLIN, Ph. D., Assistant Professor of Political Economy in Harvard University. 16mo. Cloth, $1.00.

"The existence of this little book is due to an attempt to convey, by lectures to students, an understanding of the position which political economy holds in regard, not merely to its actual usefulness for every citizen, but to its disciplinary power.... The interest which the public now manifests in economic studies led me to put the material of my lectures into a general form, in order that they might assist inquirers in any part of the country."—*From Preface.*

MILL'S PRINCIPLES OF POLITICAL ECONOMY: ABRIDGED WITH CRITICAL, BIBLIOGRAPHICAL, AND EXPLANATORY NOTES, AND A SKETCH OF THE HISTORY OF POLITICAL ECONOMY. By J. LAURENCE LAUGHLIN, Ph. D., Assistant Professor of Political Economy in Harvard University. With Twenty-four Maps and Charts. A Text-book for Colleges. 8vo. 658 pages. Cloth, $3.50.

"An experience of five years with Mr. Mill's treatise in the class-room convinced me, not only of the great usefulness of what still remains one of the most lucid and systematic books yet published which cover the whole range of the study, but I have also been convinced of the need of such additions as should give the results of later thinking, without militating against the general tenor of Mr. Mill's system; of such illustrations as should fit it better for American students, by turning their attention to the application of principles in the facts around us; of a bibliography which should make it easier to get at the writers of other schools who offer opposing views on controverted questions; and of some attempts to lighten those parts of his work in which Mr. Mill frightened away the reader by an appearance of too great abstractness, and to render them, if possible, more easy of comprehension to the student who first approaches Political Economy through this author."—*From Preface.*

POLITICAL ECONOMY. By W. STANLEY JEVONS, Professor of Logic and Political Economy in Owens College, Manchester. 18mo. Flexible cloth, 45 cents.

MONEY AND THE MECHANISM OF EXCHANGE. By W. STANLEY JEVONS. 12mo. Cloth, $1.75.

New York: D. APPLETON & CO., 1, 3, & 5 Bond Street.

New revised edition of Bancroft's History of the United States.

HISTORY OF THE UNITED STATES, from the Discovery of the Continent to the Establishment of the Constitution in 1789. By GEORGE BANCROFT. Complete in 6 vols., 8vo, printed from new type, and bound in cloth, uncut, with gilt top, $2.50; sheep, $3.50; half calf, $4.50 per volume. Vol. VI contains the History of the Formation of the Constitution of the United States, and a Portrait of Mr. Bancroft.

In this edition of his great work the author has made extensive changes in the text, condensing in places, enlarging in others, and carefully revising. It is practically a new work embodying the results of the latest researches, and enjoying the advantage of the author's long and mature experience.

"On comparing this work with the corresponding volume of the 'Centenary' edition of 1876, one is surprised to see how extensive changes the author has found desirable, even after so short an interval. The first thing that strikes one is the increased number of chapters, resulting from subdivision. The first volume contains two volumes of the original, and is divided into thirty-eight chapters instead of eighteen. This is in itself an improvement. But the new arrangement is not the result merely of subdivision; the matter is rearranged in such a manner as vastly to increase the lucidity and continuousness of treatment. In the present edition Mr. Bancroft returns to the principle of division into periods, abandoned in the 'Centenary' edition. His division is, however, a new one. As the permanent shape taken by a great historical work, this new arrangement is certainly an improvement."—*The Nation (New York).*

"The work as a whole is in better shape, and is of course more authoritative than ever before. This last revision will be without doubt, both from its desirable form and accurate text, the standard one."—*Boston Traveller.*

"It has not been granted to many historians to devote half a century to the history of a single people, and to live long enough, and, let us add, to be willing and wise enough, to revise and rewrite in an honored old age the work of a whole lifetime."—*New York Mail and Express.*

"The extent and thoroughness of this revision would hardly be guessed without comparing the editions side by side. The condensation of the text amounts to something over one third of the previous edition. There has also been very considerable recasting of the text. On the whole, our examination of the first volume leads us to believe that the thought of the historian loses nothing by the abbreviation of the text. A closer and later approximation to the best results of scholarship and criticism is reached. The public gains by its more compact brevity and in amount of matter, and in economy of time and money."—*The Independent (New York).*

"There is nothing to be said at this day of the value of 'Bancroft.' Its authority is no longer in dispute, and as a piece of vivid and realistic historical writing it stands among the best works of its class. It may be taken for granted that this new edition will greatly extend its usefulness."—*Philadelphia North American.*

New York: D. APPLETON & CO., 1, 3, & 5 Bond Street.

D. APPLETON & CO.'S PUBLICATIONS.

HISTORY OF THE PEOPLE OF THE UNITED STATES, from the Revolution to the Civil War. By JOHN BACH MCMASTER. To be completed in five volumes. Vols. I and II, 8vo, cloth, gilt top, $2.50 each.

SCOPE OF THE WORK.—*In the course of this narrative much is written of wars, conspiracies, and rebellions; of Presidents, of Congresses, of embassies, of treaties, of the ambition of political leaders, and of the rise of great parties in the nation. Yet the history of the people is the chief theme. At every stage of the splendid progress which separates the America of Washington and Adams from the America in which we live, it has been the author's purpose to describe the dress, the occupations, the amusements, the literary canons of the times; to note the changes of manners and morals; to trace the growth of that humane spirit which abolished punishment for debt, and reformed the discipline of prisons and of jails; to recount the manifold improvements which, in a thousand ways, have multiplied the conveniences of life and ministered to the happiness of our race; to describe the rise and progress of that long series of mechanical inventions and discoveries which is now the admiration of the world, and our just pride and boast; to tell how, under the benign influence of liberty and peace, there sprang up, in the course of a single century, a prosperity unparalleled in the annals of human affairs.*

"The pledge given by Mr. McMaster, that 'the history of the people shall be the chief theme,' is punctiliously and satisfactorily fulfilled. He carries out his promise in a complete, vivid, and delightful way. We should add that the literary execution of the work is worthy of the indefatigable industry and unceasing vigilance with which the stores of historical material have been accumulated, weighed, and sifted. The cardinal qualities of style, lucidity, animation, and energy, are everywhere present. Seldom, indeed, has a book, in which matter of substantial value has been so happily united to attractiveness of form, been offered by an American author to his fellow-citizens."—*New York Sun.*

"To recount the marvelous progress of the American people, to describe their life, their literature, their occupations, their amusements, is Mr. McMaster's object. His theme is an important one, and we congratulate him on his success. It has rarely been our province to notice a book with so many excellences and so few defects."—*New York Herald.*

"Mr. McMaster at once shows his grasp of the various themes and his special capacity as a historian of the people. His aim is high, but he hits the mark."—*New York Journal of Commerce.*

"I have had to read a good deal of history in my day, but I find so much freshness in the way Professor McMaster has treated his subject that it is quite like a new story."—*Philadelphia Press.*

"Mr. McMaster's success as a writer seems to us distinct and decisive. In the first place he has written a remarkably readable history. His style is clear and vigorous, if not always condensed. He has the faculty of felicitous comparison and contrast in a marked degree. Mr McMaster has produced one of the most spirited of histories, a book which will be widely read, and the entertaining quality of which is conspicuous beyond that of any work of its kind."—*Boston Gazette.*

New York: D. APPLETON & CO., 1, 3, & 5 Bond Street.

D. APPLETON & CO.'S PUBLICATIONS.

FINANCIAL HISTORY OF THE UNITED STATES, FROM 1774 TO 1789, EMBRACING THE PERIOD OF THE AMERICAN REVOLUTION. New edition, thoroughly revised. By ALBERT S. BOLLES, Professor in the Wharton School of Finance, University of Pennsylvania; Editor of "The Banker's Magazine." 8vo. Cloth, $2.50.

FINANCIAL HISTORY OF THE UNITED STATES. COMPRISING THE PERIOD FROM 1789 TO 1860. By ALBERT S. BOLLES. 8vo. Cloth, $3.50.

WORKS OF J. C. CALHOUN. Vol. I. On Government. Vol. II. Reports and Letters. Vols. III and IV. Speeches. Vols. V and VI. Reports and Letters. 6 vols. 8vo. Cloth, $15.00; sheep, $18.00.

Mr. Calhoun's life and speeches form a substantive part of American history for near half a century. He was always in public life, and stamped the impress of his genius on every great public measure, either as debater or minister.

THIRTY YEARS' VIEW; OR, A HISTORY OF THE WORKING OF THE AMERICAN GOVERNMENT FOR THIRTY YEARS, FROM 1820 TO 1850. By THOMAS H. BENTON. New edition, revised, with Copious Index. Two very large volumes, 8vo. Cloth, $6.00; sheep, $8.00.

MILITARY HISTORY OF ULYSSES S. GRANT, FROM APRIL, 1861, TO APRIL, 1865. By General ADAM BADEAU, Aide-de-Camp to the General-in-Chief. Popular edition. In 3 volumes. 8vo. Cloth, $6.00.

"General Badeau has had exceptional advantages in the preparation of this valuable work. Before the war he was a journalist of known skill and acquirements. While in the war, a member of General Grant's staff, he was military secretary, and accompanied the commander of the army from the close of the Vicksburg campaign till the surrender of Lee. He shared the confidence of the general-in-chief—a confidence which continues unbroken till the present day. He has had the assistance of the leading commanders of the armies in constructing his narrative; he has had access to the records of the War Department, both Confederate and Federal, and it is known that the sheets of his work were read in proof by General Grant, General Sherman, General Sheridan, and other officers who could contribute to the truth of the author's narrative. This military history, therefore, comes to us with every assurance of accuracy, and it may be accepted as Grant's own presentation of the claims upon which his military renown will rest. . . . *A work which will long be accepted as a classic history of the greatest war of modern times.*"—*New York Herald.*

THE SAME. With a Steel Portrait and 33 Maps. Complete in 3 vols. 8vo. Cloth, $12.00; sheep, $15.00; half turkey, $20.00. Sold by subscription only.

New York: D. APPLETON & CO., 1, 3, & 5 Bond Street.

D. APPLETON & CO.'S PUBLICATIONS.

THE FRENCH REVOLUTION. By Louis Adolphe Thiers. In 4 vols. 8vo. Vellum cloth, gilt top, in box, $8.00; half calf, $18.00.

COMPLETE HISTORY OF GERMANY. By Dr. J. Kohlrausch. 8vo. Cloth, $2.50.

THE THREE PROPHETS: CHINESE GORDON; MOHAMMED-AHMED; ARABY PASHA. Events before, during, and after the Bombardment of Alexandria. By Colonel Chaillé Long, ex-Chief of Staff to Gordon in Africa, ex-United States Consular Agent in Alexandria, etc., etc. With Portraits. 16mo. Paper, 50 cents.

THE HISTORICAL REFERENCE-BOOK, COMPRISING A CHRONOLOGICAL TABLE OF UNIVERSAL HISTORY, A CHRONOLOGICAL DICTIONARY OF UNIVERSAL HISTORY, AND A BIOGRAPHICAL DICTIONARY. With Geographical Notes. For the Use of Students, Teachers, and Readers. By Louis Heilprin. Crown 8vo. 579 pages. Half leather, $3.00.

As a book of compact reference this work is believed to possess considerable advantage in its arrangement over other books of the kind—reference being in one Part under dates, and in another under countries or events—while every effort has been made to render it absolutely accurate. The compiler had many years' experience in the editorial department of the "American Cyclopædia" in verifying historical and biographical dates.

APPLETONS' AMERICAN CYCLOPÆDIA. A POPULAR DICTIONARY OF GENERAL KNOWLEDGE. Edited by George Ripley and Charles A. Dana. 16 vols. Large 8vo. Per volume, cloth, $5.00; sheep, $6.00; half morocco, $7.00; half russia, $8.00; full morocco, or russia, $10.00.

The American Cyclopædia presents a panoramic view of all human knowledge. In its volumes is contained a vast fund of practical information on the Arts and Sciences in all their branches, including Mechanics, Mathematics, Astronomy, Philosophy, Chemistry, and Physiology; on Agriculture, Commerce, and Manufactures; on Law, Medicine, and Theology; on Biography and History, Geography and Ethnology; on Political Economy, the Trades, Inventions, Politics, the Things of Common Life, and General Literature.

The work is sold to subscribers only. It is in sixteen large octavo volumes, each containing about 800 pages, fully illustrated with several thousand Wood Engravings, and with numerous colored Lithographic Maps.

New York: D. APPLETON & CO., 1, 3, & 5 Bond Street.

D. APPLETON & CO.'S PUBLICATIONS.

BIOGRAPHY.

THE HUNDRED GREATEST MEN. PORTRAITS OF THE ONE HUNDRED GREATEST MEN OF HISTORY. Reproduced from Fine and Rare Steel Engravings, with Biographies. 8vo. Cloth, $6.00.

A General Introduction to the Work was written by RALPH WALDO EMERSON; Introduction to Section I by MATTHEW ARNOLD; Section II by H. TAINE; Section III by MAX MÜLLER and R. RENAN; Section IV by NOAH PORTER; Section V by A. P. STANLEY; Section VI by H. HELMHOLTZ; Section VII by J. A. FROUDE; Section VIII by Professor JOHN FISKE.

HOURS WITH GREEK AND LATIN AUTHORS. From Various English Translations. With Biographical Notices. By G. H. JENNINGS and W. S. JOHNSTONE. 12mo. Cloth, $2.00.

LIFE OF HIS ROYAL HIGHNESS THE PRINCE CONSORT. By Sir THEODORE MARTIN. With Portraits and Views. Complete in 5 vols. 12mo. Cloth, $10.00.

"The literature of England is richer by a book which will be read with profit by succeeding generations of her sons and daughters."—*Blackwood.*

BEACONSFIELD. A SKETCH OF THE LITERARY AND POLITICAL CAREER OF BENJAMIN DISRAELI (Earl of Beaconsfield). With Two Portraits. By GEORGE M. TOWLE. 18mo. Paper, 25 cents; cloth, 60 cents.

LIFE OF CHARLOTTE BRONTE. By E. C. GASKELL. With Engravings. Two volumes in one. 12mo. Cloth, $1.50.

Charlotte Brontë was one of the most extraordinary female characters of modern times. From perfect obscurity, and notwithstanding a most unpropitious training, she sprang at one bound to the height of popularity, founded an entirely new school of novel-writing, and, after a life of severe trial and suffering, died when she was just beginning to be happy.

LIFE AND WRITINGS OF THOMAS HENRY BUCKLE. By ALFRED HENRY HUTH. 12mo. Cloth, $2.00.

"The book deals with Mr. Buckle less as a philosopher than as a man.... Mr. Huth has done his part well and thoroughly."—*Saturday Review.*

THOMAS CARLYLE: HIS LIFE—HIS BOOKS—HIS THEORIES. By ALFRED H. GUERNSEY. 18mo. Paper, 30 cents; Cloth, 60 cents.

New York: D. APPLETON & CO., 1, 3, & 5 Bond Street.

D. APPLETON & CO.'S PUBLICATIONS.

BIOGRAPHY.

ESSAYS AND SPEECHES OF JEREMIAH S. BLACK. WITH A BIOGRAPHICAL SKETCH. By CHAUNCEY F. BLACK. With a Portrait on Steel. 8vo. Cloth, $3.75.

LIFE AND LETTERS OF EMORY UPTON, COLONEL OF THE FOURTH REGIMENT OF ARTILLERY, AND BREVET MAJOR-GENERAL U. S. ARMY. By PETER S. MICHIE, Professor U. S. Military Academy. With an Introduction by JAMES HARRISON WILSON, late U. S. A. With Portraits. 8vo. Cloth, $2.00.

"The subject of the following memoir was widely known by reputation in the military profession, and the story of his life would, at least to military men, have been a matter of passing interest. The tragic circumstances of his death seemed to demand some explanation in harmony with his established reputation and character. At the earnest solicitation of his nearest relatives, the author, although conscious of his own deficiencies, undertook the task of compiling a brief record of General Upton's life for his family and immediate personal friends."—*From Preface.*

LIFE AND LETTERS OF THOMAS GOLD APPLETON. Prepared by SUSAN HALE. With a Portrait. 12mo. Cloth, gilt top, $1.75.

Mr. T. G. Appleton, it is needless to say, was well known in social and literary circles in Europe and America, and distinguished as one of the best conversationalists of the day. The present work consists of a biographical sketch, selections from his letters, and some account of his different journeys.

LOUIS PASTEUR: HIS LIFE AND LABORS. By his SON-IN-LAW. Translated from the French by Lady CLAUD HAMILTON. With an Introduction by Professor TYNDALL. 12mo. Cloth, $1.25.

"Since the first studies of M. Pasteur on molecular dissymmetry, down to his most recent investigations on hydrophobia, on virulent diseases, and on the artificial cultures of living contagia, the author of these pages has been able, if not to witness all, at least to follow in its principal developments, this uninterrupted series of scientific conquests."—*From the Preface.*

"A record in which the verities of science are endowed with the interest of romance."—Professor TYNDALL.

MEMOIRS OF NAPOLEON: HIS COURT AND FAMILY. By the Duchess D'ABRANTES (Madame Junot). 2 vols. 12mo. Cloth, $3.00.

This book supplies many valuable and interesting details respecting the Court and Family of Napoleon, which are found in no other work. The author's opportunities for observation were excellent and long continued, and she has availed herself of them so effectually as to present us with a very lively, entertaining, and readable book, as well as to supply important materials for future historians and biographers.

New York: D. APPLETON & CO., 1, 3, & 5 Bond Street.

D. APPLETON & CO.'S PUBLICATIONS.

BIOGRAPHY.

MEMOIR OF COUSIN ALICE. By A. B. Haven. 12mo. Cloth, $1.25.

MEMORIES OF MY EXILE. By Louis Kossuth. Translated from the original Hungarian by Ferenz Jausz. Crown 8vo. Cloth, $2.00.

This important work relates to the period when the Italian Kingdom was being established, and gives the Secret Treaties and details of the understanding between England, the Emperor Napoleon, and Count Cavour.

"These 'Memories' disclose a curious episode in the inner life of English domestic politics."—*The Nation.*

THE GREAT GERMAN COMPOSERS. Comprising Biographical and Anecdotical Sketches of Bach, Handel, Gluck, Haydn, Mozart, Beethoven, Schubert, Schumann, Franz, Chopin, Weber, Mendelssohn, and Wagner. By George T. Ferris. 18mo. Paper, 30 cents; cloth, 60 cents.

THE GREAT ITALIAN AND FRENCH COMPOSERS. By George T. Ferris. 18mo. Paper, 30 cents; cloth, 60 cents.

GREAT SINGERS: FAUSTINA BORDONI TO HENRIETTA SONTAG. By George T. Ferris. 18mo. Paper, 30 cents; cloth, 60 cents.

GREAT SINGERS: MALIBRAN TO TITIENS. Second Series. By George T. Ferris. 18mo. Paper, 30 cents; cloth, 60 cents.

GREAT VIOLINISTS AND PIANISTS. CORELLI TO LISZT. By George T. Ferris. 18mo. Paper, 40 cents; cloth, 60 cents.

** The preceding five volumes by George T. Ferris are also entitled The Music Series, and are sold per set in case. Cloth, $3.00; morocco, limp, $10.00.

BIOGRAPHY SERIES. Set 6 vols., 18mo, in case. Cloth, $3.75; full calf, $12.00.

Ralph Waldo Emerson. By Alfred H. Guernsey.
Thomas Carlyle. By Alfred H. Guernsey.
Ruskin on Painting. With a Biographical Sketch.
Stray Moments with Thackeray. By William H. Rideing.
Lord Macaulay. By Charles H. Jones.
Short Life of Charles Dickens. By Charles H. Jones.

New York: D. APPLETON & CO., 1, 3, & 5 Bond Street.

BIOGRAPHY.

MEMOIRS OF MADAME DE REMUSAT. 1802–1808. Edited by her Grandson, PAUL DE RÉMUSAT, Senator. In 3 vols., paper covers, 8vo, $1.50; also, in 1 vol., cloth, 12mo, $2.00; half calf, $3.50.

"These memoirs are not only a repository of anecdotes and of portraits sketched from life by a keen-eyed, quick-witted woman; but some of the author's reflections on social and political questions are remarkable for weight and penetration."—*New York Sun.*

"Madame de Rémusat's keenness of intelligence, and her intimacy with Josephine, to which she was not only admitted but welcomed, gave her those extraordinary opportunities which she has turned to so good account in these 'Memoirs.' The work, as a whole, is at once the most interesting and the most damaging commentary on the character of Napoleon that has ever been produced."—*Dr. C. K. Adams's Manual of Historical Literature.*

A SELECTION FROM THE LETTERS OF MADAME DE REMUSAT. 1804–1814. Edited by her Grandson, PAUL DE RÉMUSAT, Senator. Uniform with "Memoirs of Madame de Rémusat," 1802-1808. 12mo. Cloth, $1.25.

"'A Selection from the Letters of Madame de Rémusat to her Husband and Son' has been published by the Appletons. Coming closely upon the fascinating memoirs of that lady, they possess the same interest, and will add to the reader's knowledge of social and political life in France in the days of the first Napoleon."—*Boston Evening Transcript.*

VOLTAIRE. By JOHN MORLEY. 12mo. Cloth, $2.00.

CONTENTS.—Preliminary; English Influences; Literature; Berlin; Religion; History; Ferney.

FRENCH MEN OF LETTERS. Personal and Anecdotical Sketches of Victor Hugo, Alfred de Musset, Théophile Gautier, Henri Murger, Sainte-Beuve, Gérard de Nerval, Alexandre Dumas, fils, Emile Augier, Octave Feuillet, Victorien Sardou, Alphonse Daudet, and Emile Zola. By MAURICE MAURIS. Paper, 35 cents. cloth, 60 cents.

HISTORY OF GENERAL JAMES A. GARFIELD'S PUBLIC LIFE. (The Republican Text-Book for the Campaign of 1880.) By B. A. HINSDALE, A. M., President of Hiram College. 8vo. Paper, 50 cents.

LIFE OF WINFIELD SCOTT HANCOCK, MAJOR-GENERAL UNITED STATES ARMY. By Rev. D. X. JUNKIN, D. D., and FRANK H. NORTON. 12mo. Cloth, $1.50.

New York: D. APPLETON & CO., 1, 3, & 5 Bond Street.

D. APPLETON & CO.'S PUBLICATIONS.

BIOGRAPHY.

THE LIFE OF SAMUEL F. B. MORSE, INVENTOR OF THE RECORDING TELEGRAPH. By S. I. PRIME. Illustrated with Steel Plates and Wood Engravings. 8vo. Cloth, $5.00; sheep, $6.00; half morocco, $7.50; morocco, $10.00.

LIFE OF EMMA WILLARD. By JOHN LORD, LL. D. With two Portraits on Steel. 12mo. Cloth, $2.00.

RECOLLECTIONS AND OPINIONS OF AN OLD PIONEER. By P. H. BURNETT, First Governor of the State of California. 12mo. Cloth, $1.75.

Mr. Burnett's life has been full of varied experience, and the record takes the reader back prior to the discovery of gold in California, and leads him through many adventures and incidents to the time of the beginning of the late war.

"I have been a pioneer most of my life; whenever, since my arrival in California, I have seen a party of immigrants, with their ox-teams and white-sheeted wagons, I have been excited, have felt younger, and was for the moment anxious to make another trip."—*The Author.*

LIFE OF JOHN RANDOLPH, OF ROANOKE. By HUGH H. GARLAND. Portraits. Two volumes in one. 8vo. Cloth, $2.00.

ELIHU BURRITT: A MEMORIAL VOLUME, CONTAINING A SKETCH OF HIS LIFE AND LABORS. With Selections from his Writings and Lectures, and Extracts from his Private Journals in Europe and America. Edited by CHARLES NORTHEND, A. M. 12mo. Cloth, $1.75.

THE LIFE AND PUBLIC SERVICES OF DR. LEWIS F. LINN. FOR TEN YEARS A SENATOR OF THE UNITED STATES FROM THE STATE OF MISSOURI. By E. A. LINN and N. SARGENT. With Portrait. 8vo. Cloth, $2.00.

OUTLINE OF THE PUBLIC LIFE AND SERVICES OF THOMAS F. BAYARD, SENATOR OF THE UNITED STATES FROM THE STATE OF DELAWARE, 1869–1880. With Extracts from his Speeches and the Debates of Congress. By EDWARD SPENCER. 12mo. Paper, 50 cents; cloth, $1.00.

New York: D. APPLETON & CO., 1, 3, & 5 Bond Street

www.ingramcontent.com/pod-product-compliance
Lightning Source LLC
Chambersburg PA
CBHW051850300426
44117CB00006B/331